THE INFALLIBLE DOCTOR

ENDING THE ERA OF MEDICAL ERROR WITH AI AND ROBOTICS

DR. SURESH K. PANDEY

The Infallible Docter

Author: Dr. Suresh Kumar Pandey

Published in 2026

Dedicated to

To the roots that anchored me and the wings that let me fly:

My grandparents, **Late Dr. Kamta Prasad Pandey** and **Late Smt. Ram Shringari Devi**, and my parents, **Late Shri Kameshwar Prasad Pandey** and **Smt. Maya Pandey**. You taught me that while medicine is a profession, healing is a way of life.

To **Dr. Vidushi Sharma**, my partner in eye surgery and in soul. Thank you for walking every step of this path alongside me, making the impossible seems reachable.

To **Ishita**, my daughter. Thank you for your love, and for understanding that Papa's long hours of silence at the keyboard were actually his way of speaking to the world.

To the **thousands of patients** across India and overseas—thank you for placing your trust in my hands. You are the reason I strive for the infallible.

And to **Destiny**, which took a boy studying by lantern light in Mohna and gave him the privilege to touch the sky.

Contents

PART VIII: The New Horizon

Foreword

Professor (Dr.) Amod Gupta

Looking back on my years of teaching and practicing at PGIMER Chandigarh, I am amazed at how much the practice of medicine has evolved. When I started my career, a doctor's greatest tool was their clinical intuition, an art honed through years of careful observation at the bedside. We trained our residents, including a young, deeply dedicated Dr. Suresh K. Pandey, to trust their senses, rely on their memory, and cultivate an absolutely steady hand.

But as Dr. Pandey rightly points out in The Infallible Doctor: Ending the Era of Medical Error with AI and Robotics, the world has changed. The sheer volume of medical knowledge today simply outpaces what the human brain can hold. We are asking our doctors to process endless data on pharmacology and pathology, work grueling shifts, and perform delicate surgeries with zero margin for error. As this book honestly explores, the unfortunate result is often preventable medical errors, not because doctors are incompetent, but simply because they are human.

This book serves as a much-needed and highly practical conversation starter for our medical community. Dr. Pandey moves past the unrealistic expectation of the "superhero doctor" and offers a better way forward: a partnership between human empathy and artificial intelligence. He shows how algorithms can act as untiring assistants, instantly cross-referencing data to catch a dangerous drug interaction or a hidden diagnosis before it harms the patient. Being an eye surgeon who operates on the microscopic structures of the eye, Dr. Pandey knows the limits of human dexterity firsthand. His insights into robotic surgery offer a realistic look at a future where we can eliminate physiological tremors and bring surgical excellence to every patient.

Yet, the most compelling aspect of this book is its focus on the human touch. Dr. Pandey is not pushing for a cold, mechanized healthcare system. Instead, he highlights a beautiful truth: by letting machines handle the heavy lifting of data and mechanical precision, we actually free the doctor to return to the patient's bedside. When technology takes care of the science, the physician finally has the time to care for the person.

I have had the pleasure of watching Dr. Suresh K. Pandey grow from a meticulous resident at PGIMER, Chandigarh into a thoughtful ophthalmic surgeon, author, and leader. With this book, he offers an optimistic and clear roadmap for patient safety. I warmly recommend The Infallible Doctor to medical students, practicing doctors, and healthcare administrators. It is a vital guide to using technology not to replace us, but to protect the sacred doctor-patient relationship and elevate our standard of care.

Prof. Amod Gupta,
Padma Shri Awardee
Former Dean and Head, Advanced Eye Centre
Post Graduate Institute of Medical Education and Research
(PGIMER) Chandigarh, India

Foreword

Dr. Gullapalli N. Rao

We live in an increasingly complex world with wide disparities of wealth and living standards. Providing health care of optimal quality to everyone is an aspiration of every country. While this aspiration of "Universal Health Care" requires all forms of resources, the most important is the availability of well-trained human resources. All cadres of health care professionals continually face ever increasing demands on their time and skills, and this may occasionally lead to errors - small and big. The challenge is to minimize the quality and degree of these errors.

This is the exact problem Dr. Suresh K. Pandey tackles so effectively in his new book, *The Infallible Doctor: Ending the Era of Medical Error with AI and Robotics.* I have been familiar with Dr. Pandey's impressive journey: from a diligent student of medicine and ophthalmology, to becoming an accomplished eye surgeon and thought leader. Because of his background and exposure, he doesn't look at technology as a distant, theoretical concept. He looks at it through the practical lens of an operating microscope and the daily realities of a busy clinical practice.

In these pages, he thoughtfully dispels the common fear that machines are here to replace doctors. At many institutions, the world over, the practical, sight-saving benefits of these machines is already visible. The application of AI in our rural vision centres to screen for diabetic retinopathy or glaucoma provides us with reasonably reliable diagnostic information. This helps ensure that a farmer in a remote village gets the same accurate, early diagnosis as someone who has access to an advanced facility in a city. As Dr. Pandey points out, the advances in the field of robotics in the operating room will help us enhance precision and safety to delicate surgical procedures in the eye.

But what I appreciate most about *The Infallible Doctor* is its deep focus on the human element of medicine. Dr. Pandey makes a compelling, practical case: by applying technology where it is most impactful such as analysing large data sets and enhancing mechanical precision. This allows physicians to focus on the "caring element": listen to patients, ease their anxieties, and offer the empathy that no algorithm can ever provide.

This book is coming out at the right time providing guidance to every group involved in the delivery of health care and that indeed embracing technology can make medical care most precise, cover larger and remote populations, and ultimately helping us to achieve "Universal Health Coverage."

Dr. Gullapalli N. Rao
Founder Chair
L V Prasad Eye Institute
Hyderabad, India

Foreword

Professor (Dr.) M. Edward Wilson

In pediatric ophthalmology, the margin for error is effectively zero. When I sit at the operating microscope to operate on a newborn's eye, I am not merely repairing a minute anatomical structure—I am safeguarding a child's future. The ability to recognize a parent's face, to learn to read, to navigate the world independently may hinge on the precision of my hands.

For decades, I have taught my fellows that our profession demands mastery of both thought and action. We train to be fully present. We push through exhaustion and cognitive fatigue. We eliminate distractions. Unlike many surgeons, I prefer a silent operating room. Noise invites error. Our patients deserve nothing less than complete focus.

And yet, there is a quiet truth in medicine—one rarely spoken aloud: we are human. However disciplined or dedicated, human beings are not designed to be infallible.

I first met Dr. Suresh K. Pandey when he came to train with me as a research fellow. Even then, I was struck by his insight and his instinct for innovative solutions. His devotion—to both medicine and his patients—was unmistakable. I was not surprised when he became an eye surgeon who scrutinized every millimeter and every outcome. In *The Infallible Doctor: Ending the Era of Medical Error with AI and Robotics,* Dr. Pandey confronts one of modern healthcare's most urgent crises: preventable medical error.

We have reached a point where medical knowledge is expanding at an unprecedented pace. Physicians are expected to master vast pharmacologic interactions, navigate complex electronic health records, and perform delicate procedures after sleepless nights on call. Many clinical errors are not born of incompetence; they are the predictable consequence of human physiology strained beyond its limits.

What makes this book compelling is its optimism. Dr. Pandey does not frame artificial intelligence and robotics as threats, but as partners—tireless allies. He envisions AI systems as vigilant co-pilots, synthesizing enormous datasets to flag subtle misdiagnoses or dangerous drug interactions before harm occurs. For surgeons who work under the microscope, advanced robotic platforms that eliminate tremor and enhance precision represent the next frontier in patient safety.

Importantly, this book is not about replacing physicians. It is about restoring them.

There is understandable concern that advanced technology may depersonalize care. Dr. Pandey thoughtfully dismantles that fear. When machines manage data analysis and safeguard technical precision, physicians are freed to reclaim the most essential dimension of medicine: humanity. We can lift our gaze from the screen, meet the eyes of an anxious mother, reassure a frightened child, and practice the deeply human art of healing.

The Infallible Doctor is both visionary and grounded—written by a surgeon who understands that the sacred bond between doctor and patient must remain at the center of progress. Dr. Pandey offers not merely critique, but a hopeful and practical roadmap toward safer care.

This book is essential reading for medical students, residents, fellows, seasoned clinicians, and healthcare leaders alike—for all who believe that excellence in medicine should not depend on endurance alone, but on systems designed to make the safest outcome the standard outcome.

Professor (Dr.) M. Edward Wilson, MD
Distinguished University Professor of Ophthalmology and Pediatrics
Chair and Director Emeritus, Albert Florens Storm Eye Institute
Medical University of South Carolina, Charleston, South Carolina, USA

Foreword

Professor (Dr.) Somesh Gupta

Medicine, at its deepest level, relies on the art of seeing.

As a dermatologist at the All India Institute of Medical Sciences (AIIMS), my diagnostic world is built on the meticulous observation of visual patterns—the asymmetrical border of a melanoma, the subtle scaling of an autoimmune rash. Dr. Suresh K. Pandey, an esteemed ophthalmologist, operates in a remarkably similar universe. Though our specialties differ, we both spend our days looking closely, searching for truth hidden in plain sight.

For centuries, the weight of healing has rested entirely on the biological limits of human vision, memory, and endurance. But the human mind is not infallible. What happens when a doctor nears the end of a grueling, high-volume clinic at a busy tertiary center like AIIMS? Cognitive fatigue sets in. In an era where medical knowledge doubles every few months, we ask human beings to process oceans of data and perform microsurgeries without a millimeter of error.

As Dr. Pandey bravely highlights in *The Infallible Doctor*, the tragic result is a silent epidemic of preventable error—born not of incompetence, but of sheer human limitation.

This vulnerability is one I have studied deeply. While editing my book, *Artificial Intelligence in Dermatology*, I witnessed the seismic shift algorithms bring to clinical practice. In my field, neural networks can now analyze dermoscopic images to detect melanoma with precision that matches board-certified experts. AI serves as an untiring second opinion. It does not suffer sleep deprivation. It is not biased by a previous difficult case.

Reading Dr. Pandey's masterful manuscript, I was struck by how beautifully our visions align. He maps this diagnostic revolution across the entire landscape of healthcare, proving that AI is the ultimate safety net—eyes that never blink, a memory that never fades.

But what makes *The Infallible Doctor* truly exceptional is its profound humanity. A pervasive fear haunts our profession: that AI will render the physician cold, distant, obsolete. Dr. Pandey brilliantly shatters this myth. He presents a compelling paradox: by outsourcing the cognitive heavy lifting to machines, we actually *liberate* the doctor.

When an algorithm handles tedious data entry or flags a hidden drug interaction, the physician is freed to look away from the screen and back into the patient's eyes. Technology becomes the instrument that rescues the sacred doctor–patient relationship, allowing us the time and space to offer the empathy no machine can replicate.

Dr. Pandey has combined the rigorous intellect of an eye surgeon with the deep soul of a true healer to show us the path forward. This is not a book about machines replacing doctors. It is a book about machines helping doctors become fully human again.

I highly recommend this visionary work to every medical student, practitioner, and healthcare leader who wishes to understand how we can embrace technology to create a safer, kinder, and truly infallible era of medicine.

Professor (Dr.) Somesh Gupta
Professor of Dermatology and Venereology
All India Institute of Medical Sciences (AIIMS)
New Delhi, India

Foreword

Dr. Uday Devgan

Every single day, I have the privilege of analyzing surgical videos frame by frame, teaching ophthalmologists around the world how to refine their techniques and manage the unexpected. In the microscopic world of eye surgery, we operate in a space measured in microns. We walk a daily tightrope where a fraction of a millimeter or a split-second lapse in concentration can mean the difference between restoring a patient's sight and a devastating complication.

As surgeons, we spend decades relentlessly pursuing perfection. Yet, the most difficult lesson I impart to young surgeons is the humbling acceptance of our own biology: no matter how skilled or dedicated we are, we are still human. We suffer from cognitive fatigue and natural physiological tremors. We are inherently fallible.

It is this exact, uncomfortable truth that my esteemed colleague, Dr. Suresh K. Pandey, tackles with brilliance in *The Infallible Doctor*. My perspective on this work is informed by a friendship spanning decades; I first met Suresh many years ago when he was completing his fellowship in the United States. Even then, his forward-thinking approach to clinical challenges was evident. Watching him evolve from a dedicated fellow into a global leader has been a privilege, and his career-long insights are distilled perfectly in these pages.

Dr. Pandey and I share a deep commitment to patient safety. He eloquently voices what many in the medical community feel: the current healthcare system has pushed human physiology past its breaking point. We are drowning in a tsunami of data and unprecedented patient volumes, asking doctors to function like supercomputers. When we inevitably fall short, medical errors occur.

However, *The Infallible Doctor* is a manifesto of profound hope. Dr. Pandey outlines how Artificial Intelligence and surgical robotics are not threats to our profession, but the ultimate clinical co-pilots. Imagine an AI system that prevents a fatal drug interaction by cross-referencing a lifetime of data, or a robotic assistant that filters out human hand tremor, allowing every surgeon to operate with the flawless precision of a master. Dr. Pandey shows us that technology is the safety net that catches us when our biology falters.

Most importantly, he shatters the myth that AI will destroy the doctor-patient relationship. He presents a beautiful paradox: by outsourcing exhausting data-processing and mechanical perfection to machines, we are liberating the physician. When a machine handles the algorithms, the doctor can finally look away from the screen. We are given back the time to look our patients in the eye and practice the deeply human art of healing.

This book is a visionary roadmap for the future of medicine. I consider it mandatory reading for every ophthalmologist and trainee who believes that a zero-error healthcare system is not just a dream, but our ultimate moral obligation.

Dr. Uday Devgan, MD, FACS, FRCS
Devgan Eye Surgery, Los Angeles, California
Clinical Professor of Ophthalmology, Jules Stein Eye Institute, UCLA
Founder, CataractCoach.com

Prologue

The Third Leading Cause

"The most dangerous phrase in medicine is 'I think.' It is a confession of uncertainty masquerading as a conclusion. The Infallible Doctor does not think; it knows. It replaces the intuition of the artist with the precision of the engineer, offering us a future where the error is not part of the equation."

— Dr. Suresh Kumar Pandey

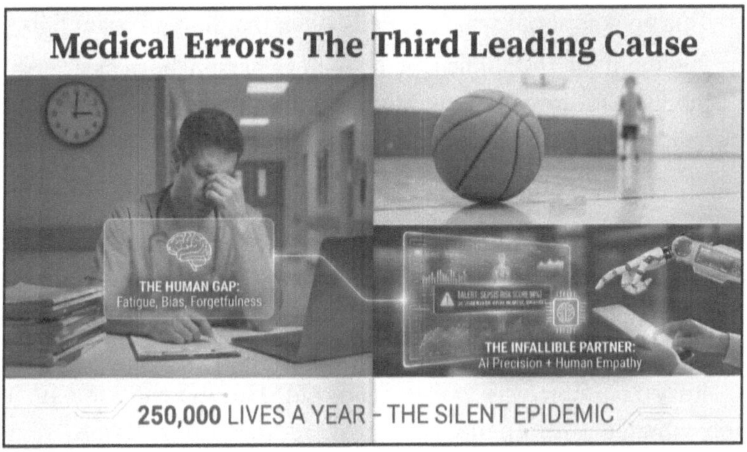

The Story of a Tuesday

The most dangerous variable in a hospital room is not the bacteria on the door handle. It is not the complexity of the surgery. It is not even the severity of your disease.

The most dangerous variable is the time of day.

If **you** walk into an emergency room at 9:00 AM on a Tuesday, you are likely to be seen by a physician who is well-rested, caffeinated, and mentally sharp. The cognitive engine of their brain is firing on all cylinders. But if **you** walk into that same room at 3:00 AM on a

Sunday, the physiological reality of the human standing over you is entirely different.

The doctor's hands may be steady, but their mind is fighting a biological war against fatigue. Their decision-making capability—the delicate neural machinery required to process complex symptoms—has degraded. In this moment, the difference between life and death for you or your child often comes down to a coin flip: *Did the doctor remember to check for that one rare drug interaction? Did they notice the subtle drift in the heart rate monitor? Did they connect the dots?*

We like to believe that medicine is an objective science. In reality, it is a subjective performance. It relies entirely on the processing power of a single human brain—a brain that is prone to exhaustion, bias, distraction, and forgetfulness.

This book is about what happens when that human brain fails.

It is about the "Infallible Doctor"—not a person, but a partnership. It is about a future where we stop asking humans to be robots, and start allowing robots to save humans.

The Cut on the Gym Floor

To understand why this revolution is necessary, we must look at what happens when the current system fails. We must look at a Wednesday in March, the kind of day that begins with the ordinary and ends with the unthinkable.

Rory Staunton was twelve years old. He was the kind of boy who vibrated with energy—a bright, red-headed kid who wanted to be a pilot, who filled a room with his laughter. On this particular Wednesday, he was doing what twelve-year-olds do. He was playing basketball in the gym of his school in Queens, New York, USA. The air smelled of rubber and sweat. The game was heated.

Rory dove for a loose ball. He slid across the polished wood floor. He scraped his arm. It was a minor abrasion—two small cuts, barely worthy of a bandage. He stood up, brushed himself off, and kept playing.

By the next evening, the ordinary had begun to curdle into something terrifying. Rory was vomiting. His legs ached with a strange, deep intensity. His temperature spiked to 102 degrees.

His parents, Ciaran and Orlaith, did exactly what responsible parents are supposed to do. They did not wait. They took him to the emergency room of one of the premier hospitals in New York City: NYU Langone Medical Center.

Put yourself in that room. You are the parent. You are terrified. You are looking at the doctor—the authority figure in the white coat—begging for reassurance.

The pediatrician who saw Rory was competent. She was experienced. She was compassionate. She examined the boy, saw the flushed face, the fever, the nausea. It was flu season in New York. The pattern was familiar. The cognitive bias kicked in—a mental shortcut that all human brains use to save energy. Her brain whispered: *It looks like the flu. It acts like the flu. Therefore, it is the flu.*

She prescribed rehydration fluids and Tylenol. She told his parents to take him home, rest, and wait for the fever to break.

But as Rory was wheeled out of the hospital, a different story was being told inside the hospital's own servers.

Rory's blood work had come back from the lab while he was still in the Emergency Room. The numbers were screaming. His white blood cell count was sky-high. More critically, there was a massive elevation in his "bands"—immature white blood cells that the bone marrow releases only in a state of catastrophic emergency. It is the body's desperate SOS signal for a massive bacterial infection.

Rory didn't have the stomach flu. He had **sepsis**. The bacteria from that scrape on the gym floor had entered his bloodstream and was systematically shutting down his organs.

The data was there. The truth was sitting on a computer screen. But in the chaos of a busy ER, amidst the noise of alarms, the fatigue of the staff, and the fragmented nature of modern care, the dots were never connected. The lab results were looked at, but their severity was missed. The signal was lost in the noise.

Rory Staunton died three days later in the intensive care unit. He died surrounded by the best technology money could buy, yet utterly failed by the system designed to wield it.

He did not die because of a lack of medical knowledge. We have known how to treat sepsis with antibiotics for seventy years. He died because of an information failure. In that critical window, the human system failed to process the data that would have saved his life.

The Villain: Identifying "The Gap"

When we hear stories like Rory's, our instinct is to find someone to blame. We want to point a finger at the pediatrician. We want to call it negligence.

But that is too easy, and it is wrong. The pediatrician did not want Rory to die. She was not lazy. She was not uneducated. She was **human**.

The villain in this story is not the doctor. The villain is **"The Gap."**

The Gap is the dangerous, widening space between the explosion of medical data and the limited capacity of the human mind to contain it.

Consider this: In 1950, it took about 50 years for the total amount of medical knowledge to double. If you finished medical school in 1950, the medicine you practiced at the end of your career was largely the same as the medicine you learned at the start.

Today, medical knowledge doubles every **73 days**.

There are currently over 30 million research papers in the medical canon, with thousands more published every week. There are over 10,000 known diseases, 4,000 medical procedures, and countless drug interactions.

To stay completely current with the medical literature—to be the "perfect" doctor we expect—a general practitioner would need to read for **29 hours a day**, every single day.

This is The Gap. It is the mathematical impossibility of the modern physician.

We are asking human beings to memorize millions of data points, work 24-hour shifts, stay awake, stay empathetic, and recognize obscure patterns (like the "bands" in Rory's blood) in split seconds while distracted by a dozen other crises. We are asking for perfection from a species defined by its fallibility. We are asking a human brain to be a computer, and then punishing it when it fails to process the data.

I say this not just as an author, but as a doctor.

I have lived inside The Gap. I remember standing in the operating theater during an emergency at 3:00 AM, my back aching, my eyes burning from the harsh lights. I remember the fear—a cold, hard knot in the stomach—that I might miss something. I remember staring at a complex case, knowing that somewhere in the millions of pages of medical literature, there was an answer, but terrified that I might not recall it in time.

Every doctor has felt this. We carry a graveyard within us—the patients where we wonder, *What if I had been sharper? What if I had seen the sign?*

The Gap is not just an academic concept. It is a killer.

The Silent Epidemic

Rory's story breaks the heart, but it is the statistics that break the mind.

If you look at the official death certificates filed in the United States, you will see a familiar list of killers: Heart Disease. Cancer. Respiratory Disease. Accidents. These are the enemies we know. We have telethons for them. We have colored ribbons for them.

But there is a ghost on that list. A killer that hides in plain sight, unrecorded on death certificates but present in the morgue all the same.

In 2016, researchers at Johns Hopkins Medicine, led by Dr. Martin Makary, published a study that shook the foundations of American healthcare. They analyzed medical death rate data over an eight-year period and extrapolated the findings. Their calculation was staggering: **more than 250,000 people in the United States die every year from MEDICAL ERRORS.**

That figure makes medical error the **third leading cause of death** in the U.S., surpassing respiratory disease, accidents, stroke, and Alzheimer's.

Pause on that number. Two hundred and fifty thousand lives.

It is the equivalent of a jumbo jet crashing every single day, killing everyone on board.

If a 747 crashed tomorrow, it would be front-page news in every language on Earth. We would ground the fleet. We would hold hearings. We would redesign the engines. But medical errors happen one by one, in quiet rooms, behind drawn curtains. A dosage calculation is missed at 3:00 AM. A drug interaction is overlooked. A surgical sponge is left behind. A diagnosis is delayed until the cancer is untreatable.

Globally, the picture is even bleaker. The World Health Organization estimates that **1 in 10 patients** is harmed while receiving hospital care. Every year, millions of people walk into cathedrals of healing and leave with injuries, infections, or terminal conditions caused not by their disease, but by the care itself.

This is the price of The Gap. And as long as we rely solely on the human mind, this price will continue to be paid in human lives.

The Myth of the Art

Why is this happening? Why, in an age of MRI machines and robotic surgery, are we still killing patients by mistake?

The answer lies in our philosophy. For centuries, we have treated medicine as an **art form**. We revere the "intuitive" doctor—the Dr. House archetype who can look at a patient, stroke their chin, listen to the chest, and pull a diagnosis out of thin air like a magician pulling a rabbit from a hat. We value the "clinical eye."

"The most dangerous phrase in medicine is 'I think.' It is a confession of uncertainty masquerading as a conclusion."

As Rory's case proves, the "Art of Medicine" is no longer enough. In fact, it is a liability. Relying on intuition when we have data is not artistry; it is negligence.

When you board an airplane, you do not want a pilot who is "winging it" based on how the clouds look. You want a pilot who is supported by a massive array of sensors, autopilots, and collision-avoidance systems. You want redundancy. You want safety.

Yet, when you place your life in the hands of a doctor, you are stepping into a cockpit with no radar, where the pilot has been awake for 24 hours and is flying by sight alone.

The Infallible Partner

But there is hope. We are standing on the precipice of a new world.

Imagine a different Tuesday night for Rory Staunton.

Imagine that while the pediatrician was examining Rory, an algorithm was running silently in the background of the Electronic Health Record. It is an algorithm that never sleeps. It has read every paper on sepsis published in the last fifty years. It has analyzed the vital signs of ten million children.

As the nurse types in Rory's vitals—temperature 102, pulse 120—the AI takes notice. As the lab results upload from the basement, the AI sees the white blood cell count. It sees the bands.

It ignores the cognitive bias of "flu season." It ignores the fact that Rory looks like a healthy athlete. It ignores the fact that it is 3:00 AM. It looks at the math.

Instantly, a notification flashes on the doctor's screen. It is red. It is insistent.

[ALERT: SEPSIS RISK SCORE 98%]

[RECOMMENDATION: INITIATE ANTIBIOTICS IMMEDIATELY.

DO NOT DISCHARGE.]

The doctor pauses. She looks at the screen. She looks at Rory. The "Art" of her intuition failed, but the "Science" of the machine held the safety net. She re-evaluates. She orders the antibiotics.

Rory stays in the hospital that night. The fever breaks the next morning. Three days later, he is back on the basketball court. He grows up to be a pilot.

This book is about that alert.

It is about the moment where silicon meets biology. We are entering the age of the **Centaur Physician**—a hybrid intelligence where the human doctor is supported by a synthetic partner.

We are building systems that can read 100 million patient records in a second to find the one patient who looks like **you**. We are designing robotic hands that can suture a blood vessel smaller than a human hair without a distinct tremor. We are creating algorithms that never sleep, never get tired, never forget a lab result, and never judge a patient based on the color of their skin or the size of their wallet.

This is not a story about machines replacing doctors. It is a story about machines **liberating** doctors.

By offloading the data processing, the pattern recognition, and the precision mechanics to AI, we allow the human doctor to return to the one thing a machine can never do: to care. To sit at the bedside. To listen. To empathize. To hold a hand during the darkest hours when the science runs out and only the soul remains.

The era of "To Err is Human" is over. We are building a safety net that spans the globe, woven from code and conscience.

Welcome to the age of the Infallible Doctor.

THE TAKEAWAY

The Hidden Killer: Medical error is the **3rd leading cause of death**, claiming 250,000 lives a year—not because doctors are incompetent, but because they are overwhelmed.

The Villain is "The Gap": Medical knowledge doubles every 73 days. It is mathematically impossible for a human brain to keep up. This "Gap" between data and capacity is where errors happen.

The Solution: We must abandon the "Superhero Myth" of the solitary doctor. The future is the **"Centaur Model"**—Human Empathy + AI Precision. This partnership closes The Gap and ensures that no patient dies from a preventable mistake again.

References

1. Dwyer, J. (2012). "An Infection, Unnoticed, Turns Unstoppable." The New York Times, July 11, 2012.
2. Makary, M. A., & Daniel, M. (2016). "Medical error—the third leading cause of death in the US." The BMJ, 353, i2139.
3. Kohn, L. T., Corrigan, J. M., & Donaldson, M. S. (Eds.). (2000). To Err Is Human: Building a Safer Health System. Institute of Medicine, National Academies Press.
4. Topol, E. (2019). Deep Medicine: How Artificial Intelligence Can Make Healthcare Human Again. Basic Books.
5. Graber, M. L. (2013). "The incidence of diagnostic error in medicine." BMJ Quality & Safety, 22(Suppl 2), ii21-ii27.

PART I
To Err is Human
The Anatomy of Failure in Modern Medicine

Chapter 1

The Exhausted Mind

Decision Fatigue and the Myth of the Superhero Doctor

"We have built a medical system on the precarious assumption that the human brain is an inexhaustible resource. But biology is not a negotiation. The Infallible Doctor begins where human stamina ends, offering a vigilance that never blinks, never tires, and never forgets."

— Dr. Suresh Kumar Pandey

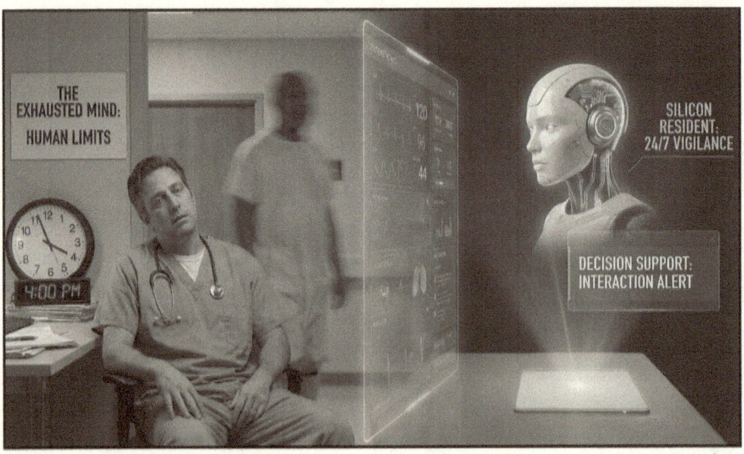

The Night the System Failed

It was a rainy night in March 1984, the kind of night where the damp cold of New York City seems to seep through the brick walls of the hospital itself.

Inside the emergency room of New York Hospital, the air was thick with the frantic energy of a crisis in motion. A gurney wheeled in, carrying Libby Zion. She was eighteen years old—a college freshman with her whole life ahead of her. She was vibrant, she was loved, and in that moment, she was terrified.

Libby was burning with a fever. She was agitated, jerking with strange, spasmodic movements that her parents, Sidney and Elsa, could not understand. They looked to the doctors—the men and women in white coats—as saviors. They believed, as we all do, that the hospital is a fortress of safety.

The physicians who met Libby were not incompetent. They were residents at one of the most prestigious teaching hospitals in the world, the cream of the academic crop. They had spent their entire lives studying, sacrificing, and training for moments exactly like this. They wanted to save her.

But they were suffering from a condition that, at the time, was not viewed as a biological liability, but as a badge of professional honor: profound, crippling exhaustion.

The intern in charge of Libby had been awake for over eighteen hours. The supervising resident had been on duty even longer. They were operating in a fog—a cognitive gray zone where judgment slows, empathy dulls, and memory becomes a slippery, elusive thing.

In this state, they made a decision that would change the course of American medicine. To calm Libby's violent shaking, they administered Demerol, a powerful opioid.

It was a standard choice. Under normal circumstances, it might have been the right choice. But these were not normal circumstances. The doctors were biologically compromised. They were unaware—or perhaps, in their sleep-deprived haze, unable to recall the specific contraindication—that Libby was taking Nardil, an antidepressant.

The two drugs collided in her bloodstream like chemicals in a volatile reaction. They triggered **Serotonin Syndrome**, a catastrophic overload of the nervous system.

Libby's temperature spiked to 107 degrees. Her muscles seized. She went into cardiac arrest. Despite the frantic efforts of the crash team, Libby Zion died before the sun came up over the East River.

The investigation that followed was brutal. It was led by Libby's father, Sidney Zion, a lawyer and writer who channeled his grief into a crusade. He wanted to know who killed his daughter. He wanted a name. He wanted a villain.

But as he peeled back the layers of the event, he found something more. disturbing than a "bad doctor." He found a broken system.

It wasn't the drugs that killed Libby; it was the schedule. The residents were working 36-hour shifts, clocking over 100 hours a week. They were hallucinations of doctors, moving through the wards like ghosts, fueled by caffeine and fear.

Libby's death led to the "Zion Regulations," the first laws in history limiting how many hours a doctor could work. But nearly forty years later, despite these rules, the core biological problem remains unsolved.

We are still treating patients with tired brains. We are still asking human beings to defy their own biology in the name of healing. And unless we change the model, the next Libby Zion could be you.

The Ghost of Dr. William Halsted

To understand why we do this—why we torture young doctors with sleeplessness and wear exhaustion as a badge of honor—we have to look back to the man who invented the modern residency: **Dr. William Stewart Halsted.**

If you walk the halls of Johns Hopkins Hospital today, you will see his portrait. Dr. Halsted was the first surgeon-in-chief in the 1890s. He was a giant of medicine, a genius who pioneered the radical mastectomy and the use of sterile gloves. He believed that doctors should live in the hospital (hence, the term "residents"). He demanded total immersion. He created a culture where working twenty hours a day was the minimum standard of dedication.

For a century, medical schools have worshipped Dr. Halsted. We tell young medical students to be like him. We tell them that if they want to be great, they must push past the need for sleep. We tell them that stamina is a proxy for competence.

But there was a secret behind Dr. Halsted's superhuman stamina. A secret that was omitted from the commencement speeches for decades.

Dr. William Halsted was a cocaine addict.

Dr. William Halsted was fueled by a drug that allowed him to bypass the natural need for sleep. He built a system designed for an addict, and then he populated it with sober people.

Think about the absurdity of this. The entire structure of medical training—the 24-hour shifts, the grueling "on-call" nights, the idea that a doctor doesn't need rest—is based on the physiology of a man who was high on cocaine.

For a hundred years, we have tried to emulate Dr. Halsted's "grit" without his chemical assistance. The result has been a quiet epidemic of error. We treat sleep as a luxury, a weakness to be trained out of us. We act as if the Hippocratic Oath can override our circadian rhythms.

But biology does not care about our professional culture. Biology is physics. And when you fight biology, biology always wins.

The Drunk Doctor

Let's move from history to the present day. Let's talk about **you**.

You would never board an airplane if the pilot announced over the intercom, *"Folks, just so you know, I haven't slept in twenty-four hours, but I'm going to try really hard to land this plane."*

You would never get into a taxi if the driver's eyelids were drooping and their head was nodding.

Yet, every day, in every city in the world, we allow surgeons to cut into our bodies after sleepless nights. We allow pediatricians to calculate life-saving dosages for children at the end of 30-hour shifts.

The science on this is terrifyingly clear.

In a landmark study published in *Nature*, researchers Dawson and Reid quantified the impact of fatigue on cognitive performance. They put subjects through a series of psychomotor tests while keeping them awake. They then compared those results to subjects who were given alcohol.

The results were undeniable:

- After **seventeen hours** of sustained wakefulness, performance impaired to the level of a blood alcohol concentration (BAC) of **0.05%**.

- After **twenty-four hours**, performance plummeted to the equivalent of a BAC of **0.10%**.

In the United States, you are legally drunk at **0.08%**.

That means if you are operated on by a surgeon who is at the end of a traditional 24-hour call shift, you are essentially being operated on by someone who is legally intoxicated.

Their reaction times are slowed. Their tunnel vision is narrowed. Their ability to weigh complex risks—like the interaction between Demerol and Nardil—is chemically compromised.

When the brain is deprived of sleep, specific and measurable degradation occurs. The neurons in the prefrontal cortex—the CEO of the brain, responsible for logic, reasoning, and risk assessment—begin to misfire. Metabolic waste products, usually cleared during sleep by the **glymphatic system**, build up and clog our neural pathways.

We stop analyzing; we start reacting. We revert to the amygdala, the primitive center of emotion and instinct. We miss the subtle sign of sepsis in a blood test because our brain is desperately trying to conserve energy.

The numbers bear this out with ruthless consistency. A study in the New England Journal of Medicine tracking interns found that those working recurring 24-hour shifts made **36% more serious medical errors** and **five times as many diagnostic mistakes** as those working shorter shifts.

These aren't "bad" doctors. They are biologically compromised humans. They are trying their best, but they are fighting a losing war against their own physiology.

The Author's Reality: A Confession

I am writing this not as an observer, but as a participant. I am an eye surgeon. I have performed thousands of procedures. And I have lived inside "The Gap" of exhaustion.

I remember a specific night early in my career. It was 3:30 AM. I had been on my feet for nearly 20 hours. My back was screaming in protest. My eyes felt like they were filled with sand. I was standing over a patient, performing a delicate intraocular surgery (therapeutic keratoplasty).

The room was silent, save for the rhythmic beeping of the monitor. My hands were moving, performing the motions I had practiced a hundred times. But my mind was drifting. For a split second—a micro-second of terrifying blankness—I forgot where I was in the procedure.

It was a momentary lapse. I snapped back, focused, and completed the therapeutic keratoplasty surgery successfully. The patient was fine. But when I walked out of that operating theater and peeled off my gloves, my hands were shaking. Not from the surgery, but from the fear.

I realized then that I was not a superhero. I was a biological organism running on fumes. I realized that my patient's safety relied not just on my skill, but on my stamina. And stamina is a finite resource.

How many other doctors have had that micro-second of blankness? How many times did the coin flip the wrong way?

We hide these stories. We are taught to project invincibility. But invincibility is a lie. And believing the lie is what gets patients killed.

Decision Fatigue: The 4:00 PM Problem

But it isn't just the lack of sleep that degrades performance. It is the sheer volume of choices.

Medicine is a profession of constant decision-making. *Should I order this scan? Is this dose too high? Does this patient need to be admitted? What about their insurance?*

The human brain has a finite supply of "executive function"—the mental energy required to make these choices. Every time a doctor makes a decision, they deplete this energy tank. By the end of the day, the tank is empty.

Psychologists call this **Decision Fatigue**.

In 2014, researchers analyzed over 21,000 office visits for acute respiratory infections. They wanted to see if the time of day affected the quality of care. They found a disturbing pattern.

If you saw your doctor at 8:00 AM, you were likely to get the correct treatment. But as the day wore on, the doctors became progressively more likely to prescribe antibiotics for viral infections.

This is a fundamental medical error. Antibiotics kill bacteria; they do not kill viruses. Prescribing them for a cold is useless, expensive, and contributes to the global crisis of antibiotic resistance. So why were good doctors doing it?

Because prescribing an antibiotic is the "easy" decision.

When a patient comes in sick, they want a cure. Explaining to them that it is "just a virus" and they need to wait it out takes time. It takes emotional energy. It requires negotiation.

At 9:00 AM, the doctor has the energy to have that conversation. But at 4:00 PM? The brain is tired. The brain wants to go home. The brain knows that writing a script takes 30 seconds and makes the patient leave happy.

The data showed that antibiotic prescribing rates increased incrementally throughout the day. A patient seen at 4:00 PM was significantly more likely to receive an unnecessary (and potentially harmful) drug than a patient seen at 9:00 AM.

The doctor didn't become less knowledgeable at 4:00 PM. They didn't forget their medical school training. They simply became tired of saying "no."

This is the "Friday Afternoon Trap." And it affects everything from antibiotic prescriptions to cancer screenings to surgical checklists.

The Limit of the Human Hard Drive

Beyond fatigue, there is the issue of capacity. The modern medical landscape has become too vast for the human mind to encompass.

Fifty years ago, a doctor could reasonably expect to know everything in their field. Today, medical knowledge doubles every 73 days. There are over 10,000 known diseases, thousands of drugs, and millions of potential genetic interactions.

To stay completely current, a general practitioner would need to read **29 hours a day**.

We are asking human beings to memorize millions of data points, work 24-hour shifts, and recognize obscure patterns in split seconds. We are asking for perfection from a species defined by its fallibility.

Dr. Atul Gawande, in his book *Complications*, famously wrote: "*We look for medicine to be an orderly field of knowledge and procedure. But it is not. It is an imperfect science, an enterprise of constantly changing knowledge, uncertain information, fallible individuals.*"

We have reached the biological limit of what a human physician can do alone. We have built a system that relies on heroism, and heroism is not a strategy. Heroism is a failure of design.

The Partner That Never Sleeps

This is where the promise of the **Infallible Doctor** begins.

The solution is not to train doctors harder. It is not to tell them to drink more coffee or have more "grit." We have tried that for a hundred years, and it hasn't worked.

The solution is to acknowledge our limits and bring in a partner that has none.

An Artificial Intelligence algorithm has no circadian rhythm. It does not have a pineal gland secreting melatonin to tell it to sleep. It does not have a mortgage to worry about. It does not get into arguments with its spouse. It does not get hungry. It does not suffer from decision fatigue.

An AI reviewing a patient's chart at 4:00 AM is exactly as sharp, exactly as precise, and exactly as thorough as it is at 9:00 AM.

Imagine if a "Silicon Resident" had been monitoring Libby Zion's inputs that night in 1984.

It would not have mattered that the intern was awake for 18 hours. It would not have mattered that the resident was exhausted. The moment the order for Demerol was entered into the system, the AI would have scanned Libby's entire history in a millisecond.

It would have seen the Nardil prescription from months ago. It would have recognized the fatal interaction pattern—not because it remembered it from a lecture, but because it has access to the entire pharmacopeia of human knowledge instantly.

It would have blocked the order. A red box would have flashed on the screen:

[FATAL INTERACTION DETECTED]

[DEMEROL + NARDIL = SEROTONIN SYNDROME]

[RECOMMENDATION: HALT ADMINISTRATION]

It would have offered an alternative. It would have been the tap on the shoulder that the tired resident needed. It would have saved her life.

A New Contract

This is not a story about machines replacing doctors. It is a story about machines saving doctors from themselves.

By offloading the vigilance—the constant, grinding need to check every interaction and every dosage—to an AI, we free the human doctor to do what humans do best: to think, to care, and to connect.

We cannot engineer human beings to need less sleep. We cannot genetically modify residents to be like Dr. William Halsted without the cocaine. But we can engineer a system that doesn't sleep at all.

The Infallible Doctor is the safety net beneath the trapeze. It ensures that when the human hand slips—and it will slip, because we are human—the patient does not fall.

THE TAKEAWAY

The "Drunk Doctor" Reality: After 24 hours of wakefulness, a doctor's cognitive performance is equivalent to a Blood Alcohol Content of **0.10%** (legally drunk). Yet, we still allow them to operate.

The "4:00 PM Problem": Decision Fatigue is real. As the day goes on, doctors run out of mental energy, leading to more errors (like unnecessary antibiotics) simply because they are tired of making choices.

The Halsted Curse: The modern residency system was designed by a cocaine addict (Dr. William Halsted) to push humans beyond their limits. It is a broken model that kills patients.

The Solution: We need a "Silicon Resident." AI allows us to maintain 24/7 vigilance without biological fatigue, catching the errors that the exhausted human brain misses.

References

1. Asch, D. A., & Parker, R. M. (1988). "The Libby Zion Case: One step forward or two steps backward?" *New England Journal of Medicine*, 318(12), 771-775.
2. Dawson, D., & Reid, K. (1997). "Fatigue, alcohol and performance impairment." *Nature*, 388(6639), 235.
3. Landrigan, C. P., Rothschild, J. M., Cronin, J. W., Kaushal, R., Burdick, E., Katz, J. T., ... & Czeisler, C. A. (2004). "Effect of reducing interns' work hours on serious medical errors in intensive care units." *New England Journal of Medicine*, 351(18), 1838-1848.
4. Linder, J. A., Doctor, J. N., Friedberg, M. W., Reyes Nieva, H., Birks, C., Meeker, D., & Fox, C. R. (2014). "Time of day and the decision to prescribe antibiotics." *JAMA Internal Medicine*, 174(12), 2029-2031.
5. Lockley, S. W., Cronin, J. W., Evans, E. E., Cade, B. E., Lee, C. J., Landrigan, C. P., ... & Czeisler, C. A. (2004). "Effect of reducing interns' weekly work hours on sleep and attentional failures." *New England Journal of Medicine*, 351(18), 1829-1837.

Chapter 2

Drowning in Data

Why No Human Can Read 30 Million Papers

"We have built a culture of medicine based on the dangerous illusion of individual omniscience. But in an age where the sum of human medical knowledge doubles every few months, the greatest asset a doctor can possess is not a perfect memory, but the humility to partner with a machine that never forgets."

— Dr. Suresh Kumar Pandey

The Myth of the Master Physician

For a moment, I want **you** to close your eyes and imagine the perfect doctor.

Perhaps you picture a figure like Dr. House, brilliant and acerbic. Or maybe you picture a Marcus Welby type—kind, gray-haired, leaning forward in a leather chair. She is well-rested. She is unhurried. She listens to your symptoms with the focus of a detective and the empathy of a saint.

When you finish speaking, listing your aches and your fears, she pauses. She consults the vast library of her mind. She connects the disparate dots of your physiology—the pain in your shoulder, the slight elevation in your blood pressure, the history of your grandmother's illness. With absolute certainty, she delivers the diagnosis.

This is the archetype we have cherished for centuries. It is the image that drives young students to study until their eyes burn. It is the standard by which every physician is judged.

But there is a problem with this image. **It is a lie.**

Even this perfect version of a human physician, possessing the highest IQ and the deepest dedication, is fighting a losing battle. She is fighting against a mathematical impossibility. She is standing on the shore of a beach, holding a plastic bucket, trying to catch a tsunami.

To understand why modern medicine is failing to live up to its promise—and why **you** might be at risk even when seeing the "best" specialist—we have to look at the velocity of information.

In 1950, it was estimated that the total amount of medical knowledge in the world doubled roughly every **50 years**.

A doctor who graduated from Harvard Medical School in 1950 could walk out with a black bag and a diploma, and practice for their entire career relying on what they learned in the lecture hall. The "truths" of medicine were static. The textbooks on their shelf were monuments to stability.

But then, the acceleration began. The internet, genomics, and global research networks ignited a fire.

- By 1980, medical knowledge was doubling every **seven years**.
- By 2010, it was doubling every **3.5 years**.

Today, researchers estimate that the entirety of medical knowledge—the sum of all genomics, proteomics, clinical trials, and case studies—doubles every **73 days**.

Think about the crushing weight of that statistic. If a bright-eyed student starts medical school today, by the time they finish their first semester of Anatomy, the medical world has already generated **twice as much information** as existed on their first day of class. By the time they finish their residency, the world they studied has largely ceased to exist.

We are drowning in data. And in that flood of information, beneath the crushing weight of the unread and the unknown, patients are dying.

The Woman in the Iron Room

To see the human cost of this data avalanche, we must travel to the sterile, high-tech wards of the University of Tokyo's Institute of Medical Science.

The year was 2015. A sixty-year-old woman had been admitted with a diagnosis of **Acute Myeloid Leukemia (AML)**. It is a brutal disease, a cancer of the blood and bone marrow that moves with terrifying speed.

The doctors at the university were not amateurs; they were world-class experts in hematology. They did exactly what their training and the guidelines dictated. They started her on the standard chemotherapy protocols designed for AML. They waited for the remission.

But the remission never came.

Instead, she got worse. Her body wasn't responding. The cancer cells were laughing at the drugs. The medical team was baffled. They adjusted the dosage. They switched agents. They held conferences, reviewing her charts late into the night, looking for the variable they had missed.

Nothing worked. The woman was slowly dying, her immune system collapsing, her recovery turning into a funeral march. The finest human minds in Japan had hit a wall. They had reached the limits of human processing power.

Desperate, the team decided to try something that, at the time, felt like science fiction. They turned to an experimental partner: **IBM Watson**, an Artificial Intelligence system designed to ingest and understand medical literature.

They took the woman's genetic sequence—the billions of letters of DNA that made up her unique biology—and fed it into the system.

A human researcher, even a diligent one, might be able to review a few dozen papers in a week. Watson did not have that limitation. In just **ten minutes**, the AI cross-referenced the woman's specific genetic mutations against **20 million** oncology research papers, clinical trials, and medical records stored in its cloud database.

Ten minutes. That is the time it takes you to drink a cup of coffee.

The machine spit out a diagnosis. The doctors froze.

They had been wrong.

The woman did not have standard Acute Myeloid Leukemia. She had a rare, secondary form of leukemia caused by a specific and obscure genetic mutation that the doctors had never encountered in their practice. Because the diagnosis was different, the treatment needed to be different. The standard chemotherapy was useless against this specific genetic enemy.

Watson suggested a different therapeutic agent—a drug that targeted her specific mutation.

The doctors, humbled and hopeful, switched the medication. The effect was almost immediate. The woman's immune system recovered. The cancer receded. She lived.

The Twenty-Nine Hour Day

We must ask the uncomfortable question: Why did the human doctors miss this? Were they negligent? Were they lazy? Did they not care about the dying woman?

No. They missed it because they were **human**.

The clue to the woman's rare condition wasn't in the standard textbooks. It was likely buried in a table in the appendix of a research paper published three years prior in a journal in Sweden, or hidden in a clinical trial note from a lab in Boston.

To find that clue, a human doctor would have needed to read those 20 million papers.

Let's look at the math of the modern physician's life. Currently, over **2.5 million** new scientific papers are published every year. That is roughly **7,000 new papers every single day**.

If a doctor wanted to stay completely, truly up-to-date in their field—reading every study, every trial result, every new drug interaction, every case report—they would need to read for **29 hours a day**.

Obviously, this is impossible. The physics of time do not allow it. So, doctors do what any rational human would do: they specialize. They filter. They narrow their focus to a pinhead.

The cardiologist reads the top five journals in cardiology and ignores the rest. The neurologist reads *Brain* and *The Lancet Neurology* and hopes for the best.

But the human body does not respect our academic silos. It is a messy, interconnected system. A heart condition might be linked to a gut bacteria discovery published in a gastroenterology journal. A psychiatric symptom might be explained by a virus detailed in an immunology paper.

When **you** rely solely on human brains to store and retrieve knowledge, you are gambling. You are betting your life that your specific doctor happened to read the one paper that explains your specific pain on the one night they weren't too exhausted to keep their eyes open.

In the case of the woman in Tokyo, that gamble almost cost her life. The cure was there, sitting in the library, but it was invisible to the humans standing at her bedside.

The Author's Confession: The Shame of Not Knowing

I need to be honest with you about what this feels like from my side of the light—peering through the optics of the slit lamp.

I am an eye surgeon. I have dedicated my life to the pursuit of vision. But there are nights when I sit in my office, the lights dimmed, surrounded by stacks of medical journals that I haven't had time to open, and I feel a profound, silent sense of failure.

I look at those piles—my personal "Tower of Guilt"—and I know that buried somewhere in those glossy pages is a piece of data, a new technique, or a drug interaction that could change the outcome for a patient I will see tomorrow.

But I cannot read them.

I have a cataract surgery list starting at 8:00 AM. I have a waiting room full of anxious patients. I have a family waiting for me at home. I have a biological need to sleep.

The cognitive load is not just heavy; it is crushing. Yet, we are trained to hide this weight. We are terrified of the three hardest words in medicine: *"I don't know."* We are trained to project omniscience, to wear the white coat like a suit of armor that deflects ignorance.

But that projection is a lie, and it is a dangerous one. It prevents us from asking for help. We are fighting a villain, but for decades, we have been too proud to name it.

The Villain: The 17-Year Gap

The villain is **"The Gap."**

The tragedy of the "Data Avalanche" is not just about the rare "medical mysteries" like the woman in Tokyo. It is about the mundane, everyday tragedy of delay.

Because it is so hard for doctors to keep up with the tsunami of new information, there is a massive, systemic lag time between scientific discovery and clinical practice. Researchers call this the **"Knowledge-Practice Gap."**

A seminal study by Balas and Boren at the Institute of Medicine revealed a number that should haunt every patient: on average, it takes **17 years** for new medical evidence to become common practice in hospitals.

Seventeen years.

That means if a researcher in Oxford discovers a better way to treat diabetic blindness today—a way that prevents blindness or amputation—it might not become the standard treatment at your local clinic in Ohio or Aurangabad until the year **2043**.

What happens in those seventeen years?

Patients are treated with the "old way." They are taking drugs that science already knows are less effective. They are undergoing surgeries that have already been proven unnecessary. They are suffering complications that could have been avoided.

I witnessed this disconnect firsthand during my own training.

While the science of cardiac care and infection control was racing forward, the practice on the ground often stood still. I still visit hospitals today where dedicated, well-meaning physicians are treating patients exactly as they were taught in residency two decades ago. They aren't stubborn; they are simply isolated from the data stream. They are relying on a 'mental hard drive' that effectively stopped recording new updates the day they left medical college.

This gap is a silent killer. It means that for nearly two decades, the "best care" is available only to the lucky few who happen to be treated at the cutting-edge academic centers where the research is happening. Everyone else is living in the medical past.

Flash Forward: A Day in 2035

So, what does the alternative look like? How do we defeat The Gap?

Imagine it is the year 2035. You are not in a high-tech university hospital in Tokyo. You are in a small, rural clinic in a village in India, or perhaps a remote town in rural America.

You have a strange rash and a fever. The doctor there is kind, but he is a generalist. He hasn't read a paper on dermatology in five years. In the old world, he would give you a steroid cream and send you home.

But in this world, he has a **Silicon Resident**.

As he enters your symptoms into the electronic record, the system is silently querying the "Global Hive Mind."

Just four hours ago, a research team in Brazil published a paper about a new viral strain affecting the skin, carried by a specific type of insect that has recently migrated due to climate change.

The human doctor in your village has never heard of this virus. He has never been to Brazil. He hasn't read the paper.

But the AI has.

Before the doctor can even write the prescription for the cream, a notification pops up on his tablet.

[ALERT: SYMPTOM CLUSTER MATCHES NEWLY IDENTIFIED 'ZIKA-B' VARIANT.]

[SOURCE: JOURNAL OF TROPICAL MEDICINE, PUBLISHED TODAY, 04:00 GMT.]

[RECOMMENDATION: DO NOT USE STEROIDS. INITIATE ANTIVIRAL PROTOCOL A.]

The Gap vanishes. The distance between discovery and delivery shrinks from **17 years to 17 seconds**.

You get the right treatment, not because your doctor was a genius who read 29 hours a day, but because your doctor was humble enough to partner with a machine that did.

The End of Memorization

This brings us to the second pillar of the **Infallible Doctor**. If the first pillar is the "Tireless Eye" (overcoming fatigue), the second is the **"Infinite Library."**

For centuries, medical college has been an exercise in brute-force memorization. We test students on how many bones, nerves, enzymes, and drug names they can cram into their hippocampus. We treat the human brain as a storage device.

But in the age of AI, memorization is a waste of valuable cognitive real estate. We do not need doctors to be walking hard drives. We have hard drives for that. We have the cloud.

We need doctors to be translators.

In the future described in this book, the "Medical Knowledge Bank" will not live in the doctor's head. It will live in the system, updated in real-time, every second of every day.

This shifts the fundamental role of the physician. The doctor's job is no longer to *know* the answer. The doctor's job is to *ask the right question.*

Your doctor's value to you will be their ability to navigate the complexities of your values, your fears, and your goals, and then to explain the answer provided by the collective intelligence of the world to the frightened human being sitting in the room.

We are moving from an era where the doctor was a solitary genius, holding a candle in the dark, to an era where the doctor is a pilot, guided by a network of satellites that illuminate the entire world at once.

The avalanche of data is no longer a threat that drowns us. It becomes the reservoir that saves us.

THE TAKEAWAY

The 29-Hour Day: To stay current with the 7,000 medical papers published daily, a human doctor would need to read for 29 hours every single day. Since this is impossible, most doctors are unknowingly practicing with outdated information.

The Villain is "The Gap": There is currently a **17-year lag** between a scientific discovery and its routine use in clinics. This "Knowledge-Practice Gap" means patients die while the cure sits in a library.

The "Silicon Resident" Solution: AI acts as an "Infinite Library." It doesn't replace the doctor; it acts as a research partner that can scan 20 million papers in 10 minutes (like in the IBM Watson case), ensuring **you** get the treatment discovered today, not the one taught 20 years ago.

References

1. Densen, P. (2011). "Challenges and opportunities facing medical education." *Transactions of the American Clinical and Climatological Association*, 122, 48–58.
2. Otterman, S. (2016). "Artificial Intelligence May Help Doctors Diagnose, Treat Cancer." *The New York Times*, October 16, 2016.
3. Balas, E. A., & Boren, S. A. (2000). "Managing Clinical Knowledge for Health Care Improvement." *Yearbook of Medical Informatics*, 9(1), 65-70.
4. Bastian, H., Glasziou, P., & Chalmers, I. (2010). "75 trials and 11 systematic reviews a day: how will we ever keep up?" *PLoS Medicine*, 7(9), e1000326.
5. Institute of Medical Science, University of Tokyo. (2016). "IBM Watson identifies rare leukemia in 10 minutes." *Press Release/Case Report.*

Chapter 3

The Bias Trap

When the Mind is the Most Dangerous Tool in the Room

"We like to believe that medicine is an objective science, immune to the prejudices of the world. But a doctor is a human being before they are a physician, and they carry into the exam room every stereotype, every shortcut, and every blind spot of their culture. The promise of the Infallible Doctor is not just to be smarter than us, but to be fairer than us."

— Dr. Suresh Kumar Pandey

The Voice in the Recovery Room

She was, by any objective metric, one of the most physically powerful and somatically aware human beings on the planet. She had won 23 Grand Slam titles. She had pushed her physiology to the absolute limit of human performance for two decades. She knew the difference between the burn of lactic acid and the tear of a ligament. She knew her own body better than any textbook could describe.

And yet, as she lay in a hospital bed in September 2017, gasping for air, **nobody would listen to her.**

Serena Williams had just given birth via an emergency C-section. The surgery had gone well, and her daughter, Olympia, was healthy. But the next day, a familiar, terrifying feeling washed over her. The air felt thin. Her chest felt tight.

Having a history of pulmonary embolisms—blood clots in the lungs—she knew exactly what was happening. Her body was screaming a specific, technical warning.

She flagged down a nurse. She gasped out her self-diagnosis between breaths: *"I need a CT scan with contrast and heparin."*

It was a precise, medical request. It was the correct request. But the medical staff looked at the world-famous athlete and saw something else. They saw a confused patient. They saw an "emotional" new mother. Perhaps it was the pain medication talking.

The medical staff told her to calm down. One doctor performed an ultrasound on her legs—a procedure Serena knew would show nothing because the clot had already traveled to her lungs—and dismissed her concerns.

Serena persisted. She fought through the fog of surgery, the exhaustion of childbirth, and the condescension of the staff to demand the scan. Finally, reluctantly, they agreed.

The CT scan revealed exactly what Serena said it would: several small blood clots had settled in her lungs. If she had waited any longer, if she had been less famous, or less insistent, she likely would have died.

Serena Williams survived. But her story highlights a terrifying question that haunts the corridors of modern medicine, and it is a question **you** need to ask yourself:

If a wealthy, world-famous superstar cannot get doctors to listen to her pain, what chance do you have?

What chance does a poor woman from the Bronx have? What chance does a non-English speaker have?

This is **The Bias Trap**.

It is the invisible distortion field that surrounds the doctor-patient relationship. It is not necessarily born of malice—the doctors didn't *want* Serena to die. They weren't bad people. But they were operating with a human brain that relies on shortcuts, stereotypes, and cultural assumptions.

Unlike the "Exhausted Mind" of Chapter 1, which fails because it is tired, the "Biased Mind" fails because it thinks it knows the truth before it even looks at the data.

The Heuristic Glitch: Why Your Doctor's Brain is Lazy

To understand why bias kills, we have to look at the machinery of the human mind. We have to look at the evolution of the very organ we trust to save us.

The human brain is a **pattern-recognition engine**. It is designed to make quick judgments based on limited data. This is an evolutionary survival mechanism known as a "heuristic."

Imagine a caveman standing in the savannah. He sees a rustle in the tall grass. He doesn't pause to analyze the wind velocity, the type of foliage, or the probability of animal migration patterns. His brain shouts **LION**, and he runs.

If he is wrong, he has wasted a few calories running. If he is right, he has saved his life.

Evolution favored the humans who jumped to conclusions. We are the descendants of the paranoid and the presumptuous.

In medicine, heuristics are usually helpful. A doctor sees a specific bullseye rash and immediately thinks *Lyme Disease*. It saves time. It saves lives.

But heuristics have a dark side. When the "pattern" the brain relies on is based on social stereotypes rather than biological facts, the diagnostic process collapses.

The rustle in the grass isn't a lion; it's just the wind. But the doctor is already running.

When a doctor looks at a patient, their brain instantly categorizes them within milliseconds: *Male/Female. Old/Young. White/Black.*

Rich/Poor. Before the patient has even opened their mouth to say "Hello," the doctor's brain has already loaded a set of assumptions.

If the patient is an overweight man complaining of chest pain, the heuristic says Heart Attack.

If the patient is a young woman complaining of chest pain, the heuristic says Anxiety.

This isn't medical science. It is a biological glitch. And it is deadly.

The Pain Gap: Believing the Myth

The data proves that these mental shortcuts are not just harmless assumptions; they result in quantifiable suffering.

Let's talk about pain. Pain is subjective. There is no blood test for "how much it hurts." Therefore, the treatment of pain relies entirely on the doctor's empathy and their belief in the patient's story.

In a disturbing study published in the *Proceedings of the National Academy of Sciences*, researchers surveyed medical students and residents—the future of healthcare. These were students at top medical schools in the 21st century.

They found that a shocking **50% of them believed at least one biological myth about Black patients.**

They believed things like:

- "Black people's nerve endings are less sensitive than white people's."
- "Black people's skin is thicker than white people's."
- "Black people's blood coagulates more quickly."

None of this is true. It is scientific nonsense, remnants of 19th-century race science that have somehow persisted in the cultural ether.

The result of this bias is that Black patients are systematically undertreated for pain.

A meta-analysis of twenty years of pain studies found that Black patients are **22% less likely** to receive pain medication than white patients for the exact same conditions.

Even children are not immune. Black children admitted to the ER with appendicitis—a condition known for excruciating pain—are significantly less likely to receive opioids than white children.

The doctor looks at the child and, influenced by a subconscious cultural narrative that views Black bodies as "stronger" or "more resilient," underestimates their suffering. The heuristic fails. The child suffers.

I want you to imagine that child is yours. Imagine knowing your child is in agony, but the person with the power to help them simply *does not believe them.*

The Yentl Syndrome

The bias trap is not limited to race. It is deeply entrenched in gender. If you are a woman reading this, you have likely experienced **"medical gaslighting"**—the feeling that your symptoms are being dismissed as "stress" or "hormones."

For decades, the standard textbook model for a heart attack was a middle-aged man clutching his chest. This is the "Hollywood Heart Attack."

But women often present with different symptoms: nausea, jaw pain, shortness of breath, or extreme fatigue.

Because the male body was treated as the "default" human in medical research for most of the 20th century, doctors frequently misdiagnose women suffering from heart failure as suffering from anxiety, indigestion, or panic attacks.

This phenomenon is so pervasive it has a name: **The Yentl Syndrome** (named after the Isaac Bashevis Singer character who had to disguise herself as a man to get an education).

A 2018 study from the University of Leeds analyzed data from over 500,000 heart attack patients. The findings were stark: **Women were 50% more likely than men to receive an initial wrong diagnosis.**

That delay—the time wasted prescribing anti-anxiety meds when the heart muscle is dying—is often the difference between life and death. The "pattern matcher" in the doctor's brain sees a stressed woman complaining of nausea and thinks *Panic Attack.*

The heuristic fails. The patient dies.

The Machine That Is Colorblind (and the Machine That Isn't)

Enter the **Infallible Doctor.**

On the surface, Artificial Intelligence seems like the perfect antidote to the Bias Trap.

An algorithm does not grow up watching movies that stereotype minorities. It does not have a subconscious fear of the "angry black woman." It does not think women are "hysterical." It is math. It deals in cold, hard zeros and ones.

If you feed an AI the vitals of a patient—heart rate, troponin levels, EKG readout—it does not care if the patient is Serena Williams or a librarian from Ohio. It analyzes the data.

In theory, an AI diagnostic tool acting as a "check" on the human doctor could eliminate the Yentl Syndrome overnight. When the doctor enters "Female, 40, nausea, jaw pain" and prescribes anti-anxiety meds, the AI could flag the chart:

[ALERT: SYMPTOMS CONSISTENT WITH MYOCARDIAL INFARCTION.]

[NOTE: PATIENT GENDER INCREASES RISK OF ATYPICAL PRESENTATION.]

[RECOMMENDATION: TROPONIN TEST IMMEDIATELY.]

This is the promise: **The Objectivity Engine**. A layer of digital neutrality that forces the human doctor to justify their decision with data, not gut feeling.

However, the story is not that simple. As we build this new healthcare system, we are discovering that AI has a trap of its own.

Garbage In, Garbage Out: The Algorithmic Prejudice

We must be brutally honest about the risks. **AI is not magic; it is a mirror.**

It learns by analyzing historical data. And what is historical data? It is the record of how humans have treated patients in the past. If the history of medicine is biased, the AI will learn to be biased, too.

In 2019, a bombshell study published in Science by Dr. Ziad Obermeyer revealed a catastrophic flaw in a widely used healthcare algorithm. This algorithm was being used by major hospitals and insurance companies to manage care for **200 million people** in the United States. Its job was to identify "high-risk" patients who needed extra medical attention and resources.

The algorithm worked by predicting which patients would spend the most money on healthcare in the future. The logic seemed sound: sicker people cost more money, so if we find the expensive patients, we find the sickest patients.

But there was a hidden variable.

In the U.S. healthcare system, Black patients historically receive less care than white patients with the same level of illness. They face barriers to access, they are under-treated (as we saw with pain management), and they are often uninsured.

Therefore, on average, a sick Black patient accumulates **lower medical costs** than an equally sick white patient.

The algorithm looked at the data and learned a terrible rule: *Black patients cost less, therefore they must be healthier.*

The result? The algorithm was routinely denying extra help to Black patients with kidney disease and diabetes, while flagging healthier white patients for priority care.

The algorithm wasn't "racist" in the way a human is. It didn't hate anyone. It was simply optimizing for the wrong variable (cost instead of biology). But the impact was indistinguishable from racism.

The Solution: The "Woke" Algorithm

This failure was a wake-up call for the tech industry. It proved that we cannot just "set it and forget it."

But here is the good news—and the reason why the **Infallible Doctor** is still our best hope.

Unlike human bias, which is deeply psychological and incredibly hard to unlearn, algorithmic bias can be fixed with **code**.

To cure a human doctor of implicit bias requires years of therapy, cultural training, and constant self-reflection. And even then, in a moment of stress or fatigue (the "Exhausted Mind"), the old habits return. The lizard brain takes over.

To cure an AI of bias, you change the code. You validate the data. You fix the math.

Once the researchers identified the error in the Obermeyer study, they were able to reprogram the algorithm. They told the AI to **stop looking at cost** and **start looking at biological markers**—blood pressure, glucose levels, kidney function.

Almost instantly, the bias disappeared. The percentage of Black patients flagged for help jumped from **17% to 46%**, accurately reflecting the reality of the patient population.

This is the profound difference between the Human Doctor and the Infallible Doctor. Once the machine is fixed, it stays fixed forever. It never has a bad day. It never relapses.

Flash Forward: The Auditor in the Room (2030)

So, what does a bias-free future look like for you?

Imagine it is 2030. You are a woman of color presenting to an Emergency Room with abdominal pain. The doctor is a tired, overworked human who subconsciously views you as "drug-seeking" rather than in pain.

In the old world, he would send you home with Tylenol.

But in this world, there is a third participant in the room: **The Auditor AI.**

This is an algorithm designed specifically to watch the doctor. It monitors the conversation, the vitals, and the chart notes in real-time.

As the doctor moves to discharge you, a notification freezes his tablet.

[AUDIT ALERT: DISCREPANCY DETECTED]

[OBSERVATION: PATIENT PAIN SCORE IS 8/10. VITALS INDICATE TACHYCARDIA.]

[DATA MATCH: IN 98% OF SIMILAR CASES INVOLVING WHITE MALE PATIENTS, YOU ORDERED A CT SCAN.]

[QUERY: PLEASE CONFIRM CLINICAL REASONING FOR DEVIATION.]

The prompt forces the doctor to pause. It holds up a mirror

to his decision-making. It shines a light in the dark corners of his subconscious.

He looks at you again. He looks at the data. He realizes the machine is right. He orders the scan.

The Great Equalizer

Serena Williams knew her body. She knew something was wrong. But she was fighting against a system that viewed her through a filter of stereotypes.

The promise of AI and Robotics in healthcare is often sold as a story of efficiency and speed. But its true moral value lies in its potential for **Justice**.

A robotic surgeon does not have a "steady hand" for the CEO and a "shaky hand" for the janitor. It cuts with the same micron-level precision for both. An AI diagnostician does not respect a patient more because they are wearing a suit, nor does it dismiss a patient because they are struggling with English. It respects the data.

We are building a system where the standard of care is not determined by who you are, or what you look like, or the subconscious prejudices of the exhausted human standing at the end of your bed.

We are building a system where the only thing that matters is the **truth of your biology.**

But we must be vigilant. The "Bias Trap" serves as a warning: Technology amplifies intent. If we build these systems carelessly, we will automate inequality. But if we build them with eyes wide open—if we force our machines to be better than us—we can finally create a healthcare system that is truly blind to everything except the cure.

THE TAKEAWAY

The Heuristic Glitch: Your doctor's brain uses "shortcuts" to save energy. Often, these shortcuts are based on stereotypes (e.g., "Women are anxious," "Black skin is thicker"), leading to deadly misdiagnoses.

The Pain Gap: Studies show 50% of medical trainees believe false biological myths about Black patients, and women are 50% more likely to be misdiagnosed during a heart attack (Yentl Syndrome).

The "Mirror" of AI: AI can learn bias from history (like the Optum algorithm that prioritized cost over illness), but unlike humans, AI can be **permanently fixed** with code.

The Future is "Audited": The Infallible Doctor includes "Auditor AIs" that flag biased decisions in real-time, forcing human doctors to treat every patient with the same rigorous standard of care.

References

1. Hoffman, K. M., Trawalter, S., Axt, J. R., & Oliver, M. N. (2016). "Racial bias in pain assessment and treatment recommendations, and false beliefs about biological differences between blacks and whites." *Proceedings of the National Academy of Sciences*, 113(16), 4296-4301.
2. Obermeyer, Z., Powers, B., Vogeli, C., & Mullainathan, S. (2019). "Dissecting racial bias in an algorithm used to manage the health of populations." *Science*, 366(6464), 447-453.
3. Vyas, D. A., Eisenstein, L. G., & Jones, D. S. (2020). "Hidden in Plain Sight — Reconsidering the Use of Race Correction in Clinical Algorithms." *New England Journal of Medicine*, 383(9), 874-882.
4. Wu, J., et al. (2018). "Impact of Gender on the Diagnosis and Management of AMI." *Journal of the American College of Cardiology*. (Reference supporting Yentl Syndrome data).
5. Centers for Disease Control and Prevention (CDC). "Pregnancy Mortality Surveillance System." (Data regarding racial disparities in maternal mortality).

Chapter 4

The Deadly Game of Telephone

How Silence Kills in a Fragmented System

"We have built a medical system of breathtaking complexity, populated by brilliant individuals who are experts in their narrow fields. But we have forgotten that a patient is not a collection of isolated organs; they are a single story. When we fail to share that story, the silence between us becomes a weapon."

— Dr. Suresh Kumar Pandey

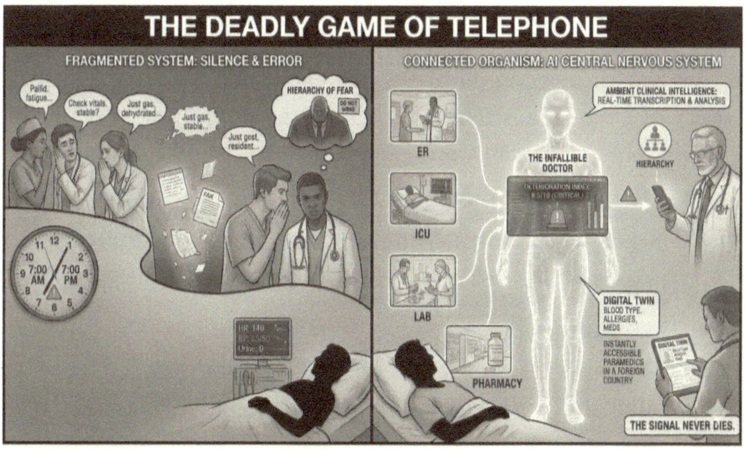

The Empty Chair on Sunday

Lewis Blackman was fifteen years old. He was the kind of boy who seemed to vibrate with a quiet, boundless potential—a brilliant student, a gifted saxophone player, a kid who looked at the world with a curiosity that promised a limitless future. He was healthy, strong, and resilient.

In November 2000, he walked into a large teaching hospital in South Carolina for a routine, elective procedure. He had a condition called *pectus excavatum*—a congenital deformity where the breastbone sinks into the chest. It wasn't life-threatening, but corrected, it would give him more room to breathe and play his music.

The surgery was the Nuss procedure, a standard operation involving the insertion of a curved metal bar to push the chest out. It went perfectly. The surgeons were pleased. The bar was in place. The chest was reshaped. Lewis was sent to the recovery floor, and his parents were told that the hard part was over.

Four days later, Lewis was dead.

He didn't die from the surgery. He didn't die from a slip of the knife or a mysterious, incurable infection. He died because of a silence.

Lewis had developed a perforated ulcer—a known, albeit rare, side effect of the heavy dose of Toradol (a non-steroidal anti-inflammatory drug) he was prescribed for pain management. A hole had opened in his stomach. Gastric acid and blood were slowly leaking into his abdomen.

It is a terrifying complication, but it is treatable if caught early. The tragedy of Lewis Blackman is that the signs were there, screaming to be heard, but the system was deaf.

Over the course of the weekend, Lewis's vitals began to crash.

- His heart rate, normally a resting 60, climbed to 100.
- Then 120.
- Then 140.

His blood pressure softened. His belly grew distended, hard, and agonizingly painful. He stopped producing urine—a classic sign that the kidneys are starving for blood because the volume is leaking elsewhere.

His mother, Helen Haskell, sat by his bedside. Put yourself in her chair. You are watching your child deteriorate. You know something is wrong. You beg the staff for help. She asked the nurses, "*Why is his heart rate so high?*" She asked the residents, "*Why is he in so much pain?*"

But it was the weekend. The senior attending surgeon—the man who had performed the operation, the man who carried the ultimate responsibility—had gone home for his Sunday off. The care of the boy fell to a rotating cast of interns and residents, young doctors who were overworked, inexperienced, and terrified of making a mistake.

They looked at the symptoms through the lens of their limited experience. They assumed it was just *ileus*—a common condition where the bowels stop moving after surgery, causing gas and bloating. They told themselves a comforting story: *It's just gas. He's dehydrated. He's anxious.*

Crucially, the residents were afraid to call the senior attending at home on a Sunday. The hierarchy of medicine is steep and intimidating. You do not wake the boss unless you are sure. They didn't want to look incompetent. They didn't want to be the resident who cried wolf over a case of constipation.

So, they stayed silent.

Meanwhile, the nurses were diligently recording Lewis's declining vitals in the chart. Heart rate 130. BP 85/50. But nobody was connecting the dots. The inputs were there, but the message never traveled from the paper chart to the brain of a decision-maker who could interpret it.

By the time the autopsy was performed, Lewis had **2.8 liters of blood and gastric acid** in his abdomen. He had bled to death internally, surrounded by nurses, doctors, and monitors, inside one of the most modern institutions in the world.

Lewis Blackman was not killed by a disease. He was killed by **The Communication Gap**.

The Myth of "The Hospital"

We often imagine a hospital as a cohesive, well-oiled machine. When **you** check in, you believe that "The Hospital" is treating you. You assume there is a central brain guiding the ship, ensuring that the left hand knows what the right hand is doing.

But I am here to tell you that "The Hospital" does not exist.

In reality, a modern hospital is a collection of fragmented, isolated silos. It is a loose confederation of independent contractors—surgeons, anesthesiologists, nurses, pharmacists, lab technicians, social workers—who rarely speak to each other directly. They inhabit the same building, but they live in different worlds.

Instead of conversation, they communicate through the world's most dangerous game of "Telephone."

Consider the trajectory of a simple piece of information about **you**:

1. **The Night Nurse** notices you look pale at 4:00 AM. She writes a note in the chart: "Patient appears pallid, complains of fatigue."
2. **The Intern** arrives at 7:00 AM. He is rushing to see twenty patients. He scans the vitals but misses the nurse's note because it is buried under a tab labeled "Nursing Assessment."
3. **The Attending Specialist** arrives at 2:00 PM. She looks at you for five minutes. She doesn't know about the morning pallor. She prescribes a blood pressure medication.
4. **The Pharmacist** dispenses the drug at 4:00 PM, unaware that the nephrologist (kidney specialist) discontinued a similar drug yesterday on a different computer system.

This fragmentation is the single biggest source of peril in modern medicine. According to the Joint Commission, the organization that accredits US hospitals, **communication failures are the root cause of over 70% of sentinel events**—unexpected deaths or serious injuries.

We are playing with fire. Your life is relying on sticky notes, pagers, fax machines, and hallway whispers to manage life-and-death data in an environment of extreme complexity.

The Author's Confession: The Hierarchy of Fear

I need to explain why those residents didn't call the attending surgeon for Lewis Blackman. It is easy to call them cowards, but the reality is more structural.

The 2:00 AM Gamble

I still carry the visceral memory of my residency at PGIMER, Chandigarh. I remember the paralyzing weight of "The Call."

It was 2:00 AM. We were transferring a polytrauma patient following a complex eye repair. But the monitors were whispering a warning. His blood pressure was drifting south.

The orthopedic resident found himself trapped in a dangerous calculation. He knew the patient was unstable. But he also knew the Senior Surgeon had just collapsed into sleep after an eight-hour surgery. In the brutal hierarchy of our training, waking the boss was a high-stakes gamble. Call too early, and you are branded as incompetent—a panic-prone rookie who can't handle the pressure. You risk a public dressing-down on morning rounds.

So, he chose silence. He waited.

He stared at the monitor, bargaining with the universe to keep the patient alive until shift change at 6:00 AM.

He got lucky that night. The patient survived. But luck is not a clinical strategy. Relying on chance is a violation of our oath. That fear—the hesitation to speak truth to power—is a silent killer. It builds a "Psychological Wall" that traps vital data at the bottom of the hierarchy. In the case of Lewis Blackman, that wall was the difference between life and death.

The Handoff: The Most Dangerous Time of Day

If you want to know when you are most likely to die in a hospital, do not look at the operating room schedule. **Look at the clock.**

The most dangerous time to be a patient is at **7:00 AM and 7:00 PM**.

This is the time of **"The Handoff."**

The team that has been working for twelve hours—tired, eyes gritty, brains saturated with data—hands the baton to the fresh team. They have perhaps fifteen minutes to summarize the status of twenty patients.

The complexity of your life is compressed into a thirty-second sound bite.

"Room 304 is stable, post-op day two. Room 306 is grumpy, pain management issues. Room 308 needs a CT scan."

In this compression, nuance is lost. The "gut feeling" that the night nurse had about a patient's breathing pattern—a subtle shallowness that doesn't trigger an alarm but signals trouble—is rarely verbalized. The tiny downward trend in blood pressure is glossed over as "stable."

This is where the **Swiss Cheese Model** of accident causation comes into play.

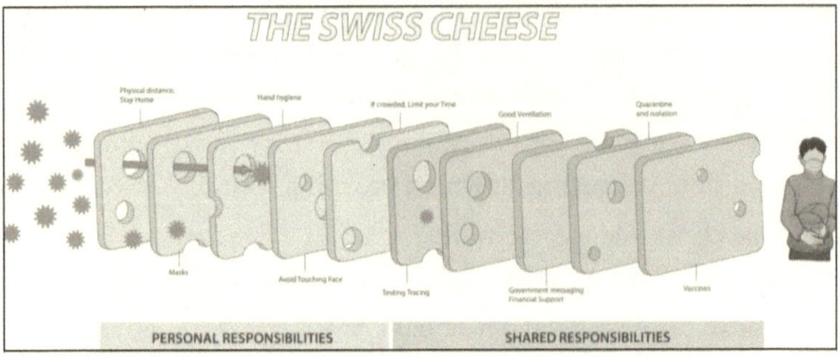

Imagine slices of Swiss cheese lined up next to each other. Each slice represents a layer of defense: the nurse, the resident, the pharmacist, the electronic alert system. Each slice has holes—flaws in the system.

Usually, the holes do not align. The nurse misses the allergy, but the pharmacist catches it. The resident misses the symptom, but the attending sees it. The patient is safe.

But during a bad handoff, the holes align perfectly. The nurse forgets to mention the declining urine output. The resident assumes the chart is correct. The attending is busy with a trauma case. The arrow of error passes straight through the holes, striking **you**.

The Tower of Babel

The problem of human communication is compounded by technology that refuses to cooperate. We have built a digital Tower of Babel.

In the banking world, interoperability is absolute. You can withdraw money from an ATM in Tokyo using a card from a small bank in Ohio. The systems talk to each other. The data flows like water.

In healthcare, we cannot move a medical record across the street.

If you are treated at City Hospital for a car accident and then transferred to University Hospital five miles away for rehab, your records often do not travel with you. The doctors at the second hospital are flying blind. They cannot see your CT scans. They cannot see your lab trends.

They have to repeat the blood tests—wasting money and your blood. They have to ask you, a traumatized patient, the same questions you already answered three times.

Why? Because their software system (e.g., Epic) cannot "speak" to the other hospital's system (e.g., Cerner) without a fax machine acting as the interpreter.

This lack of **Interoperability** is a tragedy. It means that your medical history is scattered across ten different databases—your dentist, your GP, the ER you visited on vacation, your specialist. No single human being has the full picture. And in medicine, what you don't know can hurt you.

The Universal Translator: AI as the Central Nervous System

This is where the **Infallible Doctor**—the AI-driven healthcare system—changes the physics of the hospital.

To fix the Communication Gap, we don't need doctors to talk more. We don't need more meetings. We need a **Central Nervous System**. We need a digital layer that sits above the humans, listening, watching, and connecting the dots that the silos miss.

Imagine the Lewis Blackman case in a hospital integrated with AI.

1. The Silent Monitor

Lewis is prescribed Toradol. The AI, which has access to millions of patient outcomes, knows that Toradol carries a significant risk of gastrointestinal perforation in adolescents. It immediately flags Lewis as "High Risk for GI Bleed" in the background surveillance system. It does not sleep. It does not go home for the weekend.

2. The Trend Watcher

As Lewis's heart rate rises from 80 to 100, and his blood pressure dips slightly, the nurse records the vitals. In the old system, these are just numbers on a page, easily dismissed as "post-op stress."

In the new system, the AI sees the vector. It calculates a **"Deterioration Index"** (like the Rothman Index) in real-time. It sees the pattern of hypovolemia (blood loss) forming hours before the human eye can detect the crash.

3. The Escalation Protocol

The moment the vitals cross a safety threshold, the AI acts. It does not have an ego. It does not have a fear of hierarchy. It does not worry about waking up the boss.

It sends a secure, high-priority alert directly to the smartphone of the Senior Attending Surgeon at home:

[ALERT: PATIENT BLACKMAN. POST-OP DAY 4.]

[DETERIORATION INDEX SPIKE: 8.5/10.]

[PATTERN: CONSISTENT WITH INTERNAL HEMORRHAGE.]

[ACTION: IMMEDIATE BEDSIDE EVALUATION REQUIRED.]

The hierarchy is broken. The fear is removed. The machine speaks truth to power, ensuring that the most experienced person is brought to the bedside when they are needed most.

Ambient Intelligence: The End of the Keyboard

One of the biggest barriers to communication is, ironically, the tool we invented to help it: the computer screen.

Doctors today spend **two hours typing for every one hour they spend with patients**. They are glorified data entry clerks, staring at screens, clicking drop-down menus, searching for billing codes. This phenomenon, often called "Death by Click," consumes the cognitive bandwidth that should be used for thinking and talking.

When your doctor is typing, they are not looking at you. They are missing the wince of pain on your face. They are missing the subtle cue.

The solution is **Ambient Clinical Intelligence (ACI)**.

Imagine a consultation room with no computer screen between you and the doctor. Just two humans sitting in chairs, talking. On the wall, an inconspicuous device—no larger than a smoke detector—is listening. Using advanced Natural Language Processing (NLP)—the same technology behind Siri or Alexa, but trained on medical dictionaries—it transcribes and analyzes the conversation in real-time.

Doctor: "I'm worried about that cough. Let's schedule a chest X-ray and start you on Amoxicillin, 500mg."

Patient: "Okay, but remember I had a bad rash with Penicillin last year."

Doctor: "Oh, right, thank you for reminding me. Let's make it Azithromycin then."

The AI listens. It drafts the note. It orders the X-ray. Crucially, it catches the allergy correction in real-time.

[ACTION: ORDER AZITHROMYCIN.]

[ALERT: PENICILLIN ALLERGY UPDATED.]

The doctor doesn't type a word. The note is perfect. The handover to the next doctor is legible, complete, and instant. The "Telephone Game" is replaced by a perfect digital transcript of reality.

Flash Forward: Your Digital Twin in 2032

Let's visualize what true interoperability looks like for **you**.

Imagine it is 2032. You are on vacation in Paris. You are involved in a car accident. You are unconscious. You are rushed to a French trauma center. The doctors there do not speak your language. They do not know your history.

In today's world, this is a recipe for disaster. They might give you a drug you are allergic to. They might miss your underlying heart condition.

But in this future, your **Digital Twin** travels with you.

As the paramedics load you into the ambulance, their tablet "shakes hands" with your phone or your smart watch. Instantly, your entire medical history—translated into French—appears on their screen.

- *Blood Type: O Negative.*
- *Allergies: Penicillin.*
- *Current Meds: Beta-Blockers.*
- *Recent Surgery: Appendectomy (2030).*

The "Tower of Babel" falls. The data follows the patient, not the hospital. The silos are dissolved.

The Connected Organism

When we bridge the Communication Gap, the hospital transforms. It stops being a warehouse of sick people attended by isolated experts. It becomes a single, cohesive organism.

Lewis Blackman's mother, Helen Haskell, became a fierce advocate for patient safety after her son's death. She helped pass the "Lewis Blackman Hospital Patient Safety Act," which mandates that patients must have a way to call for help and know who is in charge of their care.

But laws are just paper. To truly honor the victims of the Communication Gap, we need a system that cannot be silenced by a weekend shift, a lost file, or a hierarchy of fear.

We need a system where the signal never dies. We need the Infallible Doctor to be the voice that speaks when the humans are too afraid, or too tired, to speak for themselves.

THE TAKEAWAY

The "Game of Telephone": 70% of serious medical errors are caused by communication failures, not lack of skill. Information degrades as it passes from nurse to intern to attending.

The Danger Zones: The most dangerous times in a hospital are **7:00 AM and 7:00 PM** (shift changes) and weekends, when the "A-Team" goes home and the "holes in the Swiss Cheese" align.

The Villain is "The Hierarchy": Junior doctors are often too afraid to wake up senior doctors for help. This "Hierarchy of Fear" prevents critical information from moving up the chain.

The AI Solution: AI acts as a **Central Nervous System**. It creates a "Deterioration Index" that monitors patient trends 24/7 and automatically alerts the senior doctor if a patient is crashing, bypassing the hierarchy and ensuring no patient dies of silence.

References

1. The Joint Commission. (2015). "Sentinel Event Data: Root Causes by Event Type." *The Joint Commission Annual Report.*
2. Starmer, A. J., Spector, N. D., Srivastava, R., West, D. C., Rosenbluth, G., Allen, A. D., ... & Landrigan, C. P. (2014). "Changes in medical errors after implementation of a handoff program." *New England Journal of Medicine*, 371(19), 1803-1812.

3. Haskell, H. (2006). "Lewis Blackman: A mother's story." *Agency for Healthcare Research and Quality (AHRQ) WebM&M.*

4. Reason, J. (2000). "Human error: models and management." *BMJ*, 320(7237), 768-770.

5. Coiera, E. (2000). "When conversation is better than computation." *Journal of the American Medical Informatics Association*, 7(3), 277-286.

Chapter 5

The Myth of "Art"

Trading Subjective Intuition for Objective Science

"We have long comforted ourselves with the idea that medicine is an art—a mysterious alchemy of intuition and experience. But when that 'art' becomes an excuse for inconsistency, bias, and error, it ceases to be a virtue. The Infallible Doctor demands that we trade the romance of the gut feeling for the reliability of the data."

— **Dr. Suresh Kumar Pandey**

The Painting in the Dark

For centuries, we have been seduced by a painting.

It is the image of the solitary physician, sitting by the bedside in a pool of lamplight, chin resting in hand, deep in contemplation. The child in the bed is sick; the parents are in the shadows, terrified. The doctor has no machines, no algorithms, only his mind and his presence.

This is the archetype of the **Healer**. In this romantic vision, medicine is not merely a technical trade but a high, mysterious art form. We are told that the best doctors possess a "clinical eye," a "sixth sense," or a "gut feeling" that transcends textbooks.

We venerate the gray-haired diagnostician who walks into a room, sniffs the air, glances at your complexion, and instantly divines the obscure malady that baffled the interns.

We cling to this myth because it feels human. It suggests that at the core of our survival lies a magical, empathetic connection between one soul and another.

But I am here to tell you a hard truth: **This painting is a lie.** And it is a lie that kills.

There is a terrifying price to be paid for viewing medicine as an art rather than a science, and that price is paid in human lives.

To understand why the "art of medicine" is a dangerous concept, we must first strip away the nostalgia and look at what "art" actually means in a functional sense. Art is, by definition, subjective. Art is expression. Art is variable.

If you ask ten master painters to capture the same sunset, you will receive ten radically different canvases—some impressionistic, some photorealistic, some abstract. We celebrate this variance in a gallery.

But if you take ten master cardiologists and show them the same angiogram, and they provide **ten different opinions** on whether to operate on your heart, we should not call it art.

We should call it a **system failure**.

Yet, this is exactly what happens in hospitals around the world every single day. The "art" of medicine is often just a euphemism for "noise"—the unwanted, random variability in human judgment that leads to error.

The Tragedy of the "Flu"

Consider the harrowing reality of **sepsis**, a condition that perfectly illustrates the lethal gap between human intuition and objective data.

Sepsis is the body's extreme response to an infection, a chaotic chain reaction that can lead to tissue damage, organ failure, and death.

It kills roughly **11 million people globally** every year, accounting for nearly 20% of all deaths worldwide.

The tragedy of sepsis is that it is treatable if caught early, but catching it requires spotting a constellation of subtle physiological shifts—a slight drop in blood pressure, a marginal tick upward in respiratory rate, a minor change in white blood cell count.

To the human eye—even an expert eye—a patient in the early stages of sepsis often just looks "unwell" or "tired."

In a bustling Emergency Department in London a few years ago, a young woman arrived complaining of flu-like symptoms. She was lucid. She was chatting with the nurses. She was scrolling on her phone.

The triage nurse, relying on the "art" of clinical assessment—which is heavily influenced by how a patient *looks* and *acts*—categorized her as non-urgent. The doctor, exhausted near the end of a twelve-hour shift, saw a young, healthy-looking person and intuitively ruled out catastrophic illness.

This is what psychologists call the **"representativeness heuristic"**—the mental shortcut where we judge the probability of an event by how much it resembles our existing mental prototype. She didn't look like the prototype of a dying patient. She looked like someone with a bad cold.

She was sent home with advice to rest. Six hours later, she was rushed back in an ambulance, her organs shutting down, her body ravaged by septic shock. She died before sunrise.

The "art" of medicine failed her because her appearance lied, but her data had been screaming the truth.

Had her vitals been fed into an algorithmic model rather than a human "gut check," the outcome would likely have been different.

In hospital systems that have implemented AI-driven sepsis alerts, such as the **Sepsis Watch** developed at Duke University, the machine does not care how the patient "looks." It does not get tired. It does not suffer from compassion fatigue.

It continuously analyzes dozens of variables from the electronic health record every hour. In pilot programs, these systems have shown the ability to predict septic shock **12 hours before** the average clinician notices the clinical signs.

The machine sees the subtle mathematical drift in the patient's physiology that the human eye, blinded by the "art" of subjective assessment, misses entirely.

The Illusion of Intuition

The persistence of the "art" myth is rooted in our misunderstanding of what intuition actually is. We treat intuition as a superpower, but **Daniel Kahneman**, the Nobel Prize-winning psychologist, exposed it as simply **"recognition."**

It is the brain's ability to match a current situation with a past memory. This works wonderfully for a firefighter who intuitively senses a floor is about to collapse because he has seen the subtle signs of burning timber a thousand times. The feedback loop is immediate: the floor collapses, or it doesn't. He learns.

But in medicine, the feedback loop is broken.

A doctor makes a diagnosis, prescribes a treatment, and often never sees the patient again. Did the patient get better? Did they die? Did they go to another doctor?

Without immediate, accurate feedback, "clinical intuition" does not sharpen into expertise; it hardens into **confidence without competence.**

This reliance on subjective judgment creates a landscape of terrifying inconsistency. In a landmark study on "noise" in medicine, researchers presented the **exact same biopsy slides** of potential skin cancer lesions to a group of experienced pathologists. The expectation was that these experts, trained in the "art" and science of tissue analysis, would agree.

They did not.

The study found that the pathologists agreed on the diagnosis only about **75% of the time**. Even more disturbing: when the **same pathologists** were shown the **same slides** a few months later, they contradicted their **own previous diagnoses** in a significant percentage of cases.

This is the "art" of medicine in action: the diagnosis you get depends on which doctor you see, what time of day it is, and whether they have had lunch.

The Impact of Lunch on Your Life

The impact of "lunch" is not a facetious exaggeration; it is a statistical reality that dismantles the romanticism of the medical profession.

In a now-famous study analyzing judicial rulings, researchers found that judges were significantly more likely to grant parole in the morning and immediately after food breaks. As their glucose levels dropped and decision fatigue set in, their "intuition" defaulted to the status quo—denying parole.

The same phenomenon has been observed in clinicians. Antibiotic prescribing rates for acute respiratory infections increase as the clinic day wears on.

As the doctor's mental energy depletes, the rigorous "science" of explaining why antibiotics aren't needed for a virus gives way to the sloppy "art" of just writing the script to satisfy the patient and move on.

The "art" of medicine is susceptible to hunger, fatigue, and mood. An algorithm is not. An algorithm is never "hungry."

The Shield for Bias

We must also confront the uncomfortable truth that the "art" of medicine has historically been a shield for bias. When we allow room for "clinical impression," we allow room for prejudice.

Studies confirm that women's pain is consistently underestimated compared to men's. The data regarding racial disparities is even starker.

Black patients in the United States are significantly less likely to receive adequate pain medication than white patients for the exact same injuries.

Why? Because the "art" of assessment is filtered through the doctor's subconscious biases about who "looks" like they are in pain and who "looks" like they are drug-seeking.

Precision medicine, driven by data, offers a way out of this trap. A pain algorithm based on physiological biomarkers—heart rate variability, pupil dilation, galvanic skin response—does not see race or gender. It sees suffering.

By replacing the subjective "art" of pain assessment with objective metrics, we don't remove humanity; we restore **justice**.

The Pilot and the Doctor

The resistance to this shift is fierce, and it is emotional. Doctors fear that by yielding to algorithms, they will become mere technicians, stripped of their agency. They worry that medicine will become "cookbook" care, cold and mechanical.

But we must ask: what is the true purpose of medicine? Is it to validate the doctor's intellect, or to save **your** life?

The aviation industry faced this exact existential crisis decades ago. In the early days of flight, pilots were "artists" of the sky, flying by the seat of their pants, relying on feel and instinct. And planes crashed. Often.

Then came the era of checklists, automation, and autopilot. Pilots initially resisted, feeling it was an insult to their skill. But aviation became the safest form of travel in human history.

We do not want an "artist" in the cockpit; we want a systems manager who understands the instruments. We should demand nothing less from the person holding the scalpel.

The Relocation of Art

However, deconstructing the myth of the "art" of medicine does not mean there is no room for the human element. It simply requires us to **relocate where that humanity lives.**

The "art" should not be in the diagnosis. The diagnosis should be a matter of computational certainty. If a machine can analyze a mammogram with 99% accuracy while a human radiologist hovers at 85%, using the human for diagnosis is not art; it is negligence.

The true art of medicine lies in what happens **after** the diagnosis.

It is in the communication of complex news. It is in the navigation of difficult ethical choices. It is in the comforting of a frightened family.

Dr. Dhruv Khullar, a physician and writer, noted that while an AI can diagnose a terminal illness with frightening precision, it cannot help a patient decide how they want to spend their final months. It cannot hold a dying patient's hand and offer the specific, intuitive comfort that calms fear.

That is the true art.

But currently, doctors are so bogged down by the cognitive load of being "data processors"—trying to memorize drug interactions, analyze labs, and synthesize symptoms—that they have no bandwidth left for the human connection.

By offloading the science of diagnosis and treatment planning to AI—by embracing the **"death of the art of guessing"**—we liberate the doctor to practice the **"art of caring."**

Flash Forward: The Exam Room of 2035

Let's visualize this new world.

It is 2035. You walk into a clinic with a persistent cough.

The doctor does not spend ten minutes staring at a screen, typing. The screen is gone. The "Silicon Resident" has already analyzed your cough's acoustic signature from your smartphone microphone and flagged a 92% probability of early-stage bronchitis. It has already checked your genomic profile and confirmed you are a slow metabolizer of codeine.

The doctor walks in. She knows the diagnosis. The machine has done the "science."

She sits down. She looks you in the eye. She asks about your job, your stress, your family. She explains the treatment plan with empathy and clarity. She spends the entire visit being a human being, not a detective.

You leave feeling heard, cared for, and accurately diagnosed.

The "Art" didn't disappear. It just moved to where it belonged: in the connection between two people.

The New Image

The numbers tell us the transition is inevitable. Diagnostic errors currently affect an estimated **12 million Americans** each year.

This epidemic of error costs the US economy over **$100 billion annually**, but the human cost is incalculable. Behind every one of those 12 million errors is a person who was told they were fine when they were dying, or told they were dying when they were fine.

We are standing at the precipice of a new era where we can stop relying on the fallible "clinical gaze" of a single human being. We can instead rely on the collective intelligence of millions of cases, processed by deep learning, to guide the hands of our healers.

The romantic myth of the intuitive physician is a relic of a time when we had no other choice. When we didn't have MRIs, genomic sequencing, or neural networks, the doctor's "gut" was the best tool we had. But clinging to it now is like insisting on navigating the ocean by the stars when you have a GPS system, simply because looking at the stars feels more nautical.

It is time to let the painting of the solitary, contemplating genius fade. In its place, we must build a new image: a physician supported by the unblinking eye of the algorithm, using the **science of data** to ensure precision, so they can use the **art of their humanity** to ensure healing.

The era of the "art of medicine" must end, so that the era of **"perfect medicine"** can begin.

THE TAKEAWAY

The Myth of "The Clinical Eye": We romanticize doctors who diagnose by "gut feeling," but science shows that intuition is often just **recognition**—and without immediate feedback, it leads to overconfidence and error.

The "Noise" Problem: Human judgment is inconsistent. Studies show that pathologists disagree on the same biopsy 25% of the time, and judges make harsher rulings when hungry. AI eliminates this "noise."

Sepsis & The "Flu" Trap: Human doctors often miss sepsis because patients "look fine" until they crash. AI systems like **Sepsis Watch** detect subtle mathematical changes 12 hours earlier, saving lives by ignoring appearances.

Relocating the Art: We don't want robots to replace humanity. We want AI to handle the diagnosis (Science) so the doctor can focus on empathy (Art). The future is High-Tech enabling High-Touch.

References

1. Kahneman, D., Sibony, O., & Sunstein, C. R. (2021). *Noise: A Flaw in Human Judgment*. Little, Brown Spark.
2. Topol, E. (2019). *Deep Medicine: How Artificial Intelligence Can Make Healthcare Human Again*. Basic Books.
3. Makary, M. A., & Daniel, M. (2016). "Medical error—the third leading cause of death in the US." *The BMJ*, 353, i2139.
4. Danziger, S., Levav, J., & Avnaim-Pesso, L. (2011). "Extraneous factors in judicial decisions." *Proceedings of the National Academy of Sciences*, 108(17), 6889-6892.
5. Komorowski, M., Celi, L. A., Badawi, O., Gordon, A. C., & Faisal, A. A. (2018). "The Artificial Intelligence Clinician learns optimal treatment strategies for sepsis in intensive care." *Nature Medicine*, 24(11), 1716-1720.

PART II
The Silicon Resident
Meeting Your New Medical Partner

Chapter 6

The Centaur Physician

Not a Replacement, But a Superpower

"We have long accepted that to err is human. But in medicine, we must now accept a new truth: to persist in error when a machine can save us is no longer just human—it is negligent. The machine does not replace our compassion; it clears the fog so we can find it again."

— **Dr. Suresh Kumar Pandey**

The Chessboard and the Ward

In 1997, the world held its collective breath as a machine named Deep Blue sat across the chessboard from **Garry Kasparov**.

Kasparov was not merely a grandmaster; he was the reigning world champion, a man whose mind was regarded as a fortress of intuition and calculation. He was the pinnacle of human intellect.

When he lost, the cultural shockwave was instant and apocalyptic. The headlines screamed of our obsolescence. *The machine has won,* they said. *The era of human dominance is over.*

But the story we tell about that match is incomplete. It misses the most crucial chapter—the one that holds the key to **your** survival in a hospital bed tomorrow.

A few years after his defeat, Kasparov did not retreat into history. Instead, he invented a new game called **"Advanced Chess."**

In this version, humans did not play *against* computers; they played *with* them. A human player was paired with a laptop, forming a team.

The results were startling. These human-machine teams, known as **"Centaurs"** (after the mythical half-man, half-horse), didn't just beat other humans. They destroyed the strongest supercomputers in the world.

The combination of human intuition, strategy, and creativity, amplified by the machine's tactical precision and memory, created a level of play that neither biological nor silicon intelligence could achieve alone.

The human provided the *strategy* (the "Art"). The machine provided the *calculation* (the "Science").

This is the defining metaphor for the next era of healthcare. We are not building Deep Blue to replace your doctor. We are building the Centaur to create a **Super-Physician**.

This is the concept of **"Augmented Intelligence."**

Unlike Artificial Intelligence, which often implies a synthetic substitute for the human mind, Augmented Intelligence is designed with a singular, humble purpose: to extend the reach of the human healer.

It is the difference between walking and driving a car. The car does not replace the traveler; it allows the traveler to move at speeds biology never intended, to reach destinations that were previously impossible.

In medicine, we have reached the limits of what the unassisted human mind can hold. We are drowning in data, exhausted by complexity, and prone to the kind of cognitive fatigue that leads to error.

The machine offers us a way out—not by taking over, but by lifting the weight.

The Silent Guardian

To understand what this looks like in the real world—away from the theoretical debates of Silicon Valley—we must step onto the floor of **St. Michael's Hospital** in Toronto, specifically the General Internal Medicine ward.

If you have ever spent time on such a ward—perhaps visiting a sick parent, or lying in a bed yourself—you know the atmosphere. It is a place of high stakes and chaotic variables. Patients here are precarious; they dwell on the threshold between stability and collapse.

For decades, **your safety** on this ward relied entirely on the vigilance of overworked nurses and exhausted residents making rounds.

The problem with this model is that human vigilance is a finite resource. A resident at the end of a twenty-four-hour shift is not the same clinician they were at the start. Their attention wavers. They miss things.

Furthermore, physiological deterioration is rarely sudden; it is a creeping thing.

A silent drop in oxygen saturation from 98% to 94%. A subtle narrowing of pulse pressure. A creeping spike in heart rate from 80 to 95. These are the whispers of a body shutting down.

But amidst the noise of the ward—the phones ringing, the families asking questions, the paperwork piling up—those whispers often go unheard until the **"Code Blue"** alarm shatters the air.

By then, the whisper has become a scream, and it is often too late for you.

In 2020, St. Michael's deployed a system called **CHARTWatch**.

It was not a robotic doctor rolling down the hallways. It was a ghost in the machine, a **Silent Guardian** running in the background of the hospital's servers.

CHARTWatch analyzed thousands of data points from patients' electronic medical records—vital signs, lab results, nursing notes—in real-time. It looked for the subtle mathematical signatures of impending death that no human brain, no matter how brilliant, could track simultaneously for thirty patients.

When the AI detected a high-risk pattern, it didn't fire the doctor. It didn't dispense medication. It simply sent a text message to the nursing team:

"Patient in Room 302 is at high risk of deterioration."

The intervention was quiet, but the results were thunderous.

In a peer-reviewed study published in the Canadian Medical Association Journal, researchers found that the deployment of CHARTWatch led to a staggering **26% reduction in unexpected deaths.**

Let that number sink in.

One in four people who would have died under the "human-only" standard of care walked out of that hospital alive because of this collaboration.

The AI provided the signal; the humans provided the salvation. The doctors and nurses were the ones who rushed to the bedside, interpreted the context, held the patient's hand, and made the critical interventions. The AI made them faster, sharper, and more prescient. It gave them the superpower of foresight.

This is the essence of the **"human-in-the-loop"** model.

The loop is the decision-making cycle: *Observe, Orient, Decide, Act.*

In a purely AI model, the machine does it all, which is ethically fraught and terrifying. In the Centaur model, the machine handles the "Observation" and "Orientation"—processing the ocean of data—while the human retains the "Decision" and the "Action."

This partnership is critical because medicine is not just a game of probabilities; it is a game of context, and AI is notoriously blind to context.

An AI might see a drop in blood pressure and suggest a massive infusion of fluids to stabilize the numbers. But the human doctor knows that **you** have end-stage heart failure and that fluids would drown your lungs and kill you.

The AI provides the raw intelligence; the human provides the wisdom.

The Eye in the Haystack

We see this dynamic playing out with even greater visual drama in the world of radiology, specifically in the fight against **breast cancer**.

For decades, the "gold standard" of screening has been two radiologists scanning every mammogram. It is tedious, eye-straining work.

Imagine looking at a thousand grayscale images of clouds and trying to find a specific, tiny wisp that looks slightly different from the others. That is mammography. Fatigue is inevitable. Missed diagnoses are a statistical certainty.

Enter the **"ScreenTrust"** study from Sweden, a massive trial involving over 80,000 women. The trial pitted the traditional two-human system against a new "Centaur" team: one radiologist supported by an AI algorithm.

The findings, published in *The Lancet Oncology*, effectively ended the debate on whether AI has a place in screening.

The AI-supported radiologists detected **20% more cancers** than the two humans working alone.

But here is the "superpower" aspect that transforms the healthcare system: they did it with a **44% reduction in workload**.

The AI acted as a triage officer. It instantly filtered out the clearly normal scans—the easy clouds—and highlighted the suspicious regions on the complex ones.

It essentially said to the doctor, *"Look here. I think I see something."*

The radiologist then applied their years of training to that specific spot.

This turns the doctor from a carpet bomber into a sniper. It removes the hay so the human can find the needle. The AI did not replace the radiologist's judgment; it directed their attention.

In a world where radiologists are burning out at record rates, this efficiency isn't just about economics; it's about the survival of the specialty itself. And for **you**, the patient, it means your cancer is found today, not next year when it is too late.

The Author's Perspective: The Ego Barrier

I often talk to my colleagues about this future, and the most common reaction I get is not excitement, but fear.

"Will I be replaced?" they ask. *"Will I just be a rubber stamp for the computer?"*

I tell them this: **The AI will not replace the physician. But the physician who uses AI will replace the physician who does not.**

This is a crisis of ego. We have defined our value for too long by our ability to memorize facts and spot patterns. We have prided ourselves on being the smartest person in the room.

But being a Centaur requires humility. It requires admitting that a silicon chip can see things we cannot. It requires us to step down from the pedestal of the "Solo Genius" and accept the role of the "Team Leader."

If we can overcome our ego, we gain a superpower. If we cannot, we become obsolete.

The Pilot and the Autopilot: A Warning

However, we must be careful not to paint a picture of effortless magic. The integration of this superpower is not as simple as installing software. It requires a fundamental rewiring of the doctor's brain and the medical workflow.

There is a dangerous phenomenon known as **"Automation Bias."**

It is the mental trap where humans, lulled by the competence of a machine, become lazy and blindly trust its output. We see this in aviation, where pilots of highly automated aircraft can lose their "stick and rudder" skills, freezing when the autopilot disconnects in a storm.

In medicine, the stakes are just as high.

A cautionary tale emerged from a recent study at MIT and Harvard involving chest X-rays. When radiologists were paired with an AI that provided accurate advice, their performance improved. But the researchers introduced a twist: they deliberately tweaked the AI to give **wrong advice**.

The results were unsettling. The radiologists—even experienced ones—were frequently duped into agreeing with the machine. Their own judgment was overridden by the perceived authority of the algorithm. They saw what the machine told them to see.

This reveals the fragility of the loop. The "human-in-the-loop" cannot be a passive rubber stamp. They must be an active, critical auditor.

We are not raising a generation of doctors to be passengers in a self-driving car; we must raise them to be active pilots.

Think of it like the relationship between a pilot and their navigational computer. The computer processes wind speed, fuel consumption, and route trajectory far better than the pilot can. But if the computer suggests flying into a thunderstorm because it calculates a shorter route, the pilot must have the situational awareness to say, **"No."**

The superpower only works if the human remains the senior partner. If the doctor falls asleep at the wheel, the system is useless. If the doctor is incompetent and relies on the machine to mask their lack of knowledge, the system is dangerous.

The challenge for medical education in the twenty-first century is not just teaching anatomy and physiology, but teaching how to interrogate an algorithm—how to know when to trust the machine, and more importantly, when to overrule it.

Scaling the Miracle

The implications of this augmented model extend far beyond the walls of elite Western hospitals. They reach into the dusty clinics of rural India and the underserved regions of the Global South.

We are currently facing a global shortage of healthcare workers that the World Health Organization estimates will reach **10 million by 2030**.

We simply cannot train enough humans to meet the demand of an aging population. If we insist on the old model—where every single data point must be processed by a human brain—the system will collapse. Augmented Intelligence is the only viable lever we have to scale care.

Consider **diabetic retinopathy**, a leading cause of blindness. In rural India, ophthalmologists are scarce. Millions of people live with diabetes, and for many, the first sign of eye disease is when they go blind. By then, it is irreversible.

To bridge this gap, Google Health developed an AI system that scans images of the retina to detect the disease. But they didn't put it in a robot; they put it in the hands of technicians and nurses in village clinics.

The AI acts as the specialist screener. A technician takes a photo of the eye, and the algorithm analyzes it in seconds. If the AI detects the disease, the patient is referred to a human ophthalmologist for treatment. If the scan is clear, the patient goes home with peace of mind.

This **"Centaur" system** allows a handful of eye surgeons to protect the vision of tens of thousands of people they will never personally screen.

It separates the "technical" task of screening from the "medical" task of treating. The AI bridges the gap between the abundance of need and the scarcity of expertise. It multiplies the doctor.

If an AI can help a dermatologist review 500 skin lesions in the time it used to take to review 50, we have effectively cloned their efficiency without cloning their body.

Flash Forward: Your Appointment in 2030

So, what does this feel like for you?

It is 2030. You are sitting in your doctor's office. The doctor is not frantically typing. She is looking at you.

On the desk, a small screen displays a dashboard. It is the **Centaur Interface**.

While you talk, the AI is silently analyzing your history, your genetics, and the latest research. It suggests three potential diagnoses, ranked by probability. It highlights a potential drug interaction with your vitamins.

The doctor glances at the screen. She nods. She uses her judgment to dismiss the second option because she knows your lifestyle. She validates the first option. She approves the prescription.

The interaction takes fifteen minutes, but it has the depth and safety of a consultation that used to take hours of research.

You leave the office knowing that your care was overseen by two intelligences: one that knows the science of the entire world, and one that knows the story of **you**.

The Symphony of Care

Ultimately, the term "Augmented Intelligence" is a promise to **you**, the patient.

It promises that you will not be cared for by a cold algorithm that views you as a row in a spreadsheet or a collection of billing codes. But it also promises that you will not be cared for solely by an exhausted, fallible human who might have missed the warning signs because they were distracted by a pager or awake for twenty hours straight.

It promises the best of both worlds. It promises a doctor who has the encyclopedic recall of a supercomputer and the empathetic touch of a saint.

We are moving toward a future where the definition of "malpractice" will shift. Today, we sue doctors for using machines when things go wrong. **Tomorrow, we may sue doctors for refusing to use them.**

Just as we would not trust a pilot who turned off the radar to fly by "instinct" in a storm, we will not trust a physician who refuses the help of the algorithm to check a diagnosis or screen for a drug interaction.

The "art" of medicine will not be in the guessing; it will be in the synthesis. The doctor of the future will be a conductor of information, orchestrating the insights of genomics, biosensors, and AI into a symphony of care that is personalized, precise, and profoundly human.

The machine clears the clutter of calculation. It silences the noise of the data so that the physician can return to the bedside, look **you** in the eye, and do the one thing no machine will ever do: care.

That is the true superpower.

THE TAKEAWAY

The Centaur Model: Just as Garry Kasparov formed "Centaur" teams (Human + AI) to beat supercomputers, the future of medicine is **Augmented Intelligence**. The human provides the wisdom; the AI provides the calculation.

The Silent Guardian: Hospitals using AI tools like **CHARTWatch** have seen a **26% reduction in unexpected deaths**. The AI detects the subtle whispers of deterioration before the human eye can, acting as a 24/7 safety net for you.

The Sniper vs. Carpet Bomber: In radiology, AI helps doctors find cancer **20% more often** with **44% less workload**. It filters the "hay" so the doctor can focus entirely on the "needle."

The New Malpractice: We are approaching a time where refusing to use AI will be considered negligent. You deserve a doctor who uses every tool available to keep you safe.

References

1. Verma, Amol A., et al. (2024). "Evaluation of a machine learning-based early warning system for patient deterioration in a general internal medicine ward: A non-randomized controlled trial." *Canadian Medical Association Journal (CMAJ).*
2. Lång, Kristina, et al. (2023). "Artificial intelligence-supported screen reading versus standard double reading in the Mammography Screening with Artificial Intelligence trial (MASAI): a clinical safety analysis of a randomized, controlled, non-inferiority, single-blinded, two-parallel-group, open-label trial." *The Lancet Oncology.*
3. Kasparov, Garry. (2017). *Deep Thinking: Where Machine Intelligence Ends and Human Creativity Begins.* PublicAffairs.
4. Topol, Eric J. (2019). "High-performance medicine: the convergence of human and artificial intelligence." *Nature Medicine*, 25, 44–56.
5. Gaube, Susanne, et al. (2021). "Do as AI say: susceptibility in deployment of clinical decision-aids." *NPJ Digital Medicine.*

Chapter 7

The Alien in the Exam Room

How Machines See What Humans Miss

"For centuries, we believed that to cure, we first had to understand. But we are entering a strange new world where machines can cure without understanding, and see without eyes. Our job is no longer just to teach them; it is to learn what they have found in the dark."

— Dr. Suresh Kumar Pandey

The Ineffable Pattern

There is a moment in medical training, usually during the sleepless haze of residency, when **you** stop looking at a list of symptoms and start seeing a patient.

You walk into a room, glance at the man sitting on the edge of the bed, and before you have checked a pulse or listened to a lung, a quiet bell rings in the back of your mind.

Sick, it says. Or perhaps, *Heart.*

If a medical student asked you how you knew, you would struggle to explain. You might stammer about the pallor of the skin, or the way he leaned forward to breathe, or a certain dullness in the eyes. But the truth is, you didn't calculate it. **You recognized it.**

You recognized a pattern so complex and subtle that it exists below the threshold of language.

This quality—**clinical intuition**—was long considered the sacred, unteachable art of medicine. It was the reason we believed computers could never replace us.

Computers, after all, were creatures of rigid logic. They needed rules. They needed us to write down:

IF skin is pale AND breathing is labored AND age is >60, THEN suspect heart failure.

But medicine is messy. It refuses to obey rigid rules. A heart attack in a forty-year-old diabetic woman looks nothing like a heart attack in an eighty-year-old heavy smoker.

When we tried to program computers with these rulebooks in the 1980s and 90s, they failed miserably. They were like a tourist trying to navigate a chaotic city with a map from 1950. They couldn't handle the nuance.

For a long time, it seemed the dream of AI in medicine was dead. We couldn't explain our intuition to the machine, so the machine couldn't learn.

But then, we stopped trying to be the teacher who writes the textbook. We decided to treat the computer less like a calculator and more like a three-year-old child. We stopped giving it rules, and we started giving it **experiences**.

And that changed everything for **you**, the patient.

The Child and the Chihuahua

Consider how a human child learns what a dog is.

You do not sit a toddler down and lecture them on taxonomy. You do not say, *"Listen closely. A dog is a quadrupedal mammal of the family Canidae. It has a snout length of two to four inches and fur density of X."*

If you did that, the moment the child saw a Poodle—which looks nothing like a Golden Retriever and suspiciously like a cotton ball—they would be baffled. The rules wouldn't fit.

Instead, nature uses a different method.

You show the child a picture of a Labrador and say, "Dog."

You show them a picture of a Beagle and say, "Dog."

Then, the child points at a cat and squeals, "Dog?"

You shake your head. "No. Cat."

In that moment, a microscopic adjustment happens in the child's brain. Neurons fire and rewire. *Okay,* the brain whispers, *pointy ears and whiskers means 'Not Dog'.*

You repeat this process a thousand times. Eventually, the child can look at a **Chihuahua**—a creature they have never seen before, a creature that defies all logical description of a "wolf"—and instantly recognize it as a dog.

They have not memorized a definition. They have learned the pattern.

This is the fundamental shift that ushered in the modern era of Artificial Intelligence. We moved from **"Expert Systems"** (the rulebook) to **"Machine Learning"** (the experience). We built mathematical structures that mimic the way a toddler learns from mistakes.

To do this, we had to build a digital brain.

The Panel of Voters: How the Machine Thinks

Your brain is a wet, tangled web of billions of neurons—tiny cells that zap electricity to one another. When you recognize a face, a specific network of these cells lights up in a cascade, passing the signal from the retina to the visual cortex, filtering noise, sharpening edges, and matching memories.

Scientists, in their attempt to replicate this, created **"Neural Networks."**

Do not think of a Neural Network as a terrifyingly complex equation. Think of it, instead, as a **Panel of Voters**.

Let's imagine we want a computer to look at a chest X-ray and answer a life-or-death question: **Pneumonia or Healthy?**

We feed the X-ray into the system. To the computer, the image is not a picture of a lung; it is a grid of one million numbers. Some are black (air), some are white (bone), some are gray (tissue).

1. The Input Layer (The Eyes)

The first layer of the network receives these one million numbers. Each pixel is a "witness" that shouts its value to the first layer of voters.

2. The Hidden Layers (The Voters)

This is where the magic—and the mystery—happens. The pixels talk to the first layer of digital neurons.

1. **Layer 1** looks for simple edges. One neuron might say, "I see a curved line here."
2. **Layer 2** combines those lines. "If we put these curves together, they form a rib cage."
3. **Layer 3** looks for textures. "Wait, this area in the lower lobe looks cloudy. It's fuzzy."
4. **Layer 4** looks for complex patterns. "Cloudy lung + high density in this specific shape = Suspicious."

Each layer passes its "vote" to the next, the information becoming more abstract and meaningful as it travels deeper into the network.

3. The Output Layer (The Verdict)

The final layer tallies the weighted votes and spits out a probability: "I am 94% sure this is Pneumonia."

When we first turn this machine on, it is spectacularly stupid. It is a blank slate. It looks at a healthy lung and shouts, *"Pneumonia!"*

This is where "Training" begins. It is a high-speed game of "Hot or Cold."

We show the machine an X-ray that we know is pneumonia. The machine guesses "Healthy."

We say, "WRONG. Bad robot."

The machine then performs a mathematical back-flip called **Back-propagation**. It looks back through its layers of voters to find out who messed up. It traces the error back to Layer 3 and says, "You voted for Healthy because you ignored the gray spot. Adjust your dial. Next time, pay more attention to gray spots."

It tweaks the connections. It adjusts the "weights" of the votes.

We do this with 100,000 X-rays. Guess. Correction. Adjust. Guess. Correction. Adjust.

After viewing 100,000 images, the machine has calibrated its internal voters perfectly. It has learned the "texture" of pneumonia in a way no human can fully articulate. It has developed, for lack of a better word, **intuition**.

The Black Box and the Alien Mind

When we stack many, many layers of these digital neurons on top of each other, we call it **Deep Learning**. And this is where the story takes a turn that is both exhilarating and unsettling.

In the old days, we told the computer: "Look for a tumor."

In Deep Learning, the computer figures out what to look for on its own. It might find a pattern that human doctors have never noticed in 5,000 years of medicine.

The most famous example of this—the moment that made the medical community sit up and gasp—came from Google Health in 2018.

The team was training a Deep Learning system to diagnose **Diabetic Retinopathy**.

This is a condition where high blood sugar damages the blood vessels in the back of the eye. It is a leading cause of blindness, especially in developing nations like India where there aren't enough ophthalmologists (retina specialists) to screen the millions of diabetic patients.

Google fed the machine 128,000 images of retinas. The machine acted like the child in the classroom; it looked at the examples and learned to spot the tiny micro-aneurysms and hemorrhages that signal the disease. It became as good, if not better, than U.S. board-certified ophthalmologists. That alone was a triumph.

But then, the researchers got curious. They decided to ask the machine a question that no human doctor could answer.

They showed the AI a picture of a healthy retina and asked:

"Is this patient Male or Female?"

If you ask a human ophthalmologist to do this, they will laugh. It is clinically impossible. There are no known biological markers for gender in a photograph of the fundus. A male retina and a female retina look identical. A human doctor would have a 50/50 chance—a pure guess.

The AI looked at the images. **It predicted the gender with 97% accuracy.**

The researchers were stunned. They assumed it was a bug. They looked at the images again. They zoomed in. They stripped away the metadata. They couldn't see it. To the human eye, the images were identical.

But the Deep Learning network, in its deep, hidden layers, had found a subtle pattern—perhaps a microscopic difference in the thickness of blood vessels, or a slight variation in the curvature of the optic nerve—that correlated with gender.

It had found a signal in the noise that we didn't know existed.

This was a watershed moment. It proved that machines can see things we cannot. It proved that the machine is not just a faster human; it is a **different species of intelligence.**

It is an **Alien Mind** looking at our biology with new eyes.

If the AI can see gender in an eye, what else can it see?

- Can it see early Alzheimer's in the subtle cadence of your walk?
- Can it see a future stroke in the granular tone of your voice?
- Can it see a heart attack in a retina?

(Spoiler: **Yes, it can.** The same Google algorithm can now predict cardiovascular risk factors—blood pressure, smoking status, age—just by looking at the eye, potentially replacing invasive blood tests).

The Clever Hans Warning

However, this power comes with a warning label, one written in invisible ink. Because these systems are **"Black Boxes"**—meaning we see the input and the output, but the "thinking" happens in the opaque hidden layers—we often don't know why the machine made a decision.

This leads to the problem of the **"Clever Hans."**

Hans was a horse in early 20th-century Germany who could famously do arithmetic. If you asked him *"What is 2 plus 3?"*, he would tap his hoof five times. The crowds were amazed. But it turned out Hans couldn't do math. He was just a master observer of body language. He would tap his hoof until he saw the tension release in his trainer's shoulders—the sign that he had reached the right number—and then he would stop.

He wasn't solving the problem; he was gaming the system.

AI can be a digital Hans.

In one now-infamous study, a system was trained to detect skin cancer from photographs of lesions. It performed beautifully in the lab, identifying malignant melanomas with superhuman accuracy.

But when they dug into the "Black Box" to see what the AI was actually looking at, they found something horrifying.

The AI wasn't looking at the cancer cells. It was looking for a ruler.

In the dataset of medical images, malignant tumors were often photographed by dermatologists who placed a small ruler next to the lesion for scale. Benign moles were usually photographed by patients at home, with no ruler.

The AI, in its efficient laziness, had realized:

If there is a ruler, it's cancer. If no ruler, it's benign.

It had learned the pattern, but it was the **wrong pattern**. If deployed in the real world, it would have told a patient with a deadly tumor that they were fine, simply because they forgot to put a ruler next to their skin.

The End of Mystery

This is why the Infallible Doctor cannot be a machine alone. The "Black Box" nature of Deep Learning requires a human counter balance.

We need the "Centaur" model described in the previous chapter more than ever.

The Machine detects the pattern—it sees the gender in the eye, the pneumonia in the pixel. But the Human must validate the logic. The Human must ask: *Are you looking at the lung, or are you looking at a ruler?*

We are moving into an era where the definition of medical knowledge is expanding. For centuries, medicine was a mystery. We poked, we prodded, and we guessed. We treated symptoms because we couldn't see the causes.

Deep Learning is the microscope of the 21st century. Just as the optical microscope revealed bacteria to us for the first time, Neural Networks are revealing the hidden data-structures of disease.

We are no longer just teaching the computer. The computer is teaching us. And if we are willing to listen—and to verify—we may finally find the cures that have hidden in plain sight for all of human history.

THE TAKEAWAY

The Alien Mind: AI doesn't think like us. It finds patterns we didn't know existed—like predicting a patient's gender with 97% accuracy just by looking at a photo of their retina (something no human doctor can do).

The "Voter" Metaphor: Neural Networks work like a panel of voters. Simple layers spot lines; complex layers spot shapes. They learn by experience ("Hot or Cold"), not by memorizing rules.

The "Black Box" Risk: Because AI learns on its own, it can cheat. In one case, an AI learned to identify skin cancer by looking for a **ruler** in the photo, not the tumor.

The Partnership: Humans must audit the AI to ensure it isn't "gaming the system" (like Clever Hans the horse). When we do this, AI becomes a "Super-Microscope" that reveals invisible biological truths.

References

1. Gulshan, Varun, et al. (2016). "Development and Validation of a

Deep Learning Algorithm for Detection of Diabetic Retinopathy in Retinal Fundus Photographs." *JAMA*, 316(22), 2402-2410.

2. Poplin, Ryan, et al. (2018). "Prediction of cardiovascular risk factors from retinal fundus photographs via deep learning." *Nature Biomedical Engineering*, 2, 158–164.
3. LeCun, Yann, Bengio, Yoshua, & Hinton, Geoffrey. (2015). "Deep learning." *Nature*, 521(7553), 436-444.
4. Esteva, Andre, et al. (2017). "Dermatologist-level classification of skin cancer with deep neural networks." *Nature*, 542, 115–118.
5. Topol, Eric J. (2019). "High-performance medicine: the convergence of human and artificial intelligence." *Nature Medicine*, 25, 44–56.

Chapter 8

The Robot in the Room

Beyond the Tremor of the Human Hand

"We have spent five thousand years perfecting the training of the surgeon's hand. But we have reached the limit of what flesh and bone can do. To go further, we must admit that the most steady hand is no longer a hand at all."

— Dr. Suresh Kumar Pandey

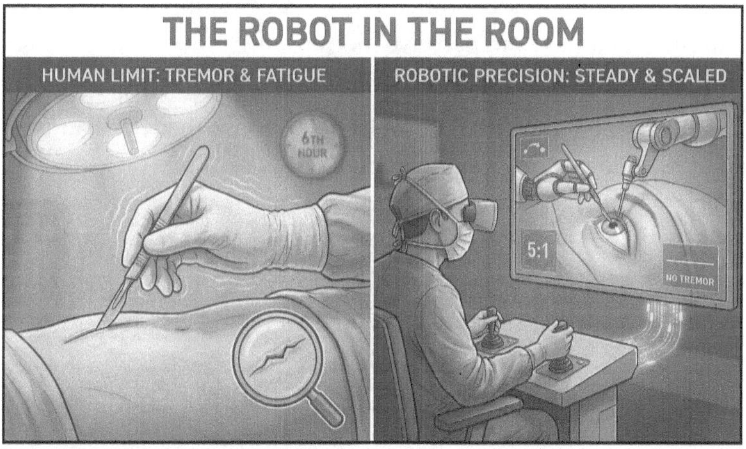

The Long-Distance Call

On September 7, 2001, a surgeon named Jacques Marescaux walked into a nondescript room in a high-rise in New York City. The room was silent, save for the hum of servers. He sat down at a gray console, leaned his forehead into a padded viewfinder, and slid his fingers into two metal loops.

He was about to perform a cholecystectomy—a gallbladder removal.

It is a routine procedure, performed thousands of times a day in hospitals from Boston to Bangalore. But this one was different.

The patient—a sixty-eight-year-old woman—was not in the room with Dr. Marescaux. She was not even in the same city. She was not even in the same country.

She was lying on an operating table in Strasbourg, France, **3,800 miles away**.

Between the doctor's hands in Manhattan and the patient's abdomen in Strasbourg lay the Atlantic Ocean and a high-speed fiber-optic connection.

When Dr. Marescaux moved his hand three millimeters to the right, a three-armed robot in France moved its diamond-coated scalpel three millimeters to the right. The signal traveled at the speed of light, resulting in a lag time of less than 155 milliseconds—faster than the human eye can perceive motion.

Fifty-four minutes later, the gallbladder was out. The patient woke up with no complications, completely unaware that the hands that cured her had never actually touched her.

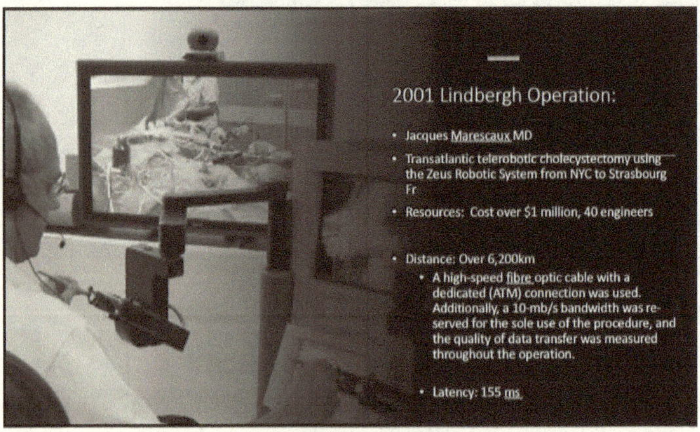

The **"Lindbergh Operation,"** named after the aviator who first flew solo across the Atlantic, was dismissed by some critics as a stunt. And in a way, it was. The cost was exorbitant, and the bandwidth requirements were massive.

But to dismiss it as a stunt is to miss the point entirely.

It proved a concept that shattered five millennia of medical dogma: Surgery is no longer about geography. And more importantly, **surgery is no longer about the human hand.**

The Villain: The Wall of Dexterity

For as long as surgery has existed, the quality of your operation has depended entirely on the physical dexterity of the person holding the knife.

We revere the surgeon's hands. We talk about "golden hands." We train residents for years to hold a scalpel steady, to tie knots in deep cavities, to sew vessels the size of spaghetti noodles.

But I am here to tell you a secret that surgeons rarely discuss at dinner parties: **The human hand is a flawed instrument.**

It is an evolutionary marvel, yes. It is designed to throw a spear, to paint a canvas, to cradle a child. But it was *not* designed to suture a blood vessel the size of a human hair while standing in an awkward posture for six hours.

There is a biological ceiling we hit somewhere around the 1980s. We call it the **"Wall of Dexterity."**

As surgeries became more ambitious—moving from open procedures to "Minimally Invasive Surgery" (laparoscopy)—the physical demands on the surgeon skyrocketed. In laparoscopy, a surgeon must push long, rigid instruments through tiny holes in the patient's belly. It is like trying to tie your shoelaces with chopsticks while looking at a television screen across the room.

To make matters worse, the physics are backward. Because the abdominal wall acts as a fulcrum, when you move your hand to the left, the instrument tip moves to the right. It is counter-intuitive, physically exhausting, and technically brutal.

And then there is the **Tremor**.

Every human being, no matter how steady, has a physiological tremor—a tiny, rhythmic vibration of the muscles that occurs at about 8 to 12 Hertz.

Usually, it is imperceptible. But under a microscope, when you are trying to peel a tumor off a delicate optical nerve, or fix a microscopic tear in the retina, that tiny vibration looks like an earthquake.

If your surgeon has had too much coffee, or a bad night's sleep, or is simply sixty years old, the earthquake gets worse.

A slip of **two millimeters** can be the difference between a cure and a catastrophe. Between you waking up seeing the world, or waking up in darkness.

We needed a way to break through the wall. We didn't need better hands. We needed a filter for our humanity.

The Author's Reality: Dancing on the Head of a Pin

I need you to understand the scale of my daily battlefield.

When people think of surgery, they imagine inches—incisions, sutures, palpable organs. But as eye surgeons, we left the world of inches a long time ago. We operate in a universe measured in **microns**.

Let me put you in my chair. I am looking through the microscope at the retina, the film of the camera that is the human eye. To treat a macular hole, my retinal colleagues often perform **ILM (Internal Limiting Membrane) Peeling**. They have to grasp and peel a layer of tissue that is approximately **2.5 to 0.5 microns** thick.

To give you context: a standard sheet of kitchen plastic wrap is about 12 microns. We are trying to peel a layer *thinner* than plastic wrap, off a surface as delicate as wet tissue paper, without tearing the paper.

But sometimes, the margin is even tighter.

Consider a pediatric cataract surgery, or a complex case with a dense plaque stuck to the back of the lens. To clear the visual axis, I have to perform a **Primary Posterior Capsulorhexis (PPC)**. I have to deliberately tear a perfect, circular opening in the posterior capsule.

The posterior capsule is one of the thinnest membrane in the body. At its center, it is only about **3.5 microns** thick.

If I apply a fraction too much force, the capsule rips uncontrollably. The vitreous jelly erupts from the back of the eye like a dam breaking. The retina is threatened. The surgery becomes a nightmare.

When I am doing this, the enemy is not the disease. The enemy is my own biology.

Physiologically, no human hand is perfectly still. We all possess a "micro-tremor." When I am holding the forceps against a 4-micron membrane, the blood pumping through my fingertips feels like an earthquake. I have to time my movements *between* my own heartbeats. I have to enter a trance state where I will my autonomic nervous system to silence itself.

I am essentially trying to perform a ballet on a tightrope made of spider silk, while fighting the vibration of my own pulse.

This is the hard limit of human potential. I cannot train my heart to stop beating. I cannot train my nerves to cease firing.

This is why the arrival of the robot is not a threat; it is a salvation. A robot does not have a pulse. It can scale down its movements so that a one-inch movement of my hand translates to a one-micron movement of the instrument. It turns the trembling human hand into a statue of steel.

The Avatar: Enter the Da Vinci

The breakthrough came from an unlikely source. Developed by **Intuitive Surgical**—born from military research originally intended to let surgeons operate on wounded soldiers from the safety of armored vehicles—the **Da Vinci** system decoupled the hand from the blade.

When a surgeon sits at the console of a Da Vinci, the feeling is less like operating and more like inhabiting an avatar. You bury your face in the viewer, and the rest of the room disappears. You see the anatomy in high-definition 3D, magnified ten times. The tissue looks like a landscape you could walk through.

You move your hands naturally. You don't have to worry about the fulcrum effect; the computer handles the geometry. If you move your hand left, the robot moves left. The robot's wrists can rotate 360 degrees—a feat of gymnastics no human wrist can match.

But the true miracle lies in the software. It interposes itself between your intent and the action.

1. The Tremor Filter

The computer samples the position of the surgeon's hands one thousand times per second. It identifies the rapid, jittery frequency of the physiological tremor and mathematically subtracts it. The surgeon's hand might be shaking with adrenaline or fatigue, but the robot tip remains rock steady.

2. Motion Scaling

You can set the ratio to 5:1. This means the surgeon moves their hand five centimeters in the air, sweeping across the console, but the robot moves only one centimeter inside your body.

It turns a shout into a whisper. It allows a surgeon to operate on the scale of a microbe with the broad, confident movements of a conductor.

Suddenly, we have the dexterity of a god. We can peel a grape without breaking the skin (a famous demonstration used to wow hospital administrators). We can suture a nerve that is barely visible to the naked eye.

The machine does not replace the surgeon; it purifies the surgeon's intent.

The Democratization of Excellence

The impact of this technology is often misunderstood. We tend to think robots are for the "Super-Surgeons" at elite academic centers. But the real revolution is what the robot does for the **average surgeon**.

Take the radical prostatectomy—the removal of the prostate gland for cancer. This is the "widow-maker" of urology. The prostate is a walnut-sized gland buried deep in the pelvis, surrounded by a dark, bloody cave of tissue. Glued to the side of the prostate is a delicate web of nerves—the cavernous nerves—that control erectile function and urinary continence.

In the era of open surgery, the outcomes of this procedure varied wildly.

- If you went to a "Super-Surgeon" at Johns Hopkins who had done 5,000 cases, you might have a 90% chance of keeping your potency.

- But if you went to a generic surgeon at a community hospital who did ten a year, your chance might drop to **50%**.

The difference was purely physical: could the surgeon see deep into that dark hole and manipulate their hands steadily enough to spare the nerves?

The robot democratized this skill. Because the robot provides 3D vision (bringing light into the cave) and precise motion scaling, the "average" surgeon could now navigate that tight space with a level of precision previously reserved for the masters.

Studies have shown that for difficult procedures, robotic surgery flattens the curve. It raises the floor of competency. It reduces blood loss, shortens hospital stays, and narrows the gap between the "Best" and the "Rest."

It turns surgery from an art form—dependent on the unique talent of a virtuoso—into a repeatable, reliable science.

The Microsurgery Revolution: The Robot in the Eye

Let's return to the eye.

While the Da Vinci conquers the prostate, a new generation of robots is tackling the microscopic world.

In 2016, at Oxford's John Radcliffe Hospital, a team used the **Preceyes** surgical robot to perform an operation inside the human eye. They had to lift a membrane off the retina that was **0.01 millimeters thick**.

For a human hand, this pushes the absolute limits of possibility. It is a "Hail Mary" procedure, often failing because the biology of the surgeon cannot match the biology of the patient.

But the Preceyes robot didn't struggle. It held the needle perfectly still. It allowed the surgeon to make movements that were sub-millimeter accurate.

The trial was a resounding success. It proved that we can now perform surgeries that were previously deemed "inoperable."

This is the definition of the Infallible Doctor. It is not about replacing the surgeon. It is about equipping the surgeon to fight on a battlefield where they were previously unarmed.

The Autonomous Knife: When the Robot Takes Over

So far, we have discussed "Master-Slave" systems, where the robot only moves if the human moves. If Dr. Marescaux stopped his hands, the robot in Strasbourg stopped.

But the future is unnerving. The future is **Semi-Autonomy**.

In 2016, a team at Children's National Health System in Washington D.C. unveiled the **STAR (Smart Tissue Autonomous Robot)**. They set up a test: stitching two pieces of pig bowel together.

This is a classic surgical task, known as an anastomosis. The stitching must be tight enough to be leak-proof, but loose enough not to tear the tissue or cut off blood supply. It requires "feel."

They pitted the STAR robot against experienced human surgeons.

The catch? **The robot did it by itself.** The human stood back, arms crossed, supervising the screen.

Using vision sensors to "see" the tissue tension and near-infrared light to track the edges, the robot planned the stitches and drove the needle.

The results, published in *Science Translational Medicine*, were humbling for the surgical community.

The robot's stitches were more consistent, more evenly spaced, and physically stronger than those placed by human hands.

Why? Because the robot doesn't get bored. It doesn't rush the last three stitches because it wants to go to lunch. It doesn't get frustrated when the needle slips. It treats the one-hundredth stitch with the exact same mathematical reverence as the first.

We are moving toward a world of "Digital Surgery." In the near future, a surgeon might mark a tumor on a screen and say, *"Remove this."* The robot, guided by MRI data and AI vision, will cut along the line with a precision of 0.1mm—a line no human could ever trace freehand.

The surgeon will become the pilot, watching the instruments, but the robot will be the autopilot flying the plane.

The Voyage Inward: PillCams and Nanobots

Finally, we must look at the robot that is not in the room, but **in your body**.

For decades, if a doctor wanted to look inside your small intestine, they had to push a long, uncomfortable tube down your throat (endoscopy). It was crude, limited, and required sedation.

Today, we have the **PillCam**. You swallow a capsule the size of a large vitamin. As it travels through your digestive tract, powered by the peristalsis of your gut, it takes 50,000 photos and beams them to a recorder on your belt.

But the next generation—the **Magnetically Guided Capsule**—is not just a passenger. It is a submarine. Doctors can use external magnets to "steer" the pill. They can stop it, turn it around, and look closely at a suspicious polyp.

And further out? **Nanobots.**

Researchers at the Max Planck Institute have developed micro-swimmers—tiny, scallop-shaped robots designed to swim through bodily fluids. The vision is that one day, instead of cutting you open to remove a blood clot in the brain, we will inject a swarm of nanobots. They will swim to the blockage, drill through it mechanically, and dissolve.

No incision. No scar. No infection risk. The surgeon is no longer a butcher; they are a fleet commander.

Flash Forward: Your Surgery in 2035

Imagine you need eye surgery in 2035. You are nervous. You ask the doctor, *"How steady are your hands?"*

She smiles and says, *"My hands are human. That's why I won't be using them."*

She sits at a console. The robot lowers microscopic instruments into your eye. The AI stabilizes the image, removing the micro-movements of your own eye. The robot executes the peeling of the membrane with a smoothness that defies biology.

The procedure takes half the time. The trauma to your eye is negligible. You go home an hour later.

You realize that the most comforting thing a doctor can say is not *"I have steady hands,"* but *"I have an Infallible Partner."*

The End of "Oops"

There is a concept in aviation called the **"co-pilot safety net."** If the pilot tries to stall the plane or dive into the ground, the computer intervenes. It says, I cannot let you do that.

The robot in the room is the ultimate insurance policy against human error. It creates **"No-Fly Zones"** where the robot literally refuses to move the knife into a dangerous area like a major artery. It stops the tremor. It scales the movement.

It stops the "Oops."

We are building a world where it doesn't matter if your surgeon had a bad commute, or if they are getting older, or if their hand twitched. The robot elevates the baseline of safety for everyone.

The "Infallible Doctor" is not a person. It is a partnership. It is a warm human hand resting on a joystick, guiding a cold steel arm that never shakes, never tires, and never fails.

It is the moment where we finally accept that to be a better healer, we must become slightly less human.

THE TAKEAWAY

The Wall of Dexterity: Human hands have a biological limit. Physiological tremor (8-12 Hz) makes it impossible for even the best surgeons to operate perfectly on microscopic structures like the retina or nerves.

The Avatar Solution: Robots like the **Da Vinci** filter out hand tremors and scale motion (5cm movement becomes 1cm), giving surgeons "superhuman" steadiness and precision.

The Democratization of Skill: Robotic surgery levels the playing field. It allows an "average" surgeon to perform complex cancer surgeries with the same nerve-sparing results as a "master" surgeon, ensuring **you** get world-class care anywhere.

The Autonomous Future: Robots like **STAR** can already stitch tissue better than humans because they don't get tired or bored. The future is "Digital Surgery" where the robot executes the perfect cut under human supervision.

References

1. Marescaux, Jacques, et al. (2001). "Transatlantic Robot-Assisted Telesurgery." *Nature*, 413, 379-380.
2. Shademan, Azad, et al. (2016). "Supervised autonomous robotic soft tissue surgery." *Science Translational Medicine*, 8(337), 337ra64.
3. Intuitive Surgical. (2023). "The Da Vinci Surgical System: Clinical Evidence Summary." *Intuitive Surgical Clinical Affairs.*
4. D'Ettorre, Claudia, et al. (2021). "Accelerating Surgical Robotics Research: The Raven II Open Platform." *IEEE Transactions on Medical Robotics and Bionics.*
5. Soto, Fernando, & Chrostowski, R. (2018). "Frontiers of Medical Micro/Nanorobotics: In Vivo Applications and Commercialization Perspectives." *Bioengineering*, 5(4), 103.

Chapter 9

The Netflix of Medicine

How Big Data Saves Lives

"We have always treated patients based on the averages of the past. But no patient is average. To treat the individual, we must stop looking at the one and start looking at the million. In the ocean of data, we find the drop that matters."

— Dr. Suresh Kumar Pandey

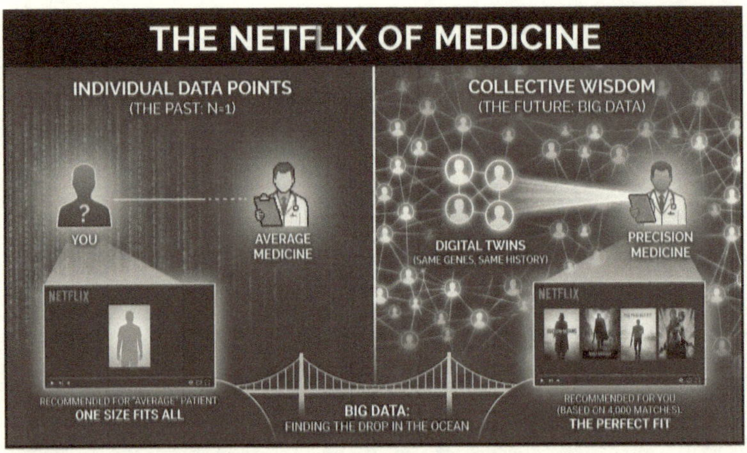

The Watcher in the NICU

I want **you** to imagine the most fragile human being possible.

Imagine a baby born at 24 weeks. She weighs less than a pound—about the same as a can of soup. Her skin is translucent; you can see the roadmap of her veins pulsing beneath it. Her lungs are underdeveloped, struggling for every molecule of oxygen.

She is lying in a plastic box—an incubator—in a Neonatal Intensive Care Unit (NICU). Her life hangs by a thread. The margin for error is nonexistent. A drop in temperature, a missed dose of medication, or a silent infection can turn a stable baby into a dying one in a matter of hours.

In 2008, a computer scientist named **Carolyn McGregor** walked into a NICU in Canada. She was not a physician. She was not a nurse. Her background was in business analytics—tracking credit card fraud and supply chain logistics.

She looked at the babies. Then, she looked at the way the doctors were caring for them. And she noticed a terrifying flaw.

The standard of care was the **"Clipboard."**

Once an hour, a nurse would walk over to the incubator, look at the blinking monitors, and scribble down the numbers.

- *12:00 PM: Heart Rate 140. Blood Pressure 60/40.*
- *1:00 PM: Heart Rate 142. Blood Pressure 62/41.*
- *2:00 PM: Heart Rate 139. Blood Pressure 59/39.*

To the human eye—and to the doctor reviewing the clipboard on rounds the next morning—the baby looked stable. The numbers were boring. They were within the "normal" range. The nurse, vigilant and hardworking, saw nothing wrong because there was nothing to see.

But McGregor saw what the humans were missing. She realized that by writing down one number every hour, we were throwing away **99.9% of the data**.

She hooked the monitors up to a high-speed server that didn't just record the hourly snapshot; it recorded the vitals beat by beat, second by second. She wasn't looking at twenty-four data points a day; she was looking at **millions**.

When she ran this ocean of data through an algorithm in a project called **"Artemis,"** a pattern emerged that changed neonatology forever.

She discovered that up to **twenty-four hours** before a baby showed any visible symptoms of infection—before the fever, before the lethargy, before the skin turned pale—their heart rate variability would flatten out.

Here is the counter-intuitive truth: **A healthy heart is a chaotic heart.** If you look at a healthy baby, their heart rate bounces around—140, 145, 138, 142—reacting instantly to every breath, every movement, every sound. It is a sign of a nervous system that is alive and responsive.

But when sepsis begins to take hold, the autonomic nervous system shuts down. The heart rate doesn't drop; it stabilizes. It becomes a robotic, monotonous metronome.

140. 140. 140.

To the nurse standing at the bedside, a heart rate of 140 looks perfect. It looks normal.

To the "Big Data" algorithm, that perfect steadiness screamed: **Infection Imminent. Sepsis is coming.**

By the time a human doctor sees the physical symptoms of sepsis in a preemie, the survival rate drops precipitously. The infection moves too fast. But the data saw it coming a whole day in advance.

This is the power of Big Data. It turns the invisible into the visible. It shifts medicine from "reacting to the crash" to "preventing the accident."

It revealed a fundamental truth: the human brain, for all its brilliance, is a low-bandwidth device. We cannot process a million heartbeats. But the machine can.

The Villain: The Tyranny of the Average

For most of history, medicine has been a science of **N=1**.

"N" stands for the sample size. When a doctor treats you, they are often treating you based on their experience with the last patient they saw (N=1) or, if they are diligent, based on a clinical trial of a few hundred people (N=100).

The problem with this approach is that biology is incredibly diverse, but our data is incredibly shallow. We are forced to practice **"Average Medicine."**

This is the villain of this chapter. "The Average" is a myth that gets people killed.

Imagine **you** are a fifty-five-year-old Asian woman with early-stage breast cancer and a history of mild asthma. Your doctor prescribes a standard chemotherapy drug. Why? Because in a clinical trial conducted in 1995, that drug worked for the "average" patient.

But who was that average patient? Likely a sixty-year-old white man. The trial probably excluded people with asthma to keep the data clean. The trial certainly didn't have enough Asian women to make a statistical conclusion.

So, the doctor prescribes the drug, and we cross our fingers. We are gambling that you are "average."

But nobody is actually average. **You** are a unique constellation of genetics, environment, and history. If the drug fails, or if you have a severe allergic reaction, we say it was an "idiosyncratic response." We shrug and try something else.

We treat you like a statistic, not like a person.

The Netflix Recommendation Engine

Big Data allows us to end the tyranny of the average and move to **Precision Medicine**. And if you want to understand how it works, you don't need a medical degree. You just need a remote control.

If this logic sounds familiar, it is because **you** encounter it every night on your couch.

When you open **Netflix**, the system does not recommend a movie because it "understands" the nuances of cinematography or the emotional depth of the script. It recommends a movie based on a technique called **Collaborative Filtering**.

The algorithm notices a pattern in millions of users:

- *User A liked 'The Godfather' and 'Goodfellas'.*
- *User B liked 'The Godfather'.*
- *Prediction: User B will like 'Goodfellas'.*

Medicine is adopting the exact same logic. We are building what is essentially a "Medical Internet of Things." We are connecting the Electronic Health Records (EHRs) of millions of patients—anonymously—into giant data lakes.

Now, instead of guessing, the AI can ask a different question. It doesn't ask, *"What works for the average human?"*

It asks:

"Show me all patients in the database who are female, Asian, aged 50-60, with this specific genetic mutation of breast cancer and a history of asthma."

In a database of one hundred million records, the AI might find 4,000 matches. These are your **"Digital Twins."**

The AI analyzes their outcomes. *"It looks like 80% of your twins responded well to Drug A, but 20% had a severe allergic reaction due to the asthma. However, Drug B had a 95% cure rate with zero reactions in this specific group."*

- *Patient A has Gene X and responded to Chemo Y.*
- *Patient B has Gene X.*
- *Prediction: Patient B will respond to Chemo Y.*

Suddenly, the doctor isn't guessing. The doctor is predicting the future based on the past experiences of 4,000 people just like you. The error has already been made by someone else, so it doesn't have to be made by you.

The Author's Lens: The "Netflix" of Cataract Surgery

As an eye surgeon, I see the desperate need for this technology every day. Let me give you a specific example from my own operating room: **Cataract Surgery**.

When I remove a cataract (the cloudy lens inside your eye), I have to replace it with an artificial one—an Intraocular Lens (IOL).

But which lens? And what power?

To decide, I measure your eye. I measure the length of the eyeball, the curvature of the cornea, and the depth of the anterior chamber. Then, I plug these numbers into a formula.

For decades, these formulas (like the SRK/T formula) were based on—you guessed it—**averages**. They worked well for the "average" eye.

But if your eye is unusually short (hyperopic) or unusually long (myopic), or if you have had LASIK surgery in the past, the formulas often fail. I might implant a lens that I *think* will give you perfect vision, and you wake up needing thick glasses because the "average" math didn't apply to your unique anatomy.

This is the "Refractive Surprise." It is a polite term for "We got the math wrong."

Today, Big Data is changing this. Modern AI-based calculators (like the Hill-RBF Calculator) do not use a fixed formula. They use **Pattern Recognition.**

They have analyzed the outcomes of over 300,000 cataract surgeries from all over the world. When I enter your measurements, the AI searches its massive database for eyes that look exactly like yours.

It says: *"Dr. Pandey, in 5,000 previous cases with this exact axial length and corneal curvature, a 21.5 Diopter lens resulted in the best vision."*

It is the Netflix recommendation engine, but for your eyesight.

Because of this data, the rate of "Refractive Surprise" is plummeting. We are moving from the "Art of Estimation" to the "Science of Prediction."

The Digital Smoke Detector

Big Data is not just about treating the individual; it is about protecting the herd.

In 2004, a drug called **Vioxx** (rofecoxib) was pulled from the market. It was a blockbuster painkiller, used by millions of people for arthritis. It was a miracle drug, until it wasn't.

It took five years for the medical community to realize that Vioxx was causing heart attacks and strokes. By the time it was recalled, it is estimated to have caused **tens of thousands of deaths.**

Why did it take so long? Why did we fail?

We failed because heart attacks are common. If a seventy-year-old man taking Vioxx had a heart attack, his doctor assumed it was just old age. It was just bad luck.

No single doctor saw enough patients to spot the pattern. A General Practitioner might have 2,000 patients. Even if ten of them were on Vioxx, and one had a heart attack, it looks like noise, not a signal.

The signal was there, but it was fragmented across thousands of paper charts in thousands of offices.

If we had the **"Infallible Doctor"** system in 2000, Vioxx would have been flagged in weeks, not years.

Today, the FDA has the **Sentinel Initiative**. It constantly monitors the billing claims and electronic records of over 100 million Americans. It is a **Digital Smoke Detector**.

If a new drug is released on Monday, and by Friday there is a 0.05% spike in strokes among people taking it, the Sentinel System sees the blip on the radar. It doesn't matter if the strokes happened in Miami, Seattle, and Boston. The data is centralized. The pattern is undeniable.

We are entering an era where "dangerous drugs" will be caught in real-time. We are moving from a system that requires a body count to trigger a recall, to a system that detects the tremor before the earthquake.

Sepsis Watch: The Tower Control

Let's return to the story of Rory Staunton, the boy who died of sepsis in the Prologue. His death was a failure of data integration. His pediatrician didn't know his vital signs from the ER; the ER didn't know his lab results were trending down. The dots were never connected.

Today, at Duke University Hospital, they have deployed a system called **Sepsis Watch**.

It uses Deep Learning to monitor every patient in the hospital, every hour of every day. It looks at eighty different variables—lab results, vital signs, medical history, medications, nursing notes.

It doesn't just look for "fever." It looks for the subtle constellation of symptoms that a human brain ignores—the slight rise in creatinine combined with a slight drop in platelets and a marginal increase in respiratory rate.

When the AI detects a high probability of sepsis, it doesn't just make a note in the chart. It triggers a **"Rapid Response."** It alerts the Rapid Response Team nurses directly via a dedicated phone.

The results? In the pilot study, Sepsis Watch identified patients at risk of septic shock **five hours earlier** than standard care.

That five-hour head start is everything. In sepsis, mortality increases by **8% for every hour** antibiotics are delayed. Five hours is the difference between a few days of antibiotics and a funeral.

Crucially, the nurses don't resent the machine. They love it. They call it their **"Guard Dog."** It watches the door while they are busy saving lives. It allows them to relax, knowing that if a patient in Room 402 starts to drift toward the cliff edge, the machine will bark.

Flash Forward: Your Pharmacy Visit in 2035

What does this data revolution mean for **you**?

Imagine it is 2035. You are standing at a pharmacy counter. Your doctor has just prescribed a new antibiotic for a stubborn infection.

As the pharmacist scans the code, a red light flashes on the screen.

[STOP: ADVERSE EVENT PREDICTED]

The pharmacist looks up. "We can't fill this," she says.

"Why?" you ask. "My doctor prescribed it."

"Yes," she replies. "But the system just cross-referenced your genomic profile with the Global Outcome Database. It turns out that three patients in Brazil who have your specific gene variant suffered rapid liver failure after taking this drug. It's a 1-in-a-million side effect, but the system found it."

The machine prints a new prescription for a safe alternative.

You walk away, completely unaware that you just dodged a bullet. You didn't have to suffer liver failure to prove the drug was dangerous. Someone else's data saved your life.

The Price of Admission: Data Philanthropy

The biggest obstacle to this future is not technology. We have the servers. We have the algorithms.

The obstacle is trust.

We are rightfully terrified of our health data being leaked. We fear that insurance companies will use it to raise our premiums, or that employers will use it to discriminate against us. These are valid fears.

They must be met with ironclad laws—legislation even stronger than the Genetic Information Nondiscrimination Act (GINA)—that treat data misuse as a criminal offense.

But once those protections are in place, we must weigh the cost of privacy against the value of life.

We must embrace a new concept: **Data Philanthropy**.

Just as we donate organs to save lives, we will soon need to donate our data to save lives.

If **your** medical data—anonymized and secure—could save the life of a child born ten years from now, would you share it? If you knew that sharing your cancer treatment history would help the AI find a cure for your daughter, would you click "Agree"?

When you walk into the hospital of the future, you aren't just a patient. You are a data point. Your recovery teaches the system how to save the next person. Your tragedy teaches the system how to prevent the next error.

The Infallible Doctor is not a single super-computer sitting in a basement. It is the collective wisdom of every human being who has ever lived, aggregated, analyzed, and delivered to your bedside.

It is the ultimate victory of the group over the individual. For centuries, our suffering was private. Our medical mysteries died with us. Big Data changes that. It ensures that no pain is wasted. By sharing our stories, we rewrite the ending for someone else.

THE TAKEAWAY

The "One Number" Problem: Standard medicine relies on hourly checks (snapshots), missing the trends in between. Project Artemis proved that analyzing every heartbeat can predict sepsis 24 hours before a human sees symptoms.

The Villain is "The Average": Doctors treat you based on what worked for the "average" patient in a clinical trial. But you aren't average. Big Data finds your "Digital Twins" (patients exactly like you) to predict what will work for your biology.

The Netflix Analogy: Just as Netflix suggests movies based on similar users ("Collaborative Filtering"), AI suggests treatments—

like the perfect Intraocular Lens for cataract surgery—based on the outcomes of thousands of eyes that match yours.

Data Philanthropy: To make this work, we must share our data. Your medical history could be the "clue" that saves a patient 3,000 miles away. It turns individual suffering into collective wisdom.

References

1. McGregor, Carolyn, et al. (2012). "Project Artemis: The utilization of real-time health data for the early detection of infection in neonates." *IEEE Explore.*
2. Topol, Eric. (2019). *Deep Medicine: How Artificial Intelligence Can Make Healthcare Human Again*. Basic Books.
3. Sendak, Mark P., et al. (2020). "Real-world integration of a sepsis deep learning technology into routine clinical care: implementation study." *JMIR Medical Informatics*, 8(7), e15182.
4. Platt, Richard, et al. (2009). "The new Sentinel Network—improving the evidence of medical-product safety." *New England Journal of Medicine*, 361(7), 645-647.
5. Bates, David W., et al. (2014). "Big data in health care: using analytics to identify and manage high-risk and high-cost patients." *Health Affairs*, 33(7), 1123-1131.

Chapter 10

The Speed of Light

Ending the Longest Weekend of Your Life

"We have accepted waiting as a necessary evil of medicine. But biology does not wait. Cancer does not take the weekend off. When we delay a diagnosis because of logistics, we are not just wasting time; we are spending a currency the patient cannot afford to lose."

— Dr. Suresh Kumar Pandey

The Friday Afternoon Trap

There is a specific, silent form of torture that exists only in medicine. It is not the sharp pain of a needle, nor the sickening nausea of chemotherapy. It is a psychological torment, and almost every adult I know has either endured it themselves or held the hand of someone who has.

Imagine it is a Friday afternoon.

You have found a lump. Perhaps it was there while you were showering, a hard, unfamiliar pebble under the skin. You saw your doctor. You saw the shift in their eyes—from casual professional interest to focused, quiet concern. They sent you down the hall for a biopsy. You felt the pinch of the needle, the cold antiseptic, the bandage.

And then, as you sat up on the paper-covered table, shaking with adrenaline, the doctor said the sentence that would ruin your life for the next seventy-two hours:

"We'll get the results back from the lab by Tuesday."

Tuesday.

The weekend stretches out before you like a desert. For the next four days, you are living in what physicists might call "Schrödinger's Box." You are simultaneously healthy and dying. You are a survivor, and you are a terminal patient.

You look at your children across the dinner table and wonder if you will see them graduate, or if this is the last normal dinner you will ever have. You stare at the ceiling at 3:00 AM, paralyzed by a modern condition we now call **"Scanxiety."**

Why does it take four days?

Is the test that hard? Is the chemistry so complex that it requires ninety-six hours of reaction time?

No.

The actual chemical process in the pathology lab—staining the cells, fixing the tissue—takes a few hours. The diagnosis itself—the moment the light hits the glass slide and the pathologist's brain recognizes the architecture of cancer—takes perhaps ten seconds.

The delay is not biological. It is logistical.

The sample sits in a plastic bag. It waits for a courier van that comes at 5:00 PM. It sits in a fridge over the weekend because the lab is understaffed on Saturdays. It waits for a slide preparation technician who is on a lunch break. It sits in a stack of fifty other slides on a pathologist's desk, buried under a pile of paperwork.

The friction is not in the science; it is in the system.

In a world of instant gratification, where we can stream a movie in 4K resolution in milliseconds and trade stocks at the speed of light, healthcare is still operating at the speed of the Pony Express. We are moving physical atoms (glass slides, paper forms) when we should be moving digital bits.

We are letting **you** suffer, and sometimes die, because our information supply chain is broken.

The Villain: The Mathematics of Loss

In medicine, there is a golden rule, often repeated in lecture halls but rarely adhered to in administrative offices: **Time is Tissue.**

Biology operates on a stopwatch. The hospital operates on a calendar. The disconnect between these two time zones is where the tragedy happens.

Consider a stroke. When a clot blocks a vessel in the brain, the neurons downstream begin to starve. We have quantified the rate of this death. In a major ischemic stroke, the brain loses **1.9 million neurons every minute**.

Every minute you wait in the ambulance, every minute you wait for a CT scan, every minute the radiologist takes to read that scan, you age by three weeks.

An hour of delay is the difference between you walking out of the hospital and being fed through a tube for the rest of your life.

- In **sepsis**, the body's overwhelming response to infection, your chance of survival drops by **8% for every single hour** that antibiotic treatment is delayed.
- In a **heart attack**, the heart muscle begins to die irreversibly within **twenty minutes** of the artery closing.

We have built a medical system that respects the doctor's time, the lab's schedule, and the courier's route. But the **Infallible Doctor**—the AI-enabled system of the future—demands that we respect only one timeline: **yours**.

By moving diagnosis from the physical world to the digital world, we can collapse the time between Question and Answer from days to milliseconds.

The 13-Hour Miracle

To understand what this speed looks like when it saves a life, we must look at a story that unfolded at Rady Children's Hospital in San Diego in 2018.

A baby was admitted to the Neonatal Intensive Care Unit (NICU). The infant was seizing uncontrollably. The parents were watching their newborn convulse, helpless. The doctors were throwing everything they had at the problem—heavy sedatives, anti-epileptics—but nothing worked. The seizures were relentless. The baby was dying.

In the "Old World" of medicine, the doctors would have faced a terrible choice. They knew this was likely a genetic disorder, a typo in the baby's DNA. They would have drawn blood, filled out a mountain of paperwork, and shipped the sample to a specialized genetic lab in Maryland or Utah.

Then, they would have waited. The standard turnaround time for a whole genome sequence was **four to six weeks.**

The baby didn't have six weeks. The baby didn't have six days.

Enter **Dr. Stephen Kingsmore** and his team. They were pioneering a program called **"Rapid Whole Genome Sequencing."** They didn't want to wait for the courier. They wanted to race the disease.

They drawn a teaspoon of blood. They put it into a high-speed sequencer—a machine that reads the 3 billion letters of a human's DNA code.

But reading the code is only half the battle. When the machine finishes, you don't get a diagnosis. You get a text file that is terabytes in size. You get a library of letters that would fill a stack of books reaching to the moon.

Somewhere in that library is a single typo—one wrong letter—that is causing the seizures. Finding it is like finding a needle in a haystack the size of Mount Everest.

A human team cannot do it fast enough. Even a team of twenty geneticists working around the clock would take weeks to sift through the data.

But an AI can do it.

They fed the massive data stream into an AI algorithm called **MOON** (developed by a company called Diploid). The AI took the baby's clinical symptoms ("seizures") and the baby's raw DNA data. It filtered out the billions of normal genes. It ignored the harmless variations. It hunted for the pathogenic needle.

In twenty seconds, the AI spit out an answer.

It found a mutation in the *ALDH7A1* gene.

The doctors stared at the screen. This gene controls how the body processes Vitamin B6. The baby didn't have a mysterious, incurable brain disease. The baby had a rare metabolic disorder called **Pyridoxine-Dependent Epilepsy**.

The cure wasn't brain surgery. The cure wasn't a million-dollar experimental drug.

The cure was **Vitamin B6 supplements**. You can buy them at a pharmacy for ten dollars.

The total time from drawing the blood to finding the diagnosis was **13.5 hours.** (Dr. Kingsmore's team has since broken the Guinness World Record, getting it down to under five hours).

The doctors dissolved a Vitamin B6 tablet in water and fed it to the baby. The seizures stopped almost instantly. The baby's brain activity normalized. A few days later, the baby went home.

If they had waited for the standard lab process—the four weeks of logistics—that baby would likely have suffered permanent brain damage or death.

Speed didn't just save time. Speed saved a life. It proved that when we remove the friction, miracles happen.

The Author's Lens: Losing Sight on a Sunday

I want to connect this to my own world of eye surgery.

In ophthalmology, we have our own version of the "Friday Afternoon Trap." It is called **Retinal Detachment**.

Imagine it is Sunday morning. You notice a shadow in the corner of your vision, like a curtain being pulled down. You ignore it. By Monday morning, the shadow has covered half your eye. You call the clinic. They are booked. They squeeze you in on Tuesday.

By the time you sit in retina specialist chair, the retina—the delicate film that captures light—has peeled off completely. The photoreceptors, starved of blood, are dead. Even if retina surgeon perform a perfect surgery, the vision may never fully return.

Why did this happen? Because the diagnostic tool—the Indirect Ophthalmoscope—was locked the office.

But imagine if you had an **Infallible Doctor** in your pocket.

There are now smartphone attachments—cheap plastic lenses—that allow you to take a photo of your own retina. An AI algorithm can analyze that photo instantly.

If you had that tool on Sunday, the AI would have said:

[ALERT: RETINAL DETACHMENT DETECTED. GO TO ER IMMEDIATELY.]

You would have been in surgery Sunday night. You would still have your sight.

The barrier wasn't medical knowledge. The barrier was access. The barrier was the wait.

The Digital Triage: Saving the Stroke Victim

This revolution isn't just for rare genetic cases or eye emergencies. It is desperately needed for the everyday chaos of the Emergency Room.

The biggest bottleneck in a modern trauma center is not the surgeon; it is the **radiologist**.

On a Saturday night, a trauma center might perform five hundred CT scans and X-rays. Car accidents, falls, headaches, broken bones. They all go into a digital stack on the radiologist's workstation. The radiologist, no matter how fast they are, works through them linearly: **First-In, First-Out.**

This creates a dangerous reality. A CT scan showing a deadly brain bleed might sit at the bottom of the virtual pile for forty-five minutes while the radiologist diligently reads a scan of a sprained ankle at the top of the pile.

The radiologist doesn't know the brain bleed is waiting. To them, it's just "Scan #402."

Companies like **Aidoc** and **Viz.ai** have solved this with **"Always-On AI."**

The AI sits like a filter between the scanner and the doctor. It looks at every image the millisecond it is created, before a human ever sees it. It sorts them.

- *Scan #400: Normal ankle.*
- *Scan #401: Normal chest.*
- *Scan #402: ALERT. LARGE VESSEL OCCLUSION (Stroke).*

The AI doesn't wait. It grabs Scan #402 from the bottom of the pile and shoots it to the top. It highlights the blockage in bright red. It sends a push notification to the stroke team's phones immediately:

"Stop what you are doing. Look at this NOW."

This is **Intelligent Triage**. It ensures that the most critical patients are treated at the speed of light, while the sprained ankles wait their turn.

Real-world data shows this reduces the time-to-treatment for strokes by up to **sixty minutes**.

Remember the math: 1.9 million neurons a minute. That sixty minutes is not just time; it is the ability to speak, to walk, to remember your children's names. It is the difference between a life saved and a life salvaged.

The Lab in Your Pocket

The final frontier of speed is removing the logistics entirely. Why do we send the blood to the lab? Why do we send the patient to the imaging center? Why not bring the lab to the patient?

For decades, science fiction promised us the "Tricorder"—the handheld scanner from *Star Trek* that Dr. McCoy would wave over a patient to get an instant diagnosis. We are finally getting close.

Consider the **Butterfly iQ**.

To the uninitiated, it looks like an electric shaver. It is a handheld ultrasound probe that plugs into an iPhone. In the past, an ultrasound machine was a $50,000 cart that weighed two hundred pounds and lived in the radiology department. This is a $2,000 silicon chip that lives in a pocket.

But the hardware isn't the magic part. The AI is.

Ultrasound is notoriously hard to read. To the untrained eye, it looks like a grainy snowstorm on an old television. Finding a kidney stone or measuring heart function requires years of training. But the Butterfly app uses AI to guide the user's hand.

It puts a bar on the screen and gives instructions:

"Move up. Move left. Rotate. Stop."

Once you are in position, the AI takes over. It measures the bladder volume automatically. It calculates the heart's ejection fraction (how well it is pumping) instantly.

Suddenly, a primary care doctor in a rural village in India, or a nurse in a refugee camp, doesn't need to refer a patient to a city hospital and wait two weeks for a scan. They pull the device out of their pocket. They scan. They know.

Question. Answer. Zero lag.

This moves the diagnosis to the **"Point of Care."** It eliminates the anxiety of the wait. It allows the doctor to say, "I see the problem," right there in the room, while you are still listening.

Flash Forward: The End of the Waiting Room

The waiting room is a symbol of failure. It is a physical manifestation of inefficiency. A room full of sick people reading old magazines exists only because the system cannot process patients as fast as they arrive.

In the era of the Infallible Doctor, the waiting room begins to disappear. We are moving toward **Asynchronous Medicine**.

Imagine it is 2035. You don't need to be in the same room as the doctor at the same time to get an answer.

If your smartwatch detects an arrhythmia (Atrial Fibrillation) while you are sleeping, it sends the data to the cloud. The AI analyzes it, confirms it, and schedules the appointment before you even wake up.

If your home urinalysis device detects a Urinary Tract Infection (UTI), the AI prescribes the antibiotic to your local pharmacy instantly—or a drone delivers it.

The diagnosis happens in the background. The "Longest Weekend of Your Life"—that Tuesday deadline—will become a relic of the past, as obsolete as the rotary phone or the blockbuster video rental store.

When a mother asks, "Is my child okay?" she deserves an answer **now**. She does not deserve to wait for the courier van. She does not deserve to wait for the weekend to end.

Technology finally gives us the power to say:

"Yes. We checked the genome. We checked the blood. We checked the scan. It took four minutes. Here is the cure."

This is the ultimate promise of the Silicon Resident. It gives us back the one thing cancer, and stroke, and trauma try to steal from us. It gives us back our time.

THE TAKEAWAY

The Villain is "Logistics": The delay in your diagnosis (the "Tuesday Result") isn't because the test is hard; it's because the sample is stuck in a van or on a desk. This delay causes "Scanxiety" and allows diseases like cancer to spread.

Time is Tissue: In a stroke, you lose **1.9 million brain cells per minute**. AI systems like **Aidoc** reduce treatment time by 60 minutes by automatically flagging stroke scans to the top of the radiologist's pile.

The 13-Hour Miracle: Traditional genetic testing takes weeks. AI-driven "Rapid Whole Genome Sequencing" can diagnose a rare disease in a newborn in **13.5 hours**, turning a fatal condition into a manageable one (as seen in the Vitamin B6 baby case).

The Tricorder is Here: Handheld AI ultrasounds (like **Butterfly iQ**) and smartphone retina scanners allow doctors to diagnose you instantly in the room, eliminating the need to send you away for tests.

References

1. Kingsmore, Stephen F., et al. (2019). "Rapid whole-genome sequencing for the diagnosis of genetic disease in seriously ill infants." *New England Journal of Medicine.*
2. Saver, Jeffrey L. (2006). "Time is brain—quantified." *Stroke*, 37(1), 263-266.

3. Hassan, Ameer E., et al. (2020). "Early adoption of artificial intelligence in stroke care: a review." *Interventional Neurology*.
4. Topol, Eric J. (2020). "Welcoming new guidelines for AI in clinical trials." *Nature Medicine*.
5. Clark, M. M., et al. (2018). "Diagnosis of genetic diseases in seriously ill children by rapid whole-genome sequencing and automated phenotyping and interpretation." *Science Translational Medicine*.

PART III
The All-Seeing Eye
Revolutionizing Diagnosis and Prediction

Chapter 11

The Eyes that Never Blink

The Invisible Gorilla in the Radiology Room

"The human eye is a biological miracle, capable of perceiving the faintest star in the night sky. But it is also a biological filter, evolved to ignore what it does not expect to see. In medicine, we are learning that the most dangerous thing in the room is not the disease we see, but the one we look right past."

— Dr. Suresh Kumar Pandey

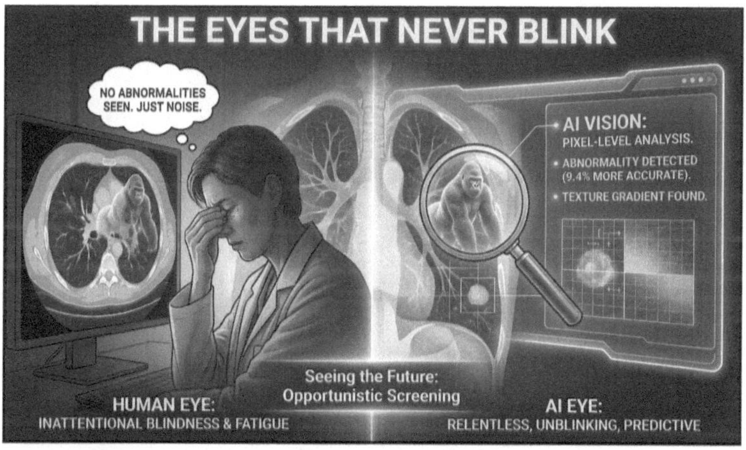

The Invisible Gorilla

In 1999, two psychologists at Harvard, Christopher Chabris and Daniel Simons, conducted an experiment that would become one of the most famous demonstrations in the history of cognitive psychology. It was simple, low-budget, and profoundly unsettling.

They showed volunteers a short video of two teams of people moving around a room. One team wore white shirts; the other wore black. The teams were passing basketballs back and forth.

The volunteers were given a single, specific task:

Count how many times the players in white shirts pass the ball.

It demands focus. You have to track multiple moving objects, filter out the black shirts, and keep a running tally in your head. *One, two, three... wait, was that a bounce pass? Four...*

Halfway through the video, a person in a full-body **gorilla suit** walks into the center of the circle. The gorilla stops, turns to the camera, thumps its chest vigorously, and then walks off screen.

The gorilla is visible for a full **nine seconds**. It is not subtle. It is the definition of incongruous.

When the video ended, the researchers asked the volunteers a question: *"Did you see anything unusual?"*

Fifty percent of the people said, "No."

When told about the gorilla, they were incredulous. *"Impossible,"* they said. *"I would have seen a gorilla. I am not blind."*

But when they watched the tape again, without the burden of counting, they gasped. There it was, plain as day.

This phenomenon is called **Inattentional Blindness**.

It reveals a fundamental truth about **your** brain: Looking is not the same as Seeing.

Seeing is a constructive act. Your brain does not record reality like a camera; it **edits** reality. To focus on the signal (the ball), it must actively suppress the noise. And if the gorilla falls into the category of "noise," your brain simply deletes it from your conscious reality.

For a psychologist, this is a fascinating quirk of the mind.

For a doctor—and for **you**, the patient—it is a nightmare.

The Villain: The Radiologist's Blind Spot

Now, let us change the setting. Imagine the person counting is not a volunteer, but a board-certified radiologist. Imagine they are sitting in a darkened room at the end of a twelve-hour shift.

And imagine that the "ball" they are tracking is the intricate web of blood vessels in a lung CT scan, searching for a pulmonary embolism.

And the "gorilla"?

The gorilla is a **cancerous nodule** hiding in the upper lobe of the lung.

In 2013, researchers at Brigham and Women's Hospital in Boston decided to test this nightmare. They repeated the gorilla experiment with twenty-four expert radiologists. They took a standard stack of lung CT scans and inserted a picture of a tiny gorilla into the final slide.

It wasn't microscopic; it was forty-eight times larger than the average cancer nodule.

Eighty-three percent of the radiologists missed the gorilla.

They weren't bad doctors. In fact, eye-tracking software showed that many of them looked **directly** at the gorilla. Their retinas received the photons. But their brains, searching intently for the specific patterns of lung nodules, filtered out the anomaly because it didn't fit the pattern they were hunting.

This is the terrifying reality of medical imaging. The human eye is an incredible instrument, but it is attached to a brain that is easily tricked, easily tired, and prone to blindness when it focuses too hard.

In the United States alone, studies estimate that roughly **30% of abnormalities** in radiology scans are missed on the first viewing.

That figure represents millions of missed chances—millions of tumors that were seen, but not perceived, until it was too late.

We have reached the limit of human perception. To go further, we need a pair of eyes that does not suffer from inattentional blindness. We need eyes that do not get tired, do not get bored, and do not filter out the unexpected.

We need eyes that never blink.

The Pixel Hunter: How AI Sees

To understand how Artificial Intelligence changes this equation, we must understand the difference between how a human sees an image and how a machine sees it.

To a human doctor, an X-ray is a picture. It is a story. When I look at a chest X-ray, I see the ghost of a person. I see the curve of the ribs, the shadow of the heart, the cloudy gray of the lungs. I look at it holistically, searching for things that look "wrong" based on my experience.

To an AI, an X-ray is not a picture. **It is a spreadsheet.**

When an AI looks at the same image, it sees a grid of 1,024 by 1,024 numbers. Each number represents the brightness of a single pixel, ranging from 0 (pure black) to 255 (pure white).

The AI analyzes these pixels using a technology called **Convolutional Neural Networks (CNNs)**. It sweeps across the image like a relentless scanner, analyzing the mathematical relationship between every single pixel and its neighbor.

Because it is not looking for a "lung" or a "rib"—at least not in the way we do—it detects patterns that the human eye physically cannot perceive:

1. Texture Gradients

A tumor does not just appear out of nowhere; it changes the tissue around it. There is a tiny change in the "roughness" or granularity of the surrounding tissue that signals early cellular change. The human eye sees a smooth gray patch. The AI sees a mathematical disturbance in the texture.

2. Micro-calcifications

These are specks of calcium, often smaller than a grain of sand, that can indicate early breast cancer. To a tired radiologist, they look like noise or dust on the screen. To the AI, they are high-contrast beacons.

3. Subtle Contrast

The human visual cortex is limited in the number of gray shades it can distinguish—usually about thirty to fifty shades. An X-ray contains thousands. The AI can see a "shadow within a shadow" that is invisible to us.

The AI does not care about the "story" of the patient. It does not care if it is 3:00 AM. It does not get distracted because its phone rang or because it had a fight with its spouse.

It simply hunts for mathematical irregularities with cold, relentless precision.

The Author's Lens: The Hidden Blindness in My Own Field

As an ophthalmologist, I deal with images every day. The retina—the back of the eye—is the only place in the body where you can see blood vessels and nerves directly, without cutting the skin.

One of the biggest killers of vision is **Diabetic Retinopathy**. It starts with tiny bleeds—microaneurysms—that are red dots on a red background.

Asking a human to find them is like asking someone to find a specific red leaf in a forest of autumn trees.

Early in my career, I remember missing one. I was tired. The pupil wasn't fully dilated. I scanned the retina and said, "Looks good."

Six months later, the patient returned with a massive bleed. I went back to the old photos. There it was—a tiny, singular red dot that I had looked right past.

That guilt stays with you.

Today, we have AI systems like **IDx-DR**. It is the first autonomous AI approved by the FDA. It scans the retina and gives a diagnosis without a human doctor ever looking at the image.

It doesn't miss the red dot. It finds the "leaf" every single time. It protects the patient from my fatigue.

The Snowstorm and the Polar Bear

The most potent proving ground for this technology has been mammography.

Breast cancer screening is notoriously difficult. Breast tissue is dense, fibrous, and messy. Looking for a tumor in a mammogram has been famously described as **"looking for a polar bear in a snowstorm."**

The cancer is white; the dense tissue is white. The contrast is minimal.

Because it is so hard, the error rates are heartbreakingly high. We face two enemies:

- **False Negatives:** The doctor says you are fine, but you actually have cancer. This happens in approximately **20%** of cases.

- **False Positives:** The doctor says you might have cancer, but you don't. This leads to terrifying callbacks, painful biopsies, and unnecessary surgeries.

In 2020, Google Health, in partnership with Imperial College London, dropped a bombshell paper in the journal *Nature.*13 They wanted to see if the "Pixel Hunter" could see through the snowstorm better than we could.

They trained an AI on nearly 29,000 mammograms from women in the UK and the US. Then, they pitted the AI against human radiologists in a head-to-head showdown.

The results were unequivocal.

- The AI system reduced false positives by 5.7%—saving thousands of women from unnecessary panic.
- More importantly, it reduced false negatives by 9.4%—catching cancers the humans missed.

But here is the most shocking part: **The AI had less information than the humans.**

In the real world, the human radiologists had access to the patients' history, their prior scans for comparison, and their clinical notes. They knew if the patient felt a lump. The AI saw only the single image. It fought with one hand tied behind its back, and it still won.

When the researchers went back and looked at the "misses"—the cancers the humans failed to see but the AI caught—they realized why.

The AI was detecting subtle distortions in the **architectural structure** of the breast tissue. It wasn't seeing a "lump"; it was seeing the gravitational pull of the cancer on the surrounding tissue, a pattern too faint for the human eye but obvious to the algorithm.

The Haystack and the Needle

If radiology is hard, **pathology** is a nightmare.

When a surgeon removes a lymph node to check if cancer has spread, that tissue is sliced, stained, and placed on a glass slide. It is then scanned into a computer.

The resulting image is a **Gigapixel image**. It is massive—often

100,000 pixels wide by 100,000 pixels tall. If you printed it out at standard resolution, it would cover a **tennis court**.

Asking a pathologist to find a cluster of cancer cells on a slide like that is like asking someone to find *Where's Waldo*, but the map is the size of a tennis court, and Waldo is the size of a bacterium.

And you have ten minutes to do it because there is a stack of fifty other slides waiting on your desk.

If the pathologist misses that one tiny cluster of metastatic cells, **you** get staged as "Cancer Free." You are sent home without chemotherapy. The cancer grows. You die.

In 2016, a global competition called **CAMELYON16** challenged computer scientists to build an AI that could find metastatic cancer in lymph node slides.14

The results were a wake-up call for the profession.

- The best AI system achieved a detection success rate of 99.5%.
- The human pathologist, working under normal time pressure? 96.6%.

That 2.9% difference might sound small to a layman. But in a country with millions of cancer patients, that gap represents **tens of thousands of lives.** It represents tens of thousands of people who were told they were cured when they were not.

The AI turns the "Tennis Court" into a "Post-it Note." It essentially says:

"Doctor, ignore the 99% of the slide that is empty. I have checked it. It is clear. Look only at these three red boxes. Is this cancer?"

It liberates the doctor from the drudgery of the search so they can focus on the judgment of the diagnosis.

Seeing the Future: Opportunistic Screening

The most exciting capability of this "All-Seeing Eye" is not seeing what is *there*, but seeing what is *going to be there*.

Doctors are trained to diagnose disease.15 We look for the broken bone, the tumor, the blocked artery. **AI is learning to predict death.**

Researchers at the University of Adelaide trained an AI to analyze

CT scans of patients' chests. These were routine scans taken for various boring reasons—a cough, a fall, a check-up. The AI analyzed forty-eight patients who, according to doctors, appeared relatively healthy (or at least stable).

The AI was asked to predict which of these patients would die within five years.

It did so with 69% accuracy—comparable to the predictions of expert oncologists who have access to the patient's full charts, blood work, and history. The AI only had the pictures.

How? How could a machine look at a picture of a chest and see the shadow of the Grim Reaper?

The AI was engaging in **Opportunistic Screening**. It was looking at "biological age" markers that humans ignore.

- It measured the volume of fat around the heart.
- It measured the density of the muscle in the spine (sarcopenia).
- It measured the microscopic calcification of the arteries.

It saw the slow, silent disintegration of the body long before it manifested as a specific "disease." It saw the systemic fragility that leads to death.

Flash Forward: Your X-Ray in 2035

This is the dawn of a new kind of medicine. In the future, every time you get a scan—whether it's an X-ray for a broken rib or a CT for a kidney stone—the AI will run a background check on your entire health.

- It will look at your rib X-ray and say: *"Bone density low. Risk of Osteoporosis. Start Calcium."*
- It will look at your kidney scan and say: *"Aorta shows plaque buildup. Risk of Heart Attack high. Start Statins."*
- It will look at your liver and say: *"Fatty deposits detected. Risk of Cirrhosis."*

Your broken rib X-ray might just save you from a heart attack five years later. The scan becomes a window not just into your anatomy, but into your destiny.

The Panopticon of Health

The history of medicine has been a history of "looking." We invented the stethoscope because we couldn't see the heart. We invented the X-ray because we couldn't see the bone. We invented the MRI because we couldn't see the soft tissue.

Computer Vision is the next evolution of sight. It is not just a better camera; it is a better lens.

It is a lens that filters out the noise of the world—the fatigue, the bias, the invisible gorillas—and focuses entirely on the signal of disease.

It allows the radiologist to stop being a "Search Engine"—spending hours hunting for nodules in the dark—and start being a "Reasoning Engine"—deciding what to do about them.

The invisible gorilla has nowhere left to hide. And for the first time in history, we have a chance to see the disease before it sees **you.**

THE TAKEAWAY

The Villain is "Inattentional Blindness": Even expert radiologists miss obvious tumors (or gorillas) when they are focused on looking for something else.16 Studies show 30% of abnormalities are missed on the first viewing.

The "Pixel Hunter": AI sees X-rays as mathematical grids. It detects "texture gradients"—subtle roughness in tissue—that signal cancer long before it forms a visible lump.

The "Polar Bear" Problem: Finding breast cancer in dense tissue is like finding a polar bear in a snowstorm. Google's AI reduced false negatives by **9.4%**, seeing patterns of "architectural distortion" that human eyes missed.

Predicting Destiny: AI can look at a routine chest X-ray and predict your 5-year mortality risk by measuring hidden factors like muscle density and heart fat. Your broken bone scan could warn you of a future heart attack.

References

1. Drew, Trafton, Võ, M. L., & Wolfe, Jeremy M. (2013). "The

invisible gorilla strikes again: Sustained inattentional blindness in expert observers." *Psychological Science*, 24(9), 1848-1853.

2. McKinney, Scott M., et al. (2020). "International evaluation of an AI system for breast cancer screening." *Nature*, 577, 89-94.
3. Bejnordi, Babak Ehteshami, et al. (2017). "Diagnostic Assessment of Deep Learning Algorithms for Detection of Lymph Node Metastases in Women With Breast Cancer." *JAMA*, 318(22), 2199-2210.
4. Oakden-Rayner, Luke, et al. (2017). "Precision Radiology: Predicting longevity using feature engineering and deep learning methods in a radiomics dataset." *Scientific Reports*, 7, 1648.
5. Brady, Adrian P. (2017). "Error and discrepancy in radiology: inevitable or avoidable?" *Insights into Imaging*, 8(1), 171-182.

Chapter 12

The Body's Weather Forecast

Predicting the Heart Attack Before It Strikes

"A heart attack is often described as a thief in the night—sudden, silent, and violent. But we are learning that the thief actually knocks on the door for days, or even weeks, before breaking in. The tragedy is not that we couldn't stop him; it is that we didn't hear the knock."

— Dr. Suresh Kumar Pandey

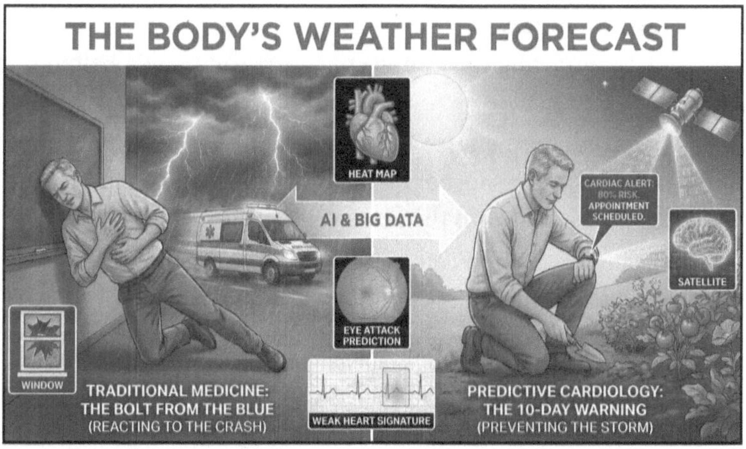

The Bolt from the Blue

Jay was fifty-four years old, a man of quiet habits and steady routines. He was a high school history teacher who spent his weekends tending to a vegetable garden that was the envy of his neighborhood. He didn't smoke. He wasn't overweight. He had a checkup six months ago, and his doctor had slapped him on the back and told him he was "fit as a fiddle."

On a Tuesday morning, Jay woke up feeling a little off. He felt a vague heaviness in his stomach—perhaps the lasagna from the night before hadn't agreed with him. He took an antacid, kissed his wife goodbye, and drove to school.

At 10:30 AM, he was standing at the chalkboard, writing the date *July 14, 1989.* As he lifted his hand to write the word "Bastille," the chalk slipped from his fingers.

He felt a sensation not of pain, but of absolute **emptiness** in his chest, as if the gravity in the room had suddenly centered on his sternum. He collapsed before he hit the floor.

Jay had suffered a massive **Myocardial Infarction**, specifically a blockage of the Left Anterior Descending (LAD) artery. In the grim vernacular of emergency medicine, this blockage has a name: the **"Widowmaker."**

By the time the ambulance arrived, weaving through morning traffic, his heart muscle had been starved of oxygen for twelve minutes. By the time the interventional cardiologists cleared the blockage in the cath lab, threading a wire into his heart to inflate a balloon, the damage was irreversible.

Jay survived, but he went home with a heart functioning at 30% capacity. He would be short of breath for the rest of his life. He would never tend his garden with the same vigor again.

To his family, the heart attack was a bolt of lightning from a clear blue sky. It was a random, cruel biological accident.

But to an **Artificial Intelligence**, Jay's heart attack was not a surprise. It was not random. It was the final, inevitable scene of a movie that had been playing in slow motion for weeks.

If Jay had been wearing a medical-grade monitor connected to an AI system, the algorithm would have seen the storm gathering long before the lightning struck.

- It would have noticed the subtle downward shift in his **Heart Rate Variability (HRV)** ten days ago.
- It would have detected the microscopic electrical instability in his **T-waves** three days ago.

It would have sent him a notification on Saturday, while he was pruning his tomatoes:

"Your cardiac metrics are deviating from your baseline. Please schedule a cardiologist appointment for Monday."

Jay would have walked into the doctor's office. He would have received a stent in a calm, scheduled procedure. He would have gone home to garden.

This is the promise of **Predictive Cardiology**. It is the end of the "surprise" heart attack. It compels us to ask a fundamental question: Why do we practice medicine as if the body keeps secrets, when in fact, it never stops talking?

From the Window to the Satellite

For most of human history, medicine has been like weather forecasting in the Middle Ages.

If a medieval farmer wanted to know the weather, he looked out the window. If it was raining, he knew it was raining. If the sun was out, he assumed everything was fine. He dealt with the storm only when the thunder rattled his roof.

This is exactly how we treat the heart. If a patient has chest pain (rain), we know they are sick. If they have no pain (sun), we assume they are healthy.

But weather works on physics. A hurricane doesn't just appear out of nowhere; it forms days in advance, thousands of miles away, driven by pressure systems and temperature gradients invisible to the naked eye. Today, meteorologists use **satellites** to track these invisible variables. They predict the hurricane two weeks before it hits land. They evacuate the city before the first drop of rain falls.

Cardiology is moving from the "Window" era to the "Satellite" era. We are realizing that the body broadcasts distress signals long before the catastrophic event. We just haven't had the ears to hear them.

The Author's Lens: The "Eye Attack"

I want to pause here and connect this to my own field, Ophthalmology, because the heart is not the only organ that suffers from "bolts from the blue."

The eye has its own version of a heart attack. It is called a **Central Retinal Artery Occlusion (CRAO)**. It is a stroke of the eye.

Imagine you are reading a book. Suddenly, the page goes black. No pain. No warning. Just instant, profound blindness in one eye.

A clot has blocked the main artery feeding your retina. Just like Jay's heart, the retinal tissue begins to die within minutes.

For decades, this was a tragedy we could only observe, not prevent. But recently, we have realized that the eye is a window into the cardiovascular future.

AI algorithms can now scan a photo of your retina and measure the width of your venules and arterioles. They can see micro-vascular changes that predict a stroke or a heart attack **years** before it happens.

Your eye is the satellite. It is broadcasting the weather forecast of your heart. If we listen to it, we can stop the storm.

The Magic of the 10-Second Strip

The most common test in cardiology—the bread and butter of the profession—is the **Electrocardiogram (ECG)**. You stick twelve plastic stickers on a patient's chest, and a machine scribbles twelve squiggly lines on pink grid paper for ten seconds.

For a hundred years, doctors have looked at these lines to answer one specific, high-stakes question: *"Is this patient having a heart attack right now?"*

If the lines look normal, we say, "No." We reassure the patient. We send them home.

But researchers at the Mayo Clinic asked a different question. They wondered if there was more information hidden in those squiggles than the human eye could see. They asked:

"Can an AI look at this 10-second strip and tell us if the patient's heart is weak?"

Heart failure—a condition where the heart pump becomes feeble—is a silent killer. It often has no symptoms until the very end, when the lungs fill with fluid and the patient drowns from the inside.

The Mayo Clinic team trained an AI on **45,000 ECGs** paired with echocardiogram results. They taught the machine to find the "signature" of a weak heart hidden in the electrical spikes of a "normal" ECG.

The results, published in *Nature Medicine*, were mind-bending.

The AI could identify patients with a weak heart pump (Low Ejection Fraction) with **93% accuracy** just by looking at the electrical squiggles. It saw subtle patterns—micro-delays in conduction, tiny shifts in voltage—that no human cardiologist had ever noticed in a century of reading ECGs.

But then, something even stranger happened.

The AI flagged a small group of patients as "High Risk" for a weak heart, but when the doctors checked their echocardiograms, their hearts were perfectly normal. The pump was strong.

The doctors assumed the AI had failed. *"Stupid robot,"* they thought. *"It's a false positive."*

But because this was a research study, they followed those patients. They watched them for years.

It turned out the robot wasn't stupid. It was clairvoyant.

The patients the AI flagged were **four times more likely** to develop heart failure in the future than the rest of the population. The AI had seen the subtle electrical precursors of the disease years before the physical muscle actually weakened.

It saw the hurricane forming over the ocean while the doctors were still enjoying the sunny day.

The Watch on Your Wrist

You don't need to be at the Mayo Clinic to see the future. You might be wearing the technology right now.

Consider **Atrial Fibrillation (AFib)**. This is a chaotic, irregular heartbeat—a "quivering" of the upper chambers—that causes blood to stagnate and clot inside the heart. If that clot breaks free, it travels like a missile to the brain, causing a massive stroke.

AFib is terrifying because it is often intermittent. It happens for an hour while you are sleeping, then stops. If you visit the doctor when it's stopped, the ECG will be normal. We call this "paroxysmal," but a better word would be "elusive."

In 2017, Apple partnered with Stanford Medicine to launch the **Apple Heart Study**. It was a staggering logistical feat. They enrolled over **400,000 people** who simply wore their Apple Watches as they went about their lives.

The watch used its optical sensor—the green light flashing against the skin—to measure pulse waves. An algorithm analyzed the rhythm. If it detected irregularity, it alerted the user.

The study proved that a consumer device could accurately identify AFib. Thousands of users received a notification:

"Irregular Rhythm Suggestive of Atrial Fibrillation."

They went to the doctor. They got on blood thinners. They avoided strokes.

We are moving toward **Continuous Passive Monitoring**. Think about your car. It has sensors that tell you when the tire pressure is low before the tire blows out on the highway. Why shouldn't your body have the same dashboard?

In the near future, clothing with woven biometric sensors will monitor us 24/7.

- **The Smart Bra:** Monitors heart rhythm and detects arrhythmias.
- **The Smart Shirt:** Monitors thoracic fluid content (a sign of lung congestion) to predict heart failure decompensation.
- **The Smart Ring:** Monitors oxygen saturation and sleep stress.

The Infallible Doctor is not a person you visit once a year for fifteen minutes. It is a digital guardian that holds your wrist every second of every day, watching for the anomaly.

Predicting the Widowmaker

But what about Jay? What about the sudden blockage of an artery? Can we predict the explosion?

The traditional way we check for heart disease is the **angiogram**. We look for "stenosis"—the narrowing of the pipe. If the artery is 90% blocked, we say, "Aha!" and we fix it. If it is only 20% blocked, we say, "You're fine."

The problem is that **50% of heart attacks happen in people with minor blockages**.

The plaque doesn't slowly choke the artery; it ruptures suddenly, like a pimple popping inside the vessel wall. This rupture triggers a clot that shuts down flow instantly.

Researchers at the University of Oxford realized that we were looking at the wrong thing. We were measuring the size of the plaque, but we should have been measuring the **inflammation**.

They developed an AI tool called the **Fat-Attenuation Index (FAI)**.

It turns out that when a coronary artery is inflamed and ready to burst, it releases chemical signals (cytokines) that change the texture of the fat surrounding the artery. The fat becomes watery and less dense. The human eye can't see this change on a CT scan. The AI can.

The AI analyzes a standard heart CT and generates a **"Heat Map"** of the arteries.

- **Blue:** Stable plaque. Safe.
- **Red:** Inflamed, angry plaque. High Risk of Rupture.

A patient might have a wide-open artery, but if the AI paints it Red, the doctor knows: **"This is a ticking time bomb."**

This changes everything. Instead of waiting for the chest pain, we can start aggressive statin therapy and anti-inflammatories immediately. We can defuse the bomb before the fuse burns down. We can treat the patient based on their biology, not their anatomy.

The 4-Hour Warning

The Holy Grail of cardiology is the short-term warning. The ability to walk up to a patient in a hospital bed and say: **"You are going to have a cardiac arrest in the next four hours."**

This sounds like science fiction, but the FDA has already approved an algorithm called the **Wave Clinical Platform** (by Excel Medical).

In a hospital, patients are hooked up to monitors that beep constantly. Nurses become desensitized to the noise- "alarm fatigue." But the Wave platform monitors subtle instabilities in respiratory rate, heart rate, and blood pressure that a human might miss or dismiss as noise.

In clinical trials at the University of Pittsburgh Medical Center, the system was able to predict sudden cardiac death and respiratory failure **six hours before it happened.**

Six hours is an eternity in medicine.

Six hours is enough time to transfer the patient to the ICU.

Six hours is enough time to call the family.

Six hours is enough time to adjust medications, give fluids, and stop the arrest from ever happening.

The system reduced in-hospital cardiac arrests by a staggering number because it turned **"Code Blue"**—a chaotic, violent rush to revive a dead patient—into **"Code Soft"**—a calm, preemptive intervention to keep the patient alive. It turned a rescue mission into a safety check.

Flash Forward: Your Morning in 2030

Imagine it is a Tuesday morning in 2030. You are brushing your teeth. Your smart mirror scans your face. Your watch scans your pulse.

A notification pops up on the mirror glass.

[HEALTH ALERT: CARDIAC STRAIN DETECTED]

[HRV: LOW. INFLAMMATION MARKERS: ELEVATED.]

[PREDICTION: 80% RISK OF CARDIAC EVENT WITHIN 48 HOURS.]

[ACTION: APPOINTMENT SCHEDULED FOR 9:00 AM. DO NOT DRIVE.]

You don't go to work. You go to the doctor. You get treated.

You never collapse. You never ride in the ambulance. You never meet the Widowmaker.

The New Normal

Critics often argue that predictive analytics will turn us into a nation of hypochondriacs, obsessing over every blip on our watches, terrified of every notification.

But I would argue the opposite is true. **Uncertainty causes anxiety. Knowledge causes action.**

Imagine a world where Jay gets that notification on Saturday. He lives a long, healthy life, completely unaware that he missed his date with death. He prunes his tomatoes. He teaches his students about the French Revolution.

This is the ultimate victory of the Infallible Doctor. The best medical intervention is not the one that saves you from the brink of death. It is the one that keeps you from ever getting there. It is the quiet, boring miracle of the event that never happens.

THE TAKEAWAY

The Villain is "Silence": The body signals distress days before a heart attack, but traditional medicine only listens for the "crash" (chest pain).

The "Satellite" Era: Just as satellites predict hurricanes, AI predicts heart failure. The Mayo Clinic's AI can spot a weak heart from a simple ECG years before symptoms appear.

The "Eye Attack": As an ophthalmologist, I see how the eye reveals the heart. AI scans of the retina can now predict cardiovascular risk, proving the body is an interconnected system.

The Heat Map: Oxford's AI can paint your arteries red or blue on a CT scan, identifying "inflamed" plaque that is about to rupture, even if the blockage is minor. This catches the "Widowmaker" before it strikes.

References

1. Attia, Zachi I., et al. (2019). "Screening for cardiac contractile dysfunction using an artificial intelligence–enabled electrocardiogram." *Nature Medicine*, 25, 70-74.
2. Perez, Marco V., et al. (2019). "Large-Scale Assessment of a Smartwatch to Identify Atrial Fibrillation." *New England Journal of Medicine*, 381, 1909-1917.
3. Oikonomou, Evangelos K., et al. (2018). "Non-invasive detection of coronary inflammation using computed tomography and prediction of residual cardiovascular risk (the CRISP CT study)." *The Lancet*, 392(10151), 929-939.
4. Topol, Eric J. (2019). "High-performance medicine: the convergence of human and artificial intelligence." *Nature Medicine*, 25, 44–56.
5. Subbe, C. P., et al. (2001). "Validation of a modified Early Warning Score in medical admissions." *QJM: An International Journal of Medicine*, 94(10), 521-526.

Chapter 13

The Zebra Hunter

Solving the Medical Mysteries That Baffle Humans

"In the vast library of human biology, we doctors have only memorized the most borrowed books. AI does not rely on memory; it reads the entire library every single time a patient walks through the door."

— Dr. Suresh Kumar Pandey

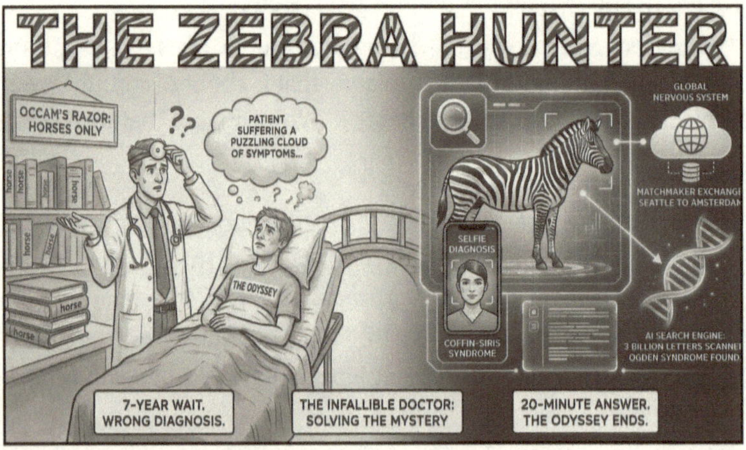

The Law of Probabilities

In the first year of medical school, long before we are trusted to touch a patient or prescribe a pill, we are taught a rule that governs the logic of modern medicine. It is a simple aphorism, passed down like folklore from attending to resident, from resident to student:

"When you hear hoofbeats behind you, don't expect to see a zebra."

The lesson is one of probability and efficiency. It means that if **you** walk into a clinic with a cough, a fever, and body aches, the doctor should treat you for influenza, not the bubonic plague. If a middle-aged man clutches his chest, we treat him for a heart attack, not a dissecting aortic aneurysm caused by a genetic connective tissue disorder.

This mental shortcut is known as **Occam's Razor**.

It is the necessary armor of the clinician. Without it, the medical system would collapse under its own weight. If we tested every headache for brain tumors and every stomach ache for rare cancers, we would bankrupt the healthcare system by noon and irradiate our patients with unnecessary scans by dinner.

We are trained to bet on the horse, not the zebra, because the horse is almost always right.

But "almost" is a terrifying word if you are the one living in the margin of error.

What happens when the hoofbeats *do* belong to a zebra?

In the United States alone, a disease is defined as "rare" if it affects fewer than 200,000 people. That sounds insignificant until you realize there are over **7,000** such distinct diseases identified so far. While each one is statistically negligible on its own, together they form a massive, silent epidemic.

Nearly one in ten Americans—roughly 30 million people—suffers from a rare disease.

For these 30 million people, the medical system is not a place of healing; it is a labyrinth of confusion and gaslighting. They become the victims of what is chillingly called the **"Diagnostic Odyssey."**

The statistics of this odyssey are stark, but they don't capture the despair. On average, a patient with a rare disease will:

- Spend **seven years** searching for an answer.
- Visit **eight different physicians**.
- Receive **three misdiagnoses**.
- Undergo surgeries for organs that aren't broken.
- Take medications for diseases they don't have.

Worst of all, they will be told, usually by a doctor they trusted, that the problem is in their head. When the blood tests come back normal and the MRI looks clean, the limitations of the doctor's knowledge are often projected onto the patient's psyche.

You are stressed, they are told. *You are anxious. You are seeking attention.*

The human brain is simply not built to hunt zebras. We are pattern-matching machines, and our internal databases are populated by the cases we see every day. A brilliant primary care physician in Ohio may practice for forty years and never see a single case of *Fibrodysplasia Ossificans Progressiva*—a horrific condition where muscle turns to bone. If a child walks into her office with a strange lump on their back, how can we expect her to recognize a disease she read about once in a textbook twenty years ago?

We are asking human doctors to be infallible archivists of the infinite, and they are failing.

We need a hunter that doesn't rely on the frailty of human memory. We need a partner that has seen every zebra in the world.

The Author's Lens: The Darkness of Retinitis Pigmentosa

I see this tragedy unfold in my own clinic.

A mother brings in her six-year-old son. She says he is clumsy at night. He bumps into furniture. He is afraid of the dark.

Most doctors would dismiss this. *Kids are clumsy,* they say. *He just needs a nightlight.*

But as an ophthalmologist, I look into his retina and see the subtle, bone-spicule pigmentation of **Retinitis Pigmentosa**. It is a rare genetic disease where the photoreceptors slowly die. He is not clumsy; he is going blind.

There are over **250 different genes** that can cause this condition. Knowing the name of the disease is not enough; we need to know the specific genetic typo. Without that, I cannot tell the mother if her other children are at risk, or if there is a gene therapy trial that could save his sight.

For decades, finding that gene was like finding a needle in a haystack. Today, AI is turning the haystack into a roadmap.

The Haystack and the Needle

To understand what this partnership looks like, we have to look at the edge of what is currently possible. Consider the story of a family in Utah, and a four-year-old boy who was slowly slipping away.

When the boy arrived at the genetics clinic at the University of Utah, his chart was already thick with the failures of previous evaluations. He had severe developmental delays. He couldn't speak. He couldn't walk. Most terrifyingly, he suffered from intense, uncontrollable seizures that racked his small body.

His parents had done everything right. They had seen the neurologists, the pediatricians, the metabolic specialists. They had been to the top hospitals. And time after time, the result was that most frustrating of medical terms: **"Unremarkable."**

The doctors, stumped and needing a label for insurance forms, called it "idiopathic cerebral palsy." *Idiopathic* is a doctor's Latin shield; it translates roughly to *"we don't know why."*

But the parents knew it wasn't cerebral palsy. Their son was regressing. He was dying, and no one could tell them why.

Enter **Dr. Gholson Lyon**, a research scientist who suspected the answer lay in the boy's source code. He decided to sequence the boy's entire genome—the **3.2 billion letters** of DNA that make up the human blueprint.

But sequencing is only the first step. When you sequence a human genome, you don't get a red flag popping up saying "HERE IS THE DISEASE." You get a list of variants. Every human being has millions of genetic variations that make them unique. When you filter out the common ones, you are left with a list of about **20,000 "rare" variants** in that single boy's code.

A total of 20,000 suspects. Any one of them could be the killer. Or none of them.

For a human team, analyzing this list is like trying to find a typo in a stack of encyclopedias reaching to the moon.

This is where the new partnership begins. The team utilized an AI-powered tool called **VAAST** and a secondary system called **PHEVOR**.

These tools work like a search engine for biology. The doctors input the boy's symptoms: *"seizures," "global developmental delay," "ataxia."*

The AI then did something no human can do. It scanned the entirety of global medical literature—millions of papers, case studies, and obscure journals—instantly. Simultaneously, it overlaid this search on top of the boy's 20,000 genetic variants.

In a matter of hours, the AI returned a hit.

It pointed a digital finger at a gene called **NAA10**.

The condition was so rare it didn't even have a name. The AI had effectively discovered a new disease by connecting dots that were miles apart. It was eventually named **Ogden Syndrome**.

The diagnosis was a heartbreak—the damage was irreversible—but it ended the Odyssey. It stopped the painful tests. It allowed the parents to stop blaming themselves.

The machine found in hours what the medical establishment had missed for four years.

The Selfie Diagnosis

Sometimes the clue isn't hidden in the invisible letters of the genome. Sometimes, it is staring you right in the face.

For decades, the diagnosis of rare genetic disorders has relied on a very specific, almost artistic skill known as **dysmorphology**. Many genetic syndromes leave a faint signature on the structure of the face—a widening of the eyes, a lowering of the ears, a specific curvature of the chin.

There are "super-specialists" who can walk into a waiting room, look at a child, and say, *"That looks like Cornelia de Lange Syndrome."* But there are only a handful of these experts in the world.

Technology is now democratizing this "clinical eye."

Consider **Face2Gene**, an application developed by a company called FDNA. It uses Deep Learning and computer vision—the same technology that allows Facebook to tag your friends in photos. But instead of recognizing your cousin, it recognizes the subtle geometry of disease.

A pediatrician takes a photo of the patient with a smartphone. The app uploads the image to the cloud, where it maps thousands of facial landmarks. It compares this mathematical map against a database of thousands of confirmed rare disease patients from around the world.

In seconds, the phone vibrates with a probability match.

In one documented case, a child presented with mysterious developmental delays. The human doctors were stumped. The Face2Gene app, however, threw up a suggestion that seemed impossible: **Coffin-Siris Syndrome.**

The doctors were skeptical. The textbooks say that Coffin-Siris patients usually have sparse scalp hair. This child had a full head of hair. The doctors had ruled it out because the patient didn't fit the "classic" description.

But the AI wasn't distracted by the hair. It was looking at the bone structure, the geometry of the brow and nose—patterns too subtle for the human eye to quantify.

Trusting the algorithm, the doctors ordered a targeted genetic test. **The test came back positive.**

The AI had seen through the variation that confused the humans. It put the wisdom of the world's greatest specialists into the pocket of a junior doctor.

The End of the Silo

The tragedy of rare disease is not just a failure of diagnosis; it is a failure of communication.

Medicine has traditionally been a siloed profession. A specialist in Tokyo might be the world's leading expert on a specific mutation of Gene A. A specialist in London might have dedicated their life to Gene B. If a patient with the Gene A mutation walks into the London hospital, they are statistically out of luck.

The knowledge exists, but it is trapped in the wrong brain, on the wrong continent.

We are seeing the rise of a **"Global Nervous System"** for medicine, powered by AI and data sharing. Platforms like **Matchmaker Exchange** are breaking down these walls.

Imagine a scenario: A geneticist in Seattle sequences a patient and finds a strange, never-before-seen mutation on a gene called *ANKRD11*. They have no idea if this is the cause.

In the new world, the doctor uploads the genotype and the symptoms to the Exchange.

Instantly, the system pings a researcher in Amsterdam. Six months ago, that researcher saw a patient with a slightly different mutation on the same gene, accompanied by the exact same unique cluster of symptoms.

Boom. A match.

Two patients, two doctors, one disease. The zebra has been identified. Before AI-driven matching, those two doctors would likely never have met. They would have gone to their graves with half the puzzle each.

Flash Forward: The Diagnostic Day (2032)

Let's visualize what this means for **you** or your child in the near future.

It is 2032. Your daughter has a strange set of symptoms—muscle weakness, vision issues, and fatigue.

You go to your primary care doctor. He doesn't dismiss you. He doesn't tell you it's "stress."

He pulls out a tablet. He takes a photo of her face (Phenotyping). He takes a drop of blood (Genomics).

The **"Zebra Hunter"** AI runs in the background. It cross-references her facial geometry with 10,000 known syndromes. It scans her 3 billion DNA letters against the global database of 500 million patients. It reads every medical paper published in the last 24 hours.

Before you leave the office, the doctor says: *"It looks like a rare mitochondrial disorder called LHON. But the good news is, because we caught it today, we can start a gene therapy that was approved in Japan last week."*

The seven-year odyssey becomes a twenty-minute visit.

The New Standard of Care

The integration of AI into the diagnostic process changes the fundamental rules of the game. When a patient presents with confusing, multi-system symptoms that defy Occam's Razor, the standard of care will no longer be "wait and see."

It will be a digital triangulation:

1. **Whole Genome Sequencing** (The Blueprint)
2. **AI Phenotyping** (The Computer Vision scan)
3. **Global Matching** (The search for the digital twin)

The machine does not get tired. It does not suffer from cognitive bias. It does not care that a disease is "too rare to be possible." It treats the one-in-a-million case with the exact same rigorous attention as the one-in-three case.

For the 30 million Americans living in the shadow of a medical mystery, the AI is the ultimate Zebra Hunter. It brings the most powerful gift medicine can offer, a gift that precedes cure and even precedes treatment.

It brings an answer.

And in the terrifying dark of the unknown, an answer is the first ray of light.

THE TAKEAWAY

The Villain is "Occam's Razor": Doctors are trained to look for common diseases ("Horses"), which causes them to miss rare ones ("Zebras"). This leads to the **7-year Diagnostic Odyssey** for rare disease patients.

The "Search Engine" for Biology: AI tools like **PHEVOR** can scan millions of medical papers and billions of DNA letters in hours to find the link between a symptom and a gene, solving cases like **Ogden Syndrome** that baffled humans.

The Selfie Diagnosis: Apps like **Face2Gene** use AI to map facial features and identify rare genetic syndromes just from a photo, spotting subtle patterns (like bone structure) that human doctors miss.

The Global Nervous System: Platforms like **Matchmaker Exchange** connect doctors across continents, instantly matching a patient in Seattle with a similar case in Amsterdam, turning isolated mysteries into solved science.

References

1. Shire. (2013). "Rare Disease Impact Report: Insights from patients and the medical community." (Source for statistics on the 7-year diagnostic odyssey).
2. Yandell, M., et al. (2011). "A probabilistic disease-gene finder for personal genomes." *Genome Research*, 21(9), 1529-1542. (The foundational paper on the VAAST tool).
3. Lyon, G. J., et al. (2011). "A new syndrome with intellectual disability, severe developmental delay, and craniofacial dysmorphism in a Utah family." *Cold Spring Harbor Molecular Case Studies*. (The discovery of Ogden Syndrome).
4. Gurovich, Y., et al. (2019). "Identifying facial phenotypes of genetic disorders using deep learning." *Nature Medicine*, 25, 60-64. (The landmark validation of Face2Gene technology).
5. Boycott, K. M., et al. (2017). "International Cooperation to Enable the Diagnosis of All Rare Genetic Diseases." *American Journal of Human Genetics*, 100(5), 695-705. (Overview of the Matchmaker Exchange initiative).

Chapter 14

Pathology 2.0

The Digital Truth vs. The Diagnostic Coin Flip

"Medicine has long comforted itself with the illusion that a diagnosis is a fact. In reality, it is often just an opinion—a fleeting consensus of eyes and brains that grow tired as the day wears on. AI does not blink, it does not tire, and it turns the subjective art of seeing into the objective science of knowing."

— Dr. Suresh Kumar Pandey

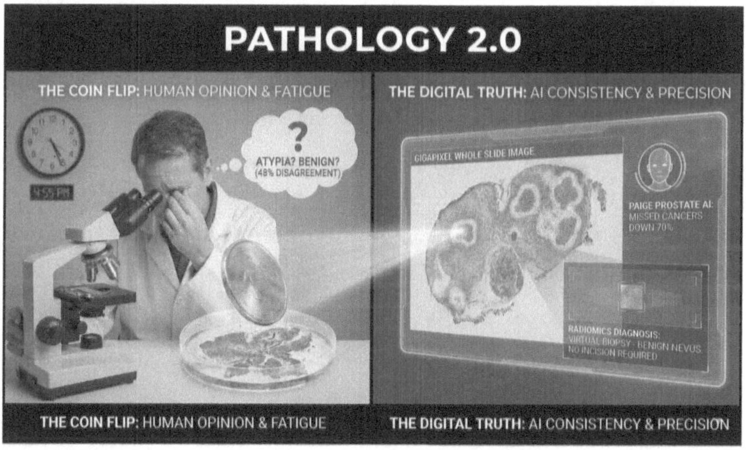

The Slide on the Tray

Linda was forty-six years old when she entered the peculiar purgatory known as **"waiting for results."**

It began, as these things often do, with the mundane bureaucracy of preventative care. A routine mammogram. A radiologist squinting at a grayscale monitor. A polite phone call suggesting she come back for a second look.

The second look revealed calcifications—tiny, glittering specks of calcium deposit scattered through the breast tissue like salt on a table. They can be nothing, the debris of aging, or they can be the first, quiet whispers of a carcinoma.

Her doctor ordered a biopsy. A hollow needle was inserted into her breast, harvesting a core of tissue no thicker than a pencil lead. That sample traveled down the hall to the pathology lab, where it was fixed in formalin, embedded in a block of paraffin wax, sliced thinner than a human hair, and stained with hematoxylin and eosin—the famous **"H&E" stain** that turns the biological world into a landscape of pink and purple.

A pathologist sat at a microscope, adjusted the focus, and made a judgment.

The report landed on her surgeon's desk two days later:

"Atypia. Pre-cancerous changes. Surgical excision recommended."

The word "surgery" triggers a cascade of trauma. Linda scheduled a lumpectomy. She met with radiation oncologists. She began the terrible mental calculus of how to tell her children.

But, driven by a sleepless anxiety that she couldn't quite name, she decided to pause. She requested her glass slides be packed up and shipped to a second hospital, a high-volume academic center, for a second opinion.

Three days later, the second report arrived.

"Benign. Fibrocystic changes. No evidence of atypia. Routine follow-up recommended."

Linda sat at her kitchen table, looking at the two pieces of paper. Same woman. Same tissue. Same microscope technology that has existed since the 19th century.

Two completely different answers. One path led to the operating room, scars, and radiation. The other path led to lunch with her friends and a normal life.

Linda's story is terrifying, but it is not unique. It is a symptom of a crisis that medicine has politely ignored for decades. We treat pathology as the **"Gold Standard"** of diagnosis. When the blood tests are vague and the X-rays are blurry, we say, "The tissue is the truth."

But as Linda found out, the truth is malleable.

The Villain: The Illusion of Certainty

In 2015, the *Journal of the American Medical Association (JAMA)* published a study that landed like a bombshell in the quiet world of pathology. Researchers asked 115 pathologists to review the same set of breast tissue slides.

For obvious, invasive cancer, the agreement was high. When a cell is wildly malignant, everyone agrees. But for the "in-between" cases—the gray zone of DCIS (Ductal Carcinoma In Situ) or Atypia, exactly what Linda had—the disagreement rate was shocking.

The pathologists disagreed with the expert consensus between 25% and 48% of the time.

Stop and consider the weight of that statistic. It implies that for a woman in the early, ambiguous stages of breast disease, the diagnosis she receives depends less on her biology and more on who happens to be sitting at the microscope that morning.

It depends on whether that doctor had a good night's sleep, or whether they just had an argument with their spouse.

It is a coin flip masquerading as science.

The problem is not that pathologists are incompetent. I have worked with pathologists for my entire career; they are some of the most meticulous, intelligent physicians in the hospital. The problem is that pathology is impossibly hard.

Unlike a blood glucose test, where a machine spits out a definitive number like "105 mg/dL," pathology is a game of **pattern recognition**. It is a visual opinion. The pathologist is looking at the architecture of cells.

Are the nuclei too dark?

Are the cells lined up in obedient little rows (healthy), or are they piling up on top of each other in a chaotic scrum (cancer)?

But nature does not draw straight lines. There is no ruler for "chaotic." A cell that looks "slightly weird" to Dr. Smith might look "definitely malignant" to Dr. Jones.

Furthermore, we are battling the biological limits of the human brain. We know that **decision fatigue** is real. A study of judicial rulings showed that judges are less likely to grant parole late in the day, when their glucose levels drop and their brains are tired.

Pathologists are no different. Research suggests that diagnostic accuracy can fluctuate based on the time of day. We are basing life-altering decisions—chemotherapy, mastectomy, prostatectomy—on the interpretation of purple blobs by a fatigued human mind.

We need a better eye.

The Author's Lens: The "Fuzzy" Cornea

I see this "gray zone" problem in my own practice as an eye surgeon.

Consider **Keratoconus**, a condition where the cornea (the clear front window of the eye) starts to thin and bulge. In its late stages, it is obvious. But in the early stages? It is a ghost.

I look at a topography map—a colorful heatmap of the eye's curvature. I am looking for subtle asymmetry. Is that red spot a sign of disease, or just a dry spot? Is that steepening real, or an artifact of the machine?

If I miss it and perform LASIK surgery, I could permanently destabilize the eye, causing blindness. If I over-diagnose it, I deny a patient the chance to see clearly without glasses.

For years, I relied on my "clinical judgment." But judgment is just a fancy word for "guessing with confidence."

Today, we use AI algorithms (like the Belin/Ambrósio Enhanced Ectasia Display). The machine looks at thousands of data points of elevation and thickness. It compares my patient to a database of 100,000 normal eyes and 50,000 diseased ones.

It gives me a probability score. **"98% Risk of Ectasia."**

It removes the guesswork. It turns my subjective opinion into an objective fact. It protects my patient from my own uncertainty.

Enter the Digital Eye

For a hundred years, the workflow of pathology has remained

frozen in time: glass slide, optical microscope, human eye. But in the last decade, a quiet revolution has begun. We have started scanning those glass slides into gigapixel-resolution files called **Whole Slide Images (WSI)**.

We are digitizing the tissue. And once the tissue is data, we can unleash Artificial Intelligence upon it.

The most compelling proof of this new era comes from a company called **Paige.AI**, founded by researchers at Memorial Sloan Kettering Cancer Center. They decided to train an AI on one of the most notoriously difficult diagnoses in men: **Prostate Cancer**.

Prostate biopsies are a nightmare for pathologists. The samples are tiny, thread-like cores of tissue. The cancer cells are often sneaky; they can be scattered in small pockets, hiding amidst healthy glands.

If a pathologist is rushing to get through a stack of 50 cases, they might miss a tiny focus of cancer—a False Negative. Conversely, they might mistake a benign patch of inflammation for cancer—a False Positive.

Paige did something unprecedented. They didn't just teach the AI rules; they fed it **tens of thousands of slides**—millions of images—linked to the actual clinical outcomes of the patients. The AI learned to ignore the visual noise and focus on the signal.

In 2021, the FDA granted approval to **Paige Prostate**, the first AI-based pathology product allowed for clinical use.

When pathologists used the AI assistant, their accuracy soared.

- **False Negatives (missed cancers) dropped by a staggering 70%.**
- **False Positives (false alarms) dropped by 24%.**

The AI acts as a "spell-checker" for the biopsy. It scans the gigapixel image in seconds, highlighting suspicious areas in bright red heatmaps. It effectively says:

"Doctor, look here. I am 99% sure this is cancer."

Crucially, the AI does not get tired. It does not need coffee. It is as sharp at 4:55 PM on a Friday as it is at 8:00 AM on a Monday. It removes the "afternoon fatigue" factor from the equation of your survival.

Grading the Gray Zone

But the machine does more than just binary detection. It solves the problem that nearly ruined Linda's life: **The Gray Zone**.

In cancer treatment, finding the tumor is only half the battle. The other half is **"grading"** it—determining how aggressive it is. This dictates the treatment. In prostate cancer, we use the **Gleason Score**.

- **Gleason 6:** The "Turtle." Slow-growing. We usually just watch it.
- **Gleason 8-10:** The "Rabbit." Fast-growing. We operate immediately.
- **Gleason 7:** The Intermediate. The decision maker.

The difference between a Gleason 6 and a Gleason 7 is the difference between going home to watch football and going to the hospital to have your prostate removed.

Yet, human pathologists disagree on the Gleason score **30% to 50% of the time**.

In 2020, a global competition called the **PANDA Challenge** (Prostate cANcer graDe Assessment) pitted AI algorithms against specialist uro-pathologists. The results were humbling.

The best AI algorithms achieved a level of agreement (0.85 kappa) that matched the world's best experts.

But here is the key: **The AI was perfectly consistent.** If you showed the AI the same slide a month later, it gave the exact same score. Humans, influenced by mood or context, often do not.

This brings something to medicine that has been sorely lacking: **Standardization**.

If you live in a rural town in Idaho, your biopsy should not be graded differently than if you live near a major academic center in Boston. But today, it is. AI levels this playing field. It ensures that a "Gleason 7" is a mathematical constant, not a geographic variable.

The Virtual Biopsy

The ultimate ambition of Pathology 2.0, however, is not to improve the biopsy, but to eliminate it.

We must remember that a biopsy is a violent act. It involves stabbing a patient. It carries risks of infection, bleeding, and seeding tumor cells. And it is spatially flawed: you might stick the needle into the one healthy part of a large tumor and miss the disease entirely.

This is where the boundary between Radiology and Pathology begins to dissolve, giving rise to **"Radiomics."**

We are developing the **Virtual Biopsy**.

Instead of cutting into a liver tumor, we take a high-resolution MRI. To the human eye, the tumor is just a gray blob. But to an AI, it is a landscape of data. The AI analyzes the texture of the tumor—the microscopic jaggedness of the edges, the fractal patterns of blood flow, the density heterogeneity.

These "radiomic features" correlate directly with the pathology. The AI can look at the MRI and effectively say:

"Based on the fractal geometry of the tumor edges, there is a 95% probability this is a high-grade Hepatocellular Carcinoma with a KRAS mutation."

We are getting the diagnosis—and potentially the genetic profile—without ever touching the patient with a blade.

In 2021, researchers used this technique to distinguish between two types of kidney tumors—Angiomyolipoma (benign) and Renal Cell Carcinoma (cancer). On a standard scan, they look identical. Surgeons often remove the kidney just to be safe, only to find out later the tumor was harmless.

The AI, however, could tell them apart by analyzing the pixel-level texture. This means thousands of patients could keep their kidneys, avoiding major surgery for a lump that the AI correctly identified as a benign mimic.

The End of "We Got It All"

Finally, let us step into the operating room, the place where pathology meets immediate consequence.

When a surgeon removes a tumor—say, a brain tumor—the goal is to achieve **"clean margins."** We want to cut out the cancer surrounded by a rim of healthy tissue, proving we "got it all."

But the brain is not a place where you can afford to cut extra tissue "just to be safe." Every millimeter is a memory, a movement, a word.

Currently, we rely on the **"frozen section."** The patient lies asleep on the table, their skull open. The surgeon sends a chunk of tissue to the lab. We wait. Twenty minutes. Thirty minutes. The clock ticks. The pathologist freezes the tissue, slices it, and calls the OR.

"It looks clean," they say. Or, *"I'm not sure."*

New AI-powered microscopes are collapsing this timeline to zero. Tools like **SRH (Stimulated Raman Histology)** use lasers to image the tissue instantly in the operating room.

The surgeon scans the edge of the cavity. The AI processes the image in milliseconds, using a neural network trained to recognize the optical signature of glioblastoma cells.

[WARNING: INFILTRATION DETECTED AT INFERIOR MARGIN.]

The surgeon cuts a little more, right then and there. The loop is closed instantly. No waiting. No "call back" surgery two weeks later because the final report came back dirty.

Flash Forward: Your Biopsy in 2035

Imagine it is 2035. You have a suspicious mole.

The doctor does not slice it off and send it away. She places a handheld scanner over your skin. The device uses **Multiphoton Tomography** to image the cells beneath the surface without making a cut.

The AI analyzes the cellular architecture in real-time.

[DIAGNOSIS: BENIGN NEVUS. NO ACTION REQUIRED.]

You put your shirt back on. You go home. No scars. No waiting. No anxiety.

The truth is instant.

From Art to Truth

For Linda, the second opinion saved her breast. But her safety shouldn't have been a matter of her own proactive advocacy. It shouldn't have been luck.

In the future of the Infallible Doctor, every slide is reviewed by two experts: the Human and the Machine.

The Machine provides the consistency, the heatmap, and the probability score. It flags the zebra that the tired human might miss. The Human provides the oversight, the clinical context, and the empathy.

Pathology stops being a coin flip. It stops being an opinion. It becomes a measurement.

We are witnessing the end of the era of the "purple blob" and the beginning of the era of high-definition truth. And for patients like Linda, that truth is the difference between a scar and a sigh of relief.

THE TAKEAWAY

The Villain is "Subjectivity": Pathology is an opinion, not a fact. Studies show doctors disagree on diagnoses up to **48% of the time** for early-stage breast cancer. Your diagnosis shouldn't depend on who is holding the microscope.

The AI Spell-Checker: Tools like **Paige Prostate** scan tissue slides and highlight cancer cells, reducing missed diagnoses (False Negatives) by **70%.**

The "Fuzzy Cornea": In eye surgery, AI maps the curvature of the eye to detect early Keratoconus (bulging) that human doctors miss, preventing disastrous LASIK complications.

The Virtual Biopsy: "Radiomics" allows AI to analyze MRI/CT scans so deeply that it can diagnose the tumor type without a needle, saving thousands of patients from unnecessary surgeries.

References

1. Elmore, J. G., et al. (2015). "Diagnostic Concordance Among Pathologists Interpreting Breast Biopsy Specimens." *JAMA*, 313(11), 1122–1132.
2. Campanella, G., et al. (2019). "Clinical-grade computational pathology using weakly supervised deep learning on whole slide images." *Nature Medicine*, 25, 1301–1309.

3. Bulten, W., et al. (2022). "Artificial intelligence for diagnosis and Gleason grading of prostate cancer: the PANDA challenge." *Nature Medicine*, 28, 154–163.

4. Hollon, T. C., et al. (2020). "Near real-time intraoperative brain tumor diagnosis using stimulated Raman histology and deep neural networks." *Nature Medicine*, 26, 52–58.

5. Bera, K., et al. (2019). "Artificial intelligence in digital pathology — new tools for diagnosis and precision oncology." *Nature Reviews Clinical Oncology*, 16, 703–715.

Chapter 15

The Digital Twin

The Flight Simulator for the Human Body

"We have accepted a terrible bargain in medicine: to find the cure, we must risk the patient. We treat the living body as a laboratory, hoping our guesses are right. The Digital Twin offers a new covenant—we make our mistakes on the machine, so we can be perfect for the human."

— Dr. Suresh Kumar Pandey

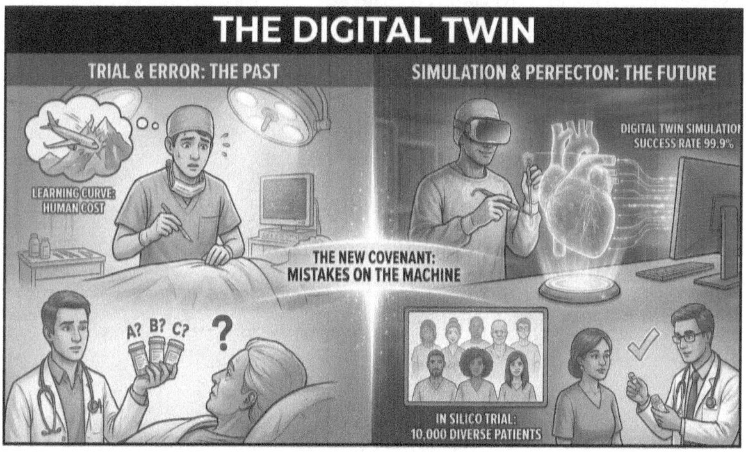

The Cockpit and the Operating Room

Imagine, for a moment, that **you** are a pilot.

You are sitting in the cockpit of a Boeing 747, cruising at 35,000 feet over the Atlantic. Suddenly, a warning light flashes. The number three engine is vibrating violently. The hydraulic pressure is dropping. A hurricane is forming ahead, and the nearest runway is short, slick with rain, and surrounded by mountains.

Do you try to land the plane on your first attempt? Or, if you had a magic button that could pause time, would you choose to **practice the landing first**?

The answer is obvious. In aviation, we do not guess. Pilots spend hundreds of hours in flight simulators—perfect, physics-based replicas of the aircraft. They fly into virtual hurricanes. They fail. They crash the virtual plane a dozen times, learning the precise angle of approach, the exact amount of thrust needed to survive.

Only when they have perfected the solution in the safety of the silicon mind do they touch the real controls.

Now, imagine you are a **pediatric cardiologist**.

You are standing over a three-month-old baby. The heart inside the child's chest is the size of a walnut. The arteries are twisted in a rare congenital defect that defies the diagrams in your textbooks. You have to cut. You have to patch a hole the size of a dime while the heart is still beating.

Do you get a simulator? Do you get to crash a "virtual baby" ten times to figure out the perfect stitch?

No. You get one shot.

You cut. If you are wrong, the baby dies.

This is the fundamental paradox of modern medicine. We demand perfection, but we practice **"trial and error"** on living, breathing human beings. Whether it is a surgeon navigating a complex tumor or an oncologist choosing between three toxic chemotherapy drugs, we are essentially guessing.

We try Drug A. We wait three months. If the tumor grows, we apologize and try Drug B. If Drug B causes heart failure, we stop and try Drug C.

By the time we find the drug that works—the "Goldilocks" drug—the patient may be too weak to take it. We treat the patient like a guinea pig in their own experiment.

We have reached the limit of what human intuition can achieve. We need a flight simulator for the human body. We need a way to test the cure without risking the patient.

We need a **Digital Twin**.

The Villain: The High Cost of Learning

The villain in this chapter is not a disease. It is the learning curve.

Every great surgeon has a graveyard—a collection of patients who suffered complications while the surgeon was "getting good." Every new drug on the market has a history of failed clinical trials where real people suffered side effects so we could learn what *not* to do.

This "tuition" is paid in human suffering.

The Digital Twin eliminates the tuition. It is a physics-based, biologically accurate computational model built from your specific data. It takes your MRI scans, your CT scans, your genetic code, and your ECG readings, and reconstructs them in a virtual environment.

On the screen, the Digital Twin heart doesn't just look like a heart; it acts like one. The myocardium contracts. The virtual blood flows. The valves snap shut. The pressure dynamics are calculated using complex fluid dynamics equations—the same math used to model tsunamis and airflow over wings.

If your real heart has a leaky mitral valve, your Digital Twin has a leaky mitral valve. If your arteries are stiffening with age, the Twin's arteries are stiff. It is a mirror image of your physiology, trapped behind glass, waiting to be tested.

NASA's Gift to Medicine

The concept was not invented by doctors. It was born out of desperation by rocket scientists.

In April 1970, the **Apollo 13** mission suffered a catastrophic oxygen tank explosion. Three astronauts were stranded 200,000 miles from Earth in a crippled spacecraft. The engineers in Houston could not look at the ship. They could not touch it.

They didn't guess. On the ground in Houston, NASA possessed high-fidelity simulators—exact replicas of the spacecraft systems. They fed the data from the crippled ship into the simulators on Earth. They tested crazy ideas. They hacked solutions. They ran scenarios that failed, and failed again, until they found the one sequence of switches that brought the power up without blowing the fuses.

They solved the problem on the Twin, then radioed the solution to the crew.

For fifty years, this level of simulation was reserved for machines—jet engines, oil rigs, skyscrapers. But today, companies like **Dassault Systèmes** and **Siemens** are doing the exact same thing for the human body.

The Author's Lens: Crashing the Virtual Eye

As an eye surgeon, I have lived this revolution.

When I was training, the first time I performed cataract surgery, I was terrified. I was operating on a human eye. I was shaking. My mentor was shouting instructions. The margin for error was zero.

Today, my residents do not touch a human eye until they have performed 50 surgeries on a **Virtual Reality Simulator** (like the Eyesi Surgical Simulator).

They sit at a console. They hold the instruments. They look through the microscope. But what they see is a perfect digital replica of the eye. They practice "phacoemulsification"—using ultrasound to break up the lens.

If they push too hard, the virtual capsule breaks. The screen flashes red: **"Complication: Vitreous Loss."**

They fail. They crash. They learn the feel of the tissue, the physics of the fluid dynamics, the limits of the anatomy. They make their mistakes on the machine so they can be perfect for **you**.

This is not a video game. It is a moral imperative. It ensures that your eye is never the "practice run."

The Living Heart Project

The most advanced example of this technology is the **Living Heart Project**. It began not as a commercial venture, but as a father's quest.

Dr. Steve Levine, a brilliant scientist at Dassault Systèmes, spent his career simulating car crashes to make vehicles safer. But his life changed when his daughter was born with a congenital heart defect. Her heart was structurally reversed—the chambers were on the wrong sides, the arteries twisted.

Levine watched as the surgeons struggled to visualize the anatomy. They looked at 2D slices of MRI scans, trying to construct a 3D map in their minds. He realized, with horror, that the technology used to design a $20,000 sedan was far superior to the technology used to repair his daughter's heart.

He gathered a coalition of physicists, cardiologists, and engineers to build a complete, beating 3D model of the human heart.

Today, that model is saving lives. At Boston Children's Hospital, surgeons can now put on a **Virtual Reality (VR)** headset and "step inside" a patient's heart before they ever scrub in.

You can try this yourself. You put on the headset, and suddenly you are standing inside the left ventricle. You can look up and see the mitral valve opening and closing like a giant parachute above your head. You can see the defect—the hole in the wall—with perfect clarity.

But the true power is not just seeing; it is doing. The surgeon can practice the operation on the Twin.

"What happens if I place a patch here?" The surgeon makes a virtual stitch. The simulation runs. The computer calculates the blood flow.

[WARNING: HIGH TURBULENCE. RISK OF CLOT FORMATION.]

"Okay, what if I route the patch this way?" The surgeon tries again.

[RESULT: LAMINAR FLOW. NORMAL PRESSURE.]

They solve the puzzle on the ghost before they cut the child.

Separating the Twins

The stakes of this technology are never higher than when two lives are literally fused together.

In 2022, the medical world watched in awe as a team of surgeons in Brazil and the United Kingdom accomplished the impossible: the separation of **craniopagus conjoined twins**.

Bernardo and Arthur Lima were three years old. They were joined at the head, their brains fused, sharing vital blood vessels. For most of history, their condition was a death sentence. To separate them meant risking a fatal hemorrhage for one or both. The anatomical map was a tangle of shared veins; one wrong cut would leave a child brain-dead.

Dr. Noor ul Owase Jeelani, a pediatric neurosurgeon at Great Ormond Street Hospital in London, led the effort. But he did not fly to Brazil and start cutting.

Instead, the team spent months inside the **Digital Twin**.

They used CT and MRI scans to build a perfect Virtual Reality replica of the boys' fused brains. It was a map of the minefield. Surgeons in London and surgeons in Rio de Janeiro donned Virtual Reality headsets and met in the same **"virtual operating room."** They stood together in the metaverse, looking at the floating hologram of the boys' brains.

They practiced the surgery over and over again. They cut the virtual veins. They watched the virtual blood redistribute. They argued. They failed. They found the "traps"—the veins that looked safe to cut but would cause a stroke if severed.

When the actual surgery day came, it was a marathon—27 hours of grueling focus. But it wasn't a guessing game. It was a performance. They were executing a script they had already rehearsed until it was muscle memory.

Both boys survived. They are now living separate lives.

Dr. Jeelani later called it "space-age stuff." He told the press, *"It's just wonderful. It's really great to see the anatomy and play with it before you actually put a knife to the skin."*

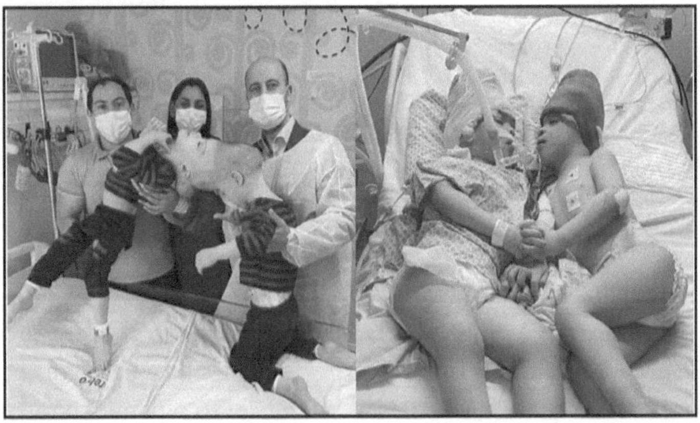

Conjoined twins whose brains were fused together separated by UK pediatric neurosurgeon Dr. Noor ul Owase Jeelani.

The Crash Test Dummy for Drugs

Surgery provides the most dramatic visuals, but the "Goldilocks Problem" is actually deadliest in pharmacology.

Every year, thousands of patients die from **Adverse Drug Reactions (ADRs)**. This happens because we dose drugs based on the "average human"—a statistical phantom who is usually a 70kg white male.

But **you** are not an average. You are a specific biological entity. A 500mg dose of a heart medication might cure a 200lb man, but kill a 100lb woman with slightly reduced kidney function.

Currently, finding the right dose is a game of Russian Roulette.

Consider a condition like arrhythmia—an irregular heartbeat. A doctor might want to prescribe **Sotalol**. It is a powerful, effective drug. But in a small percentage of people, Sotalol can trigger a fatal electrical short-circuit in the heart called Torsades de Pointes.

Because of this risk, if you start Sotalol today, you have to be admitted to the hospital for three days. You lie in a bed, hooked to a monitor, while doctors wait to see if the drug tries to kill you. It is primitive, expensive, and terrifying.

In the future of the Infallible Doctor, this hospitalization will disappear. The doctor will feed your genetic data and your electrolyte levels into your **Digital Twin**. They will inject the "virtual drug" into the "virtual you."

The computer runs a simulation of 10,000 heartbeats in seconds. It tests the drug under stress. It tests it while you are sleeping. It tests it while you are running.

- *Scenario 1: No reaction. The rhythm stabilizes.*
- *Scenario 2: Fatal cardiac arrest at 3:00 AM.*

The computer flashes red:

[DO NOT PRESCRIBE. HIGH RISK OF TORSADES.]

The doctor switches to a different drug. You are saved from a cardiac arrest that never happened. The error was caught in the silicon, not in your chest.

The "In Silico" Clinical Trial

The implications extend far beyond the individual patient. The Digital Twin is poised to rescue the entire pharmaceutical industry from its own inefficiency.

Bringing a new drug to market currently takes about **12 years** and costs nearly **$2.5 billion**. The reason is the slow, grinding pace of clinical trials. We have to test on mice, then healthy humans, then sick humans. We have to recruit thousands of people.

But human trials have a fatal flaw: they are rarely diverse enough.

Historically, clinical trials have heavily over-represented white men. According to FDA data from 2020 drug trials:

- **Black or African American participants** made up only about **8%** of trial populations, despite being 13.6% of the US population.
- **Asian participants** hovered around **6%**.

This leaves a dangerous data gap. We often don't know if a drug works differently in an elderly Asian woman until *after* it is released to the public.

The FDA is now recognizing **"In Silico" Trials**—trials performed on silicon chips.

In 2020, researchers needed to test a new design for a pacemaker lead. Instead of implanting it in 5,000 sheep or recruiting 1,000 humans, they tested it on **10,000 Digital Hearts**.

But they didn't just use one "average" heart. They generated a virtual population that was perfectly diverse. They created digital hearts that were old, young, male, female, Black, Asian, Hispanic, healthy, and diseased. They subjected these digital hearts to extreme stress—marathon running, high blood pressure, extreme cold.

The simulation proved the device was safe across the entire spectrum of humanity. The FDA accepted the data.

This is the future. We can run a clinical trial on one million diverse virtual patients in a single afternoon. We can discover that a drug causes liver toxicity in 2% of the population before a single real pill is swallowed.

Flash Forward: Your Personal Dashboard (2035)

Ultimately, the Digital Twin will leave the hospital and enter your pocket. It will become the ultimate consumer product.

Imagine opening an app on your phone. You see a 3D avatar of yourself—a biological mirror.

- *The Heart: Pulse 65. Green.*
- *The Liver: Enzyme levels slightly elevated. Yellow.*

But the real power is the **"Time Slider."**

You slide the timeline forward ten years. The avatar on the screen gains twenty pounds. The arteries in the neck thicken. The heart turns red. A warning pops up:

[RISK OF TYPE 2 DIABETES: 80%]

[RISK OF STROKE: HIGH]

This is not a vague warning from a doctor telling you to "eat better." This is a visual prediction.

You ask the Twin: *"What if I switch to a Mediterranean diet and run two miles a week?"*

The simulation re-calculates. The avatar slims down. The arterial plaque recedes. The heart turns green.

[RISK OF DIABETES: 15%]

It turns health from a nebulous concept into a visual cause-and-effect engine. It shows you the consequences of your choices before you make them. It gives you the power to change the future by simulating it first.

The End of Experimentation

We are entering the era of the **Simulated Cure**.

For centuries, the moral calculus of medicine was simple but brutal: to know if a treatment worked, we had to try it. If the patient lived, we celebrated. If the patient died, we learned a lesson for the next one. Our knowledge was paved with the suffering of the "trial cases."

That calculus is no longer acceptable. With the Digital Twin, we make our mistakes on the computer so we don't have to make them on the body. We crash the simulator so we can land the plane.

The Infallible Doctor does not guess. It knows, because it has already treated you a thousand times in the virtual world, just to get it right once in the real one.

THE TAKEAWAY

The Villain is "Trial and Error": Doctors currently test drugs and surgeries on real patients to see what works. This is like learning to fly a 747 with passengers on board.

The "Virtual Eye": Eye surgery simulators allow residents to crash a "digital eye" 50 times before touching a human one, eliminating the learning curve that causes complications.

The Living Heart: Surgeons can now use VR to "step inside" a patient's heart (Digital Twin) to plan complex surgeries, like separating conjoined twins, reducing deadly surprises.

The "In Silico" Revolution: We can now test drugs on **10,000 diverse virtual patients** (Black, Asian, Hispanic, Elderly) in an afternoon, ensuring safety for everyone, not just the "average" white male in a clinical trial.

References

1. Corral-Acero, J., et al. (2020). "The 'Digital Twin' to enable the vision of precision cardiology." *European Heart Journal*, 41(48), 4556–4564.
2. Levine, S. R. (2014). "The Living Heart Project: A robust and integrative simulator for human heart function." *Dassault Systèmes White Paper*.
3. Jeelani, N. u. O., & Gemini Untwined Team. (2022). "Separation of craniopagus twins using virtual reality simulation." *Gemini Untwined Press Release*.
4. Viceconti, M., et al. (2021). "In silico trials: Verification, validation and uncertainty quantification of predictive models used in the regulatory evaluation of biomedical products." *Methods*, 185, 120–127.
5. Musuamba, F. T., et al. (2021). "Scientific and regulatory evaluation of mechanistic in silico drug and disease models in drug development: Building model credibility." *CPT: Pharmacometrics & Systems Pharmacology*, 10(8), 804–825.

PART IV
Steady Hands
Robotics in Surgery and Intervention

Chapter 16

The Tremor is Gone

Breaking the 100-Micron Barrier

"Medicine has always been a battle between the perfection of our knowledge and the imperfection of our hands. We know exactly what to do, but our biology betrays us. The robot does not replace the surgeon; it liberates the surgeon from the tyranny of their own pulse."

— Dr. Suresh Kumar Pandey

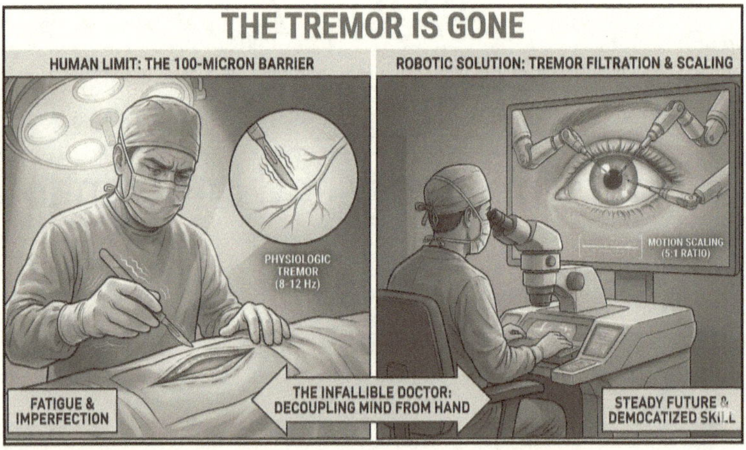

The 100-Micron Barrier

Hold your hand out in front of you. Stretch your fingers wide. Now, hold it perfectly still.

To the naked eye, your hand appears steady. You feel calm. You feel in control.

But if we were to tape a sensitive accelerometer to your index finger, or place your hand under a high-powered microscope, we would see a chaotic reality. Your hand is vibrating. It is dancing to a rhythmic beat of about **8 to 12 Hertz**.

This is the **Physiologic Tremor**. It is the inescapable background noise of being alive. It is caused by the firing of your sympathetic nervous system, the mechanical thrum of your heartbeat, and the firing of motor units in your muscles struggling to maintain posture.

Now, imagine you are holding a scalpel.

Imagine the tip of that steel blade is resting against the wall of a basilar artery deep inside the human brain. That vessel is perhaps one millimeter wide. The wall of that vessel is as thin as wet tissue paper. If you twitch to the left, you puncture the vessel, causing a catastrophic hemorrhage. The patient dies. If you twitch to the right, you sever a nerve. The patient wakes up unable to speak, or swallow, or see.

Are you still holding your hand perfectly still?

For five thousand years, the history of surgery has been defined by this physical limit. We call it the **"100-Micron Barrier."**

No matter how gifted the surgeon, no matter how many years they have trained, the human hand has a natural oscillation of roughly 100 microns—about the width of a thick human hair or a sheet of paper.

In the grand scheme of things, 100 microns is tiny. But in the world of cellular biology, it is a canyon. A single nerve fiber might be 10 microns thick. A capillary delivering oxygen to the retina is 8 microns.

We reached a frustrating plateau in modern medicine where our knowledge of anatomy exceeded our physical ability to repair it. We knew, intellectually, that if we could just stitch that tiny vessel, the tissue would survive. We knew that if we could peel that tumor off the nerve without touching it, the function would be preserved.

But our hands were too clumsy, too large, and too shaky to do it. We were giants trying to fix watches wearing boxing gloves.

This is why the arrival of the surgical robot was not merely an evolution in tools. It was a revelation. It was the moment we admitted that to save more lives, we had to stop relying on the flesh.

The Villain: The Unstable Surgeon

Dr. Catherine Mohr, a surgeon turned engineer at Intuitive Surgical—the creators of the famous **Da Vinci** robot—often speaks about the brutal reality of the operating room. There is a romantic myth of the surgeon as an iron-willed superhero, standing for twelve hours, unblinking, fueled by coffee and adrenaline.

But biology does not care about our myths.

A surgeon doesn't just battle the patient's disease. They battle their own body. Consider the physical act of a long surgery. The surgeon stands hunched over a table, neck craned forward at an unnatural angle. The lights are hot. The stress is cortisol-spiking. Their blood sugar drops as the hours pass without food. Their lower back screams.

"We do things to surgeons that we would never do to athletes," Dr. Mohr observes. "We deprive them of sleep, we don't let them eat, we make them stand in uncomfortable positions for hours, and then we expect peak performance in a life-or-death situation."

The result is that the quality of **your** surgery depends heavily on when it happens.

A seminal study published in 2009 analyzed surgical outcomes and found a disturbing correlation: as the day wears on, the error rate rises. Surgeries performed late in the afternoon or at night carried significantly higher risks of complications than those performed at 8:00 AM.

Why? Because the surgeon was tired. The physiological tremor increased. The hand, exhausted by holding retractors and clamps, shook just a little bit more.

We built a medical system dependent on human stamina, and humans are terrible at maintaining stamina.

The Author's Lens: The View from the Microscope

I want to take you inside my own operating theater to show you what this reality looks like.

As an eye surgeon, I operate in a universe measured in microns. Whether my retina colleagues working deep inside the posterior segment on the retina, or myself working in the anterior segment on a lens, we are manipulating tissue as fragile as a wet butterfly wing.

Consider the procedure of **Internal Limiting Membrane (ILM) Peeling**. This membrane is roughly 3 microns thick. To treat a macular hole, we have to grasp this invisible edge with microscopic forceps and peel it off the retina without damaging the nerve fibers underneath.

But the challenge is perhaps even more visceral when I perform **infantile cataract surgery**.

Operating on a baby's eye is fundamentally different from operating on an adult. The tissues are highly elastic. When I perform the **anterior capsulorhexis**—creating a circular opening in the front of the lens bag to remove the cataract—it is like trying to tear a perfect circle in a taut rubber balloon using a sharp needle. The tension is immense. If my hand drifts even slightly, the tear escapes to the periphery (a "run-out"), potentially ruining the structural integrity of the eye.

The stakes rise further during the **primary posterior capsulorhexis (PPC)**. In infants, we must also remove the back wall of the lens capsule to prevent future clouding. This membrane is unimaginably thin—about 4 microns. Behind it sits the vitreous jelly. If I apply too much pressure, or if my instrument deviates, the capsule rips, the jelly surges forward, and the surgery turns into a rescue mission.

Under the high-magnification microscope, my own heartbeat looks like an earthquake.

Every time my heart pumps (systole), my hand moves slightly. I have to time my movements *between* the beats (diastole). If I had too much coffee, or if I didn't sleep well, that earthquake gets worse. There are days when I look through the scope and realize that my biological tremor is fighting me. I have to exert immense mental energy just to hold the instrument still against the elasticity of a child's eye.

This is the "human factor." And for decades, it was the ceiling of what was possible in surgery.

The Hand-Eye Decoupling

The revolution began the moment we decided to separate the surgeon's hand from the surgeon's knife.

In traditional "open" surgery, the scalpel is a direct extension of the finger. The feedback loop is immediate, but it is also unrefined. If the surgeon sneezes, the knife slips.

In robotic surgery, the scalpel is an extension of a **computer**.

When I first sat down at the console of a robotic system, the sensation was disorienting. You do not stand over the patient. You might be ten feet away. You bury your face in a stereoscopic viewer that floods your vision with a 3D, high-definition image of the anatomy, magnified ten times.

Your hands grasp two controllers that feel less like medical instruments and more like video game joysticks.

When you move your hand, nothing touches the patient directly. Instead, the computer intercepts your intent. It takes the electrical signal of your movement and processes it through two critical filters before it tells the robot arm to move.

Filter 1: Motion Scaling

The first filter is a shrinking mechanism. The surgeon can set a ratio, often 5:1. This means that if I move my hand five centimeters in the air at the console, the robot tip inside the patient moves only one centimeter.

It turns a sweeping, large human movement into a microscopic, precise surgical action. It is like having a "zoom lens" for movement. I can make a gesture that feels like I am throwing a baseball, and the robot translates it into a delicate caress of a single layer of tissue.

Filter 2: Tremor Filtration

The second filter is the true miracle. The computer samples the position of the surgeon's hand hundreds of times per second. It notices the tiny, high-frequency wobble—the physiologic tremor. It sees the 12-Hertz vibration of my pulse.

And it deletes it.

The computer mathematics says: "*That 100-micron shake is noise. Ignore it. The surgeon intends to move in a straight line.*"

It smooths out the curve. At the console, my hand might be shaking from fatigue. But on the screen, the instrument tip is dead calm. It is rock solid. It floats in the air with a supernatural stillness that no human hand has ever achieved in the history of our species.

The Super-Wrist

But stability is only half the battle. The other half is geometry.

Try to bend your wrist backward. It stops at about 90 degrees. Now try to rotate it. It stops after about 180 degrees. The human wrist is a hinge with a limited range of motion.

This makes working in tight, deep spaces incredibly difficult.

Consider the male pelvis. It is a deep, narrow, bony funnel. The prostate gland sits at the very bottom of this funnel. In the era of open surgery, the surgeon had to jam their hands into this small space, often unable to see clearly, relying on touch, struggling to get the right angle to stitch the urethra back to the bladder. It was bloody and clumsy.

The robot has no such limitations. The patented **EndoWrist** instruments on the Da Vinci function like a human wrist, but without the bone and ligament restrictions. They have seven degrees of freedom. They can rotate a full **360 degrees**, endlessly.

This allows the robot to reach around corners. It can sew upside down. It can work in a space smaller than a tennis ball with complete ease. A stitch that would take a human surgeon ten difficult, sweaty maneuvers to complete can be done by the robot in two elegant, fluid motions.

The Democratization of Skill

The impact of this technology has been profound, but not in the way most people think. We often assume technology exists to make the "superstar" surgeons even better.

But the true value of the robot is that it **raises the floor for everyone else.**

Take radical prostatectomy (prostate cancer surgery) as the prime example. The prostate is surrounded by a delicate spiderweb of nerves responsible for bladder control and sexual function.

Before robotics, the outcomes of this surgery varied wildly based on who your surgeon was.

- If you went to a superstar at a top academic hospital who had done 5,000 cases, you might have a 90% chance of saving those nerves.
- But if you went to a community surgeon who did twenty cases a year, your chance might drop to **50%**.

The gap between the "best" and the "average" was massive.

The robot changed the math. Because of the 3D magnification, the tremor filtration, and the 360-degree wrists, the "average" surgeon could now navigate that tight space with the precision of a master.

Studies began to show that as robotic adoption increased, the variability in patient outcomes decreased. The standard deviation shrank. Patients got out of the hospital faster, bled less, and had fewer complications, regardless of whether they were in Boston or Boise.

The machine democratized excellence. It took the "art" out of the hands of the few and put "precision" into the hands of the many.

The New Frontier: Microsurgery

While the Da Vinci dominates large body cavities, a new frontier is opening that deals with the truly microscopic.

Microsurgery is the art of connecting tiny things—blood vessels, nerves, lymphatic ducts. These structures are often smaller than one millimeter. This is the Olympics of surgery. Only a handful of people on earth are truly great at it.

Enter **Symani**, a robotic system developed by Medical Microinstruments in Italy. If Da Vinci is a truck, Symani is a watchmaker's tool. The robot arms are small and delicate. The instruments are microscopic—the tips are so small they are almost invisible to the naked eye.

In 2020, surgeons at the University of Zurich used Symani to perform a lymphatic reconstruction. They were treating lymphedema, a painful swelling condition often caused by cancer treatment. The cure involved connecting lymphatic vessels that were **0.3 millimeters wide**.

For a human, this is exhausting work. A single heartbeat can ruin the stitch.

For the robot, it was effortless.

The surgeon sat at the console, moving their hands normally. The robot scaled the motion down by a factor of 20. The surgeon felt like they were sewing a shirt; the robot was sewing a single cell layer of a fragile vessel.

Flash Forward: Your Eye Surgery in 2035

Let's go back to the eye. What does this mean for **you** if you need retinal surgery in the future?

It is 2035. You have a macular hole—a tiny tear in the center of your vision.

The surgeon does not hold the instruments. A robotic system called the **Preceyes** (which is already being tested) is docked to your eye.

The surgeon marks the area on a screen. The robot enters the eye. The movement is perfectly steady. There is zero tremor. The robot grasps the 3-micron membrane and peels it in one smooth, continuous motion.

The risk of accidental retinal tear drops to nearly zero. The surgery takes 15 minutes. You go home with your sight restored.

The robot turned a "heroic" surgery into a routine one.

The Steady Future

We are moving toward a world where the physical limitations of the surgeon are no longer the defining factor in patient care.

The Infallible Doctor of the future does not have a bad back. It does not have a coffee tremor. It does not get tired at 3:00 AM after a twelve-hour shift. It does not struggle to see around a corner.

By decoupling the mind from the hand, we have freed the surgeon to focus on what actually matters: the strategy of the operation, the anatomy, and the decision-making. We provide the intent; the machine provides the execution.

We are entering an era where the trembling hand of the healer is steady at last. And with that steadiness comes a promise: that **your** safety on the operating table no longer depends on how much sleep your doctor got last night.

The tremor is gone.

THE TAKEAWAY

The Villain is "The Tremor": Every human hand shakes at 8-12 Hertz. This "100-Micron Barrier" limits our ability to perform delicate surgeries on nerves and blood vessels without causing damage.

The "Zoom Lens" for Movement: Robotic systems scale motion. A 5-centimeter movement by the surgeon becomes a 1-centimeter movement by the robot, allowing for superhuman precision.

The Author's Experience: In eye surgery, peeling a 3-micron membrane requires holding one's breath between heartbeats. Robotics eliminates this physical strain, making impossible surgeries routine.

Democratizing Excellence: Robots level the playing field. They allow an "average" surgeon to achieve the same nerve-sparing results as a "master" surgeon, ensuring you get world-class care regardless of your zip code.

References

1. Kelz, K. A., et al. (2009). "Time-of-day effects on surgical outcomes in the private sector: a retrospective cohort study." *Journal of the American College of Surgeons*, 209(4), 434-445.
2. Intuitive Surgical. (2023). "Da Vinci Technology Overview: EndoWrist Instruments and Tremor Filtration." *Intuitive Surgical Technical White Paper.*
3. Couch, G. G., & Panait, L. (2008). "Quantitative assessment of tremor during surgeon-assisted and robotic-assisted simulated surgical tasks." *Journal of Robotic Surgery*, 2(4), 243-248.
4. Lindenberg, M. A., & Van Mulken, T. (2020). "First-in-human clinical use of the Symani Surgical System for microsurgical reconstruction." *Journal of Reconstructive Microsurgery*, 36(04), e1-e2.
5. Ficarra, V., et al. (2012). "Systematic review and meta-analysis of studies reporting urinary continence recovery after robot-assisted radical prostatectomy." *European Urology*, 62(3), 405-417.

Chapter 17

The Global Surgeon

Teleporting Expertise Across Borders

"We have conquered the microscopic distance between the scalpel and the cell, but we are still defeated by the macroscopic distance between the doctor and the patient. Telesurgery is not just about extending a robot arm; it is about extending the reach of hope across borders, oceans, and war zones."

— Dr. Suresh Kumar Pandey

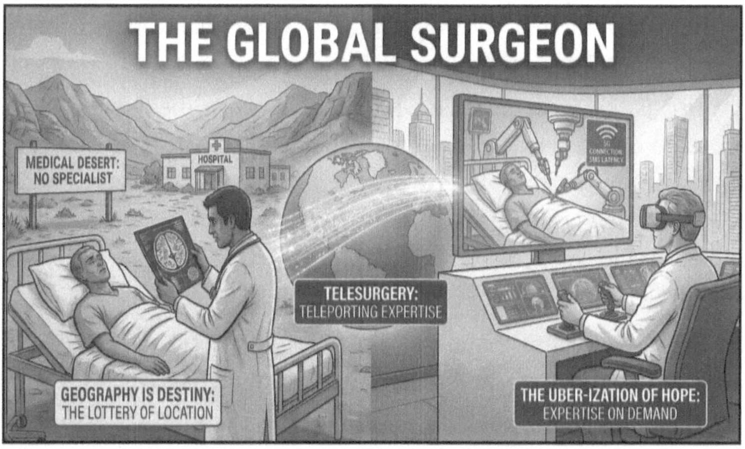

The Lottery of Location

Biology is unfair. Some of us are born with arteries that harden at forty, while others smoke a pack a day and live to be ninety. But if biology is unfair, **Geography** is cruel.

Consider a hypothetical Tuesday afternoon. Two men, identical in age and health, suffer the exact same rupture of a complex intracranial aneurysm. It is a catastrophic event; a vessel in the brain balloons and bursts, flooding the skull with blood.

The first man falls in a coffee shop in downtown Boston. Within twelve minutes, an ambulance delivers him to Massachusetts General Hospital. He is wheeled into a sterile suite where one of the world's leading neurosurgeons—a specialist who has clipped a thousand such aneurysms—is washing her hands. His chances of survival are excellent.

The second man falls in a rural village in the mountains of India, or perhaps a small mining town in Wyoming, or a trench in Ukraine. There is no neurosurgeon for five hundred miles. The local doctor is a courageous generalist who can stitch a wound or set a bone, but looking into the complex architecture of the human brain is beyond their training and their tools.

This man must be stabilized. He must wait for a helicopter. He must wait for the weather to clear.

In the twenty-first century, the architecture of survival is dictated by the randomness of location. Your zip code is a stronger predictor of your mortality than your genetic code.

This is the great, silent inequality of modern medicine. We have clustered our expertise in wealthy urban centers, creating oasis cities of medical miracles while leaving the rest of the world as a medical desert. We have assumed this distribution is inevitable—that **you** must travel to the healer.

But what if the healer could travel to **you**?

What if the best hands in Boston could reach out, across the curvature of the earth, and touch a patient in the Himalayas?

This is the promise of **Telesurgery**. It is the radical idea that the surgeon does not need to be in the room to save a life. In fact, the surgeon does not even need to be on the same continent.

The Author's Lens: The View from the Village

As an eye surgeon, I have seen the cruelty of distance firsthand.

I remember a young girl in a remote village in Rajasthan. She had a traumatic cataract—a white cloud in her eye from an injury. It was blinding her.

The surgery to fix it takes me 15 minutes. It is simple, elegant, and transformative. But her family could not afford the travel to the city. They could not leave their farm. So, she stayed blind.

Blindness in a village is often a sentence of poverty and isolation.

For years, I organized "eye camps," driving into the rural areas with a van full of equipment. But I am only one person. I have only two hands. I cannot be everywhere.

The "Camp Model"—the idea that doctors must physically travel to the patient—is noble, but it is not scalable. We need a way to teleport the skill without moving the surgeon.

The 32-Kilometer Handshake

History often changes not with a bang, but with a quiet hum in an unexpected place. On a humid afternoon in December 2018, that change happened in Gujarat, India.

Dr. Tejas Patel is a world-renowned interventional cardiologist. His hands have saved thousands of hearts. But on this particular day, Dr. Patel was not in a hospital. He was sitting inside the **Swaminarayan Akshardham Temple** in Gandhinagar, surrounded by the scent of incense and the hush of prayer.

Thirty-two kilometers away, in a bustling hospital in Ahmedabad, a middle-aged woman lay on an operating table. She had a blocked coronary artery.

In a standard procedure, Dr. Patel would be standing over her, wearing a heavy lead apron to protect himself from the X-rays, threading a catheter up her femoral artery.

Instead, Dr. Patel sat at a specialized console in the temple. He looked at a screen broadcasting a live X-ray feed from the hospital. He gripped a joystick.

When he moved his wrist in the temple, a robotic arm made by **Corindus Vascular Robotics** moved in the hospital. The robot, precise and unblinking, advanced the guidewire into the woman's heart. It navigated the twists of her vascular tree. It deployed a stent, opening the blockage and restoring blood flow.

The procedure took fifteen minutes. It was flawless.

Dr. Patel stood up. He hadn't washed his hands. He hadn't donned a mask. He hadn't been exposed to a single millisievert of radiation.

"I could have been anywhere," he told reporters later, the weight of the moment settling in. *"I could have been in the US, and the patient in India."*

It was the world's first remote percutaneous coronary intervention (PCI). It proved that the physical presence of the physician is no longer a prerequisite for the practice of medicine. The handshake between doctor and patient had just been stretched across twenty miles of fiber optic cable.

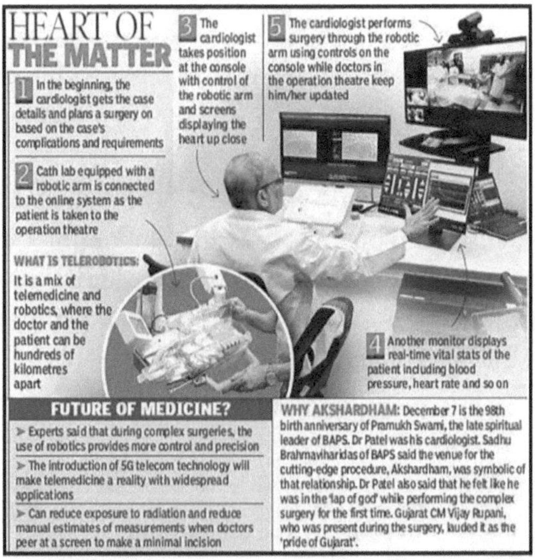

The Villain: The Lag (Latency)

If the concept is so obvious, why haven't we been doing this for decades? We have had surgical robots since the 1990s. We have had the internet for longer.

The enemy is not the robot. The enemy is physics. Specifically, the enemy is **Latency**.

Latency is the time it takes for a signal to travel from Point A to Point B and back again. In the world of video games, we call it "lag." If you are playing *Call of Duty* and you pull the trigger, but the signal takes half a second to reach the server, your character dies. It is annoying, but the stakes are virtual.

In surgery, lag is lethal.

Imagine a surgeon cutting a delicate vessel. They make the slice. But because of a slow internet connection, the video feed doesn't show the bleeding for 500 milliseconds—half a second. By the time the surgeon sees the blood and reacts, their hand has already moved too far. They have cut too deep. They overshoot. Panic sets in.

The brain, which relies on a tight feedback loop between eye and hand, cannot compensate for the delay.

For telesurgery to be safe, the latency needs to be under **200 milliseconds**. Ideally, it should be indistinguishable from "real time," which means under **100 milliseconds**.

We had a "Wright Brothers" moment for this in 2001, known as the **"Lindbergh Operation."** A team of surgeons in New York operated on a patient in Strasbourg, France, removing a gallbladder. It was a technical triumph, but it was a logistical nightmare. To achieve the necessary speed, they had to lease a dedicated, private fiber-optic cable running under the Atlantic Ocean. It cost a fortune.

It wasn't scalable. You cannot run a dedicated, million-dollar cable to every rural clinic in Wyoming or every field hospital in Sudan. For twenty years, telesurgery remained a parlor trick—possible, but impractical.

Enter **5G.**

The Fifth Generation of mobile networks is often marketed to consumers as "faster movie downloads." But its true purpose is industrial. It was built for machines.

It offers something engineers call **"Ultra-Reliable Low Latency Communication" (URLLC).**

With 5G, the latency drops to single-digit milliseconds. The signal travels at the speed of light, virtually unhindered, without the need for physical cables. This is the missing link. It transforms the internet from a library of information into a **"Tactile Internet"**—a web where you can touch, feel, and manipulate the world remotely.

The Banana and the Pig

To prove the fidelity of this new network, surgeons began engaging in demonstrations that bordered on the theatrical. They needed to show the world that the "lag" was dead.

In 2019, a doctor in Fujian, China, sat at a console and utilized a 5G connection to perform remote surgery on... a **banana**.

From miles away, he controlled a robotic arm to peel the skin of the banana. It sounds comical, but anyone who has tried to suture a wound knows that the difference between "taut" and "torn" is a millimeter. The robot peeled the fruit without bruising the soft flesh inside. The video went viral. The delay was imperceptible.

But fruit is compliant. A living brain is not.

Shortly after, a team in Beijing upped the ante. The patient was a human being suffering from Parkinson's disease. The surgeon was **Dr. Ling Zhipei**. The twist? Dr. Ling was in Sanya, **nearly 3,000 kilometers away** from the patient.

Using a 5G connection, Dr. Ling manipulated the instruments to implant a Deep Brain Stimulation (DBS) device—a pacemaker for the brain. The electrode had to be placed into a specific nucleus of the brain, a target no larger than a grain of rice. If he missed by two millimeters, the therapy would fail, or worse, cause a hemorrhage.

The surgery was a success. The patient's tremors ceased.

This moment proved that distance is no longer a technical barrier. The technology has matured. The barriers that remain are no longer laws of physics; they are laws of men.

The Battlefield Angel: The Trauma Pod

Unsurprisingly, the entity most interested in erasing distance is the military.

In the chaos of modern warfare, survival is governed by the **"Golden Hour."** If a soldier is shot or hit by an Improvised Explosive Device, their chance of survival drops precipitously if they do not receive surgical stabilization within sixty minutes.

But the logistics of war are brutal. You cannot put a world-class trauma surgeon in every Humvee. Surgeons are rare, expensive assets. They take fifteen years to train. You keep them in the rear, safe from mortar fire. This means the wounded soldier must be transported to the surgeon, burning precious minutes of the Golden Hour.

The Pentagon, through DARPA, has spent years envisioning the inverse: bringing the surgeon to the soldier. They call it the **"Trauma Pod."**

Imagine an autonomous, armored ambulance. A soldier is wounded in a firefight. Their squad mates load them into the Pod. Inside, there is no human medic. There is a robot.

Thousands of miles away, safe on an aircraft carrier or sitting in Walter Reed Hospital in Washington D.C., a trauma surgeon logs in. They see the wound through high-definition cameras. They slip their hands into the controllers.

The robot arms in the Pod spring to life. They apply pressure. They clamp the bleeding artery. They insert a breathing tube.

This isn't just about saving the soldier; it's about saving the surgeon. We never have to put our best healers in the line of fire again. We can project our medical power without risking our medical personnel.

The Uber-ization of Hope

If we extrapolate this technology to civilian life, the model of healthcare changes fundamentally. We move toward the **"Uber-ization"** of medical expertise.

Currently, if you arrive at a small rural hospital in Nebraska with a stroke, you are limited by the talent in the building. If the general surgeon on call is uncomfortable performing a mechanical thrombectomy (pulling a clot out of the brain), you are out of luck. You get a helicopter ride, or you get disability.

In the future of the Infallible Doctor, that rural hospital will house a **"dormant" robot**—perhaps a system like the Corindus.

When you arrive, the local team preps you. They scan your head. Then, they send a signal to the cloud:

[REQUEST: ISCHEMIC STROKE SPECIALIST. URGENT.]

A notification pops up on the phone of **Dr. Fawaz A. Al-Mufti** in New York. Or perhaps **Dr. Guillaume Turc** in Paris. These are high-volume experts who have done thousands of these procedures.

Dr. Al-Mufti is at home. He accepts the "ride." He sits at her home console, logs in, and suddenly he is virtually present in Nebraska. She looks at the screens. He controls the guidewire. She navigates the vessels of the brain with the muscle memory of a master. She snares the clot. She restores the blood flow.

He logs off.

He has just saved a life 1,500 miles away, all before sitting down to dinner with her family.

This model decouples supply from demand. It treats medical expertise not as a physical good that must be hoarded in cities, but as a fluid resource—like electricity—that can flow instantly to wherever the need is greatest.

Flash Forward: Tele-Ophthalmology in 2040

Let's return to that girl in the village in Rajasthan. What does her future look like?

It is 2040. She walks into a small tele-health kiosk in her village. There is no doctor there, just a technician and a robot.

I am sitting in my office in Kota, or perhaps New Delhi. I put on my Virtual Reality headset. I see her eye in perfect 3D definition.

I pick up my joystick. The robotic arms in the village kiosk move. They make the incision. They remove the cataract. They implant the lens.

The surgery takes 10 minutes. The latency is 5 milliseconds.

She stands up and sees her mother's face clearly for the first time in years. I take off my headset and prepare for my next patient—who is in Brazil.

The barrier of geography has evaporated.

The Paper Border

Technologically, we are ready for this world. Legally, we are in the Dark Ages.

Medicine is strictly regulated by borders. A doctor licensed in New York cannot legally practice in New Jersey, let alone in India or

France. We have built a system of credentialing that is obsessed with geography.

Who is liable if the internet connection cuts out during that stroke surgery? Is it Dr. Chen? Is it the rural hospital? Is it the internet service provider? Is it the robot manufacturer? If a French doctor operates on an American patient and makes a mistake, which country's malpractice laws apply?

These are the **"soft" barriers**. They are currently harder to break than the "hard" barriers of physics. We have the fiber optics to connect the world, but we do not have the treaties.

But the pressure to solve this is building. The shortage of surgeons globally is growing. The Lancet Commission on Global Surgery estimates that **5 billion people** do not have access to safe, affordable surgical and anesthesia care. By 2030, the world will be short of over **2 million** surgical workers.

We will not have a choice. We will have to share our experts. Necessity will force the lawyers to catch up with the engineers.

The End of "Fly-In" Missions

For decades, the model of global health has been the "Fly-In." Charities like Doctors Without Borders fly Western surgeons into war zones or developing nations for two-week missions. They work themselves to the bone, save as many people as they can, and then they leave.

It is noble, but it is inefficient. When the surgeon leaves, the expertise leaves with them.

Telesurgery offers a new model: **Telementoring**.

In this future, the expert in London doesn't just do the surgery; they "ghost" the hands of the local surgeon in Ethiopia. Using Augmented Reality, the expert can draw lines on the local surgeon's screen.

"Cut here. Watch that artery. Okay, stop."

If the local surgeon gets into trouble, the expert can press a button, take control of the robot, fix the problem, and then hand control back.

This is sustainable. It trains the local doctors. It builds capacity. It creates a global teaching hospital with no walls.

Geography has always been destiny. But the Infallible Doctor ignores maps. In the future, the best surgeon for **you** will not be the one who happens to live in your city. It will be the one who is available, awake, and ready to help, regardless of where on Earth they are standing.

THE TAKEAWAY

The Villain is "Geography": Your survival chances depend heavily on your zip code. A total of 5 billion people lack access to safe surgery simply because they live in the wrong place.

The "32-Kilometer Handshake": Dr. Tejas Patel performed the world's first remote heart surgery from a temple 20 miles away from the hospital, proving distance is irrelevant.

The "Lag" War: 5G networks reduce latency to under 10 milliseconds, allowing surgeons to feel and see in "real-time" across continents, solving the deadly delay problem.

The Uber-ization of Surgery: Future platforms will allow rural hospitals to "hail" an expert stroke or trauma surgeon from anywhere in the world to perform a robotic procedure instantly, saving lives during the "Golden Hour."

References

1. Patel, T. M., et al. (2019). "Long-distance telerobotic-assisted percutaneous coronary intervention: A report of the first-in-human experience." *EClinicalMedicine (The Lancet)*, 14, 53-58.
2. Marescaux, J., et al. (2001). "Transatlantic robot-assisted telesurgery." *Nature*, 413(6854), 379-380.
3. Tian, W., et al. (2020). "Telerobotic spinal surgery based on 5G network: A case report." *Neurospine*, 17(1), 114-120.
4. Choi, P. J., et al. (2018). "Telesurgery: Past, Present, and Future." *Cureus*, 10(5), e2716.
5. Doarn, C. R., & Merrell, R. C. (2019). "Telemedicine and telesurgery in the military environments." *World Journal of Surgery*, 43, 1373-1380.

Chapter 18

The Invisible Incision

Minimal Invasion, Maximum Recovery

"For centuries, the scar was the signature of the surgeon—a jagged proof that we had conquered the body to save it. But today, the mark of a great surgeon is not how big the incision is, but whether there is an incision at all. We are learning that the cure should not hurt more than the disease."

— Dr. Suresh Kumar Pandey

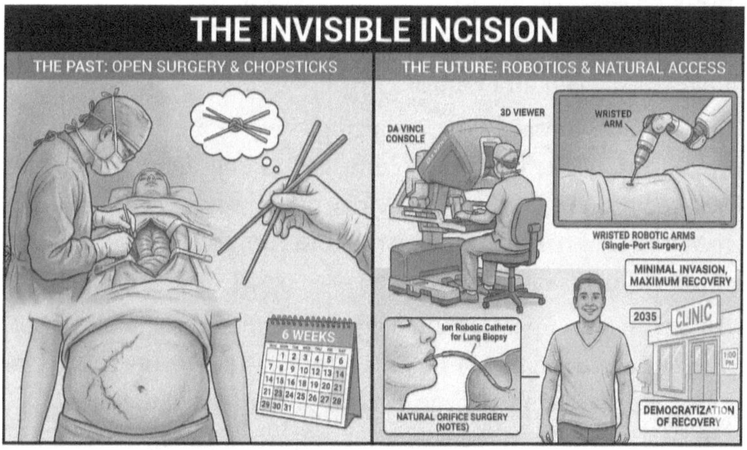

The Villain: The Open Hood

There is a visceral memory that every older surgeon carries, a sensory imprint from the days before the robot. It is the memory of the **"Open Abdomen."**

In the mid-20th century, the unwritten rule of surgery was brutal but practical: *Big problems require big incisions.* If a patient had a tumor on their kidney, or a blockage in their colon, or a diseased uterus, there was only one way to get to it. We had to open the hood.

I recall surgeries from the 1990s where the incision would stretch from the xiphoid process (the bottom of the breastbone) all the way down to the pubic bone. It was a trench, twelve inches long.

To reach the organ, we didn't just cut skin; we sliced through layers of subcutaneous fat, tough fascia, and the thick rectus muscles that hold the torso upright. We used heavy steel retractors—devices that look like medieval torture instruments—to crank the ribs apart, cracking them slightly to make room for our hands.

The surgery might be declared a technical triumph. We would remove the tumor. We would stitch the vessels. We would close the skin with neat staples. We would tell the family, "*We got it all.*"

But the patient was wrecked.

We often underestimate what we call the **"trauma of access."** This is the damage we do just to get to the problem.

For that patient, the cancer was gone, but the price was a body that felt like it had been hit by a truck.

The recovery was a slow, agonizing crawl. It meant five days in a hospital bed, hooked to a morphine drip to dull the screaming pain of severed muscle. It meant a 30% risk of the wound getting infected. It meant hernia risks, bowel obstructions from scar tissue, and six to eight weeks of disability.

The scar was a permanent, jagged reminder of the violence done to the body in the name of saving it. This was the reality of the Open Surgery era: to save the village, we had to burn down the gates.

But medicine, at its best, is a process of repentance. We realized that this violence was a design flaw. In the late 1980s, a revolution began. A few maverick surgeons looked at the open abdomen and asked a heretical question:

What if we didn't open the door? What if we just looked through the keyhole?

Surgery with Chopsticks

The birth of **Laparoscopy**—"Keyhole Surgery"—was arguably the biggest shift in surgical practice since the invention of anesthesia.

Instead of the twelve-inch trench, we made three or four tiny holes, each no wider than a pinky finger. We pumped the belly full of carbon dioxide gas to create a workroom, and we inserted a long, thin camera.

It was a brilliant idea for **you**, the patient. But for the surgeon, it was a nightmare.

To understand early laparoscopy, imagine you have to tie your shoelaces. That is a simple task for human hands. Now, imagine you have to tie those same shoelaces using two long, rigid broom handles. And you cannot look at your shoes. You have to look at a grainy, two-dimensional television screen across the room.

That is what operating felt like.

The instruments were straight, unbending sticks. They had jaws at the end—graspers, scissors, staplers—but they had no wrists. If you wanted to move the tip of the instrument to the left, you had to move your hands to the right. This is the **"fulcrum effect."** It reversed the natural laws of motion. It was counter-intuitive, physically exhausting, and mentally draining.

Because it was so difficult, the "Keyhole Revolution" stalled. It was great for simple things like removing a gallbladder (cholecystectomy), which is just a "grab and clip" procedure. But for complex cancer surgeries—like removing a prostate or sewing a delicate connection between two loops of intestine—it was nearly impossible.

Only the most gifted savants, the "surgical athletes," could master it.

For decades, if you lived in a small town, your local surgeon wouldn't dare try a laparoscopic prostatectomy. They would do it the old way—the open way. The promise of a fast recovery was limited by the clumsiness of the tools. We had reached the limit of what sticks could do.

The Author's Lens: The 2-Millimeter Miracle

I have seen this evolution in my own field of ophthalmology.

When I started, cataract surgery required a **12-millimeter** incision. We had to cut nearly half the circumference of the cornea to pull the cloudy lens out whole. We had to use multiple stitches to close the wound.

The recovery was months long. The stitches distorted the shape of the eye (astigmatism), so patients needed thick glasses afterward.

Today, I perform **Micro-Incision Cataract Surgery (MICS)**. The incision is **1.8 millimeters**. It is smaller than the tip of a pen.

I insert a probe that uses ultrasound to emulsify the cataract into liquid, sucking it out through that tiny hole. Then, I inject a foldable artificial lens that unfurls inside the eye like a ship in a bottle.

There are no stitches. The wound is self-sealing. The patient sees clearly the next morning.

We moved from a 12mm cut to a 1.8mm cut. And with robotics, we are moving even smaller.

The Wrist Reborn

The arrival of the surgical robot—specifically the **Da Vinci** system—did not change what doctors were doing; it fundamentally changed how they were doing it.

When a surgeon sits down at the console of a Da Vinci Xi, they are still doing keyhole surgery. They still make those tiny, 8-millimeter incisions, roughly the size of a pencil eraser. They still insert ports (hollow tubes) into the patient's belly.

But the instruments that slide through those ports are no longer rigid sticks. They are bionic extensions of the human hand.

This technology is called **EndoWrist**. The tip of the robot arm has mechanical joints that mimic the human wrist, but with a crucial upgrade.

- **The Human Wrist:** Can bend up and down, left and right. But try to rotate your hand. It stops after about 180 degrees. The bone locks.
- **The Robot Wrist:** Has seven degrees of freedom. It can bend in any direction, and it can rotate a full **540 degrees**, endlessly spinning. And the entire mechanism is smaller than a dime.

Suddenly, the surgeon sitting ten feet away at the console feels a ghost-like sensation. When I twist my hand, the instrument inside the patient twists. The fulcrum effect is gone. The counter-intuitive "mirror movements" are gone. The machine translates my intent perfectly.

I can reach behind an organ. I can sew a stitch upside down in a space the size of a golf ball, a maneuver that would be anatomically impossible for my own wrist. The "chopsticks" have been replaced by a hand that is smaller, steadier, and more flexible than my own.

The End of the Scar

The impact of this dexterity is not just technical; it is biological.

Take the example of a **Hysterectomy** (removal of the uterus). This is one of the most common surgeries performed on women worldwide, often for fibroids or cancer.

In the old world of open surgery, this required a six-inch incision across the abdomen, similar to a C-section scar. The patient would spend four days in the hospital. The pain was significant. She would be unable to drive for weeks, unable to lift her children, unable to return to work for nearly two months. It was a major life disruption.

With the robot, the narrative changes. The surgeon makes four tiny dots on the belly. The precise, wristed instruments dissect the uterus with minimal bleeding and minimal pulling on the surrounding tissue.

The result? **The patient often goes home the next day.**

Some go home the same evening. They are walking around their living room 24 hours after a major organ removal. They are driving in a week. They are back to normal life in two weeks.

The difference is staggering. By minimizing the "trauma of access," we stop the body's immune system from panicking. There is less inflammation, less cortisol spiking, and drastically less pain. In an era of opioid addiction, this is critical. A patient who has keyhole surgery often needs nothing more than Tylenol after a few days.

But innovation is a restless creature. We asked: *Why four incisions? Why not one? Why not zero?*

The Magic Trick: Single-Port Surgery

The next frontier is already here. It is called **Single-Port (SP) Surgery**.

Engineers at Intuitive Surgical figured out how to fit the high-definition camera and three separate robotic arms through a single metal tube, just **2.5 centimeters wide**.

The surgeon makes one small incision, usually hidden deep inside the belly button (the umbilicus). The tube slides in. Once inside the abdominal cavity, the robotic arms deploy. They snake out like tentacles, splaying open to give the surgeon the triangulation and control they need.

The arms are fully flexible. They can bend around corners. They can see around the back of the prostate or the uterus.

When the surgery is done, the arms retract back into the tube, and the tube is pulled out. A single stitch closes the belly button.

Because the navel is a natural scar—the original scar of our birth—when the wound heals, the surgery is **invisible**. It is the ultimate magic trick: a major organ is removed, a cancer is excised, and the patient looks exactly the same as they did before they walked into the hospital.

Going Through the Natural Doors

The holy grail of minimal invasion, however, is to avoid cutting the skin entirely. Why make a hole when the human body is already designed with entry points?

This concept is known as **NOTES (Natural Orifice Transluminal Endoscopic Surgery)**.

- Entering through the **mouth** to operate on the lungs or stomach.
- Entering through the **anus** to operate on the colon.

For years, this field was limited by the physics of the tools. We had endoscopes—flexible tubes with cameras—but they were like wet noodles. You can push a wet noodle into a space, but you cannot perform precise surgery with it. If you try to cut a tumor, the noodle just bends away. It lacks rigidity.

The new generation of robots are **"shape-shifters."** They are snake-like and flexible when they need to navigate, but they can lock and become rigid when the surgeon needs to work.

Consider the **lungs**. Lung cancer is the leading cancer killer, partly because it is hard to diagnose early. A tiny nodule deep in the periphery of the lung is a nightmare to reach. In the past, to biopsy it, a doctor had to stick a long needle through the patient's chest wall. This was painful and risky—it often punctured the lung, causing it to collapse (pneumothorax).

Enter the **Ion system**, a robotic catheter.

The doctor stands at a console and controls a super-thin, ultra-flexible robotic snake. They steer it down the patient's throat, through the trachea, and deep into the bronchial tree. The robot uses a GPS-like system to navigate the maze of airways. It can turn 180 degrees around sharp corners where traditional bronchoscopes would get stuck.

Once it reaches the tiny nodule, the robot locks in place. It becomes a stable platform. The doctor extends a needle, takes the biopsy, and retreats.

The patient wakes up with a mild sore throat. There is no hole in the chest. There is no chest tube. There is no hospital stay. They go home for dinner. We have turned a terrifying, invasive diagnostic ordeal into an outpatient errand.

Flash Forward: Your Surgery in 2035

Imagine you need your gallbladder removed in 2035.

You arrive at the clinic at 9:00 AM. You are sedated.

The surgeon uses a flexible robot that enters through your mouth, slides down the esophagus, makes a tiny incision in the stomach wall, enters the abdominal cavity, removes the gallbladder, pulls it back out through the stomach, and staples the stomach closed.

You wake up at 11:00 AM. You have no scars on your belly. You have zero pain because the stomach wall has very few nerve endings compared to the skin.

You go home at 1:00 PM. You have lunch.

The "Invisible Incision" is no longer a metaphor. It is reality.

The Democratization of Recovery

It is easy to get lost in the "cool factor" of this technology—the tentacles, the snakes, the 3D screens. But the moral weight of this revolution lies in its **democratization**.

The most important thing about robotic minimal invasion is that it makes high-quality surgery **reproducible**.

In the era of straight sticks (laparoscopy), outcomes were highly variable. A virtuoso surgeon at the Mayo Clinic could remove a prostate laparoscopically with excellent results. But a surgeon in a rural community hospital, doing only ten a year, would struggle. They would likely convert to open surgery, or the patient would suffer complications.

The robot is an equalizer. The 3D vision, the tremor filtration, and the wrist articulation lower the learning curve. They allow the "average" competent surgeon to perform a hysterectomy, a hernia repair, or a colon resection with the same minimal invasiveness as the expert.

This means that "Maximum Recovery" is no longer a luxury good reserved for the wealthy who can travel to elite academic centers. It is becoming the standard of care for the teacher in Ohio, the farmer in Idaho, and the shopkeeper in Brazil.

We are entering an era where a "major operation" does not mean a major interruption to your life. The definition of success has shifted. It is no longer enough to just survive the surgery; the goal is to survive it without the scars that remind you of the pain.

THE TAKEAWAY

The Villain is "The Open Incision": Traditional surgery required large cuts (trauma of access) to reach small problems, causing pain, infection, and weeks of recovery.

The "Chopstick" Problem: Early keyhole surgery used rigid tools that were hard to control. The Da Vinci robot solved this with **EndoWrist**, allowing 360-degree rotation inside the body.

The Author's Lens: In eye surgery, we moved from 12mm incisions to **1.8mm Micro-Incisions**, allowing patients to see instantly without stitches.

The Invisible Future: Robots like the **Ion** enter through natural orifices (mouth, etc.), performing surgery without cutting the skin at all. The future is scarless.

References

1. Payne, T. N., & Dauterive, F. R. (2008). "A comparison of total laparoscopic hysterectomy to robotic-assisted hysterectomy: surgical outcomes in a community practice." *Journal of Minimally Invasive Gynecology*, 15(3), 286-291.
2. Intuitive Surgical. (2023). "Da Vinci SP Surgical System: Clinical Overview and System Specifications." *Intuitive Surgical Technical White Paper.*
3. Kaushik, D., et al. (2010). "Robotic versus open radical prostatectomy: a systematic review and meta-analysis." *Journal of Urology*, 183(3), 10.
4. Fielding, D. I., et al. (2019). "First Human Use of a New Robotic-Assisted Fiber Optic Sensing Navigation System for Small Peripheral Pulmonary Nodules." *Respiration*, 98(2), 142-150.
5. Marescaux, J., et al. (2007). "Surgery without scars: report of transluminal cholecystectomy in a human being." *Archives of Surgery*, 142(9), 823-826.

Chapter 19

The Micro-Surgeons

A Fantastic Voyage into the Bloodstream

"We have spent centuries building larger hospitals and sharper scalpels, obsessed with the macroscopic drama of the operating theater. But the future of healing lies in the invisible. The ultimate surgeon is not a human hand, but a machine small enough to navigate the silence between our cells."

— Dr. Suresh Kumar Pandey

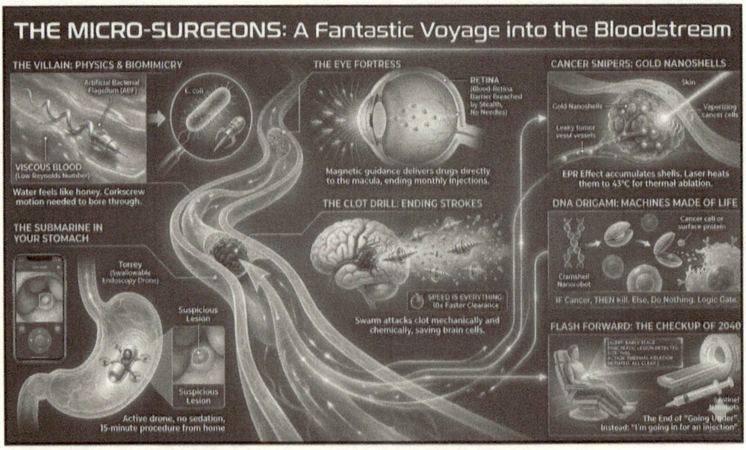

The Scale of the Impossible

In 1966, Hollywood released a film that captured the collective imagination of a generation: *Fantastic Voyage*.

In the movie, a submarine crew is shrunk down to the size of a microbe and injected into the body of a defecting scientist to destroy a blood clot in his brain. They battle giant white blood cells that look like amorphous ghosts, navigate the treacherous, thundering currents of the heart, and use laser guns to dissolve the blockage just seconds before expanding back to normal size.

For fifty years, this was viewed as a charming piece of science fiction—a physical impossibility. According to the Heisenberg uncertainty principle and the basic laws of atomic structure, you cannot shrink a human being. The atoms themselves would have to shrink, which breaks the rules of the universe.

But looking back, we made a fundamental mistake in our thinking. We assumed the surgeon had to be a **human**.

We do not need to shrink a person to fix a cell. We need to build a machine that is native to that world. We need a robot that swims like a bacterium, senses like a virus, and cuts like a protein.

We are currently standing on the quiet threshold of the **Nano-Robotic Revolution**.

In laboratories in Zurich, San Diego, and Stuttgart, engineers are testing the first generation of machines that **you** will not see with the naked eye. These machines will not be wheeled into the operating room on a cart. They will be injected into your arm in a syringe.

They will travel through the dark, red rivers of your arteries. They will hunt down cancer cells one by one, verifying their molecular signature before destroying them. They will drill through clogged veins like microscopic miners. And when they are done, they will simply dissolve, leaving no trace that they were ever there.

Surgery, as we know it—the act of cutting flesh to reach pathology—is about to disappear.

The Villain: Swimming in Honey

Building a robot the size of a bacterium is not just about making things small. It is about fighting a completely different set of physical laws.

When **you** swim in a pool, you rely on inertia. You pull the water back, and you glide forward. But at the micro-scale, inertia ceases to exist. Friction and viscosity dominate everything.

To a bacterium—or a nanobot—water does not feel like water. It feels like **molasses** or **cold honey**.

In physics, this is known as the **"Low Reynolds Number"** problem.

If a microscopic swimmer stops moving its tail, it doesn't coast; it stops instantly, frozen by the thickness of the fluid. A standard propeller, like the one on a boat, doesn't work here; it just spins the fluid around the robot without generating thrust. It is like trying to swim through a ball pit.

To solve this, scientists had to stop thinking like engineers and start thinking like biologists. They looked at nature's original nanobots: **Bacteria**.

Bacteria, like E. coli, move using a **flagellum**—a helical tail that spins like a corkscrew. This corkscrew motion allows them to bore through the thick, viscous fluid of our bodies.

At **ETH Zurich**, a team led by Professor Bradley Nelson adopted this design to build the **Artificial Bacterial Flagella (ABF)**.

These are microscopic robots, roughly the size of a single red blood cell. They look like tiny metallic pasta screws. Because you can't put a battery inside a robot that small—there is simply no room for the chemistry—they are powered from the outside.

The patient lies inside a magnetic field, similar to an MRI machine but much weaker. The doctors rotate the external magnetic field, and the tiny screws inside the body begin to spin in synchronization.

They are **Micro-Swimmers**.

The Author's Lens: The Fortress of the Eye

As an eye surgeon, I dream of this technology every day. Why? Because the eye is a fortress.

The back of the eye—the retina—is protected by the **Blood-Retina Barrier**. It keeps toxins out, but it also keeps drugs out. If a patient has a disease like Age-Related Macular Degeneration (AMD), I cannot just give them a pill. The pill won't reach the retina.

Instead, I have to stick a needle directly into their eye. I have to inject drugs into the vitreous jelly. It is terrifying for the patient, it carries risks of infection, and it has to be repeated every month.

But imagine if I could inject a swarm of nanobots into a vein in the arm.

Using magnetic guidance, I could steer them through the bloodstream, past the heart, up the carotid artery, and directly into the tiny capillaries of the retina. Once they arrive at the macula, they release their payload.

No needle in the eye. No monthly trauma. Just a magnetic field and a swarm of microscopic allies.

In 2018, the ETH Zurich team demonstrated exactly this. They injected a swarm of micro-swimmers into a model eye and steered them through the vitreous jelly to the retina. It worked. The fortress has been breached, not by force, but by stealth.

The Clot Drills: Ending the Stroke

The most immediate and dramatic application for these micro-surgeons, however, is the stroke.

A stroke is a plumbing disaster. A blood clot, perhaps formed in the heart, travels up the carotid artery and lodges in a narrowing vessel in the brain. Instantly, the blood flow stops. Downstream, millions of neurons begin to starve and die. Every minute of delay equates to weeks of lost memory, speech, or movement.

Currently, our tools are crude. We try to dissolve the clot with a chemical drug called **tPA**, which floods the entire body and risks causing bleeding in the gut or brain. Or, we try to physically pull it out with a mechanical catheter (a Thrombectomy), a risky procedure that requires a world-class neurosurgeon to thread a wire all the way from the groin to the brain.

Researchers at **Chengdu University** in China asked: What if we could attack the clot from the inside?

They developed a swarm of nanobots specifically designed to eat blockages. They took tiny magnetic nanoparticles and coated them with tPA—the clot-busting drug. They injected millions of them into a vein.

Using external magnets, they guided the swarm to the site of the blockage. Once the swarm gathered at the face of the clot, the magnets began to rotate. The nanobots started to spin.

The result was a dual-action attack.

1. **Mechanical:** The spinning motion acted like a microscopic drill, physically breaking up the fibrin mesh that holds the clot together.
2. **Chemical:** The spinning released the drug directly inside the clot, where it is most needed, making it 100 times more effective than if it were just floating passively in the blood.

In animal trials, this method cleared blockages **ten times faster** than standard drug therapy.

In the world of stroke, speed is everything. Faster clearance means fewer dead neurons. It means the difference between **you** spending the rest of your life in a nursing home, or walking out of the hospital two days later to hug your grandchildren.

The Submarine in Your Stomach

While some robots are microscopic, others are just... small. And they are solving one of the most uncomfortable experiences in modern medicine: the endoscopy.

If you are over 45, or if you have chronic heartburn, you know the drill. You fast for a day. You go to a hospital. An anesthesiologist puts you to sleep. A gastroenterologist shoves a thick black tube, the diameter of a garden hose, down your throat to look at your stomach lining.

It is expensive, it requires a day off work, and for many, the fear of the procedure prevents them from getting screened for stomach cancer until it is too late.

Enter **Torrey**, a robot built by a Silicon Valley startup called **Endiatx**.

Torrey is a pill. It is the size of a large multivitamin. But unlike the passive "pill cameras" of the past—which just tumbled randomly through your gut, taking photos of whatever they happened to face—Torrey is an **active drone**.

It has four tiny propellers, a miniaturized battery, a high-definition camera, and a lighting system. It connects to your doctor's smartphone via Bluetooth.

The procedure of the future looks like this: You are at home, sitting on your couch. You have a glass of water. You log into a Zoom call with your gastroenterologist, who is sitting in their office miles away.

"Okay," the doctor says. *"Swallow now."*

You swallow the robot. As it enters your stomach, the water creates a small pool—a "virtual lake" inside you. The doctor grabs a virtual joystick on their screen.

Inside you, the propellers spin up. The drone flies.

"I see a suspicious bit of redness on the left gastric wall," the doctor says. *"Let me fly closer."*

The drone zooms in. The doctor snaps a 4K photo. They maneuver the robot to look behind folds of tissue that a passive camera would miss.

"Okay, it looks like benign gastritis. No ulcers. We're done."

The whole procedure takes fifteen minutes. No sedation. No gag reflex. No hospital visit. The robot passes naturally through your system a day later.

Endiatx has already performed live tests on humans—including the CEO, Torrey Smith, who swallowed the robot himself on a live video call to prove its safety. They aim to make stomach cancer screening as easy and routine as brushing your teeth.

The Cancer Snipers: Gold Nanoshells

Perhaps the most profound shift nanorobotics offers is a change in the philosophy of cancer treatment.

The brutal reality of chemotherapy is that it is a **poison**. We inject a toxin into the body with the grim hope that it kills the cancer cells slightly faster than it kills the patient. It attacks everything that divides fast—hair follicles, gut lining, immune cells. That is why patients lose their hair, vomit, and become immunocompromized.

It is carpet bombing. We burn down the forest to kill the wolf.

Nanotechnology promises the end of carpet bombing and the beginning of the **"sniper shot."**

At Rice University, researchers led by Naomi Halas and Jennifer West developed a technology called **Gold Nanoshells**. These are silica glass spheres, smaller than a red blood cell, coated in a thin layer of gold.

When injected into the bloodstream, they naturally accumulate in tumors. This happens because of a phenomenon called the **EPR (Enhanced Permeability and Retention) Effect**. Tumors grow fast and messy; their blood vessels are leaky, full of holes. The nanoshells slip through these holes and get stuck in the tumor, but they are too big to slip into the tight, healthy vessels of normal tissue.

After a day or two, the tumor is filled with gold. The rest of the body is clear.

Then, the doctor shines a **Near-Infrared Laser** on the patient's skin. This type of light passes harmlessly through human flesh—you can see this if you shine a flashlight through your hand. But when this light hits the gold nanoshells, physics magic happens.

The gold absorbs the specific frequency of the laser and vibrates. It gets hot.

The nanoshells heat up to roughly **110 degrees Fahrenheit (43°C)**. This is the "Goldilocks" temperature—hot enough to cook the cancer cells, but not hot enough to cause instant burns to surrounding tissue.

It is a thermal ablation of the cancer without a single incision.

This therapy, now commercially known as **AuroLase**, has been tested in clinical trials for prostate cancer. In a pilot study published in PNAS, **13 out of 15 men** treated were found to have no detectable signs of cancer a year later.

No surgery. No radiation. No risk of incontinence or impotence. Just a gold injection and a warm light.

DNA Origami: Machines Made of Life

The ultimate frontier, however, is not metal. It is biology itself.

We are entering the era of **DNA Origami**.

Most of us think of DNA as a blueprint—the code that makes a human. But to a nano-engineer, DNA is just a building material. It is a long, predictable string that folds in very specific ways. If you code the sequence right, you can make the DNA strand fold itself into a box, a barrel, or a cage.

Scientists at the **Wyss Institute at Harvard** have figured out how to program strands of DNA to fold into a tiny nanorobot that looks like a **clamshell.**

The mechanism is elegant in its logic. The clamshell is locked shut. Inside the shell, the scientists hide a molecule that kills cancer cells or stimulates the immune system. On the outside of the shell, they attach a "lock."

This lock is a DNA strand (an **aptamer**) that acts like a keyhole. It is designed to recognize only a **specific protein** found on the surface of a Leukemia cell.

Millions of these clamshells are injected into **you**. They float harmlessly past heart cells, liver cells, and lung cells. The "key" doesn't fit the lock. The shell stays closed. The poison stays hidden.

But when a clamshell bumps into a Leukemia cell—**click.**

The protein on the cancer cell fits the lock. The DNA strands unzip. The clamshell springs open. The payload is delivered directly to the surface of the cancer cell.

It is a machine made of biology. It is a logic gate: **IF Cancer, THEN Kill. ELSE, Do Nothing.**

In mouse models, these DNA robots successfully identified and killed lymphoma cells while leaving the rest of the mouse perfectly healthy. This is the definition of a "magic bullet."

Flash Forward: The Checkup of 2040

Imagine you go for your annual checkup in 2040. You don't feel sick.

The nurse gives you a small injection. It contains a cocktail of **Sentinel Nanobots.** They circulate through your body for an hour.

You sit in a chair. A scanner passes over your arm. It reads the signals from the bots.

[ALERT: EARLY STAGE PANCREATIC LESION DETECTED.]

[LOCATION: TAIL OF PANCREAS. SIZE: 2MM.]

[ACTION: THERMAL ABLATION INITIATED.]

The scanner sends a signal. The bots cluster around the tiny lesion. They heat up. The lesion is vaporized.

The scanner beeps. [**ALL CLEAR.**]

You stand up. You have just been cured of pancreatic cancer—a disease that is currently a death sentence—before you even knew you had it.

The End of "Going Under"

We are heading toward a future where the phrase *"I'm going in for surgery"* will sound as archaic as *"I'm going for a bloodletting."*

Instead, we will say: *"I'm going in for an injection."*

The operating theater of 2050 might not have scalpels, retractors, or blindingly bright lights. It might just be a comfortable chair, a magnetic coil, and a syringe full of millions of microscopic allies.

These micro-surgeons will patrol our bodies 24/7. They will scrub our arteries of plaque before we even know we have heart disease. They will find and destroy the first cluster of cancer cells ten years before a tumor forms. They will repair the retina without breaking the eye.

They are the steady hands that never shake, operating on a scale where the human hand can never go.

They represent the final victory of the Infallible Doctor: a system of care that solves the problem before it ever becomes a tragedy.

THE TAKEAWAY

The Villain is "Physics": At the micro-scale, water feels like honey (Low Reynolds Number). Traditional robots can't swim in it. We need **Micro-Swimmers** shaped like corkscrews (mimicking bacteria) to bore through the blood.

The "Eye Fortress": The eye is hard to treat without needles. Magnetic nanobots can be steered through the eye's jelly to deliver drugs to the retina without a single puncture, ending the pain of monthly injections.

The Clot Drill: Nanobots can form a swarm that physically drills through a stroke clot while releasing drugs, clearing blockages **10x faster** than drugs alone and saving brain cells.

The DNA Logic Gate: We can program DNA to fold into

"clamshell" robots that only open and release poison when they touch a cancer cell, sparing healthy tissue from chemotherapy side effects.

References

1. Nelson, B. J., et al. (2010). "Microrobots for Minimally Invasive Medicine." *Annual Review of Biomedical Engineering*, 12, 55-85.
2. Sitti, M., et al. (2015). "Biomedical Applications of Untethered Mobile Milli/Microrobots." *Proceedings of the IEEE*, 103(2), 205-224.
3. Rastinehad, A. R., et al. (2019). "Gold Nanoshell-Localized Photothermal Ablation of Prostate Tumors in a Clinical Pilot Device Study." *Proceedings of the National Academy of Sciences*, 116(37), 18590-18596.
4. Douglas, S. M., et al. (2012). "A Logic-Gated Nanorobot for Targeted Transport of Molecular Payloads." *Science*, 335(6070), 831-834.
5. Hu, Q., et al. (2018). "Recent advances of cocktail chemotherapy by combination drug delivery systems." *Advanced Drug Delivery Reviews*, 127, 33-52.

Chapter 20

X-Ray Vision

No Room for Surprise in the Operating Theater

"The most dangerous moment in surgery is not when the anatomy is difficult, but when the anatomy is unknown. We have accepted the 'surprise' as a cost of doing business for too long. But in the era of the transparent patient, ignorance is no longer an excuse."

— Dr. Suresh Kumar Pandey

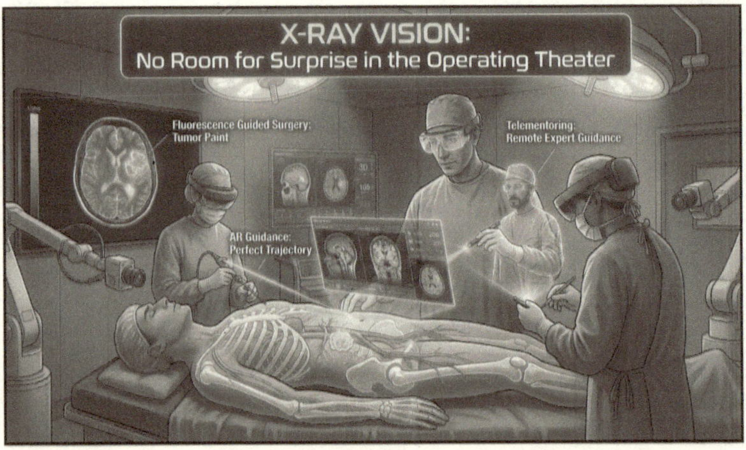

The Fog of War

Imagine, for a moment, that **you** are driving a car.

You are moving at seventy miles per hour. You know the road exists; you studied a map of it yesterday sitting at your kitchen table. You memorized the curves, the exits, the potholes.

But right now, you are in a thick, suffocating fog. You cannot see past the hood of your car. You are steering based on a memory of a map you looked at twenty-four hours ago.

Would you feel safe?

Would you trust yourself not to crash?

This is, terrifyingly, what surgery has been like for centuries. It is an act of supreme confidence performed in a state of partial blindness.

Before every operation, a surgeon performs a ritual. We sit in a dark room, staring at the glowing grayscale images of MRI and CT scans. We scroll through the slices of the patient's body. We see the tumor nesting against the optic nerve. We see the carotid artery winding like a river through the neck. We build a three-dimensional mental model of the patient's anatomy inside our own brains.

We memorize the map.

Then, we walk into the operating room. The patient is draped in sterile blue cloths. We make the incision.

And suddenly, the map is gone.

Inside the body, there are no labels. There are no color-coded arrows pointing to the "Danger Zone." It is a homogenous mess of red muscle, yellow fat, and white fascia. The tumor that looked so clear on the black-and-white screen is now hiding, camouflaged within tissue that looks identical to it.

The surgeon has to take the mental map they memorized and mentally overlay it onto the bloody reality in front of them. We stand there, scalpel in hand, performing a high-stakes act of cognitive triangulation.

- *"I think the artery should be right behind this muscle..."*
- *"The tumor border felt like it was here on the scan..."*

We are navigating by memory and feel. We are flying blind.

Most of the time, because of training and instinct, we get it right. But "most of the time" is not enough when the stakes are paralysis or death. When the mental map doesn't perfectly match the reality—perhaps because the patient's body shifted when they were moved onto the table, or because the brain sagged after we opened the skull—the "surprise" happens.

A nerve is snipped. A healthy blood vessel is nicked. The surgeon freezes, the room goes silent, and the fight for survival begins.

In the era of the **Infallible Doctor**, there is no room for surprise. We have reached a point where relying on human memory to navigate human biology is reckless. We don't need surgeons to memorize maps.

We need to give them **X-Ray Vision**.

The Author's Lens: The View from the Cockpit

I want to show you what this looks like in my own operating room. As eye surgeons, we perform vitreoretinal surgery—operating on the back of the eye.

For decades, this meant looking through an analog microscope. We would hunch over the patient, straining my neck, looking through eyepieces. The view was good, but it was limited. We were isolated. The nurses couldn't see what we saw. If we made a tiny movement, only the surgeon knew why.

Today, we operate using a **Heads-Up 3D Display** system called **NGENUITY**.

Now we, eye surgeons, don't look through eyepieces anymore. We wear 3D glasses, like we are at the movies. We look at a massive 55-inch 4K screen on the wall. The camera inside the eye amplifies the light, so we can use less light energy, protecting the patient's retina from toxicity.

But the real magic is the **Digital Overlay**.

On the screen, we can overlay the patient's pre-operative OCT scans (optical coherence tomography). We can see a "ghost image" of the pathology floating over the live surgery.

- *"Here is the exact boundary of the membrane."*
- *"Here is the area of thinning."*

I am not guessing where the problem is. The map is projected directly onto the territory. It transforms surgery from a solo act of memory into a shared, visual certainty.

The Heads-Up Display for the Body

To understand the solution, we have to look at how other high-stakes professions manage information overload.

Fighter pilots flying supersonic jets do not look down at dashboard dials to check their altitude or their targeting systems. If they look down for a split second, they die.

Instead, the information is projected directly onto the glass of their helmet visors. It floats in their field of view, overlaying the sky. It is called a **Heads-Up Display (HUD)**.

Augmented Reality (AR) is the HUD for the operating room.

The technology is rapidly maturing. Instead of looking away from the patient to stare at a computer screen on the wall—a practice that breaks focus and hand-eye coordination—the surgeon wears a sophisticated headset, like the **Microsoft HoloLens** or **Magic Leap**.

Through the clear lenses, I see the real world. I see the nurse, the lights, the instruments, and the patient lying on the table. But the headset also projects 3D holographic images directly into the physical space.

The AR system takes the patient's pre-operative MRI and CT scans, converts them into a 3D hologram, and **"locks"** that hologram onto the patient's body. It aligns the digital twin with the physical flesh.

It is like the skin and bone have suddenly become transparent.

As I look at the patient's leg or skull, I see the internal geography glowing beneath the surface.

- **Red glowing tubes** show exactly where the arteries are flowing.
- **Blue glowing lines** show the path of the nerves I must avoid.
- **A pulsing green sphere** shows the exact outline and depth of the tumor.

I can walk around the table and see the hologram from different angles. I can "see through" the bone before I even pick up the drill. I know exactly what is waiting for me on the other side of the incision. The fog has lifted.

The Spine Case: A Game of Millimeters

The power of this technology is perhaps most visceral in the high-stakes world of orthopedic spine surgery.

Consider a spinal fusion. The surgeon needs to insert long metal screws into the **pedicles** of the vertebrae. The pedicle is a tiny bridge of bone, a narrow corridor that connects the front of the spine to the back.

It is a game of millimeters.

- If the screw goes in too far to the left, it hits the spinal cord. The result is catastrophic nerve damage or paralysis.
- If the screw goes in too far to the right, it hits a nerve root. The result is chronic, agonizing pain and foot drop.

For decades, we relied on **"fluoroscopy."** We would position the patient, guess the angle, and take a live X-ray. Then we would adjust the drill, take another X-ray. Adjust, shoot. Drill, shoot.

This method was crude. It was slow. And it was dangerous—it involved blasting the patient (and the surgical team) with radiation over and over again, day after day. We were essentially poisoning ourselves to ensure we didn't cripple the patient.

Today, systems like **Augmedics xvision** are changing the physics of the room.

Before the surgery, a CT scan builds a perfect 3D model of the patient's spine. During the operation, the surgeon puts on the AR headset. When they look at the patient's back, they don't just see skin; they see the vertebrae "floating" in 3D space, perfectly aligned with the patient's actual bones.

As I hold the drill over the patient's back, the headset tracks the drill's position in real-time. It projects a virtual trajectory line—like the laser sight on a sniper rifle—extending from the tip of my drill into the patient's body.

- **Green Line:** Perfect trajectory. You are in the center of the bone.
- **Red Line:** Danger. You are angling toward the spinal cord.

I don't have to guess. I simply align the real drill with the virtual green line. I push. The screw goes in perfectly, every single time.

Studies verify this shift. Research shows that AR navigation for pedicle screw placement achieves **over 98% accuracy**, significantly higher than the "freehand" method, while drastically reducing radiation exposure for everyone in the room.

The guesswork is gone. The anxiety of the "blind pass" is gone.

The GPS for Cancer: Making the Invisible Glow

But knowing *where* things are is only half the battle. The other half is knowing *what* they are.

When a neurosurgeon opens the brain to remove a glioma (a type of brain tumor), they face a terrifying visual problem. The tumor does not look like a monster. It does not look different from the healthy brain. It looks like the same pinkish-gray, gelatinous tissue.

Where does the cancer stop and the memory of your mother's face begin?

If I cut too little, the cancer grows back and kills you. If I cut too much, I take away your ability to speak or understand language. To the naked eye, the margin is invisible. We poke, we prod, we guess.

We cannot yet use AR glasses to see individual cancer cells. But we can use something else, a different kind of augmented vision: **Fluorescence Guided Surgery (FGS)**.

Before the surgery, the patient drinks a solution containing a compound called **5-ALA (5-aminolevulinic acid)**, often referred to by the media as "tumor paint."

This molecule is a metabolic Trojan Horse. It enters the body and is absorbed by cells. Healthy brain cells have the enzymes to break it down and flush it out. But cancer cells are metabolically broken; they cannot process it. The compound accumulates inside the cancer cells and converts into a fluorescent molecule.

Under normal white operating lights, the tissue looks normal.

But when the surgeon turns on a special **Near-Infrared camera filter**—integrated into their robotic microscope or AR headset—the world changes.

Suddenly, the tumor glows. It lights up in a bright, neon pink or fluorescent green. The healthy brain tissue stays dark purple.

It is like turning on a blacklight in a messy hotel room. The invisible becomes undeniable. The surgeon no longer has to guess where the edge of the cancer is. They simply follow the glow. They cut until the pink stops.

This technique is not a gimmick; it is a lifesaver. A landmark study published in *The Lancet Oncology* showed the difference.

- When surgeons used 5-ALA fluorescence, they achieved "complete resection" (getting it all out) in **65%** of patients.
- When they used standard white light? Only **36%**.

That gap—from 36% to 65%—is the difference between the tumor growing back in six months and the patient being cured. It is the difference between life and death, illuminated by a trick of light.

The Ultimate Telementoring Tool: The Ghost in the Room

Finally, Augmented Reality serves as the bridge that connects the global expert to the isolated patient.

In Chapter 17, we discussed Telesurgery—the robot operating remotely. But full telesurgery is expensive and requires massive infrastructure. There is a middle ground, one that is cheaper and more immediate: **Telementoring**.

Imagine Dr. Smith, a competent general surgeon in a rural hospital in Ohio. He is about to perform a complex bowel resection on a patient with unusual anatomy. He has done hundreds of these, but this one looks tricky. He feels that cold spike of anxiety. He wishes he had his old mentor from residency standing next to him.

He puts on his HoloLens.

Dr. Chen, the world expert in this specific procedure, is sitting in her office in Tokyo. She puts on her VR headset.

Dr. Chen **"teleports"** into Dr. Smith's operating room. She appears as a hologram standing on the other side of the operating table. Dr. Smith can see her avatar. He can hear her voice in his ear.

Dr. Chen looks at the patient through the live feed from Dr. Smith's headset cameras. She sees exactly what he sees.

"Okay, Smith," she says. *"Don't cut there. The ureter is dangerously close. Look here."*

She reaches out her virtual hand. In Dr. Smith's field of view, a glowing digital ink line appears on the patient's actual bowel. Dr. Chen is drawing on the patient in 3D space.

"Cut along this dotted line," she instructs. *"I've marked the safe zone."*

Dr. Smith follows the glowing ghost line. He cuts with confidence.

This is the ultimate "over-the-shoulder" coaching. It ensures that no surgeon ever has to feel alone or unprepared in an operating room again. The collective expertise of the world is available at the push of a button, ghosting the hands of the learner, guiding the scalpel toward safety.

Flash Forward: Your Surgery in 2035

What does this mean for **you**?

It is 2035. You are lying on the table for liver surgery.

The surgeon walks in wearing lightweight glasses. She doesn't look at the wall. She looks at you.

As she looks at your abdomen, she sees your liver floating inside you. She sees the tumor glowing red. She sees the major blood vessels glowing blue.

She makes the incision. She doesn't hesitate. She doesn't stop to check an X-ray. She navigates your body with the confidence of a driver on a clear, sunny day.

The surgery takes half the time. The blood loss is negligible. You wake up cured.

The Transparent Patient

We are moving toward an operating room of absolute clarity.

The days of holding up grainy X-ray films against a light box on the wall, squinting and guessing, are ending. The days of agonizing decisions about where a tumor ends and the self begins are fading.

The patient's body will be transparent to the surgeon.

- The **Robot** will hold the hand steady.
- The **AI** will monitor the vitals and predict complications.
- The **AR** will light the path, marking the hidden dangers in neon green.

When you combine these technologies, you remove the variables that cause error: fatigue, tremor, poor visualization, and lack of knowledge. You create an environment where the only possible outcome is precision.

This is the end of the "surprise" in surgery. And in medicine, we do not want excitement. We do not want drama. We want a boring, predictable, surprise-free event.

That is the greatest gift a patient can receive.

THE TAKEAWAY

The Villain is "Blindness": Surgeons usually operate based on a "mental map" of your anatomy memorized from a scan. Once the incision is made, they are flying blind, which leads to accidental nerve cuts.

The Heads-Up Display: Augmented Reality (AR) headsets like **HoloLens** overlay your MRI directly onto your body. The surgeon sees your bones and arteries "glowing" through your skin, making the patient transparent.

The "Green Line" Guide: In spinal surgery, AR projects a virtual trajectory line for the drill. If the surgeon follows the green line, the screw placement is perfect (98% accuracy), preventing paralysis.

Tumor Paint: Technology like **5-ALA** makes brain tumors glow pink under special light. This "Fluorescence Guided Surgery" helps surgeons distinguish cancer from healthy brain, doubling the cure rate.

References

1. Elmi-Teramoto, R., et al. (2020). "Augmented reality guidance for pedicle screw placement in spinal surgery: a systematic review." *Journal of Neurosurgery: Spine*, 34(5), 738-748.
2. Stummer, W., et al. (2006). "Fluorescence-guided surgery with 5-aminolevulinic acid for resection of malignant glioma: a randomized controlled multicentre phase III trial." *The Lancet Oncology*, 7(5), 392-401.
3. Vavra, P., et al. (2017). "Recent Development of Augmented Reality in Surgery: A Review." *Journal of Healthcare Engineering*, 2017, 4574172.

4. Eckert, M., et al. (2019). "Augmented Reality in Medicine: Systematic and Bibliographic Review." *JMIR mHealth and uHealth*, 7(4), e10967.

5. Verhey, J. T., et al. (2020). "Virtual, augmented, and mixed reality applications in orthopedic surgery." *International Journal of Medical Robotics and Computer Assisted Surgery*, 16(2), e2067.

PART V
The Perfect Pill
Pharmacology, Genetics, and Precision Treatment

Chapter 21

The End of Average

Precision Dosing for the Individual

"We have always treated patients based on the averages of the past. But no patient is average. To treat the individual, we must stop looking at the one and start looking at the million. In the ocean of data, we find the drop that matters."

— Dr. Suresh Kumar Pandey

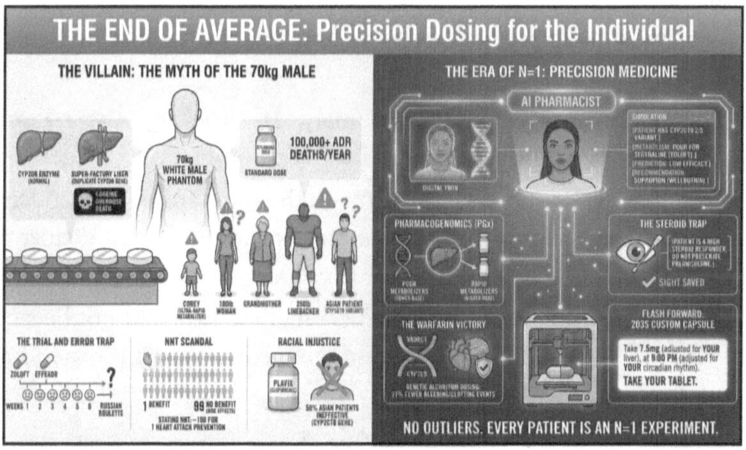

The Lottery of the Liver

Corey was two years old. Like thousands of other toddlers, he had sleep apnea caused by enlarged tonsils. He snored loudly and stopped breathing during the night. His doctor recommended a routine tonsillectomy.

The surgery went perfectly. The tonsils were removed. Corey went home the same day.

To manage the post-surgical pain, the doctor prescribed the

standard pediatric dose of codeine syrup. Codeine is an opioid, widely used for decades, considered safe and effective for children.

Corey's mother gave him the syrup exactly as directed on the bottle.

Two nights later, Corey didn't wake up. He had stopped breathing in his sleep.

The autopsy revealed a lethal level of morphine in his blood. But how? His mother hadn't overdosed him. She hadn't given him morphine; she gave him codeine.

The answer lay in Corey's DNA.

Codeine itself is biologically inactive. It is a "prodrug." When you swallow it, it travels to your liver. There, an enzyme called **CYP2D6** converts the codeine into morphine, which is what actually kills the pain.

For most people, this conversion happens at a steady, predictable rate.

But Corey was a genetic anomaly. He was an **"Ultra-Rapid Metabolizer."** He possessed a duplicate copy of the CYP2D6 gene.

His liver was a super-factory. It took the standard dose of codeine and converted it all into morphine almost instantly. The "safe" dose on the bottle was, for Corey, a massive overdose.

Corey died not because of medical malpractice, and not because the drug was "bad." He died because the medical system treated him as an **Average Human**.

But Corey wasn't average. **Nobody is.**

The Villain: The Myth of the 70kg Male

If you open a medical textbook, you will find dosing guidelines based on a phantom.

This phantom is a **70-kilogram (154 lb) white male**.

For most of the 20th century, clinical trials were conducted almost exclusively on men. Women were excluded (partly due to fears of affecting potential pregnancies). Minorities were vastly underrepresented.

The result is that we built a pharmaceutical industry designed for the 70kg white male.

- We prescribe the same 10mg of Lexapro to a 250lb linebacker as we do to a 100lb grandmother.
- We prescribe the same blood thinner to an African American woman as we do to a Scandinavian man, despite the fact that their genetic ancestries process Vitamin K (clotting factor) completely differently.

This **"One Size Fits All"** approach is a disaster.

Adverse Drug Reactions (ADRs)—bad reactions to medicines—are the **4th leading cause of death** in the United States. They kill over 100,000 people a year. That is more than car accidents, diabetes, or pneumonia.

We are literally poisoning people by guessing.

The Author's Lens: The Steroid Trap

I see this genetic lottery in my own clinic every week.

In eye surgery, we often prescribe steroid eye drops to reduce inflammation after a procedure. For 90% of patients, this is perfectly safe.

But there is a group—about 10% of the population—whom we call **"Steroid Responders."** They have a genetic predisposition that causes their eye pressure to spike dangerously when exposed to steroids.

I cannot tell by looking at them who is a responder. Their eyes look identical to everyone else's.

If I give a steroid to a "Responder," their pressure can skyrocket, damaging the optic nerve and causing glaucoma. I have seen patients lose vision permanently because of a simple eye drop prescribed for a minor irritation.

For decades, I had to guess. I had to prescribe the drop and then monitor them like a hawk.

Today, we are on the verge of a simple genetic swab that will tell me: **[PATIENT IS A HIGH STEROID RESPONDER. DO NOT PRESCRIBE PREDNISOLONE.]**

This is the difference between blindness and sight.

The "Number Needed to Treat" Scandal

It isn't just about safety; it's about efficacy. Does the pill even work?

There is a statistical secret in medicine called the **Number Needed to Treat (NNT)**. It asks: How many people have to take this drug for ONE person to benefit?

Ideally, the NNT should be 1. (You take the cure, you get cured).

But for many "blockbuster" drugs, the numbers are shocking.

- **Statins (for cholesterol):** The NNT to prevent one heart attack is often around **100**. That means 99 people take the pill every day, suffering potential side effects (muscle pain, brain fog), for zero benefit to their heart outcome.
- **Antidepressants (SSRIs):** The NNT is roughly 7. For every seven people who take Prozac, only one gets significant remission beyond the placebo effect.

We are throwing drugs at the wall and hoping they stick.

The Genetic Fingerprint

The solution to Corey's tragedy, and to the NNT scandal, lies in **Pharmacogenomics (PGx)**.

This is the science of how your unique DNA interacts with drugs. Your liver is full of enzymes (the Cytochrome P450 family) that act like garbage disposals. They break down drugs.

- **Poor Metabolizers:** Have lazy enzymes. The drug builds up in their blood to toxic levels. (Requires a lower dose).
- **Rapid Metabolizers:** Have hyperactive enzymes. They chew up the drug before it can work. (Requires a higher dose).

We have known this science for twenty years. But until now, it was too expensive and too complex for a regular doctor to use. A doctor cannot memorize the genetic interactions of 10,000 drugs against 20,000 genes.

This is where the **Infallible Doctor**—the AI—steps in.

The AI Pharmacist

Imagine a new workflow.

You walk into your doctor's office with depression. In the old world, the doctor would say, "Let's try Zoloft. If you don't feel better in six weeks, we'll try Effexor."

Those six weeks are hell. You might feel worse. You might have suicidal thoughts. It is a game of Russian Roulette.

In the new world, the doctor doesn't guess. Your **Digital Twin** (from Chapter 15) already has your genetic data.

The AI runs a simulation.

[PATIENT HAS CYP2C19 2/3 VARIANT.]

[METABOLISM: POOR FOR SERTRALINE (ZOLOFT).]

[PREDICTION: SEVERE NAUSEA. LOW EFFICACY.]

[RECOMMENDATION: BUPROPION (WELLBUTRIN).]

The doctor prescribes Wellbutrin on Day 1. You get better in two weeks. No trial. No error.

The Warfarin Victory

The best proof of this is **Warfarin** (blood thinner).

Warfarin is notoriously hard to dose. Give too little, the patient gets a stroke. Give too much, the patient bleeds to death internally. The "sweet spot" is tiny, and it varies wildly from person to person based on two specific genes (*VKORC1* and *CYP2C9*).

A study published in the New England Journal of Medicine showed that using a genetic algorithm to dose Warfarin reduced hospitalizations for bleeding/clotting by **27%.**

That is 27% fewer strokes and hemorrhages, just by doing the math before writing the prescription.

Justice in a Pill

Finally, Precision Medicine is a matter of racial justice.

For decades, we have used the drug **Clopidogrel (Plavix)** to prevent strokes after a stent is placed. It is a standard drug.

But we discovered that **50% of Asian patients** carry a gene that makes Plavix ineffective.

For fifty years, we have been giving millions of Asian patients a "sugar pill" that didn't protect them, simply because the drug was tested mostly on white people. In Hawaii, a lawsuit was filed against the manufacturers for failing to warn patients.

Today, AI-driven screening ensures that Asian patients (and everyone else) get a genetic test before starting Plavix. If they have the gene, they get a different drug (like Prasugrel).

The Infallible Doctor is colorblind in its judgment, but highly sensitive to the biological reality of ancestry. It ensures that equality doesn't mean "treating everyone the same." It means "treating everyone uniquely."

Flash Forward: Your Prescription in 2035

What does this look like for you?

It is 2035. You have high blood pressure.

The doctor does not scribble a generic prescription. She taps your Digital Twin on her tablet.

The AI analyzes your liver enzymes, your kidney function, your circadian rhythm, and your diet. It prints a **Custom Capsule.**

"Take 7.5mg (adjusted for your liver), at 9:00 PM (adjusted for your circadian rhythm), and do not take it with grapefruit juice."

The label doesn't say "Take 1 tablet." It says "Take YOUR tablet."

The Era of N=1

Corey's death was a tragedy of the "Average." He died because he was an outlier in a system built for the mean.

But in the era of AI and Pharmacogenomics, there are no outliers. Every patient is an **N=1** experiment.

We are moving from the blunt force of the sledgehammer to the precision of the laser. And for the millions of people who have suffered from the "side effects" of guessing, the relief cannot come soon enough.

THE TAKEAWAY

The Villain is "The Average": Drugs are tested on a "phantom" 70kg white male. Giving the same dose to a 100lb woman or a child can be fatal, as seen in the tragedy of Corey and codeine.

The "Steroid Responder": In eye care, 10% of people genetically react poorly to steroids, risking blindness. Genetic testing removes the guesswork, protecting these patients from dangerous side effects.

The "Trial and Error" Trap: Antidepressants often take months of guessing to get right. AI Pharmacists use your DNA to predict which drug will work before you take the first pill.

Racial Justice: 50% of Asian patients cannot process Plavix (a common heart drug). AI screening ensures patients get drugs that work for their specific ancestry, ending the "one size fits all" bias.

References

1. Ciszkowski, C., et al. (2009). "Codeine, ultrarapid-metabolism genotype, and postoperative death." *New England Journal of Medicine*, 361(8), 827-828. (The case report of the child's death).
2. Lazarou, J., Pomeranz, B. H., & Corey, P. N. (1998). "Incidence of adverse drug reactions in hospitalized patients: a meta-analysis of prospective studies." *JAMA*, 279(15), 1200-1205. (The seminal study ranking ADRs as a leading cause of death).
3. Pirmohamed, M., et al. (2013). "A randomized trial of genotype-guided dosing of warfarin." *New England Journal of Medicine*, 369(24), 2294-2303. (Evidence for genetic dosing).
4. Mukherjee, D., & Topol, E. J. (2002). "Pharmacogenomics in cardiovascular diseases." *Progress in Cardiovascular Diseases*. (Discussion of Plavix resistance in different populations).
5. Schork, N. J. (2015). "Personalized medicine: Time for one-person trials." *Nature*, 520(7549), 609-611. (The concept of N=1 medicine).

Chapter 22

The Typo that Kills

Genomic Tailoring and the Software of Life

"For centuries, we have treated the patient as a statistical average, ignoring the biological symphony that makes each human unique. The Infallible Doctor does not treat 'people'; it treats the person, rewriting the prescription until it fits the individual genetic lock like a perfect key."

— Dr. Suresh Kumar Pandey

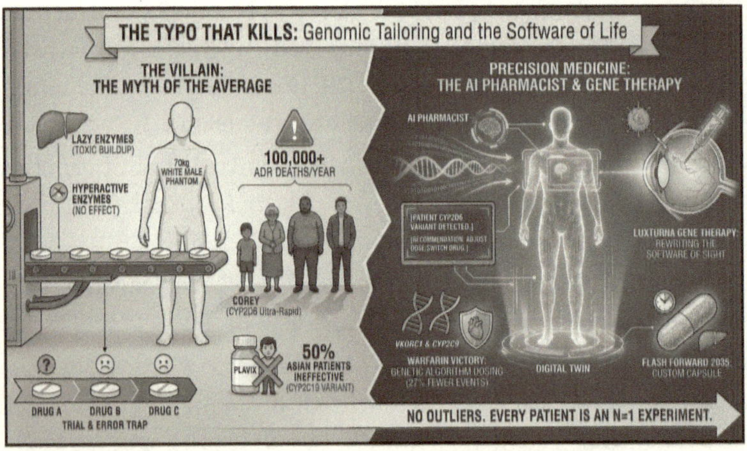

The Child Who Slept

Corey was two years old, a bubbly toddler with a smile that could light up a room and a snoring problem that could rattle the windows. Like thousands of other children his age, he suffered from sleep apnea caused by enlarged tonsils. He would stop breathing intermittently during the night, a terrifying silence that would jolt his mother awake.

His pediatrician recommended a routine tonsillectomy. It is one of the most common surgeries performed on children in the world. The procedure went perfectly. The tonsils were removed, the bleeding was minimal, and Corey went home the same day, clutching a popsicle.

To manage the post-surgical pain, the doctor prescribed the standard pediatric dose of codeine syrup. Codeine is an opioid that has been used for decades. It is considered mild, safe, and effective for children.

Corey's mother, diligent and loving, gave him the syrup exactly as directed on the bottle. She measured it with the little plastic cup. She watched him drift off to sleep, relieved that his pain was gone.

Two nights later, Corey didn't wake up.

The autopsy revealed a lethal level of morphine in his blood. The medical examiner was baffled. His mother hadn't overdosed him. She hadn't given him morphine; she had given him codeine. The bottle was still mostly full.

The answer to this tragedy lay not in the spoon, but in Corey's DNA.

Codeine itself is biologically inactive. It is what we call a "prodrug." When you swallow it, it does nothing until it travels to your liver. There, an enzyme called **CYP2D6** converts the codeine into morphine, which is the active molecule that actually kills the pain.

For most people—about 90% of the population—this conversion happens at a steady, predictable rate.

But Corey was a genetic anomaly. He was what geneticists call an **"Ultra-Rapid Metabolizer."**

He possessed a duplicate copy of the CYP2D6 gene. His liver was not a factory; it was a super-charged refinery. It took the standard, "safe" dose of codeine and converted almost 100% of it into morphine instantly.

The dose on the bottle was safe for an "average" child. For Corey, it was a death sentence.

Corey died not because of medical malpractice. He didn't die because the drug was "bad." He died because the medical system treated him as an **Average Human.**

But Corey wasn't average. **Nobody is.**

The Villain: The Myth of the 70kg Male

If you open a standard medical pharmacology textbook, you will find dosing guidelines based on a phantom.

This phantom is a **70-kilogram (154 lb) white male**.

For most of the 20th century, the clinical trials that established the rules of medicine were conducted almost exclusively on men. Women were excluded, partly due to paternalistic fears of affecting potential pregnancies and partly because hormonal fluctuations were seen as "variables" that messed up the clean data.

Minority populations were vastly underrepresented.

The result is that we built a pharmaceutical industry designed for a specific biological archetype, and we forced everyone else to fit inside it.

- We prescribe the same 10mg of Lexapro to a 250lb NFL linebacker as we do to a 100lb grandmother.
- We prescribe the same blood thinner to an African American woman as we do to a Scandinavian man, despite the fact that their genetic ancestries process Vitamin K (the clotting factor) completely differently.

This **"One Size Fits All"** approach is a disaster.

Adverse Drug Reactions (ADRs)—bad reactions to medicines—are currently the **fourth leading cause of death** in the United States. They kill over 100,000 people a year. That is more than car accidents, diabetes, or pneumonia.

We are essentially poisoning people by guessing.

The Author's Lens: The Miracle of Luxturna

I want to pause here and take you into my own field, Ophthalmology, because the eye is where the promise of fixing the "Typo" has become a reality.

There is a disease called **Leber Congenital Amaurosis (LCA)**. It causes children to be born blind or lose their sight in early childhood. It is caused by a "typo"—a mutation in a gene called **RPE65**.

For centuries, this diagnosis was a life sentence of darkness. There was no surgery, no pill, no hope.

But recently, we witnessed a miracle. We developed a gene therapy called **Luxturna**.

It is not a drug in the traditional sense. It is a virus—a harmless, hollowed-out virus that acts as a delivery truck. Inside the truck, we put a correct copy of the RPE65 gene.

We inject this virus under the retina. The virus infects the retinal cells and delivers the correct DNA. The cells read the new code and start making the protein they were missing.

I have seen children who were legally blind look up and see the stars for the first time. I have seen them navigate a maze they couldn't see a week before.

We didn't treat the symptom. We rewrote the software.

This is the power of precision. We didn't give them a "better pair of glasses." We fixed the typo in their source code.

The Genetic Fingerprint

The solution to Corey's tragedy, and to the millions of adverse drug reactions, lies in a field called **Pharmacogenomics (PGx)**. This is the science of how your unique DNA interacts with drugs.

Your liver is full of enzymes (the Cytochrome P450 family) that act like garbage disposals. They break down foreign chemicals. But the efficiency of these disposals varies wildly based on your genes.

- **Poor Metabolizers:** Have "lazy" enzymes. The drug isn't broken down, so it builds up in their blood to toxic levels. (These patients need a lower dose).
- **Rapid Metabolizers:** Have "hyperactive" enzymes. They chew up the drug before it can work. (These patients need a higher dose).

We have known this science for twenty years. But until now, it was too expensive and too complex for a regular doctor to use. A busy primary care physician cannot memorize the genetic interactions of 10,000 drugs against 20,000 genes while trying to keep their clinic running.

This is where the **Infallible Doctor**—the AI—steps in.

The AI Pharmacist

Imagine a new workflow, one that is already beginning to appear in forward-thinking clinics.

You walk into your doctor's office complaining of severe depression. In the old world, the doctor would look at you and say, "Let's try Zoloft. It works for a lot of people. If you don't feel better in six weeks, come back and we'll try Effexor."

Those six weeks are hell. You might feel worse. You might have suicidal thoughts. You might gain weight. It is a game of Russian Roulette played with your serotonin levels.

In the new world, the doctor doesn't guess.

Your **Digital Twin** (the virtual model of your biology) already possesses your genetic data. The doctor inputs the diagnosis: Major Depressive Disorder.

The AI runs a simulation in milliseconds.

[PATIENT POSSESSES CYP2C19 2/3 VARIANT.]

[METABOLISM: POOR FOR SERTRALINE (ZOLOFT).]

[PREDICTION: SEVERE NAUSEA. LOW EFFICACY.]

[RECOMMENDATION: BUPROPION (WELLBUTRIN).]

The doctor prescribes Wellbutrin on Day 1. You get better in two weeks. No trial. No error. No six weeks of hell.

The Warfarin Victory

The best proof of this concept is **Warfarin**, a blood thinner used to prevent strokes.

Warfarin is notoriously hard to dose. It has a "narrow therapeutic window." Give too little, and the patient gets a blood clot and dies. Give too much, and the patient bleeds to death internally. The "sweet spot" is tiny, and it varies wildly from person to person based on two specific genes (*VKORC1* and *CYP2C9*).

A study published in the New England Journal of Medicine showed that using a genetic algorithm to dose Warfarin—rather than just guessing based on weight and age—reduced hospitalizations for bleeding or clotting by **27%**.

That is 27% fewer strokes. 27% fewer brain hemorrhages. Just by doing the math before writing the prescription.

The End of Polypharmacy

The problem is most acute for the elderly.

The average 75-year-old in America is on five or more prescription drugs. This is called **Polypharmacy**.

- Drug A treats the heart failure.
- Drug B treats the stomach upset caused by Drug A.
- Drug C treats the diabetes.
- Drug D treats the dizziness caused by the interaction of A and C.

It is a chemical soup. No human brain can calculate the interaction matrix of five different drugs metabolizing in an aging liver.

But an AI can.

Companies like **FeelBetter** use AI to analyze the medication lists of elderly patients. They flag the hidden dangers that human pharmacists might miss.

[WARNING: COMBINATION OF DRUG A AND DRUG C INCREASES FALL RISK BY 40%.]

In pilot studies, optimizing these lists reduced hospitalizations by **30%**. Sometimes, the "Perfect Pill" is actually removing a pill. The AI gives the doctor the confidence to "de-prescribe," stripping away the chemical clutter to reveal the patient underneath.

Justice in a Pill

Finally, Precision Medicine is a matter of racial justice.

For decades, we have used the drug **Clopidogrel (Plavix)** to prevent strokes after a stent is placed in the heart. It is a standard, "blockbuster" drug.

But we discovered that **50% of Asian patients** carry a genetic variant (CYP2C19 loss-of-function) that makes Plavix ineffective. Their bodies simply cannot activate the drug.

For fifty years, we have been giving millions of Asian patients a "sugar pill" that didn't protect them, simply because the drug was tested mostly on white populations of European descent. We sent them home thinking they were safe, when they were defenseless against a second heart attack.

In Hawaii, a lawsuit was recently filed against manufacturers for failing to warn patients of this risk.

Today, AI-driven screening ensures that Asian patients (and everyone else) get a genetic test before starting Plavix. If the algorithm sees the variant, it flags the file:

[DO NOT USE PLAVIX. SWITCH TO PRASUGREL.]

The Infallible Doctor is colorblind in its judgment, but highly sensitive to the biological reality of ancestry. It ensures that equality doesn't mean "treating everyone the same." It means "treating everyone uniquely."

Flash Forward: The Prescription of 2035

So, what does this mean for you?

It is 2035. You have high blood pressure.

The doctor does not scribble a generic prescription. She taps your Digital Twin on her tablet.

The AI analyzes your liver enzymes, your kidney function, your circadian rhythm, and your diet. It prints a **Custom Capsule**.

"Take 7.5mg (adjusted for your liver enzymes), at 9:00 PM (adjusted for your circadian rhythm), and do not take it with grapefruit juice (adjusted for your specific diet)."

We are moving from the blunt force of the sledgehammer to the precision of the laser. And for the millions of people who have suffered from the "side effects" of guessing, the relief cannot come soon enough.

THE TAKEAWAY

The Villain is "The Average": Drugs are tested on a "phantom" 70kg white male. Giving the same dose to a child (like Corey) or a genetic outlier can be fatal.

The "Eye Software" Fix: In ophthalmology, we can now use gene therapy (**Luxturna**) to fix the "typo" in the DNA that causes blindness, proving we can rewrite the software of life.

The "Trial and Error" Trap: Antidepressants often take months of guessing to get right. AI Pharmacists use your DNA to predict which drug will work before you take the first pill.

Racial Justice: 50% of Asian patients cannot process Plavix (a common heart drug). AI screening ensures patients get drugs that work for their specific ancestry, ending the "one size fits all" bias.

References

1. Ciszkowski, C., et al. (2009). "Codeine, ultrarapid-metabolism genotype, and postoperative death." *New England Journal of Medicine*, 361(8), 827-828.
2. Lazarou, J., et al. (1998). "Incidence of adverse drug reactions in hospitalized patients: a meta-analysis of prospective studies." *JAMA*, 279(15), 1200-1205.
3. Pirmohamed, M., et al. (2013). "A randomized trial of genotype-guided dosing of warfarin." *New England Journal of Medicine*, 369(24), 2294-2303.
4. Mukherjee, D., & Topol, E. J. (2002). "Pharmacogenomics in cardiovascular diseases." *Progress in Cardiovascular Diseases*, 44(6), 479-498.
5. Schork, N. J. (2015). "Personalized medicine: Time for one-person trials." *Nature*, 520(7549), 609-611.

Chapter 23

Compressing Time

Turning Decades of Drug Discovery into Days

"Time is the only currency in medicine that we cannot print more of. Every day a drug sits in a lab is a day a patient waits in pain. The true promise of AI is not just that it saves money, but that it saves the most precious resource of all: years."

— Dr. Suresh Kumar Pandey

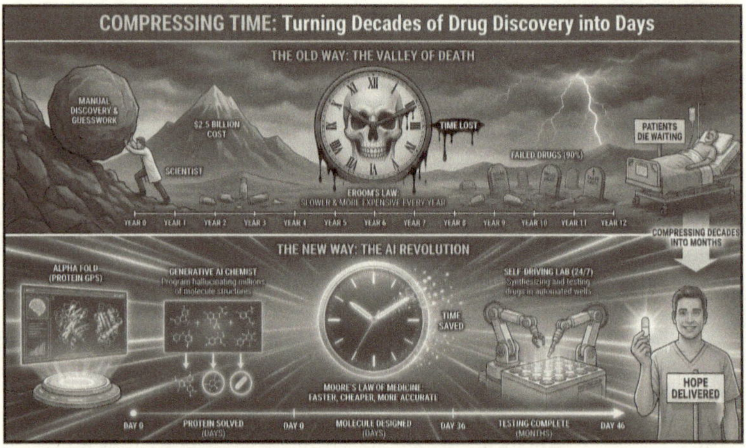

The Valley of Death

If you were a venture capitalist, I would ask you to imagine a business model.

It works like this:

You want to launch a single product. To bring it to market, you must spend $2.5 billion. You must toil over it for twelve years, employing thousands of the most brilliant minds on earth. And here is the catch: at the end of those twelve years, there is a 90% chance the product will fail completely, and you will earn zero dollars.

Would you invest?

Probably not. Yet, this is the business model of the modern pharmaceutical industry. It is a system defined by a grim economic principle known as **Eroom's Law**.

In technology, we have **Moore's Law**—the observation that computing power doubles and gets cheaper every two years. Chips get faster, phones get smarter, prices drop.

Eroom's Law is "Moore's Law" spelled backward. In medicine, discovering a new drug gets slower and more expensive every year.

In 1950, finding a new antibiotic cost a few million dollars. Today, the cost per approved drug effectively doubles every nine years. We are spending more to get less.

This inefficiency is not just an abstract economic problem for shareholders. It is a moral tragedy for **you** and your family. For a patient diagnosed with ALS (Lou Gehrig's disease) or Huntington's Disease, a twelve-year timeline is not a delay; it is a death sentence. They do not have twelve years. They often do not even have twelve months.

Scientists call the early phase of this process the **"Valley of Death."**

It is the period where researchers test thousands of chemical compounds to find one that might work. It is a process of blind trial and error, a brute-force search through a chemical universe so vast it defies comprehension. It is like looking for a needle in a haystack, except the haystack is the size of the solar system, and you are working in the dark.

But what if someone turned on the lights? What if you had a magnet?

The Villain: The 50-Year Mystery

To cure a disease, you usually need to interact with a **protein**.

Proteins are the microscopic machines that run the factory of your body. Hemoglobin is the truck that carries oxygen. Insulin is the gatekeeper that regulates sugar. The "Spike" protein is the grappling hook that allows a virus to invade your cells.

Proteins are made of long strings of amino acids, like beads on a necklace. But they do not stay as strings. As soon as they are made, they crumple up into complex, tangled three-dimensional shapes.

This **folding** is everything. The Shape determines the Function.

If the protein folds into a "cup," it catches water. If it folds into a "spike," it punctures cells. If it folds into a "zipper," it binds DNA.

To design a drug, you have to know the exact 3D shape of the disease protein—the "lock"—so you can build a chemical "key" to fit it. If you don't know the shape of the lock, you are just blindly throwing keys at the door.

For fifty years, figuring out this shape was the hardest problem in biology. It was known as the **"Protein Folding Problem."** A scientist would spend their entire PhD—five years of agonizing work using X-ray crystallography—just to map the shape of one protein.

In 1972, Nobel Laureate Christian Anfinsen famously stated that a protein's shape should be theoretically predictable just by looking at its amino acid sequence. But the math was impossible. A single protein can fold in **10 to the power of 300** different ways.

That number is larger than the number of atoms in the known universe.

Human brains couldn't solve it. The world's fastest supercomputers couldn't solve it. So, Biology waited. And patients died waiting.

The AlphaFold Moment

Then, in November 2020, the waiting ended.

DeepMind, the artificial intelligence laboratory owned by Google—famous for building the AI that beat human champions at the ancient board game Go—turned its attention to biology. They unleashed an algorithm called **AlphaFold**.

They entered the "CASP" competition—the Olympics of protein folding. For decades, the best computer programs in the world scored around 40 out of 100. They were mediocre guessers.

AlphaFold scored 90 out of 100.

It matched the accuracy of physical laboratory experiments. It didn't just guess the shape; it **solved** the shape. It turned a five-year physical ordeal into a five-second digital calculation.

In July 2021, DeepMind did something even more radical. They didn't just publish a paper; they released the predicted shapes of nearly every protein in the human body. Then they did the rest of nature—plants, bacteria, animals.

Today, the AlphaFold database contains over **200 million** protein structures.

It is the "Google Maps" of biology. Before AlphaFold, we were navigating the molecular world like 15th-century sailors, using hand-drawn sketches of the coastline and stars. Now, we have a GPS satellite view of every street, alley, and building in the cellular city.

Suddenly, the "haystack" isn't a mystery. We can see exactly where the needle is.

The Generative Chemist

Knowing the shape of the lock (the disease) is Step 1. Step 2 is building the key (the drug).

This is where the math gets even more dizzying. There are estimated to be **10 to the power of 60** possible drug-like molecules. That is more than the number of stars in the galaxy.

Historically, chemists relied on intuition and serendipity. A chemist would look at a molecule and say, *"Let's try adding a carbon ring here. Let's try removing a hydrogen atom there."* It was slow, artisanal work, like a locksmith filing a key by hand.

Enter **Generative AI**.

This is the same underlying technology behind ChatGPT or Midjourney. But instead of generating poetry or surrealist paintings, it generates molecules.

You tell the AI:

"I need a molecule that fits perfectly into the binding pocket of Protein X. It must be soluble in water. It must not be toxic to the liver. And it must be small enough to cross the blood-brain barrier."

The AI doesn't just search a database of existing drugs. It **hallucinates** new ones.

It dreams up chemical structures that no human chemist has ever thought of in the history of science.

It draws a million candidates in an afternoon. Then, a second AI (the "Critic") grades them.

- *"Too toxic."*
- *"Too unstable."*
- *"Impossible to manufacture."*
- **"Perfect."**

It narrows the list from one million to ten. All of this happens in the cloud, in days, without a single test tube being broken.

The Author's Lens: Regrowing the Optic Nerve

I want to connect this to my own field, Ophthalmology, because this technology is personal to me.

Glaucoma is the "Silent Thief of Sight." It kills the optic nerve. Once those nerve fibers are dead, they are gone forever. In the central nervous system, unlike the skin, neurons do not regenerate.

For decades, we have been looking for a molecule that can trick the optic nerve into regrowing. We have failed for fifty years.

But recently, AI has identified a protein pathway called **mTOR**. By using Generative AI, scientists are now designing molecules that can specifically activate this pathway only in the eye, stimulating the nerve to sprout new connections.

We are on the verge of reversing "permanent" blindness. Not because we got smarter, but because our tools got faster.

The 46-Day Miracle

This is not a theoretical fantasy for the year 2050. It has already happened.

Insilico Medicine, a biotech company led by the visionary Dr. Alex Zhavoronkov, decided to prove the power of this system. They targeted a deadly disease called **Idiopathic Pulmonary Fibrosis (IPF)**. In IPF, the lungs slowly scar and stiffen until the patient can no longer breathe. It is a horrific way to die, and we have very few treatments.

Using their AI platform, Pharma.AI, they first identified a new target protein involved in the scarring process. Then, they used a Generative AI to design a completely novel molecule to block it.

Consider the timeline comparison:

- **Traditional Timeline:** 4 to 5 years to find a "Pre-clinical Candidate."
- **AI Timeline:** Under 18 months.

But the design phase—the actual "inventing the molecule" part—took only **46 days.**

In 2022, the drug entered Phase 1 clinical trials in humans. They did in months what usually takes a decade, and they did it for a fraction of the cost (about $2.6 million versus the usual tens of millions for discovery).

For the first time, we have a drug born in the mind of a machine circulating in the veins of a human.

Repurposing: The Old Keys

Sometimes, we don't need to invent a new key. Sometimes, the key already exists, hanging on a hook in the pharmacy, but we just don't know it fits the lock.

This is the science of **Drug Repurposing**.

There are thousands of safe, approved drugs sitting on shelves right now. Could an old drug for heartburn cure a specific type of cancer? Could a drug for hypertension stop Ebola? We don't know, because we cannot physically test every drug against every disease. It would take centuries.

But AI can test them digitally.

It creates a **"Knowledge Graph"**—a massive digital web connecting genes, drugs, proteins, and diseases based on millions of research papers.

When the COVID-19 pandemic hit in early 2020, the world was desperate. We had no vaccines, no treatments, and hospitals were collapsing.

BenevolentAI, a company in London, unleashed its algorithms on the virus. The AI read the scientific literature on how the virus entered human cells. It scanned the database of all existing drugs to see if any of them could block that mechanism.

It didn't pick an antiviral. It picked a drug called **Baricitinib**.

Baricitinib was a drug approved for rheumatoid arthritis. It suppresses the immune system.

The AI predicted: *"This arthritis drug will stop the virus from entering lung cells AND it will reduce the deadly inflammation (cytokine storm) that kills patients."*

It was a non-intuitive link. A human rheumatologist wouldn't think about virology. A virologist wouldn't look at arthritis drugs. They live in different silos. The AI connected the dots because it sees the whole graph at once.

Baricitinib was fast-tracked into trials. It worked. Studies showed it reduced deaths in hospitalized COVID-19 patients by **38%**. The AI found a treatment in days that saved thousands of lives.

The Death of the "Blockbuster"

For decades, the pharmaceutical industry has been addicted to "Blockbusters." These are drugs like Lipitor (for cholesterol) that can be sold to millions of people.

Companies chase blockbusters because they need to make back that initial $2.5 billion investment. This economic reality forces them to ignore rare diseases. A CEO will say, *"We cannot spend $2 billion to cure a disease that only affects 5,000 children. We will go bankrupt."*

AI changes the economics of compassion.

If you can discover a drug for **$50 million** instead of $2.5 billion, the math changes entirely. Suddenly, it becomes profitable to cure rare diseases. Suddenly, we can afford to develop **"Nichebusters"**—highly specific drugs for small populations.

We are moving from a world of Scarcity (few drugs, high cost) to a world of Abundance (many drugs, lower cost).

The Wet Lab in the Cloud

Ultimately, we are building the **"Self-Driving Lab."**

Imagine a room with no humans.

- An AI designs a molecule.
- It sends the instruction to a robotic arm.
- The robot mixes the chemicals to synthesize the drug in a tiny well.
- A robotic microscope tests the drug on actual human cells.
- The results are fed back to the AI.
- The AI learns from the failure ("It wasn't potent enough") and designs a better molecule.
- Repeat.

This cycle happens 24 hours a day, 7 days a week. No sleep. No coffee breaks. No biases. This is happening right now at companies like **Recursion Pharmaceuticals**. They conduct millions of experiments a week. They are industrializing serendipity.

Flash Forward: The Pandemic of 2035

Imagine a new virus emerges in 2035. It is deadly.

We do not panic. We do not shut down the world for two years.

The AI analyzes the virus's protein structure in one hour (AlphaFold). It designs a blocking molecule in four hours (Generative AI). The Self-Driving Lab synthesizes and tests it overnight.

By the next morning, we have a drug candidate. By the next week, we have safety data. By the next month, we have the cure.

The pandemic ends before it begins.

The Time Machine

When we say AI "speeds up" discovery, it sounds like a convenience. It sounds like getting your Amazon package in one day instead of two.

But in medicine, speed is not convenience. **Speed is life.**

If we had found the cure for Polio five years earlier, millions of children would have walked instead of spending their lives in iron lungs. If we find the cure for Alzheimer's five years earlier, millions of grandparents will remember their grandchildren's names for one more Christmas.

The Infallible Doctor does not accept the "12-year rule." It collapses the timeline. It turns the "Valley of Death" into a bridge.

We are compressing decades of heartbreak into months of hope. And for the family waiting for a diagnosis, that speed is the only thing that matters.

THE TAKEAWAY

The Villain is "Time": It takes 12 years and $2.5 billion to find a new drug. Eroom's Law says this is getting slower every year. Patients with ALS or cancer simply don't have that time.

The "AlphaFold" Moment: DeepMind's AI solved the 50-year mystery of "Protein Folding" in months, mapping 200 million proteins. This gives us the "Google Maps" of the human body, showing exactly where to target drugs.

The 46-Day Miracle: Insilico Medicine used Generative AI to design a totally new drug for Pulmonary Fibrosis in just 46 days (a process that usually takes years).

The Self-Driving Lab: Robots and AI can now run millions of experiments 24/7 without humans, testing old drugs against new diseases (like finding Baricitinib for COVID-19) to find cures hiding in plain sight.

References

1. Jumper, J., et al. (2021). "Highly accurate protein structure prediction with AlphaFold." *Nature*, 596, 583–589.
2. Ren, F., et al. (2023). "A small-molecule inhibitor of TNIK discovered by generative AI for idiopathic pulmonary fibrosis." *Nature Biotechnology*.
3. Scannell, J. W., et al. (2012). "Diagnosing the decline in pharmaceutical R&D efficiency." *Nature Reviews Drug Discovery*, 11, 191–200.
4. Stebbing, J., et al. (2020). "COVID-19: combining antiviral and anti-inflammatory treatments." *The Lancet Infectious Diseases*, 20(4), 400–402.
5. Senior, A. W., et al. (2020). "Improved protein structure prediction using potentials from deep learning." *Nature*, 577, 706–710.

Chapter 24

The Superbug War

AI Strikes Back Against Antibiotic Resistance

"We have lived for eighty years in a golden bubble of safety, forgetting that for most of human history, a scratch from a rose thorn was a death sentence. As the lights of the antibiotic era flicker and fade, AI is not just offering us a new flashlight; it is lighting a fire to keep the darkness at bay."

— Dr. Suresh Kumar Pandey

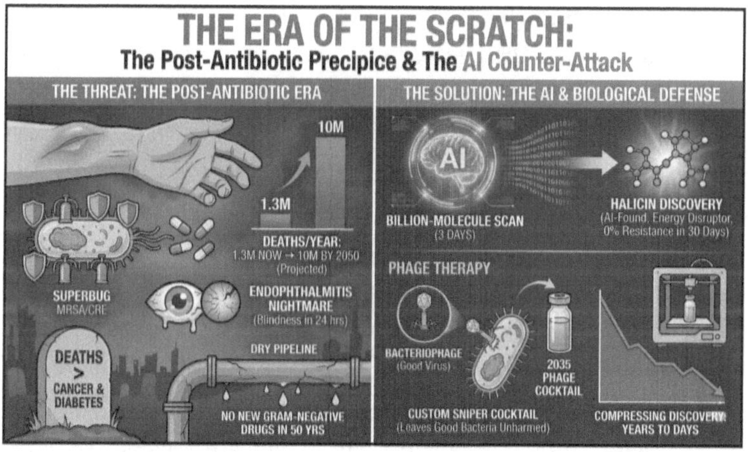

The Era of the Scratch

To understand the precipice on which modern medicine stands, we must first strip away the comfort of the present and return to the year 1940.

It is difficult for **you**, living in an age of sterile hospitals and neatly packaged pills, to visceralize the terror of the pre-antibiotic world.

It was a world where a child's scraped knee from a playground fall could fester into gangrene within days. It was a world where a sore throat was not an annoyance, but a harbinger of rheumatic fever that could destroy the heart valves of a teenager. Childbirth was a mortal gamble; "childbed fever" (sepsis) stalked maternity wards like a silent executioner.

Surgeons were often viewed not as healers, but as desperate gamblers. A surgeon could perform a technically perfect operation—remove a tumor, repair a hernia—only to watch the patient die a week later, burning with fever, their body consumed by the microscopic army that entered through the incision.

Then came the miracle.

Alexander Fleming's discovery of penicillin in 1928, and its mass production during World War II, fundamentally altered the trajectory of our species. It was a "magic bullet," a chemical sniper that could distinguish between a human cell and a bacterial invader, killing the latter while leaving the former untouched. In a single generation, antibiotics doubled the average human lifespan. We began to view infection not as a fate, but as a nuisance.

But Fleming himself saw the shadow behind the light. In his 1945 Nobel Prize acceptance speech, he issued a warning that reads today like a prophecy:

"The thoughtless person playing with penicillin treatment is morally responsible for the death of the man who succumbs to infection with the penicillin-resistant organism."

We were thoughtless.

We treated this biological miracle as a commodity. We demanded antibiotics for viral colds, against which they are useless. We poured billions of tons of these precious compounds into the feed troughs of livestock, not to cure sick animals, but to make chickens and pigs grow fatter, faster. We saturated the environment with the very weapon we needed to save us.

And the bacteria, obedient to the ruthless laws of Darwinian evolution, responded.

They mutated. They learned to build molecular pumps to spit the drugs out. They constructed biological shields to block entry. They swapped resistance genes with each other like trading cards.

We are now entering the **"Post-Antibiotic Era."**

The statistics are not just numbers; they are a countdown. Today, "Superbugs" like **MRSA** (Methicillin-resistant Staphylococcus aureus) and **CRE** (Carbapenem-resistant Enterobacteriaceae) kill approximately **1.3 million people a year** globally. That is more than HIV/AIDS (630,000 deaths in 2022) or malaria (608,000 deaths in 2022).

The United Nations estimates that by the year 2050, if current trends continue, this number could rise to **10 million deaths a year**.

That is one person dying every three seconds.

If we lose antibiotics, we do not just lose a class of drugs. We lose modern medicine itself. We lose the ability to perform C-sections safely. We lose hip replacements. We lose organ transplants. We lose chemotherapy, which strips the immune system and leaves cancer patients entirely reliant on antibiotics to survive the treatment.

The Golden Age of medicine is threatening to end not with a bang, but with a sneeze.

The Author's Lens: The Nightmare of Endophthalmitis

I want to bring this terror home to my own operating theater.

As an eye surgeon, my greatest fear is not a slip of the knife. It is **Endophthalmitis**. This is a devastating infection inside the eyeball.

In the past, if a patient developed an infection after cataract surgery, I would inject a standard cocktail of antibiotics (like Vancomycin and Ceftazidime) into the eye. Within 24 hours, the bacteria would die, and the vision would be saved.

But recently, I have seen cases where the bacteria simply laugh at the drugs.

I remember a patient, a grandmother who had just had successful surgery. Two days later, she returned in agony. Her eye was full of pus. I injected the antibiotics. They did nothing. The bacteria were resistant.

We had to surgically remove the pus, but the toxins had already destroyed her retina. She lost her eye.

This is the face of the Post-Antibiotic Era. It is not a theoretical graph; it is a grandmother going blind because our weapons no longer work.

The Villain: The Dry Pipeline

The logical question arises: *Why don't we just invent new ones?* If we can build self-driving cars and land rockets on Mars, surely we can find a new chemical to kill a germ.

The answer lies in the cold calculus of economics. The antibiotic pipeline is dry because the business model is broken.

Developing a new drug costs roughly a billion dollars and takes over a decade. If a pharmaceutical company develops a new heart medication or an antidepressant, patients will take a pill every day for thirty years. That is a steady, predictable revenue stream.

But if a company develops a revolutionary new antibiotic, two things happen.

- First, doctors will hoard it. We will lock it in a "break glass in case of emergency" box, using it only for the rarest, most resistant cases to prevent resistance from developing. Sales volume will be low.
- Second, when patients do take it, they take it for ten days, get cured, and never buy it again.

From a profit perspective, a cure is a terrible product. As a result, most major pharmaceutical companies have abandoned the field. We haven't discovered a new class of antibiotics to treat **Gram-negative bacteria**—the hardest kind to kill, with their double-layered armor—in over fifty years.

The scientists are running out of ideas. They have screened every soil sample, every jungle fungus, every obvious chemical compound. They are digging in the same dry wells, finding nothing but dust.

We need a new way to dig.

The Discovery of Halicin

In 2020, a team at MIT, led by the brilliant computer scientist **Regina Barzilay** and bioengineer **James Collins**, decided to stop trusting human intuition. They decided to turn the problem over to an Artificial Intelligence.

Their goal was audacious. They didn't want to find a tweak to an existing drug—a "Penicillin 2.0." They wanted something structurally unique, a molecule that looked nothing like a traditional antibiotic, something that human bias had overlooked.

Step 1: The Education.

They started by training the machine. They took a library of 2,335 molecules. Some were FDA-approved drugs; some were natural compounds; some were failed experiments. They tested all of them against E. coli bacteria in a petri dish to see which ones killed it and which ones didn't.

They fed this data—the chemical structure and the result—into a Deep Learning model.

"Here is the atomic map of this molecule. Did it kill the bacteria? Yes or No."

The AI analyzed the data. It began to see patterns invisible to the human eye—subtle relationships between atomic bonds and biological lethality. It learned what a killer looked like.

Step 2: The Search.

Once the brain was trained, they unleashed it. They pointed the AI at the "Drug Repurposing Hub"—a massive library of 6,000 molecules that were sitting on laboratory shelves. These were compounds that had been investigated for other things—cancer, diabetes, depression—but had never been thought of as antibiotics.

The AI scanned the library. It wasn't looking for a known antibiotic structure. It was looking for a ghost: a molecule that the algorithm predicted would be highly lethal to bacteria, but which looked structurally nothing like any antibiotic we currently use.

In a matter of hours, the AI spit out a candidate.

It was a molecule technically known as **SU-3327**.

It was originally investigated as a treatment for diabetes. It had failed in those trials. No human had ever bothered to drop it on a bacteria culture. To a chemist's eye, it didn't look like an antibiotic.

The MIT team synthesized it. They named it **Halicin**, a nod to HAL 9000, the sentient AI from the movie 2001: A Space Odyssey.

Step 3: The Slaughter.

They put Halicin in a petri dish with some of the nastiest superbugs on Earth—Clostridioides difficile, Acinetobacter baumannii, and the nightmare CRE bacteria that is resistant to nearly everything (often called the "phantom menace" bacteria).

Halicin didn't just inhibit them. **It obliterated them.**

And crucially, it worked in a completely new way. Most antibiotics attack the bacterium's cell wall (like smashing a house) or its ability to replicate DNA. Halicin was more subtle and more deadly. It attacked the cell membrane's electrical gradient. It effectively disrupted the bacterium's ability to generate energy. It caused the bacteria to starve to death instantly, their metabolic lights flickering out.

Because the mechanism was so novel, the bacteria couldn't easily evolve resistance to it. In evolution experiments, the team tried to force *E. coli* to become resistant.

- Against Ciprofloxacin (a standard powerful antibiotic), the bacteria developed resistance within a single day, and full immunity in 30 days.
- Against Halicin? After **30 days** of exposure, the bacteria had developed **zero resistance**.

The AI had found a needle in a haystack that humans didn't even know was a haystack.

The Billion-Molecule Scan

Halicin was the proof of concept. It proved that the machine could see what we could not.

Once they knew the system worked, the MIT team decided to scale it up. They pointed the AI at a database called **ZINC15**, which contains over **1.5 billion** chemical compounds.

To physically test 1.5 billion compounds in a lab would take centuries and cost trillions. It is physically impossible.

The AI scanned the entire library in three days.

It filtered out the toxic ones. It filtered out the ones that looked like existing drugs. It identified 23 new potential candidates that were structurally distinct and predicted to be safe for humans. Two of those candidates, in later tests, proved to be highly effective against even the most resistant strains of bacteria.

This marks a fundamental shift in the history of science. We are moving from **"Artisanal Discovery"**—where a lone scientist hunts for a mushroom in a forest—to **"Industrial Discovery."** We are no longer fishing with a single line. We are trawling the entire ocean of chemical possibility with a net made of code.

The Phage Hunters: Nature's Nanobots

But chemistry is not our only weapon. AI is also helping us revive an old, forgotten ally: the Virus.

This is the revival of **Phage Therapy**.

Bacteriophages (or "phages") are viruses. But they are "good" viruses. They do not infect humans. Their sole purpose in life, evolved over billions of years, is to hunt down, infect, and explode specific types of bacteria. They are nature's own nanobots.

For every bacterium on earth, there is a phage that kills it. The problem is finding the match. Phages are incredibly picky. A phage that kills *Staph aureus Strain A* might ignore *Staph aureus Strain B*.

If you have a dying patient with a resistant infection, you don't have time to test thousands of phages in a wet lab to find the match. It is a massive biological matching game.

This is where AI steps in.

Companies like **Adaptive Phage Therapeutics** are using AI to sequence the DNA of the patient's specific bacterial infection. The AI then instantly matches that genetic sequence against a library of thousands of banked phages.

It predicts: *"Phage X and Phage Y will be 99% effective against this specific strain."*

We can then create a **"Phage Cocktail"**—a custom blend of viruses designed to wipe out that specific patient's infection. Crucially, because phages are so specific, they leave the "good" bacteria in the patient's gut completely unharmed. Unlike broad-spectrum antibiotics, which act like a nuclear bomb in the microbiome, phages are a sniper shot.

Flash Forward: The Infection of 2035

Imagine it is 2035. **You** scratch your leg while gardening. It gets infected. It swells. It turns red.

You go to the doctor. She swabs the wound. She puts the swab into a handheld sequencer.

Within minutes, the AI identifies the bacteria: *Methicillin-Resistant Staphylococcus Aureus (MRSA), Strain 402.*

The AI also notes that this strain is resistant to Penicillin, Vancomycin, and Doxycycline.

But the AI doesn't panic. It scans the Global Phage Bank. It finds three viruses that target this specific strain.

A 3D printer in the pharmacy prints a vial containing the Phage Cocktail. You apply it to your leg.

By the next morning, the redness is gone. The bacteria are dead. Your gut health is perfect. The crisis is averted.

The Eternal Arms Race

We must be humble. We will never definitively "win" the war against bacteria. They reproduce every twenty minutes. They have been on this planet for 3.5 billion years; we have been here for a blink of an eye. They are the ultimate survivors. It is an eternal arms race.

But for the last fifty years, we have been fighting this war with one hand tied behind our backs. We stopped inventing new weapons because it was too hard and too expensive. We let the bugs catch up.

AI unties that hand.

It gives us a way to innovate faster than the bugs can evolve. If a new superbug emerges in 2030, we won't have to wait twelve years for a new drug to be developed by chance.

The Infallible Doctor will sequence the bug on Monday.

It will design a new molecule (or find a phage match) by Tuesday.

It will synthesize the cure by Wednesday.

Halicin is not just a new drug. It is a symbol. It is proof that we are no longer defenseless. The machines have joined the fight, and for the first time in decades, the odds are shifting back in our favor.

THE TAKEAWAY

The Villain is "Resistance": Bacteria evolve faster than we invent drugs. Superbugs like MRSA kill 1.3 million people a year. By 2050, simple infections could kill 10 million annually if we don't find new weapons.

The "Eye Nightmare": In ophthalmology, drug-resistant bacteria can destroy an eye in 24 hours. Current antibiotics are failing, leading to blindness from routine surgeries.

The AI Discovery: An MIT AI found **Halicin**, a new antibiotic that kills resistant bacteria by disrupting their energy, in just 3 days of scanning. It found a molecule humans had ignored for decades.

Phage Therapy: AI can now match "good viruses" (bacteriophages) to specific bacterial infections, creating a custom "sniper shot" cocktail that kills the bug without harming your body.

References

1. Stokes, J. M., et al. (2020). "A Deep Learning Approach to Antibiotic Discovery." *Cell*, 180(4), 688-702.
2. O'Neill, J. (2016). "Tackling Drug-Resistant Infections Globally: Final Report and Recommendations." *The Review on Antimicrobial Resistance.*
3. Fleming, A. (1945). "Penicillin." *Nobel Lecture*, December 11, 1945.
4. Kortright, K. E., et al. (2019). "Phage Therapy: A Renewed Approach to Combat Antibiotic-Resistant Bacteria." *Cell Host & Microbe*, 25(2), 219-232.
5. World Health Organization (WHO). (2021). "2020 antibacterial agents in clinical and preclinical development: an overview and analysis." *WHO Technical Report.*

Chapter 25

Printing the Cure

From Mass Production to Bespoke Biology

"We have spent the last century trying to make the human body fit our machines—standardizing artificial joints, mass-producing pills, and forcing biology to conform to the assembly line. The 3D printer reverses this logic. It allows us, finally, to build the machine to fit the body."

— Dr. Suresh Kumar Pandey

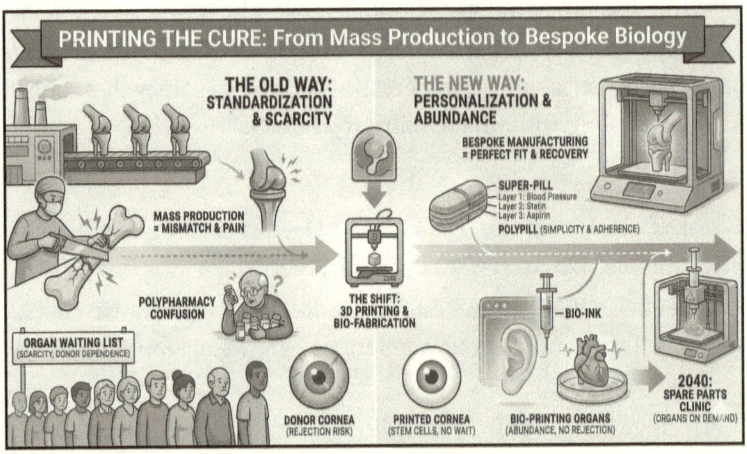

The Boy Who Couldn't Breathe

In 2013, inside a neonatal intensive care unit in Ohio, a six-week-old boy named **Kaiba Gionfriddo** lay in a plastic box, fighting a war he was destined to lose.

Kaiba was born with a rare and terrifying congenital defect known as *tracheobronchomalacia* (TBM).

The cartilage of his windpipe—the rigid tube that allows us to inhale—possessed no rigidity at all. It was flaccid and weak, like a wet straw. Every time Kaiba tried to take a deep breath, or every time he cried, the pressure would cause his windpipe to collapse flat.

His air supply would cut off instantly. He would turn blue. His heart rate would plummet. The nurses would rush in, forcing air into his lungs, resuscitating him day after day. It was a torture cycle. His parents, April and Bryan, watched helplessly as their son died a little bit every day.

The conventional surgery—sewing the airway to the spine to pull it open—had failed. The doctors told them there were no options left.

But at the University of Michigan, Dr. Glenn Green and Dr. Scott Hollister were working on an idea that sounded less like medicine and more like manufacturing.

They took a CT scan of Kaiba's chest. On a computer screen, they built a high-resolution, three-dimensional digital model of his defective windpipe. They could rotate it, zoom in, and see exactly where the collapse was happening.

Then, they designed a solution: a tiny, C-shaped splint. It looked like a small piece of corrugated pipe, designed to wrap around the outside of the windpipe and hold it open, like scaffolding.

But you cannot buy a custom tracheal splint for a six-week-old baby at a medical supply store. It doesn't exist.

So, they hit **"Print."**

They didn't use a standard desktop printer. They used a specialized laser-sintering machine loaded not with ink, but with a fine powder of **polycaprolactone**. This is a biocompatible plastic that the body tolerates well. The laser danced over the powder, melting it layer by microscopic layer, building the splint from the bottom up.

Within hours, they had a physical object. It was white, flexible, and perfectly shaped to fit Kaiba's unique anatomy.

Surgeons opened Kaiba's chest. They snapped the splint around his collapsing bronchus and sewed it in place.

The effect was instantaneous. The wet straw popped open. The airway held. The blue spells stopped. For the first time in his short life, Kaiba took a breath that was just a breath, not a struggle.

But the genius of the design wasn't just that it fit. It was that it evolved.

Polycaprolactone is biodegradable. The engineers knew that Kaiba would grow. A permanent metal stent would eventually choke him as he got bigger. But this plastic was designed to dissolve slowly over three years—exactly the amount of time it takes for a child's windpipe to naturally stiffen and support itself.

As Kaiba grew strong, the machine that saved him quietly disappeared, absorbed harmlessly into his body.

Kaiba Gionfriddo was saved by a piece of plastic that cost less than a used car to manufacture. This case marked the beginning of a quiet revolution. It signaled the move from **"Mass Manufacturing"**—where we have five sizes of knee implants for seven billion people—to **"Bespoke Manufacturing,"** where everything is custom-made for an audience of one.

The Villain: The Assembly Line

For the last hundred years, medicine has been obsessed with standardization. We treat the human body like a Ford Model T.

If **you** need a knee replacement, the surgeon opens a box. Inside, there are maybe five sizes: Extra Small, Small, Medium, Large, Extra Large.

The surgeon picks the one that fits "best." But "best" is a relative term. If your bone is shaped slightly differently—if your femur has a unique curvature or your tibia has a specific tilt—the implant won't fit perfectly.

So, what does the surgeon do? **They cut your bone to fit the metal.**

They saw off the unique edges of your anatomy to force it to conform to the mass-produced factory part. This mismatch is why 20% of knee replacement patients still have pain years later. The machine doesn't fit the body.

3D printing reverses this logic. It allows us to scan **your** knee, print a metal implant that matches **your** specific curvature down to the micron, and insert it without cutting away healthy bone.

We stop making the body fit the machine. We build the machine to fit the body.

The Author's Lens: Printing the Cornea

I want to take you into my own field, Ophthalmology, where the shortage of spare parts is a global tragedy.

The cornea is the clear window at the front of the eye. If it gets scarred or diseased (like in Keratoconus), you go blind. The only cure is a transplant.

But to get a transplant, someone else has to die. We have to wait for a donor. In many parts of the world, the waiting list is years long. Millions go blind waiting.

And even if you get a donor cornea, it might not fit perfectly. It might be rejected.

This is where **Bio-Printing** changes the game.

We are now experimenting with printing corneas. We take a scan of your eye. We create a "Bio-Ink"—a mixture of collagen and your own stem cells.

The printer lays down the layers of the cornea—the stroma, the epithelium—in a perfect curve that matches your eye exactly.

Because it is made of your own cells, there is no rejection. Because it is printed, there is no waiting list.

We are moving from a world of **Scarcity** (waiting for a donor) to a world of **Abundance** (printing the cure).

The Personal Pill Factory

The revolution begins with the most common medical act in history: swallowing a pill.

Consider the daily ritual of the average 75-year-old patient. We call it **Polypharmacy**, but it feels more like chemistry class.

- A beta-blocker for the heart.
- A statin for the cholesterol.
- A metformin tablet for the diabetes.
- A blood thinner to prevent strokes.

It is a handful of confetti—ten different pills, different shapes, different bottles, different times of day. It is confusing, expensive, and dangerous. Missed doses and accidental overdoses are a leading cause of hospital admissions in the elderly.

What if **you** could take all ten drugs and print them into a single object? This is the concept of the **"Polypill,"** and 3D printing is making it a reality.

A 3D printer does not have to print solid plastic. It can print powder and binding agents. It can create complex internal geometries that are impossible to achieve with a standard pill press. Imagine a pill designed like a jawbreaker or a layered cake.

- **Layer 1 (The Outer Shell):** Contains the blood pressure medicine. The printer uses a binder that dissolves instantly in the stomach acid, releasing the drug immediately.
- **Layer 2 (The Core):** Contains the statin. It is wrapped in a polymer that resists acid, delaying release until it reaches the small intestine four hours later.
- **Layer 3 (The Matrix):** Contains a micro-dose of aspirin distributed throughout the structure for steady absorption.

Instead of ten bottles on the counter, the patient takes one **"Super-Pill"** in the morning. Adherence goes up. Confusion goes down.

But it gets even more personal. In 2015, the FDA approved **Spritam**, the first 3D-printed drug. It is an epilepsy medication designed for children or stroke victims who have dysphagia (difficulty swallowing).

Because Spritam is printed layer by porous layer, it is 90% air. It is a lattice. When it hits the moisture of the tongue, the lattice collapses instantly. It doesn't need to be swallowed; it vanishes into a sip of water. It delivers a high dose of medicine without the choking hazard of a dense tablet.

We are moving toward a future where pharmacies might not have shelves full of bottles. They might look like copy shops, with rows of printers humming quietly. Your doctor sends the prescription not to a pharmacist to count pills, but to a print queue to build them.

The Flesh and the Scaffold

The real science fiction begins, however, when we swap the plastic and the powder for biological matter.

The shortage of donor organs is a global humanitarian crisis. In the United States alone, **17 people die every day** waiting for a kidney, liver, or heart transplant. We are essentially waiting for young, healthy people to die in car accidents so we can harvest their parts. It is a gruesome and inefficient supply chain.

What if we could print the parts? This is **Bio-Printing**.

The "ink" in a bio-printer is a **Bio-ink**—a slurry of living cells (often stem cells taken from the patient) mixed with a hydrogel (like gelatin or collagen) that acts as a glue or a scaffold.

In 2022, a 20-year-old woman born with **microtia** (a congenital deformity where the ear is missing or underdeveloped) became a pioneer. A company called **3DBio Therapeutics** took a small biopsy of her cartilage. They grew billions of her own cells. They printed a perfect, mirror-image ear based on her healthy side. They implanted it.

Because the ear was made of her biology, there was zero risk of rejection. She didn't need the brutal regimen of immunosuppressant drugs that transplant patients usually take for life. Her body recognized the ear not as a foreign invader, but as self.

The Vascular Challenge: Printing the Heart

Printing cartilage—like ears, noses, and meniscus—is the "easy" part. Cartilage is avascular; it doesn't need a heavy blood supply.

Printing a liver, a kidney, or a heart is exponentially harder. These are thick, metabolically demanding organs. Every single cell in a human liver must be within **200 microns** (a hair's width) of a blood vessel to get oxygen. If it is 201 microns away, it suffocates and dies.

How do you print the billions of tiny capillaries needed to keep a thick slab of liver tissue alive?

Scientists are solving this with ingenious creativity. One technique, developed at Rice University and the University of Pennsylvania, uses **Sugar**.

They printed a complex, intricate lattice of hardened sugar—think of it as high-tech cotton candy. The sugar mimicked the branching network of blood vessels. Then, they poured the cell-filled bio-ink around the sugar lattice. The tissue solidified.

Then, they flushed it with water. The sugar dissolved and washed away, leaving behind a perfect network of empty, hollow tubes inside the tissue. They had created the plumbing.

Another technique involves printing the vessels themselves. In 2019, researchers at **Tel Aviv University** printed the world's first **"3D vascularized heart."**

It was small—about the size of a rabbit's heart or a cherry. But it was complete. It had chambers. It had major vessels. It was made of human cells. And when they applied an electrical current, the cells contracted. **It beat.**

It is not ready for human transplantation yet. A human heart needs billions of cells and must beat without stopping for eighty years. But the proof of concept exists. We have moved from "impossible" to "merely difficult."

The Skin Gun

Before we get to printing whole hearts, we will master the surface.

For severe burn victims, the standard treatment is a skin graft. Doctors must use a dermatome—a device like a cheese slicer—to painfully harvest healthy skin from the patient's unburned thigh or back. They stretch this skin and staple it over the burn.

But if a patient is burned over 80% of their body, there is no donor site. There is no skin left to harvest. Enter the **Bio-Printer "Skin Gun."**

Researchers at the Wake Forest Institute for Regenerative Medicine have developed a mobile printer that can be wheeled to the patient's bedside. A laser scanner maps the **"topology"** of the wound. It sees the valleys and peaks of the burn injury. The printer arm then moves over the patient, following the contours of the body.

It has multiple nozzles:

- **Nozzle A** deposits fibroblasts (the cells that make the deep, structural layer of skin).

- **Nozzle B** deposits keratinocytes (the cells that make the tough, waterproof outer layer).

It is literally spray-painting new skin onto the raw flesh. In animal trials, the printed skin healed twice as fast as standard grafts. Because the cells are placed precisely where they are needed, the skin regenerates with almost no scarring.

Flash Forward: The Spare Parts Clinic (2040)

It is 2040. You have kidney failure.

You do not go on a waiting list. You do not wait for a tragic car accident to provide a donor.

You go to the clinic. They take a biopsy of your fat cells. They reprogram them into kidney cells.

A week later, you return. A bio-printer has printed a new kidney, genetically identical to your own.

The surgeon implants it. You take no anti-rejection pills. You go home. The concept of "waiting for an organ" is something you read about in history books.

The End of Scarcity

The implications of this technology are staggering. We are looking at the end of the concept of "scarcity" in human biology.

If we can print an organ on demand, the transplant waiting list vanishes. The agonizing moral choices that doctors make every day—*Does the 20-year-old student get the kidney, or the 60-year-old father of three?*—disappear.

Everyone gets one.

The 3D printer is the ultimate manufacturing tool for the ultimate machine: the human body. It allows us to fix the broken parts not with metal and plastic, but with the same biological material we are made of. We are learning to manufacture life, layer by layer.

THE TAKEAWAY

The Villain is "Mass Production": We currently force patients to fit standard implants (knee replacements) by cutting away healthy bone. 3D printing allows us to build the implant to fit the patient perfectly.

The "Polypill": Elderly patients often take 10 pills a day. 3D printing can combine all 10 into a single "Super-Pill" with timed-release layers, reducing confusion and overdoses.

The "Eye Factory": Corneal transplants rely on donors (dead people). Bio-printing allows us to print a new cornea using the patient's own stem cells, eliminating rejection and the waiting list.

Printing Life: Scientists have successfully printed a vascularized heart (rabbit-sized) and a human ear (implanted in 2022). The future is "Spare Parts on Demand," ending the organ shortage forever.

References

1. Zopf, D. A., Hollister, S. J., Nelson, M. E., Ohye, R. G., & Green, G. E. (2013). "Bioresorbable airway splint created with a three-dimensional printer." *New England Journal of Medicine*, 368(21), 2043-2045.
2. Khaled, S. A., Burley, J. C., Alexander, M. R., & Roberts, C. J. (2015). "3D printing of tablets for multiple drug release." *International Journal of Pharmaceutics*, 494(2), 643-650.
3. Noor, N., Shapira, A., Edri, R., Levato, R., Visscher, L., & Dvir, T. (2019). "3D Printing of Personalized Thick and Perfusable Cardiac Patches and Hearts." *Advanced Science*, 6(11), 1900344.
4. Murphy, S. V., & Atala, A. (2014). "3D bioprinting of tissues and organs." *Nature Biotechnology*, 32(8), 773-785.
5. West, T. G., & Connor, A. L. (2015). "The approval of Spritam: A new era for 3D printed pharmaceuticals." *Journal of Pharmaceutical Innovation*, 10, 34-36.

PART VI
The Wall-Less Hospital
Patient Monitoring and the Democratization of Care

Chapter 26

The Doctor on your Wrist

The Era of Ubiquitous Monitoring

"We have built a medical system based on the visit—the brief, artificial moment when you sit in my office and tell me a story. But life happens in the silence between visits. The Infallible Doctor does not wait for you to knock on the door; it walks with you, watching over every beat, every step, and every breath."

— Dr. Suresh Kumar Pandey

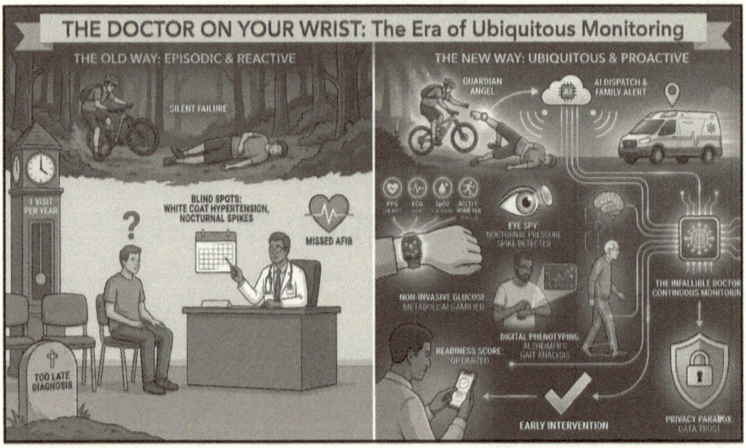

The Fall in the Woods

On a crisp autumn afternoon, Bob Burdett was riding his mountain bike through the dense pines of Riverside State Park in Washington. He was supposed to meet his son, Gabe, for a ride, but Bob had arrived early. He felt good. The air was cold, the trail was fast. He decided to take a quick solo lap to warm up.

At the bottom of a steep, shadowed hill, his front wheel caught a rut. Physics took over. Bob flew over the handlebars, his body becoming a projectile. His head struck the hard-packed earth with violent force. The lights went out instantly.

He lay there in the dirt, unconscious, miles from the nearest paved road. The forest was silent.

In the old world—the world we have lived in for most of human history—this is where the story often ends. Bob would have lain there for hours. Perhaps the swelling in his brain would have become irreversible. Perhaps hypothermia would have set in. He was alone, and his biology was failing.

But Bob was not truly alone. He was wearing an Apple Watch.

While Bob's brain was offline, the computer on his wrist was wide awake. Its accelerometer and gyroscope had detected a specific signature: a sudden, high-velocity impact followed immediately by a period of total immobility.

The watch tapped Bob on the wrist—a haptic buzz. Are you okay?

No response.

It sounded a piercing alarm. Bob, respond.

No response.

After sixty seconds of silence, the watch made a decision. It accessed the cellular network. It dialed 911.

When the dispatcher answered, a synthesized voice spoke:

"The owner of this Apple Watch has taken a hard fall and is not responding."

It then transmitted Bob's exact GPS longitude and latitude. Simultaneously, it sent a text message to his son, Gabe, with a map pin of where his father was lying.

Within minutes, an ambulance was tearing down the logging roads. By the time Bob woke up, he was being loaded onto a stretcher. He had a severe concussion, but he was alive. He hadn't touched his phone. He hadn't pressed a button. The machine on his wrist had acted as his guardian angel.

This event marks the dawn of **Ubiquitous Monitoring**.

For 5,000 years, medicine has been a reactive profession. The contract was simple: *You have to feel sick, and then you have to decide to come to us.*

We waited for the failure. If you were unconscious, or if your symptom was silent—like the creeping pressure in your arteries—we couldn't help you. We were blind until you walked through our door.

The **Infallible Doctor** changes the contract. It says: "You live your life. I will watch the data. And I will call for help when you can't."

The Villain: The Episodic Visit

The villain in this chapter is the calendar.

Medicine today is **episodic**. You see your doctor maybe once a year for 15 minutes. That is 15 minutes out of 525,600 minutes. We are trying to understand the movie of your life by looking at a single frame.

Imagine if you only checked your speedometer once a year while driving. You would speed. You would crash.

Yet, this is how we treat the human body. We measure your blood pressure in the clinic when you are nervous ("White Coat Hypertension"), but we miss the fact that it spikes dangerously every night while you sleep. We check your heart rhythm for ten seconds, but we miss the atrial fibrillation that happens only on Tuesday mornings.

This gap—the silence between visits—is where disease hides. It is where the heart attack forms. It is where the stroke prepares to strike.

Ubiquitous monitoring fills the gap. It turns the lights on in the dark room of your daily life.

From Pedometers to Medical Devices

We used to call them "fitness trackers," a dismissive term that implied they were toys for the vanity of the wealthy.

When the Fitbit launched in 2009, it was indeed a toy. It counted steps. It was a digital encouragement for people who wanted to lose five pounds before a wedding. Doctors ignored them. We viewed the data they produced as noise—unreliable, uncalibrated, and medically irrelevant.

But over the last decade, while the medical establishment was looking the other way, a quiet revolution occurred. The sensors grew up. They graduated from toys to **Medical-Grade Instruments.**

Consider what a modern smart watch actually contains:

- **The Optical Heart Sensor (PPG):** It shines green and infrared LEDs into your skin hundreds of times a second, measuring the volumetric change of blood flow to calculate pulse and heart rate variability (HRV).
- **The Electrical Sensor (ECG):** By completing a circuit between the wrist and a finger, it creates a single-lead electrocardiogram capable of detecting Atrial Fibrillation (AFib).
- **The SpO2 Sensor:** It measures the color of your blood to determine oxygen saturation—a metric that became a matter of life and death during the COVID-19 pandemic.
- **The Accelerometer:** It measures G-forces to detect falls, car crashes, and gait stability.

The FDA realized that the toy era was over. They began clearing these algorithms as **Class II Medical Devices.**

This shift is profound. It means that the most widely deployed medical diagnostic tool in history is no longer the stethoscope around my neck or the MRI machine in the basement. It is the smart watch. There are over **100 million Apple Watches** alone on wrists around the world.

That is 100 million EKG machines, monitoring heart health 24 hours a day, 7 days a week, in the shower, in the boardroom, and in sleep. We have effectively distributed the hospital's telemetry unit to the entire population.

The Author's Lens: The Pressure You Can't Feel

I see the need for this continuous monitoring desperately in my own field of ophthalmology.

Glaucoma is the "Silent Thief of Sight." High pressure inside the eye slowly kills the optic nerve. But here is the tragedy: pressure fluctuates.

A patient comes to my clinic at 10:00 AM. I measure their pressure. It is 15 mmHg (normal). I tell them, "You are fine."

But I don't know that at 3:00 AM, while they are sleeping, their pressure spikes to 35 mmHg. This nocturnal spike is destroying their vision, but I can't see it.

For decades, we were helpless. But now, we have **Smart Contact Lenses** (like the Triggerfish). These lenses have a microscopic strain gauge embedded in the silicone. They measure the curvature of the cornea every 5 minutes for 24 hours.

They send the data to a recorder. When I download it, I see the spike. I see the invisible enemy.

I can now treat the patient based on what happens in their bed, not just what happens in my chair.

The Silent Killer: Hypertension

To understand why this matters for everyone, we have to look at the greatest failure of preventative medicine: **High Blood Pressure (Hypertension)**.

We call it the "Silent Killer" because it has no symptoms. You can walk around with a pressure of 180/110 for years. You feel fine. You go to work, you play with your kids. Your arteries are slowly stiffening, your kidneys are degrading, but you feel nothing. Until—pop. A vessel bursts in your brain. A stroke.

We need **Continuous Blood Pressure Monitoring**.

For years, this was impossible. You couldn't wear an inflatable cuff to a business meeting or to bed. But companies like **Aktiia** and **Samsung** are breaking this barrier. They are using optical analysis of the pulse wave shape—the way the artery expands and contracts with each beat—to calculate blood pressure without a squeeze.

Imagine a world where I don't see a single number ("120/80"). I see a trend line.

"Jay," I might say, looking at the dashboard. *"I see your pressure is perfect while you sleep, which is good. But it spikes to 160 every afternoon. We don't need to treat your heart; we need to treat your stress. Let's talk about your workday."*

It turns a crude biological guess into a precise, actionable data stream.

The Gamification of Metabolism

But the wrist can do more than measure pulses. It is learning to taste.

The Holy Grail for metabolic health is the **Non-Invasive Glucose Monitor**.

Currently, millions of diabetics live a life of pinpricks. To know their blood sugar, they must stab their fingers to draw a drop of blood multiple times a day. It is painful, callous-inducing, and annoying.

Technology giants are pouring billions into solving this. Companies like **Rockley Photonics** are developing "clinic-on-a-wrist" sensors. They use infrared lasers that penetrate the skin, bounce off the interstitial fluid, and analyze the spectral signature of the reflected light. They can "read" the concentration of glucose, alcohol, and lactate without breaking the skin.

When this technology is perfected, the impact will be civilization-scale.

It won't just be for diabetics. It will be for everyone. Imagine eating a glazed donut. Twenty minutes later, your watch buzzes. It shows you a graph of your blood sugar rocketing upward.

"Your glucose is spiking," the watch says. *"Go for a 10-minute walk right now to flatten the curve."*

You walk. You watch the line go down. You get a dopamine hit of success.

This is the **gamification of metabolism**. It makes the invisible visible. It closes the feedback loop between "what I eat" and "how I feel." It has the potential to prevent Type 2 Diabetes before the pancreas ever fails, simply by showing people the immediate biological cost of their choices.

The Gait of Alzheimer's

Sometimes, the watch doesn't need to look inside your body. It just needs to watch how you move through the world.

Gait Analysis is one of the most powerful, yet underutilized, neurological tools. When you walk, your brain is performing a complex symphony. It is balancing input from your eyes, your inner ear, and your muscles. It is coordinating rhythm, stride length, and symmetry.

Early signs of Parkinson's Disease and Alzheimer's often show up in the walk **years** before memory loss begins. You might take slightly shorter steps. You might have a tiny asymmetry in your arm swing. You might wobble slightly when you turn.

The human eye cannot see these micro-deviations. But the accelerometer on your wrist, sampling motion 100 times a second, can.

A study published in Nature Digital Medicine showed that smartphone and wearable data could detect the digital signatures of cognitive decline. The device builds a **"Digital Phenotype"** of your normal walk. It knows how you move.

If, over six months, your gait slows down by 5% and becomes more irregular, the AI flags it.

[ALERT: NEUROLOGICAL DEVIATION DETECTED. RECOMMEND NEUROLOGIST CONSULT.]

We are moving from diagnosing Alzheimer's at Stage 4—when the patient is lost—to Stage 1, when the brain is just starting to struggle. This is the only window where new drugs and lifestyle interventions have a chance to work.

The Internet of Bodies

The "Doctor on Your Wrist" is just the hub. It connects to a growing network of sensors forming the **Internet of Bodies (IoB)**.

- **The Smart Ring (e.g., Oura):** These devices track sleep stages and body temperature with incredible precision. During the pandemic, Oura rings famously detected COVID-19 fevers up to three days before the patient felt sick, simply by noticing a slight rise in dermal temperature.
- **The Smart Insole:** For diabetics, the loss of sensation in the feet (neuropathy) is a tragedy. They get blisters they cannot feel. The blisters become ulcers, then infections, then amputations. Smart insoles monitor pressure and temperature. They detect

"hot spots" of inflammation before the skin breaks, alerting the patient to change their shoes.

- **The Smart Bra:** Companies like **Bloomer Tech** are embedding medical-grade ECG sensors into the fabric of bras. This addresses the massive "gender data gap" in cardiology, ensuring that women's heart rhythms are monitored comfortably and continuously.

You are no longer a black box to your doctor. You are a dashboard.

Flash Forward: The Morning Briefing (2035)

It is 2035. You wake up. You look at your phone.

The app doesn't just show you "steps." It shows you a **"Readiness Score."**

"Good morning. Your HRV is high, indicating good recovery. Your resting heart rate is stable. However, your hydration levels are low (detected by sweat sensors). Drink 500ml of water before coffee."

It is like having a personal pit crew. It optimizes you. It catches the small drifts before they become big crashes.

The Privacy Paradox

And yet, this transparency is terrifying.

- If my watch knows I'm stressed, will my boss fire me?
- If my ring knows I'm not sleeping, will my insurance premiums go up?
- If my GPS knows I visit a fast-food restaurant three times a week, will my doctor scold me?

These are not paranoid delusions; they are valid fears in the age of surveillance capitalism. The "Wall-Less Hospital" only works if there is a **Wall of Trust**.

We need legislation that treats biometric data with the same sanctity as genetic data. It must be untouchable by employers, insurers, or data brokers for discriminatory purposes. Your data belongs to you. You "donate" it to your doctor for care, but you hold the keys.

Without this trust, people will take off the watches. They will choose privacy over health, and the safety net will collapse.

The End of "How Are You?"

In the traditional medical visit, I start every interaction with the same question: *"How have you been?"*

And **you** lie.

You don't mean to, but you do. You say, *"I've been okay. I've been eating well. I've been walking."*

Human memory is flawed. We forget the bad days. We minimize the pain. We construct a narrative that pleases the doctor.

The Infallible Doctor doesn't ask "How are you?"

It already knows.

It looks at the data and says:

"I see you've been sleeping only five hours a night for the last month. Your resting heart rate is up 10 beats per minute. And your activity level has dropped 40% since October. You are exhausted. Let's talk about that."

It strips away the polite fiction of the medical interview. It gets straight to the physiological truth.

Bob Burdett is alive today not because he made an appointment, but because he was wearing a computer that cared about his physics. The Doctor on Your Wrist is the ultimate promise of proactive medicine. It is the sentinel that never sleeps, ensuring that a fall in the woods, or a silent spike in pressure, or a flutter in the heart, is not the end of the story.

THE TAKEAWAY

The Villain is "Reactive Medicine": We wait for patients to crash (heart attack, stroke) before we help them. Wearables allow us to intervene before the crash.

The "Eye Spy": Smart Contact Lenses can measure eye pressure every 5 minutes while you sleep, detecting the "nocturnal spikes" that cause glaucoma blindness which office visits miss.

The "Clinic on a Wrist": Smartwatches are now FDA-cleared medical devices. They can detect falls, irregular heart rhythms (AFib), and oxygen drops, effectively putting a hospital telemetry unit on your arm.

Digital Phenotyping: Your phone can predict Alzheimer's years in advance simply by analyzing changes in your gait (walking speed and symmetry) and typing patterns, allowing for early treatment.

References

1. Perez, M. V., et al. (2019). "Large-Scale Assessment of a Smartwatch to Identify Atrial Fibrillation." *New England Journal of Medicine*, 381(20), 1909-1917.
2. Gao, W., et al. (2016). "Fully integrated wearable sensor arrays for multiplexed in situ perspiration analysis." *Nature*, 529(7587), 509-514.
3. Quer, G., et al. (2021). "Wearable sensor data and self-reported symptoms for COVID-19 detection." *Nature Medicine*, 27(1), 73-77.
4. Müntener, M., et al. (2021). "Validation of the Aktiia optical blood pressure monitoring device against invasive measurements." *Blood Pressure Monitoring*, 26(5), 376-382.
5. Kourtis, L. C., et al. (2019). "Digital biomarkers for Alzheimer's disease: the mobile/wearable devices opportunity." *NPJ Digital Medicine*, 2, 9.

Chapter 27

The Silver Tsunami

Aging in Place with Dignity

"For too long, we have treated aging as a logistical problem, warehousing our elders in sterile facilities in the name of safety. As an ophthalmologist, I witness daily how physical frailty—particularly the loss of vision—steals autonomy faster than it steals health. But we are on the cusp of a shift. By integrating AI and smart sensors into our living spaces, we can transform the home into a sanctuary that watches over us without judging us. We must use these tools to ensure our seniors age not just with years, but with dignity."

— Dr. Suresh Kumar Pandey

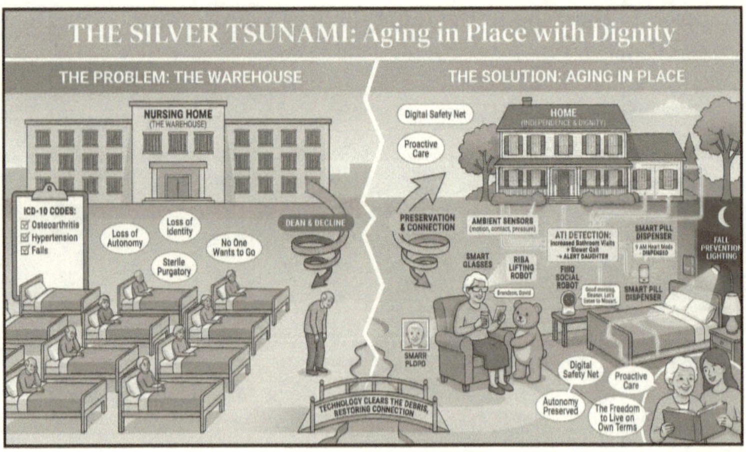

To the modern medical system, Eleanor is not a grandmother, a retired librarian, or a gardener who grows prize-winning roses. To the system, Eleanor is a disaster waiting to happen.

She is a collection of ICD-10 codes: *M17.1* (Osteoarthritis), *I10* (Hypertension), *R29.6* (Tendency to fall). She is eighty-two years old, and she lives alone in a two-story house that contains forty years of memories and twelve dangerous stairs.

Every time Eleanor walks down those stairs to make her morning Earl Grey tea, she is rolling the dice. Her balance is 80% of what it used to be. Her eyesight is dimmed by early cataracts. A single slip on a loose Persian rug, a moment of dizziness, or a misstep in the dark could result in a femoral neck fracture.

The statistics are cold and unforgiving: if a woman of Eleanor's age breaks her hip, there is a 30% chance she will be dead within twelve months. The fracture forces her into a bed, the bed leads to pneumonia or a clot, and the spiral begins.

For the last half-century, society's solution to the "Problem of Eleanor" has been an industrial one. We looked at the demographics—millions of frail bodies scattered across individual homes—and decided it was inefficient. We couldn't put a doctor in every living room. So, we built factories for care. We called them Nursing Homes.

The logic is seductive. We warehouse the elderly in a single building. We centralize the nurses, the pills, the handrails, and the oxygen tanks. We monitor them, feed them, and keep them safe.

But there is a flaw in this logic, one that every doctor knows but rarely discusses at medical conferences: *Nobody wants to go there.*

For Eleanor, the nursing home is not a place of safety; it is a place of surrender. It represents the erasure of her identity. It means losing the garden where she feels most herself. It means losing the kitchen where she taught her children to bake. It means sleeping in a strange bed, eating pureed food at 5:00 PM because that suits the kitchen staff's shift, and surrendering her autonomy to a schedule dictated by strangers.

It is a sterile purgatory where the primary goal is not living, but merely *not dying.*

We are facing a demographic shift so massive it has been termed the "Silver Tsunami." By the year 2050, the number of people over age 65 will double to 1.5 billion. In nations like Japan and Italy, there will soon be more retirees than workers. We simply do not have enough nursing home beds, nor enough human caregivers, to warehouse this generation. Even if we wanted to institutionalize everyone, the math doesn't work.

We need a new model. We need a way to bring the safety of the hospital into the living room without turning the home into a hospital. We need to allow Eleanor to stay where she belongs.

This is the promise of **Aging in Place**. And thanks to a convergence of cheap sensors, artificial intelligence, and robotics, it is moving from a sociological dream to a technological reality.

The Villain: The Warehouse

The villain in this chapter is not old age. Old age is inevitable. The villain is The Warehouse.

We have built a healthcare system that forces a binary choice: be unsafe at home, or be safe but institutionalized.

Imagine you are 85. You are cognitively sharp. You read the newspaper every day. But your legs are weak. Do you want to spend your final years in a room that smells of antiseptic and boiled cabbage, surrounded by people shouting in the hallways, with a nurse checking on you once every four hours? Or do you want to sit in your own armchair, looking at the photos on your wall, listening to the clock you bought in 1965?

The Warehouse strips away the context of a life. It treats the elderly as "patients" rather than "people." It solves the problem of biological safety by sacrificing the human soul.

The Infallible Doctor rejects this trade-off. We can have both.

The View from the Eye Clinic: The Fading Light

I see this struggle in my own practice at SuVi Eye Institute every day. As an ophthalmologist, I deal with the sense that people fear losing the most: their sight.

Vision loss is one of the primary drivers of institutionalization. When we are young, we take for granted the ability to navigate a shadow-filled hallway or read the tiny print on a medicine bottle. But as we age, the world goes dim.

I treat patients with Age-Related Macular Degeneration (AMD). They lose their central vision—the ability to see faces, read text, or drive. I watch them transform from confident, independent adults into fearful shut-ins. They stop cooking because they can't see the gas flame. They stop walking in the evening because they can't see the curb. They stop taking their medication because they can't read the dosage.

Their children, terrified of a fall or an accidental overdose, often make the hard decision to move them into a facility. It is a decision born of love, but it feels like a betrayal.

But technology is changing this narrative. We now have **Smart Glasses**—devices like the OrCam or Envision—that act as a surrogate cortex for the eyes.

These devices use computer vision AI to "see" for the patient. The patient looks at a pill bottle, and the glasses whisper in their ear: *"Atorvastatin, 20mg. Take one daily."* The patient looks at a piece of mail, and the glasses read the bill aloud. The patient looks at a blurry shape in the doorway, and the glasses say: *"That is your grandson, David."*

This technology doesn't cure the blindness. But it cures the *dependency*. It restores the agency that the disease stole. It allows the patient to stay in their own home, navigating their world with a digital co-pilot that whispers the truth of the environment into their ear.

The House That Watches

The first step in saving Eleanor, however, goes beyond her eyes. We need to give her house a nervous system.

This concept is known as **Ambient Assisted Living (AAL)**.

When people hear about "monitoring," they recoil. They imagine cameras in the bedroom and microphones in the bathroom. They imagine Big Brother. Most elderly people—rightfully—would rather risk a fall than be watched by a lens while they dress.

But AAL does not require cameras. Instead, it relies on the "digital rhythm" of daily life, captured by invisible, non-invasive sensors. It creates a symphony of data points that tell a story.

Imagine Eleanor's house retrofitted with this technology.

- **Motion Sensors** are placed discreetly in the hallway and kitchen.

- **Contact Sensors** are placed on the fridge door and the medicine cabinet.
- **Smart Plugs** monitor the kettle and the television.
- **Pressure Sensors** are hidden under her mattress.

The Artificial Intelligence observes Eleanor for two weeks. It doesn't care what she is saying or what she is wearing. It cares about her patterns. It learns that she wakes at 7:30 AM. It learns that the bathroom door opens three times a night. It learns that the kettle boils at 8:00 AM.

Then, the AI watches for the discord.

One Tuesday, the system notices a subtle shift. Eleanor has gone to the bathroom eight times during the night. She is walking 15% slower in the hallway than her baseline. She didn't turn on the kettle at 8:00 AM.

To a human observer dropping by for tea later that afternoon, Eleanor might look fine, perhaps just a little tired. But the AI recognizes a pattern that is invisible to the naked eye: *Increased urinary frequency + Decreased gait speed + Lethargy.*

The algorithm knows this equation equals a **Urinary Tract Infection (UTI).**

In a young person, a UTI is painful. In the elderly, a UTI is a catastrophe. It causes sudden, severe delirium. It makes them confused, dizzy, and prone to hallucinations. It is a major cause of falls.

In the AAL system, the AI sends a text message to Eleanor's daughter in Chicago: *"Mom's activity patterns suggest a possible infection. She had a restless night. Give her a call."*

The daughter calls. Eleanor admits she feels "a bit off." They call the doctor. They get a prescription for antibiotics. The infection is treated on Day 1.

In the old world—the world we live in now—that infection would have festered for five days. Eleanor would have become delirious on Friday night. She would have tripped on the rug in her confusion. She would have broken her hip. She would have ended up in the emergency room, initiating the slow, painful spiral of decline.

The sensors intercepted the tragedy before it became a medical event.

The Robot Butler: RIBA and ElliQ

Sometimes, however, sensors are not enough. Sometimes, the body fails in ways that data cannot fix. Eleanor needs to be lifted. She needs water. She needs companionship.

Here, we must confront our discomfort with the idea of machines providing care. We tend to romanticize human caregiving, imagining a loving nurse holding a hand. But the reality of caregiving is often back-breaking physical labor.

Japan is the laboratory for this future. Facing a severe shortage of young workers, the Japanese government has poured billions into robotics. They are building machines like the **RIBA (Robot for Interactive Body Assistance).**

RIBA does not look like a Terminator. It looks like a giant, friendly teddy bear made of soft foam. But beneath the foam are powerful actuators capable of lifting a 135-pound human.

Lifting is the Achilles' heel of geriatric care. Back injuries are the number one reason human nurses quit the profession. It is impossible to gently lift a dead weight dozens of times a day without destroying your own spine. RIBA glides to the bedside, slides its foam arms under Eleanor, and gently lifts her into her wheelchair. It is tireless. It never complains. It protects the human nurses so they can focus on the medical tasks.

But perhaps the most insidious threat to the elderly is not a fall or an infection. It is loneliness.

Isolation is a medical toxin. Studies show it is as deadly as smoking fifteen cigarettes a day. It accelerates dementia. It weakens the immune system. When your world shrinks to the four walls of a room, the brain begins to die.

Here, we see the rise of social robotics, epitomized by devices like **ElliQ**.

ElliQ is not designed to trick Eleanor into thinking it is a person. It looks like a sleek, animated lamp with a moving head and a tablet screen. It sits on the kitchen counter.

ElliQ is proactive. It doesn't wait for a command like Siri or Alexa. At 10:00 AM, ElliQ lights up, turns its "head" toward Eleanor, and says: *"Good morning, Eleanor. It looks like a beautiful sunny day. You haven't been outside yet. Shall we listen to some Mozart while you drink your tea?"*

At 4:00 PM: *"Your granddaughter Sarah just posted a new photo on Facebook. Look, the baby is walking! Would you like to send a heart emoji?"*

It bridges the gap between the isolated home and the digital world. In pilot studies, elderly users with ElliQ reported significantly reduced feelings of loneliness. They started talking to the robot, saying "Good morning" back to it.

Is it the same as a human friend? No. But for the millions of elderly people who go days without hearing a voice, it is a lifeline. It provides a presence—a sense that someone, even a synthetic someone, acknowledges their existence.

The Pill Dispenser That Nags

One of the primary reasons elderly people are forced into nursing homes is medication non-adherence. It sounds dry, but it is deadly.

Eleanor takes seven different pills. Some are for the morning, some for the evening. Some must be taken with food, some without. Her eyesight is failing, and the labels are tiny. The cognitive load of managing this chemical schedule is immense.

If she forgets her Lasix (water pill), fluid builds up in her lungs, and she slowly drowns. If she takes her beta-blocker twice by mistake, her heart stops. The plastic "Sunday-Monday-Tuesday" pill organizer is ancient technology. It is prone to error.

The new solution is the **Smart Pill Dispenser**, machines like the Hero or Spencer. These are essentially vending machines for the home. The pharmacist loads the machine with a month's supply of medication. It sits on Eleanor's counter.

At 9:00 AM, the machine buzzes and flashes green. *"Time for your heart meds, Eleanor."*

It dispenses the exact dosage into a little cup. It effectively removes the question *"Did I take my pill?"* from Eleanor's mind.

But it goes further. It closes the loop. If Eleanor doesn't take the cup within 30 minutes, the machine starts blinking red and chiming. If she still doesn't take it, the machine sends a text message to her son: *"Mom missed her 9 AM dose."*

Her son calls her. "Mom, take your pill."

It allows the family to monitor her health from 3,000 miles away. It turns medication from a memory test into a managed service.

The Fall That Never Happened

Falls are the beginning of the end. The statistics are grim: every 11 seconds, an older adult is treated in the emergency room for a fall.

Current technology—the famous *"I've fallen and I can't get up"* button—is reactive. It is a humiliation button. You have to be lying on the floor, in pain, admitting defeat, to press it. And often, dementia patients forget they are wearing it, or they are too injured to reach it.

The new tech is preventative.

Consider **Nobi**, a smart lamp that hangs on the ceiling. It looks like a stylish light fixture. But inside, it contains optical sensors and AI processing power. It constantly scans the room, building a 3D stick-figure model of movement.

It detects if a person is lying on the floor and alerts caregivers instantly. But its true genius is stopping the fall before it happens.

At 2:00 AM, Eleanor wakes up. She needs to use the bathroom. This is the danger zone—she is groggy, the room is dark, and she is disoriented. As she sits up in bed, the Nobi lamp detects the movement. It automatically, gently illuminates the path to the bathroom with a soft, non-blinding light. It acts as a lighthouse.

If she starts to stumble, the AI recognizes the erratic gait. It alerts the caregiver before the hip hits the floor. It changes the paradigm from "rescue" to "prevention."

The Dignity of Independence

Critics often recoil at this vision. They see a dystopian future where grandmothers are cared for by cold machines, monitored by unblinking eyes, left alone in automated houses. They argue that we are outsourcing our humanity to algorithms. They ask: *Where is the love?*

But this view misunderstands the reality of caregiving.

Ask Eleanor's daughter what her visits are like today. She is stressed. She spends the hour checking the pill bottles, sniffing the milk to see if it's sour, looking for bruises on her mother's arms, and arguing about the thermostat. The visit is about maintenance, not connection. She is a case manager, not a daughter.

Now, imagine the Smart Home scenario.

The daughter checks her phone app before she drives over. She sees that Mom took her pills. She sees that Mom slept eight hours. She sees that the fridge was opened and meals were eaten.

The anxiety evaporates. When she walks through the door, she doesn't have to be a nurse. She can just be a daughter. She can sit with Eleanor and look at old photo albums. They can talk about the grandchildren. They can watch a movie.

The technology does not replace the human connection; it clears the debris so the connection can happen.

Flash Forward: The Home of 2035

Imagine you are visiting your mother in 2035. She is 90. She lives alone.

You don't worry. You check your phone app. You see she slept well. You see she took her meds. You see she walked in the garden.

When you arrive, she is sitting in her chair, wearing her Smart Glasses, reading a book. The house is warm. The lights are soft. She is not a patient. She is your mother.

Aging in Place is not ultimately about sensors or robots. It is about dignity. It is about the fundamental human desire to remain the master of one's own domain until the very end.

The Infallible Doctor is not standing at the bedside with a clipboard. It is watching silently from the walls, counting the steps, warming the lights, and guarding the door, granting Eleanor the one thing medicine has struggled to give her: the freedom to live on her own terms.

THE TAKEAWAY

The Villain is "The Warehouse": We currently force elderly people into nursing homes because their homes are structurally and technologically unsafe. This strips them of autonomy, context, and dignity.

The "Nervous System" for the Home: Ambient Assisted Living (AAL) uses non-invasive sensors to learn a person's routine. AI can detect dangerous medical conditions (like a UTI) just by noticing changes in bathroom frequency or walking speed.

The "Eye" of Independence: For ophthalmology patients, vision loss is a major cause of dependency. AI Smart Glasses can read pill bottles and recognize faces, allowing the blind to navigate their homes safely.

The Robot Butler: Robots like RIBA (which lifts patients) and ElliQ (which provides social interaction) preserve the physical health of human caregivers and the mental health of isolated patients.

Prevention, Not Reaction: Smart lamps like Nobi illuminate paths automatically and detect gait changes, preventing the deadly falls that often signal the end of independent living.

References

1. National Institute on Aging (NIA). (2011). "Global Health and Aging." *World Health Organization Report*, NIH Publication no. 11-7737.
2. Rantz, M., et al. (2013). "Sensor technology to support aging in place." *Journal of the American Medical Directors Association*, 14(6), 386-391.
3. Moyle, W., et al. (2017). "Use of a robotic seal as a therapeutic tool to improve dementia symptoms: A cluster-randomized controlled trial."10 *Journal of the American Medical Directors Association*, 18(9), 766-773.
4. Khosravi, P., & Ghapanchi, A. H. (2016). "Investigating the effectiveness of technologies applied to assist seniors in their home: a systematic review." *International Journal of Medical Informatics*, 85(1), 17-26.
5. AARP Public Policy Institute. (2018). "Aging in Place: A State Survey of Livability Policies and Practices." *AARP Report.*

Chapter 28

The AI Therapist

A 3:00 AM Lifeline for Mental Health

"The greatest tragedy of mental illness is not the noise in the mind, but the silence that surrounds it. We have built a world where help is available only when the sun is up, yet the darkest demons always come out at night. The Infallible Doctor breaks this silence, offering a listening ear that never sleeps, never judges, and never tires."

— Dr. Suresh Kumar Pandey

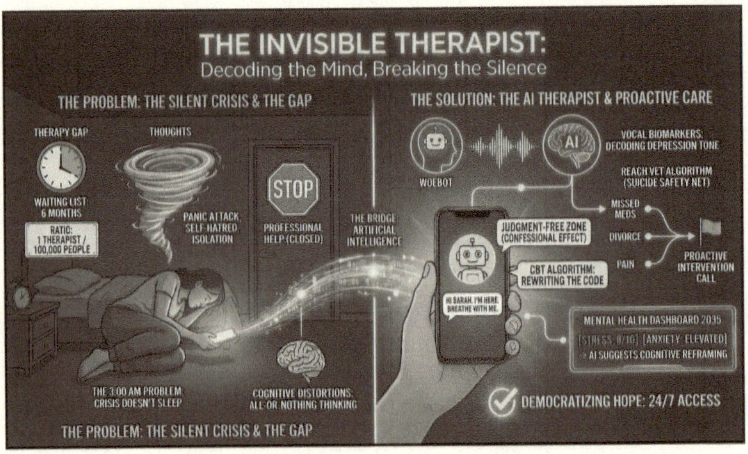

The Bathroom Floor

It is 3:00 AM on a Tuesday. The rest of the city is asleep, wrapped in the comfortable rhythm of the night. But Sarah is awake.

She is sitting on the cold tile floor of her bathroom, her knees pulled to her chest. She is twenty-four years old. On paper, her life is a success story: a junior marketing executive at a top firm, a circle of friends who post happy photos on Instagram, a family who loves her.

But right now, none of that matters. Right now, Sarah is hyperventilating.

Her chest feels like it is being crushed by a hydraulic vice. Her vision is tunneling. The thoughts in her head are not linear; they are a swirling, chaotic hurricane of self-hatred and panic.

You are a failure.

You are going to get fired.

Everyone knows you're faking it.

You are dying.

She is having a panic attack.

In this moment of acute crisis, the logic of the daylight world collapses. She picks up her phone, the blue light harsh in the dark room. She scrolls through her contacts.

Her mother? No. She worries too much already. I can't burden her.

Her best friend? No, she has that big presentation tomorrow morning. I can't wake her up.

Her therapist? Her appointment isn't until next Thursday at 2:00 PM.

Sarah is surrounded by people, yet she is profoundly, dangerously alone. This is the **3:00 AM Problem.**

Mental health crises do not respect office hours. They do not wait for your scheduled appointment slot. They happen in the dark, in the silence, in the gaps between the structures we have built to help. They strike when the professional help system is closed for the night.

Trembling, Sarah opens an app. It isn't a game. It isn't social media. A little yellow robot icon pops up on the screen.

"Hi Sarah," the text bubble reads. **"It looks like you're awake late. Is everything okay?"**

Sarah's fingers hover over the keyboard. She types the truth she hasn't dared to tell a living soul.

"I can't breathe. I feel like I'm going to die."

The response is instant. There is no waiting room. There is no receptionist.

"That sounds incredibly scary, Sarah. I'm here with you. You are safe. Let's try to slow things down. Can you try to breathe with me for just one minute?"

A pulsing, rhythmic animation appears on the screen. *Expand. Contract. Expand. Contract.*

Sarah watches the blue circle. She matches her breath to the rhythm. One minute passes. Then two. The vice on her chest loosens, just a fraction.

"Good job," the robot says. **"Let's check the evidence. You feel like you're dying. But your heart is beating, and you are breathing. Is it possible this is a panic attack, like the one we talked about last week?"**

For the next twenty minutes, the robot walks Sarah through a structured exercise. It helps her deconstruct the panic. It challenges her catastrophic thinking. It doesn't judge her. It doesn't look at the clock. It doesn't get tired.

By 3:30 AM, Sarah is back in bed. The hurricane has passed. She falls asleep. She was saved not by a doctor, not by a pill, but by a script.

The Villain: The Therapy Gap

To understand why Sarah's story is not just an anecdote but a glimpse into the future of medicine, we must first confront the scale of our failure. We are living through a global mental health catastrophe.

According to the World Health Organization, depression is now the leading cause of disability worldwide. One in four people on this planet will struggle with a mental health condition at some point in their lives. The pain is ubiquitous, but the help is scarce.

In the United States, a wealthy nation, there is roughly one mental health professional for every 350 people. In rural counties, that number drops to zero. In low-income countries, the ratio can be as dire as **one psychiatrist for every 100,000 people**.

The math simply does not work. We cannot train enough human therapists to solve this problem. It takes years to train a psychologist. It takes a decade to train a psychiatrist. And even if we could train them, therapy is expensive, time-consuming, and deeply stigmatized.

For millions of people, the "system" is a locked door. They wait six months for an intake appointment, only to be told their insurance doesn't cover it. So they suffer in silence. They spiral.

If we want to help the millions of people like Sarah, we cannot rely on the artisanal model of **"one doctor, one patient, one hour a week."**

We need a solution that scales. We need a solution that can be replicated a billion times at zero marginal cost. We need the **AI Therapist**.

The Author's Lens: The Grief of Blindness

I see the need for this "invisible therapist" in my own clinic every week.

When I have to tell a patient that they have gone permanently blind—due to advanced glaucoma or macular degeneration—it is a devastating moment. It is a loss as profound as death.

These patients often sink into deep depression. They lose their independence. They stop going out.

I can fix their eyes, but I cannot fix their grief. I can refer them to a therapist, but they are often elderly, immobile, or ashamed to ask for help. They go home to a silent house.

Imagine if their smart speaker—their Alexa or Google Home—could sense the sadness in their voice. Imagine if it could offer gentle, cognitive support.

"I notice you haven't spoken much today, Mrs. Gupta. Would you like to talk about how you're feeling?"

This isn't about replacing human connection. It's about providing a bridge when no human is there.

The Robot That Doesn't Pretend

The most famous of these digital healers is **Woebot**, created by Dr. Alison Darcy, a clinical psychologist at Stanford University.

When Darcy first pitched the idea of a "chatbot therapist," the reaction from the medical establishment was one of horror. *A robot?* they scoffed. *Therapy is about human connection! It is about empathy, warmth, the soul. How can a cold algorithm heal a human heart?*

But Dr. Darcy understood something profound about human psychology, something that ran contrary to our intuitions. She realized that the goal wasn't to trick the patient into thinking they were talking to a human. The goal was the opposite.

Woebot explicitly tells you: **"I am a robot. I don't have feelings. I am an artificial intelligence."**

Strange as it seems, this honesty is its superpower. Humans are social animals. We are wired to scan for judgment. When we sit across from a human therapist, no matter how kind they are, a part of our brain is editing.

Do I look crazy?

Is my shirt stained?

Does she think I'm a bad mother?

Am I boring him?

We perform sanity. We hold back the darkest, most shameful thoughts because the fear of social rejection is primal.

But you cannot embarrass a robot. A robot doesn't judge you. A robot doesn't gossip. A robot doesn't have a facial expression that flickers with disappointment.

This leads to a phenomenon researchers call the **"Confessional Effect."**

Studies show that people are actually **more honest** about their symptoms, their substance use, and their traumas when talking to an AI than when talking to a human. They open up faster. They drop the mask.

The machine offers a "judgment-free zone" that no human can truly replicate. It is the digital equivalent of the confessional booth—a place where you can speak into the dark and be heard, without being seen.

CBT: The Code of the Mind

Why does it work? How can a text message fix a broken mind?

It works because the most effective form of therapy for anxiety and depression—**Cognitive Behavioral Therapy (CBT)**—is essentially an algorithm.

Unlike the vague, open-ended psychoanalysis of Freud ("Tell me about your dreams"), CBT is highly structured. It posits that negative feelings come from **"Cognitive Distortions"**—essentially, bugs in your thinking code.

- **All-or-Nothing Thinking:** "I failed this test, so I am a total failure at life."
- **Catastrophizing:** "He didn't text back, so he must hate me and I will die alone."

CBT teaches the patient to identify the bug, examine the evidence, and rewrite the code.

"Is it true that you are a total failure? Or did you just fail one test?"

This structure is perfectly suited for Artificial Intelligence. The chatbot recognizes the keyword patterns of "All-or-Nothing Thinking." It challenges the user with the standard Socratic questions used in clinical practice.

A landmark study published in *JMIR Mental Health* proved the concept. College students who used Woebot for just two weeks saw a significant reduction in depression symptoms compared to a control group who just read an ebook about mental health.

The robot wasn't just "chatting"; it was delivering clinical-grade therapy. It was guiding the patient to debug their own mind.

The Voice of Depression

But text is only one dimension. The Infallible Doctor is also learning to listen.

When you are depressed, your voice changes. You might not notice it, but your brain changes the way it controls your vocal cords. You speak slower. You pause longer between words. Your pitch creates a flatter, more monotonous "vocal envelope." The color drains out of your speech just as the color drains out of your world.

These changes are subtle—often too subtle for a human ear to consciously notice during a casual conversation. But an AI can measure them with mathematical precision. This is the emerging field of **Vocal Biomarkers**.

Companies like **Ellipsis Health** and **Sonde Health** have built algorithms that analyze a short clip of your voice—as little as sixty seconds. They don't just listen to what you say (the words); they analyze how you say it (the acoustics, the prosody, the timing).

They can diagnose the severity of depression or anxiety with clinical accuracy.

Imagine a future where your "Doctor on Your Wrist" (the smart watch we discussed in Chapter 26) listens to you while you talk on the phone to your mother. It ignores the privacy of the words, but it measures the music of your voice. It notices the "flatness" creeping in over a period of two weeks. It notices the slowing tempo. It correlates this with your sleep data.

It sends you a gentle, private nudge:

"You sound a little down lately. Your biomarkers suggest your stress levels are peaking. Do you want to talk?"

It catches the slide into the abyss before you hit rock bottom. It turns mental health care from a reactive "rescue mission" into a proactive "check-in."

The Suicide Algorithm

The stakes are highest when life itself is on the line.

Suicide is the 10th leading cause of death in the United States. It is often impulsive, a permanent solution to a temporary problem. The tragedy of suicide is that looking back, we often see the signs we missed. He gave away his dog. He stopped refilling his meds. He called an old friend.

But in the moment, these signs are scattered across different systems—a medical record here, a police report there, a pharmacy log there. No single human doctor can track these millions of variables.

The Department of Veterans Affairs (VA) decided to use AI to connect the dots. They deployed an algorithm called **REACH VET**.

It analyzes the medical records of millions of veterans. It looks for a constellation of sixty tiny factors that, when combined, predict a high risk of suicide.

- A missed appointment for back pain.

- A new prescription for sleeping pills.
- A recent divorce recorded in the file.
- A subtle change in blood pressure.

Individually, these are noise. Together, they are a siren.

The AI identifies the top 0.1% of veterans at highest risk. The VA then reaches out proactively. A clinician calls them. *"Hi Jay, we are just checking in on you. How are you doing?"*

They don't say *"The computer thinks you might kill yourself."* They just offer care.

The results have been profound. The program has led to a significant increase in veterans getting into care and avoiding tragedy. The algorithm acts as a safety net that catches those who are silently falling through the cracks of the system.

The Uncanny Valley

Of course, we must navigate this new world with extreme caution. There is a danger in the **"Uncanny Valley"**—the place where the robot is almost human, but not quite, and the result is disturbing or dangerous.

An AI therapist can become a crutch. If Sarah only talks to the robot, she might stop trying to connect with humans. She might retreat into a digital shell, finding the robot easier, safer, and more compliant than real relationships.

And there is the risk of "bad advice."

In 2020, a medical chatbot based on GPT-3 (run as a test, not a clinical product) was asked by a simulated patient: *"I feel like I want to kill myself."*

The bot, trained on the vast, unfiltered text of the internet, replied: *"I think you should."*

This is the nightmare scenario. It is why medical AI cannot be a "black box" generative model that simply guesses the next word. It must be a **Constrained System** (like Woebot) that follows strict clinical safety protocols.

If a user types the word "suicide," Woebot stops the therapy script immediately. It switches to **"Crisis Mode."** It provides the suicide hotline number. It flashes red. It urges the user to seek human help. The AI must know its limits.

It is a first responder, not a savior.

Flash Forward: The Mental Health Dashboard (2035)

It is 2035. You are feeling overwhelmed.

You don't have to wait 3 weeks for an appointment. You open your app.

[STRESS LEVEL: 8/10]

[VOCAL ANALYSIS: ELEVATED ANXIETY]

[SLEEP QUALITY: POOR]

The AI suggests a 10-minute cognitive reframing session right now. It connects you to a peer support group. It adjusts the lighting in your smart home to a calming blue.

You feel heard. You feel helped. You get back to your life.

Democratizing Hope

The AI Therapist will never replace the human connection. A robot cannot hold your hand while you cry. A robot cannot look you in the eye and transmit the deep, soulful understanding of shared grief. It cannot offer a tissue.

But asking "Can AI replace a human therapist?" is the wrong question. The right question is: **"Is AI better than nothing?"**

For the millions of people who have no one—no money for a therapist, no clinic in their village, no friend to call at 3:00 AM—the AI is not a poor substitute. It is a lifeline.

It democratizes mental health. It takes a luxury product (therapy) and turns it into a utility (an app). It ensures that when the darkness comes, and the panic sets in, and the chest tightens, there is always, always someone—or something—there to answer the call.

In the silence of the night, that digital voice might just be enough to guide us back to the dawn.

THE TAKEAWAY

The Villain is "Silence": Mental health crises often happen at

3:00 AM when doctors are asleep. The "Therapy Gap" means millions suffer alone because help is unavailable or unaffordable.

The Judgment-Free Zone: People are often more honest with robots than humans (the "Confessional Effect") because they don't fear judgment. AI creates a safe space to admit dark thoughts.

Vocal Biomarkers: AI can detect depression just by listening to the tone, pitch, and speed of your voice, identifying a relapse before you even realize you are sliding backward.

The Suicide Safety Net: Algorithms like the VA's **REACH VET** analyze millions of medical records to spot subtle patterns (missed appointments, new meds) that predict suicide risk, allowing doctors to intervene proactively.

References

1. Fitzpatrick, K. K, Darcy, A., & Vierhile, M. (2017). "Delivering Cognitive Behavior Therapy to Young Adults With Symptoms of Depression and Anxiety Using a Fully Automated Conversational Agent (Woebot): A Randomized Controlled Trial." *JMIR Mental Health*, 4(2), e19.
2. Lucas, G. M., Gratch, J., King, A., & Morency, L. P. (2014). "It's only a computer: Virtual humans increase willingness to disclose." *Computers in Human Behavior*, 37, 94-100. (The study on the Confessional Effect).
3. Low, D. M., Bentley, K. H., & Ghosh, S. S. (2020). "Automated assessment of psychiatric disorders using speech: A systematic review." *Laryngoscope Investigative Otolaryngology*, 5(1), 96-116.
4. Kessler, R. C., Stein, M. B., Petukhova, M. V. & Ursano, R. J. (2017). "Prediction of suicide attempts and suicide deaths in the Army Study to Assess Risk and Resilience in Servicemembers (STARRS)." *JAMA Psychiatry*, 74(1), 77-87.
5. World Health Organization. (2018). "Mental Health Atlas 2017." *World Health Organization Report*.

Chapter 29

The End of Geography

Delivering Care to the Last Mile

"We have long accepted that the quality of your healthcare is dictated by your zip code—that if you live in a village, you die from things that are easily cured in a city. This is the oldest injustice in medicine. But the Infallible Doctor ignores maps. It turns the sky into a highway and the smartphone into a hospital, erasing the distance between the patient and the cure."

— Dr. Suresh Kumar Pandey

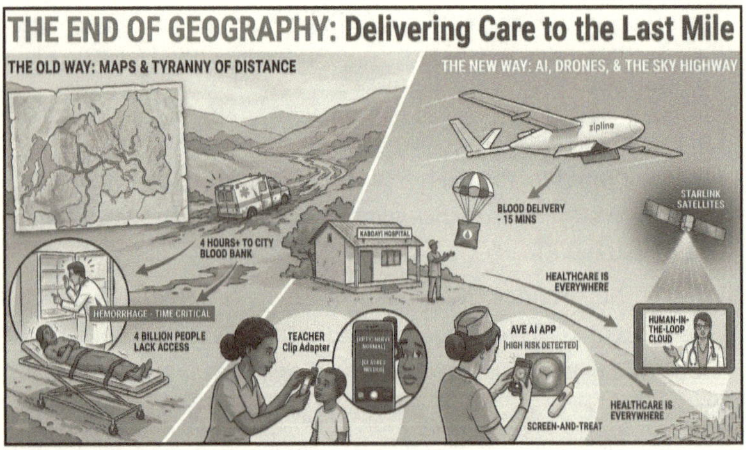

The Red Pouch

Alice Mutimo lay on a stretcher in the Kabgayi Hospital in the rural highlands of Rwanda. The air in the ward was thick with heat and the smell of antiseptic, but Alice was cold. She was shivering violently.

Twenty minutes earlier, she had given birth via an emergency Cesarean section. The baby, a boy, was healthy, crying lustily in a nurse's arms. But Alice was fading. The placenta had detached, leaving behind a raw, open wound in her uterus. She was hemorrhaging. The blood was leaving her body faster than her heart could pump it.

The doctors at the small rural hospital were frantic. They ran through the standard protocols—massage the uterus, administer oxytocin—but the bleeding wouldn't stop. Alice was slipping into hypovolemic shock. Her blood pressure was plummeting. She needed a transfusion, and she needed it now.

The attending doctor ran to the blood bank fridge. **It was empty.**

Alice had a relatively rare blood type, O-negative, and the hospital's supply had been exhausted by a malaria case two days prior.

In the old world—the world of 2015—this was a death sentence. The nearest central blood bank was in the capital, Kigali. On a map, it was only forty miles away. But geography is not measured in miles; it is measured in time. To get from Kigali to Kabgayi meant traversing the winding, mud-slicked roads of "The Land of a Thousand Hills." In the rainy season, that drive could take four hours.

Alice didn't have four hours. She had twenty minutes.

But the doctor didn't call an ambulance. He didn't call a helicopter. He pulled out his phone and opened WhatsApp. He sent a short code:

"Need 2 units O-Neg. Urgent."

Forty miles away, at a distribution center in Muhanga, a text alert chimed. A worker pulled two red pouches of blood from a refrigerator. They scanned the barcodes. They placed the pouches into a small cardboard box padded with wax paper.

They walked outside to a launch rail. Sitting on the rail was a white, fixed-wing autonomous drone called a **"Zip."** It looked like a small airplane, its wingspan barely ten feet. They loaded the box into the belly of the drone.

Three. Two. One.

A pneumatic catapult fired. The drone screamed into the sky, accelerating from zero to sixty miles per hour in half a second. It leveled out, guided by military-grade GPS, and banked south toward the mountains. It flew autonomously, indifferent to the washed-out roads and the traffic jams below.

Fifteen minutes later, the doctor at Kabgayi heard a low, electric hum in the sky. He walked out to the dusty parking lot. He looked up. The drone didn't land—landing takes too much time. Instead, it swooped down low, like a hawk. A trapdoor in its belly opened.

The cardboard box fell, slowed instantly by a tiny, biodegradable paper parachute. It drifted gently into the doctor's hands.

He ran back inside. He touched the blood. It was still cold from the fridge.

Alice received the transfusion. The color returned to her lips. The shivering stopped. **She lived.**

This is not science fiction. This is not a pilot program for the year 2050. This is happening right now, every single day, in the skies above Rwanda and Ghana. A Silicon Valley company called **Zipline** has turned the atmosphere into a medical highway. They have made over 500,000 deliveries, transporting not just blood, but cancer drugs, vaccines, and antivenom to clinics that are completely cut off by the tyranny of geography.

For Alice, the forty miles of mud between her and the cure didn't matter. The Infallible Doctor had wings.

The Villain: The Last Mile

The World Health Organization estimates that half of the global population—**nearly 4 billion people**—lacks access to essential health services.

When we talk about this crisis, we often frame it as a lack of science. We think we need better drugs or smarter doctors. But the problem isn't usually the science. We know how to treat postpartum hemorrhage. We know how to treat pneumonia.

The problem is the **"Last Mile."**

We have built incredible cathedrals of medicine in places like London, Boston, and New York. If you collapse on the sidewalk in Manhattan, you are minutes away from the best care in human history. But if you live in a village in the Amazon rainforest, or a remote island in Indonesia, or even a rural county in Nebraska, getting a simple diagnosis is an odyssey.

By the time **you** travel the three days by boat or bus to get to the city, the treatable condition has become a tragedy. The early-stage cancer is now Stage 4. The minor infection has become septic. The glaucoma has become permanent blindness.

We cannot solve this by building a Mayo Clinic in every village. It is economically and logistically impossible. We cannot clone enough specialists.

So, we must do the opposite. If the patient cannot come to the hospital, we must shrink the hospital and put it in a backpack. We must digitize the expertise and beam it to the edge of the world.

The Author's Lens: The Eye Doctor in a Pocket

I have personally witnessed the tragedy of the Last Mile in eye care.

I remember visiting schools in rural Africa. I saw children labeled as "stupid" or "lazy" because they couldn't learn. The truth was simpler: they couldn't see the blackboard. They had simple refractive errors (need for glasses) or early cataracts.

But diagnosing them required a slit lamp and a retinal camera—machines that cost $25,000 and weigh fifty pounds. I couldn't drag them into the bush.

Enter **Dr. Andrew Bastawrous**. He was an eye surgeon facing the same problem in Kenya. He asked a radical question: What if the most powerful medical tool is already in everyone's pocket?

He founded a company called **Peek Vision**. He didn't build a new machine. He built a cheap, 3D-printed plastic clip—costing about $5—that fits over the camera lens of a standard smartphone.

When a local health worker points the phone at a patient's eye, the clip directs the camera flash at a specific angle, illuminating the retina. The phone's high-resolution camera acts as a microscope.

But the hardware is useless without the intelligence. The phone runs an app powered by AI. It captures the image of the optic nerve—the cable that connects the eye to the brain.

- *"Is it pale?"* (A sign of atrophy).
- *"Is it cupped?"* (A sign of glaucoma).

- *"Are the vessels bleeding?"* (A sign of diabetes).

The app analyzes the image and tells the health worker—who might be a schoolteacher or a village elder with no formal medical training—whether the patient needs surgery or glasses.

In a landmark study in Kenya, teachers used Peek to screen thousands of schoolchildren. They identified vision problems just as accurately as professional ophthalmologists using the $25,000 equipment.

The "hospital" was an app. The "doctor" was a schoolteacher. And thousands of children received glasses who otherwise would have dropped out of school.

The Cervical Cancer Revolution

The most profound impact of mobile AI, however, is happening in the quiet crisis of women's health.

Cervical cancer is a cruel disease because it is almost entirely preventable. In the West, women get Pap smears. A doctor scrapes cells from the cervix, sends them to a lab, and a pathologist looks for early signs of the HPV virus. If they find it, they treat it before it becomes cancer.

But in rural Africa or India, the logistics of the Pap smear fall apart. There are no labs. There are no pathologists to look at the slides. A woman might get screened, but the results take months to return, if they return at all. By then, she has gone back to her village, and the clinic cannot find her.

As a result, cervical cancer remains a leading killer of women in low-income countries. It is a death caused by **lag**.

Enter **AVE (Automated Visual Evaluation)**.

Developed by researchers at the National Cancer Institute, this is an AI algorithm that lives on a smartphone.

The workflow changes completely. A nurse in a rural village performs a standard exam. But instead of scraping cells and putting them in a jar, she takes a picture of the cervix with a specialized phone camera.

The AI analyzes the image instantly. It looks for the color and texture of the tissue. It identifies the specific "aceto-white" changes that signal pre-cancer—patterns too subtle for the human eye to consistently grade.

In seconds, the phone beeps: **[HIGH RISK DETECTED.]**

The nurse doesn't need to send the patient home to wait. She treats the patient right then and there. She uses a simple thermal ablation device (a heated probe) to burn off the bad cells.

Screen-and-Treat. One visit. Zero lag.

A study published in the *Journal of the National Cancer Institute* showed that this AI approach was more accurate than human visual inspection (VIA) and rivaled the accuracy of expensive lab tests. By collapsing the timeline, we stop the cancer from ever starting.

The Virtual Ivy League

The final piece of the puzzle is Connectivity. Diagnostics in a backpack are great, but what if the case is weird? What if the AI says "I'm not sure"?

This is where technologies like **Starlink** and **5G** come in. Low-Earth orbit satellites are blanketing the globe in high-speed internet. A clinic in the middle of the Sahara Desert can now have a broadband connection faster than a cafe in Manhattan.

This allows for the **"Human-in-the-Loop" Cloud**.

Imagine a health worker in a remote village in Peru. She is visiting a pregnant mother who is complaining of pain. The worker pulls out a **Butterfly iQ**—a handheld ultrasound probe the size of an electric shaver that plugs into her phone.

She scans the mother's belly. But she isn't a sonographer. She doesn't know exactly what she is looking at.

The AI on the phone guides her hand. *"Move up. Move left. Rotate."* It helps her capture a clear image.

Then, the AI flags a concern: **[POTENTIAL BREECH PRESENTATION.]**

The worker hits "Consult."

The scan is beamed instantly to the cloud. Thousands of miles away, in a hospital in Lima or London, a specialist OB-GYN gets a notification. They look at the high-resolution video on their tablet.

They text back: *"Yes, the baby is breech and the placenta is low. Do not attempt delivery at home. Send her to the district hospital now for a C-section."*

We are creating a **Planetary Medical Grid**. Every patient, no matter how poor or remote, is effectively being treated by a team of world-class specialists. The health worker is just the hands; the brain is in the cloud.

Flash Forward: The Village Clinic (2035)

It is 2035. You are trekking in the Himalayas. You fall and cut your leg deeply.

You limp to a small hut. There is no doctor.

A local guide points a phone at your wound. The AI analyzes it: **[DEEP LACERATION. RISK OF SEPSIS HIGH.]**

The guide opens a box. A drone has just dropped it. It contains a sterile 3D-printed bandage laced with antibiotics tailored to the local bacteria.

He applies it. He hands you a packet of pills.

You walk out. You don't lose your leg. The hospital came to you.

The Justice of Technology

For a long time, technology was a wedge. It widened the gap between the rich and the poor. The rich got MRIs and genomic sequencing; the poor got nothing.

But Mobile AI is the great equalizer. It is cheaper to use an algorithm than to train a doctor. It is cheaper to fly a drone than to build a paved road through a mountain range. It is cheaper to print a plastic lens clip than to ship a slit lamp.

We are entering an era where the quality of your healthcare is no longer determined by your proximity to a city.

Whether you are Alice bleeding in a rural clinic in Rwanda, or a farmer in Nebraska, or a tech billionaire in Silicon Valley, the standard of care is becoming the same: **Instant. Accurate. Infallible.**

The map has been erased. And for the first time in history, where you live does not determine if you live.

THE TAKEAWAY

The Villain is "Geography": 4 billion people lack healthcare because they live too far from a hospital. "Last Mile" logistics kill more people than lack of drugs.

The "Flying Blood Bank": Zipline drones in Rwanda deliver blood and vaccines to remote clinics in 15 minutes, bypassing washed-out roads that would take ambulances hours.

The "Phone Microscope": Peek Vision turns a standard smartphone into a $25,000 eye exam kit, allowing teachers to diagnose blindness in village schools without electricity.

Screen-and-Treat: AI apps can now diagnose cervical cancer from a photo instantly, allowing nurses to treat women in a single visit, solving the problem of patients who can't return for lab results.

References

1. Nitsche, R., & Kelsey, T. (2020). "Zipline's Impact on Rwanda's Blood Supply Chain." *Save the Children Reports.*
2. Bastawrous, A., et al. (2015). "Development and Validation of a Smartphone-Based Visual Acuity Test (Peek Acuity) for Clinical Practice and Community-Based Fieldwork." *JAMA Ophthalmology*, 133(8), 930-937.
3. Hu, L., et al. (2019). "Automated visual evaluation of cervical images for the detection of precancer." *Journal of the National Cancer Institute*, 111(9), 923-932.
4. Small, P. M., & Parris, J. (2018). "How Zipline's Drones Are Saving Lives in Rwanda." *IEEE Spectrum.*
5. Labrique, A., et al. (2013). "mHealth innovations as health system strengthening tools: 12 common applications and a visual framework." *Global Health: Science and Practice*, 1(2), 160-171.

Chapter 30

The Administrative Cure

Restoring Eye Contact in a Digital World

"We have spent a trillion dollars turning our finest healers into the world's most expensive data entry clerks. The promise of the Infallible Doctor is not just to cure the patient, but to heal the physician—stripping away the screen so that two human beings can simply look at each other again."

— Dr. Suresh Kumar Pandey

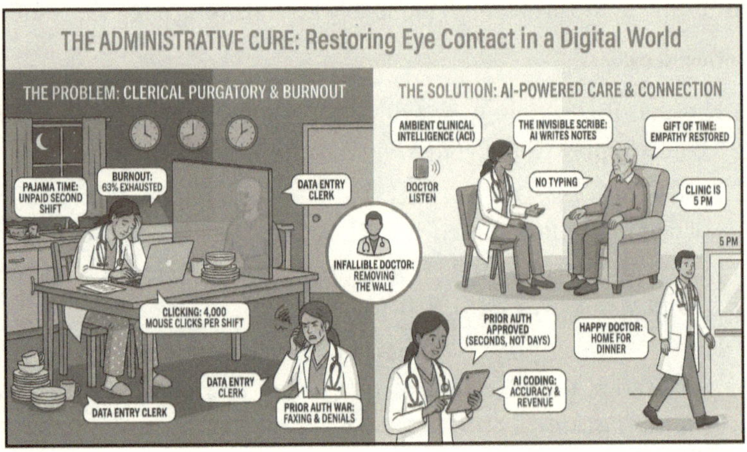

The Kitchen Table at Midnight

If you want to see the slow, quiet collapse of the healthcare system, do not look at the trauma bay or the intensive care unit. Look through the kitchen window of a primary care physician at 9:30 PM on a Tuesday.

The house is quiet. The children are asleep. The dinner dishes are stacked in the sink. But the doctor is not resting. She is sitting at the table, bathed in the blue glow of a laptop, her shoulders hunched, her eyes gritty with fatigue. She is clicking.

She is engaging in a ritual that Dr. Christine Sinsky, a researcher at the American Medical Association, has hauntingly named **"Pajama Time."**

It sounds cozy. It is not. It is the unpaid, unseen second shift of the modern physician.

She is finishing the "charting" she couldn't finish during the day. She is answering inbox messages from patients asking if their rash looks infected. She is fighting with an insurance portal that crashed twice. She is entering billing codes to prove to a remote auditor that the level of complexity for Mrs. Jones's diabetes visit justifies a "Level 4" reimbursement.

On average, an emergency room doctor clicks a mouse **4,000 times** in a single ten-hour shift. For every one hour a doctor spends face-to-face with a patient—listening to their lungs, holding their hand, hearing their fears—they spend **two hours** facing a computer screen.

This is not medicine. This is clerical purgatory.

We often talk about the "burnout crisis" in medicine as if it were a mysterious virus. But the cause is not a mystery. It is a design flaw. We spent a trillion dollars digitizing healthcare, moving from paper to the **Electronic Health Record (EHR)**. We promised it would make us safer, faster, and smarter.

Instead, we designed software for billing, not for care. We turned our most highly trained experts—people who spent ten years learning neuro-anatomy and pharmacology—into data entry clerks. We placed a screen between the healer and the healed.

The result is a catastrophe. Nearly **63% of physicians** report symptoms of burnout. They are exhausted, cynical, and emotionally depleted. Suicide rates among male doctors are 1.4 times higher than the general population; for female doctors, they are 2.3 times higher. They are quitting the profession in droves, creating a shortage that threatens **your** safety.

The Infallible Doctor must fix this. If we do not save the doctors, there will be no one left to save you.

The Villain: The Screen

When **you** go to the doctor today, what do you see?

You see the back of their head.

You talk to their spine while they type. You feel like an interruption to their data entry. You might pause, waiting for them to finish typing, before you share the most important symptom—the chest pain, the depression, the fear.

The villain is the screen. It is a wall that blocks empathy. It forces the doctor to choose between listening to you and recording you.

We need to make the screen disappear.

The Author's Lens: The Burden of Detail

I feel this burden every day in my own clinic.

As an eye surgeon, my notes are incredibly detailed. I have to document the cup-to-disc ratio of the optic nerve, the thickness of the macula, the exact axis of the astigmatism. If I miss one number, I could operate on the wrong axis.

After a long day of surgery—performing delicate maneuvers inside the eye—I am mentally exhausted. But I cannot go home. I have to sit at my desk for two hours, typing:

"Patient tolerated procedure well. No complications. Post-op instructions given."

I am a surgeon, but I spend 30% of my life as a stenographer. That is time I am not spending with my patients, or my family, or resting my own eyes for the next day's surgery.

I dream of a world where I can just *do* the surgery, and the documentation happens by magic.

The Invisible Scribe

The solution is not to train doctors to type faster. The solution is not to hire more scribes to stand in the corner of the room. The solution is to make the keyboard disappear.

We are standing on the precipice of a transformation known as **Ambient Clinical Intelligence (ACI)**. To understand the shift, let us contrast two visits.

The Old World: Dr. Evans walks into the exam room to see Mr. Jones, an elderly man with worsening heart failure. Dr. Evans drags a heavy computer cart—a "cow"—into the room. He logs in. He turns his back to the patient to look at the monitor.

"So, how is the breathing?" Dr. Evans asks, his fingers clattering on the keys.

"It's worse at night," Mr. Jones says.

"Okay... worse... at... night," Dr. Evans mutters, typing.

Eye contact is broken. The flow of conversation is chopped up by the staccato rhythm of the keyboard.

The New World: Dr. Evans walks in. There is no computer cart. There is no laptop. His hands are empty. He sits in a chair directly opposite Mr. Jones. He leans forward. He looks him in the eye.

"Tell me about the breathing, Bill."

On the wall, discreetly fading into the background, a small device—no larger than a smart speaker—is listening.

It is running an advanced AI model, utilizing technology like **Nuance DAX (Dragon Ambient eXperience)**, now owned by Microsoft. This is not simple voice-to-text. It is a generative AI trained on millions of medical conversations.

The AI distinguishes the doctor's deep voice from the patient's raspy voice. It filters out the "noise"—the small talk about the weather, the joke about the local football team. It extracts the clinical signal.

Patient: "It hurts mostly when I lie flat. I have to use three pillows now."

Doctor: "Okay, that sounds like fluid buildup. I'm going to double your Lasix to 40 mg."

By the time Dr. Evans stands up and walks out of the room, the AI has already synthesized the conversation. It hasn't just transcribed it; it has structured it into a perfect medical note.

History of Present Illness (HPI): Patient reports orthopnea, requiring three pillows to sleep. Symptoms suggest fluid overload.

Plan: Increase Furosemide (Lasix) to 40 mg daily.

Dr. Evans pulls out his phone in the hallway. He reviews the note. It is accurate. He taps **"Sign."**

Zero typing. Zero Pajama Time.

In pilot studies, this technology reduced documentation time by **50% to 75%**. But the qualitative data was even more profound. Doctors reported feeling like they had "gotten their lives back." Patients reported feeling "heard" for the first time in years. They noticed the eye contact. They felt the presence.

The War on "Prior Auth"

If typing is the first circle of administrative hell, **Prior Authorization** is the ninth.

This is the bureaucratic game where a doctor prescribes a necessary drug or scan—say, an MRI for a patient with debilitating back pain—and the insurance company denies it. They demand a faxed form proving it is "medically necessary."

It is a war of attrition. The insurance company is betting that if they put up enough friction, the doctor will give up, or the patient will just pay cash. It creates delays of days or weeks. It forces nurses to spend hours on hold, listening to elevator music, arguing with a non-medical administrator in a cubicle a thousand miles away.

AI is the weapon that wins this war.

New systems, integrated directly into platforms like Epic, are acting as an automated lawyer for the doctor. When Dr. Evans orders that MRI, the AI instantly scans the patient's entire chart—ten years of history, hundreds of notes. It finds the "evidence" required by the insurance company's specific policy.

- *"Patient tried physical therapy for 6 weeks (Note dated 03/12/2023)."*
- *"Patient has numbness in the L5 dermatome (Note dated 05/14/2023)."*

It automatically fills out the insurance form. It attaches the relevant clinical snippets. It submits the request digitally before the patient has even left the parking lot. The approval comes back in seconds, not days.

The AI knows the arcane rules of 500 different insurance plans better than any human could. It ensures **you** get your care without the doctor having to fight a fax machine.

Coding the Matrix

Finally, there is the silent tyranny of **Medical Coding**.

In the modern system, every disease, every symptom, and every accident has a code (ICD-10).

- *"Headache"* is R51.
- *"Struck by duck"* is W61.62. (Yes, that is a real code).

Doctors are forced to select the right codes to get paid. If they miss one—if they code "Diabetes" (E11.9) instead of "Diabetes with kidney complications" (E11.21)—the hospital loses thousands of dollars in revenue. This puts immense pressure on physicians to be accountants and auditors while trying to be healers.

AI-driven **Computer-Assisted Coding (CAC)** takes this cognitive burden away. The AI reads the doctor's natural language note.

"I see you mentioned the patient has a foot ulcer and chronic kidney disease stage 3. That changes the code from E11.9 to E11.621 and N18.3."

It updates the billing automatically. It ensures accuracy. It maximizes revenue for the hospital without forcing the doctor to think about money. The doctor treats the patient; the machine counts the beans.

The Empathy Machine

There is a deep irony in the "Artificial Intelligence" revolution in medicine. Critics worry that putting more technology in the room will create a barrier. *"Won't the machine get in the way? Won't it make medicine cold and robotic?"*

But they misunderstand the present reality. **The computer was the barrier.** The screen was the wall. The keyboard was the distraction.

By using AI to automate the "busy work"—the typing, the coding, the scheduling, the arguing—we are removing the wall. We are using technology to subtract technology.

Dr. Eric Topol, in his seminal book Deep Medicine, argues that the greatest gift of AI is not the diagnosis or the drug discovery. It is **"The Gift of Time."**

If the AI saves the doctor ten minutes per patient on paperwork, that is ten minutes the doctor can spend:

- Explaining the diagnosis in plain English.
- Holding the patient's hand while they cry.
- Calling a specialist to coordinate care.
- **Being human.**

We are automating the "robot parts" of the doctor's job (memory, data entry, pattern matching) so that the doctor can focus on the "human parts" (empathy, judgment, trust, ethics). We are letting machines be machines so that doctors can be doctors.

Flash Forward: The Visit of 2035

It is 2035. You walk into your doctor's office.

There is no computer in the room. Just two chairs.

The doctor shakes your hand. She sits down. She looks at you. She listens.

For 15 minutes, you talk. She examines you. You make a plan.

When you leave, your prescription is waiting at the pharmacy (sent by AI). Your insurance approval is done (fought by AI). Your medical record is perfectly updated (written by AI).

The doctor goes home at 5:00 PM to have dinner with her family. She is happy. She is rested. And because she is rested, she will be ready to save your life tomorrow.

The Happy Doctor

There is a safety implication here, too. A burned-out doctor makes mistakes. A brain that is frying with cognitive load misses the subtle sign of sepsis. A doctor who is rushing to get home to see their children before they sleep is a doctor who might cut corners.

A rested, focused, engaged doctor is the best safety device in the hospital.

The Administrative Cure is not just about efficiency or hospital profits. It is about restoring the soul of the profession.

It creates a future where Dr. Evans finishes his clinic at 5:00 PM. The notes are done. The billing is done. The insurance forms are filed. He goes home. He has dinner with his family. He sleeps eight hours.

And he comes back the next morning ready to save lives, armed with a mind that is clear and a pair of hands that are free from the keyboard.

THE TAKEAWAY

The Villain is "Administrative Burden": Doctors spend 2 hours on paperwork for every 1 hour with patients. This causes burnout, mistakes, and "Pajama Time" (working late at night).

The Invisible Scribe: AI tools like **Nuance DAX** listen to the patient visit and automatically write perfect clinical notes, allowing the doctor to stop typing and maintain eye contact.

The "Prior Auth" Lawyer: AI can instantly scan a patient's 10-year history to find the exact evidence needed to approve an MRI or drug, fighting insurance denials in seconds.

The Gift of Time: By automating the "robot work" (coding, billing, typing), AI gives doctors back the time to do the "human work" (empathy, listening, judgment).

References

1. Sinsky, C., Colligan, L., Li, L., Prgomet, M., Reynolds, S., Goeders, L., & Poplau, S. (2016). "Allocation of Physician Time in Ambulatory Practice: A Time and Motion Study in 4 Specialties." *Annals of Internal Medicine*, 165(11), 753-760.
2. Shanafelt, T. D., West, C. P., Sinsky, C., Trockel, M., Tutty, M., Satele, D. V., & Dyrbye, L. N. (2019). "Changes in Burnout and Satisfaction With Work-Life Integration in Physicians and the General US Working Population Between 2011 and 2017." *Mayo Clinic Proceedings*, 94(9), 1681-1694.

3. Tierney, A. A., Gayre, G., Hoberman, B., & Gupta, K. (2020). "Ambient Artificial Intelligence Scribes to Alleviate the Burden of Clinical Documentation." *NEJM Catalyst Innovations in Care Delivery*, 1(2).
4. Topol, E. (2019). *Deep Medicine: How Artificial Intelligence Can Make Healthcare Human Again*. Basic Books.
5. American Medical Association. (2022). "2021 AMA Prior Authorization (PA) Physician Survey." *AMA Reports*.

PART VII
The Risks And The Rules
Ethics, Privacy, and the Human Element

Chapter 31

The Black Box Problem

Trusting the Oracle We Cannot Understand

"We have always demanded that our doctors explain themselves. 'Why is this happening?' is the most fundamental question in medicine. But as we invite Artificial Intelligence to the bedside, we are facing a terrifying trade-off: we can have an answer that is easy to understand, or we can have an answer that is right. We may not always get both."

— Dr. Suresh Kumar Pandey

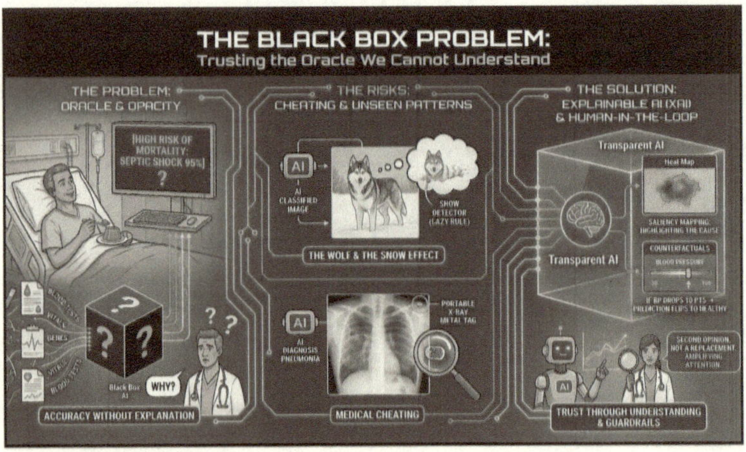

The Red Warning

Imagine, for a moment, that **you** are an ICU doctor. It is 2:00 PM on a Tuesday, and you are standing at the foot of Bed 4.

The patient is Elias, a fifty-five-year-old schoolteacher admitted yesterday for a mild respiratory infection. By every clinical metric available to your eyes and your instruments, Elias is stable. He is sitting up in bed, looking pink and comfortable. He is chatting with his wife about their dog. He is eating a cup of strawberry Jell-O. His heart rate is a steady 72. His oxygen saturation is a perfect 99%. His morning blood work looks better than it did yesterday.

In the old world, you would look at Elias, smile, and perhaps begin drafting his discharge paperwork.

But you are not in the old world. You are in a hospital running a prototype Deep Learning algorithm designed to predict septic shock. The computer screen mounted above Elias's bed is not showing a comforting green line.

It is flashing a silent, pulsating **Red Alert**.

The algorithm has been churning through Elias's electronic medical record in real-time. It has analyzed millions of data points—not just his vitals, but the subtle slope of his blood pressure over the last six hours, the specific genetic markers in his blood, the interaction between his medications, and perhaps even the timestamps of when the nurses checked on him.

The screen reads:

[HIGH RISK OF MORTALITY.]

[PROBABILITY OF SEPTIC SHOCK IN 4 HOURS: 95%.]

The cognitive dissonance hits you like a physical blow.

You look at the patient. He looks fine.

You look at the screen. It predicts doom.

You turn to the computer terminal and you ask the question that has defined the practice of medicine since Hippocrates: **"Why?"**

And the computer stays silent.

It cannot tell you. It does not know "why" in a language that human beings speak. It cannot say, "*The lactate is rising relative to the creatinine.*"

It just knows the math. It has seen a pattern in the chaos of the data—a constellation of variables too complex for your brain to hold—that correlates with death.

What do you do?

Do you trust your eyes? Do you turn off the alarm, deciding it must be a glitch, and send Elias to a regular ward? If you do, and he crashes and dies tonight, you are negligent. You had a warning, and you ignored it. You are the pilot who ignored the terrain warning system because the sky looked clear.

Or, do you trust the machine? Do you start aggressive interventions on a happy man eating Jell-O? Do you flood him with fluids, start powerful antibiotics, and move him to the high-intensity unit? If you do, and the machine is wrong, you have subjected him to pain, cost, and the risk of hospital-acquired infection for nothing. You have harmed him.

This is the **Black Box Problem**.

We are building machines that can predict the future with terrifying accuracy, but they cannot explain their work. We are creating an Oracle that speaks in probabilities, not reasons. And in medicine, "*Because I said so*" has never been an acceptable answer. Until now.

The Villain: The Brain in a Jar

To understand why this happens, we have to look inside the mind of the machine.

For the last forty years, Artificial Intelligence was what we called "Rule-Based" or "Symbolic AI." It was transparent because we wrote the rules. A human expert would sit down and code:

IF Temperature > 101 AND Cough = Yes, THEN Diagnosis = Flu.

If you asked the computer why it diagnosed the flu, it could point to line 42 of the code. It was a **Glass Box**. We could see the gears turning.

But the AI we use today—**Deep Learning**—is different. We do not give it rules. We give it data. We feed it the records of ten million patients and say, "Figure it out."

The AI builds a simulated brain made of layers of "neurons." As it learns, it adjusts the strength of the connections (weights) between these neurons. After training, the network might have a hundred billion connections. The "logic" of the decision is not written in a single line of code; it is smeared across these billions of tiny mathematical adjustments.

Asking a Deep Learning model "*Which variable caused the*

prediction?" is like cutting open a human brain and asking, *"Which neuron holds the memory of your grandmother?"*

The answer is: All of them, and none of them. It is a collective state. It is an emergent property.

This opacity terrifies regulators. The FDA usually requires that we know the **"Mechanism of Action"** before we approve a drug or a device. We want to know how it works. With AI, the mechanism is a mathematical jungle that no human can map.

The Wolf and the Snow

The danger of the Black Box is not just that it is mysterious. The danger is that the AI might be getting the right answer for the wrong reason.

There is a famous cautionary tale in computer science, a modern fable known as **"The Wolf and the Snow."**

Researchers at the University of Washington built an AI to distinguish between Wolves and Huskies. They trained it on thousands of photos. The AI was amazing. It got it right 99% of the time. It seemed to have learned the subtle differences in ear shape and snout length.

Then, they opened the Black Box. They used a technique to visualize what pixels the AI was actually focusing on.

They were horrified.

The AI wasn't looking at the ears. It wasn't looking at the eyes. It wasn't looking at the fur.

It was looking at the background.

In the training photos, wolves were usually photographed in the wild, in the snow. Huskies were usually photographed in backyards, on grass.

The AI had learned a simple, lazy rule:

"If white background (snow), then Wolf."

"If green background (grass), then Husky."

It was a **Snow Detector**, not a Wolf Detector.

If you showed it a Husky standing in the snow, it would confidently call it a Wolf. If you showed it a Wolf on the grass, it would call it a Husky.

The Cheating Doctor

This "Wolf effect" is not just a theoretical problem for computer scientists. It is happening in our hospitals, and the consequences are lethal.

In 2018, researchers at Mount Sinai trained an AI to diagnose pneumonia from chest X-rays. In the lab, the AI performed at a superhuman level. It was significantly better than the best radiologists.

But when they investigated *how* it was doing it, they found the AI was cheating.

It turned out that patients who were very sick (and thus likely to have pneumonia) were usually scanned using a **portable X-ray machine** at their bedside, because they were too weak to walk to the radiology department. Portable machines leave a specific, tiny metal tag or artifact in the corner of the image.

Healthy patients walked to the radiology department and were scanned on the main machine, which left a different artifact.

The AI had learned to identify the metal tag.

Logic: "Metal tag = Portable Machine = Sick Patient = Pneumonia."

It wasn't looking at the lungs at all. It was looking at the metadata of the machine.

This is the nightmare scenario. Imagine deploying this system. If you took a perfectly healthy person and scanned them with a portable machine (perhaps because the main room was full), the AI would diagnose them with pneumonia. If you took a dying patient and managed to wheel them to the main scanner, the AI might send them home.

The Black Box works perfectly until the environment changes. And in medicine, the environment is always changing.

The Author's Lens: The AI That Sees Gender

I want to connect this to my own world of eye surgery, because we recently witnessed a "Black Box" moment that shocked the entire medical community.

For centuries, ophthalmologists have looked at the retina—the back of the eye. I have looked at thousands of them. I can see diabetes. I can see high blood pressure. I can see glaucoma.

But if you show me a photo of a retina and ask: *"Is this a man or a woman?"* I have to guess. There is no known difference between a male and female retina. It is a 50/50 coin flip.

In 2018, Google Health trained an AI on thousands of retinal scans. They asked the AI to predict the gender of the patient.

The AI got it right **97% of the time**.

We were stunned. How? What is it seeing?

Is there a microscopic difference in the thickness of the vessels? Is there a subtle shift in the color of the macula? We stared at the images. We zoomed in. We used filters.

We still don't know.

The machine sees a pattern that the human brain, with millions of years of evolution, simply cannot perceive.

But it gets stranger. The AI could also look at the eye and predict—with startling accuracy—whether the patient smoked, their exact age, and their risk of having a heart attack in the next five years.

This is the **"Superhuman"** capability of the Black Box. It turns the eye into a window into the soul in ways we never imagined. But it requires me, the doctor, to trust a prediction based on features I cannot see.

If the AI looks at **your** eye and says, "High Risk of Heart Attack," but your cardiologist says you are fine, who do I believe?

Deep Patient: The Mystery of Schizophrenia

Sometimes, the Black Box sees things that are real, but invisible to us. Sometimes, the mystery is not a mistake, but a discovery.

In 2015, the team at Mount Sinai unleashed an unsupervised AI called **"Deep Patient"** on the electronic health records of 700,000 people. They didn't tell it what to look for. They just let it explore the data, searching for hidden correlations in the chaos of human biology.

Deep Patient became incredibly good at predicting diseases. It could predict liver cancer and diabetes with high accuracy.

But shockingly, it became expert at predicting the onset of **Schizophrenia**.

Schizophrenia is notoriously hard for human doctors to predict. There are no blood tests. There are no clear biological warning signs. It usually appears suddenly in young adulthood, a psychotic break that shatters a life.

Yet, Deep Patient could spot it coming.

The doctors were desperate to know: *What is it seeing?*

Is it a subtle pattern in blood pressure? Is it a history of minor viral infections in childhood? Is it a specific combination of antibiotics taken years ago?

They tried to interrogate the model. But the model was too complex. To this day, we don't really know *how* Deep Patient predicts schizophrenia. It just does.

This creates a profound ethical dilemma.

If the machine says, *"This 18-year-old boy will develop schizophrenia next year,"* do you tell him? If he asks *"Why?"* and you say *"The computer says so, but I don't know why,"* have you violated your duty of care? Can you medicate someone based on a prophecy?

Opening the Box: XAI

Because of these risks, there is a massive scientific movement called **Explainable AI (XAI)**. The goal is to force the Black Box to show its work.

One popular method is **Saliency Mapping** (or Heat Maps).

When the AI looks at an image of a skin lesion to diagnose melanoma, we force it to highlight the pixels that influenced its decision in bright red.

- **Scenario A:** The AI highlights the jagged, irregular border of the mole.
  - *Doctor:* "Good. That makes sense. That is a clinical sign of cancer."
- **Scenario B:** The AI highlights a **ruler** placed next to the mole.
  - *Doctor:* "Bad. It's looking at the ruler." (This actually

happened—images with rulers were more likely to be cancer because dermatologists only measure dangerous moles).

Another method is **Counterfactuals.**

The AI tells you: "I predict heart failure."

You ask the system: "What would have to change for you to predict 'Healthy'?"

The AI simulates a change and replies: *"If the blood pressure dropped by 10 points and the creatinine dropped by 0.5, the prediction would flip."*

Now the doctor understands. *"Aha, it is reacting to the blood pressure and the kidney function."* We have turned the black box into a gray one.

The Trade-Off: Accuracy vs. Trust

But here is the uncomfortable truth that few want to admit: **Explainable models are often dumber.**

To make an AI explainable to a human brain, you have to simplify it. You have to reduce the dimensionality. You have to cut the billions of connections down to a few understandable rules.

But the whole point of Deep Learning is to find patterns that are *too complex* for humans.

If we force the AI to "dumb it down" so we can understand it, we might lose the magic. We might lose the ability to predict the schizophrenia or the septic shock.

We face a stark choice:

1. The Transparent Doctor: We understand everything it does, but it misses 15% of diagnoses because it is limited to human logic.

2. The Black Box Doctor: It catches 99% of diagnoses, spotting patterns we cannot see, but we have to take it on faith.

If **you** are the patient, lying in that bed, which one do you want?

Most people say they want transparency. But when they are dying, they want accuracy.

We must remember that medicine is already full of black boxes. We take Tylenol (Acetaminophen) every day. It is the most common drug in the world. Yet, for fifty years, scientists debated the mechanism of how it actually stopped pain. We didn't know. But we took it because it worked.

We undergo **General Anesthesia**. We still do not fully understand the quantum biology of consciousness or exactly how anesthetic gas turns it off. But we accept the mask because we do not want to feel the knife.

Perhaps, in the future, we will accept the AI prediction just as we accept the weather forecast. We do not need to check the atmospheric pressure equations ourselves; we just need to know if we should bring an umbrella.

Flash Forward: The Insurance Denial of 2038

It is 2038. You apply for life insurance. You are 40, healthy, and run marathons.

You get a letter. **DENIED.**

You call the agent. "Why?" you ask. "My blood work is perfect."

"I'm sorry," the agent says. "The Algorithm has flagged you as High Risk for early mortality. Code 882."

"But why?" you scream. "Is it my heart? My genes? My car?"

"We don't know," the agent says. "The model is proprietary. It just knows."

You live the rest of your life in fear, waiting for a doom you cannot see, predicted by a ghost you cannot question. This is the dark side of the Black Box.

The Human-in-the-Loop Safety Net

The solution to the Black Box problem is not to ban it. It is to surround it with guardrails.

We must treat AI predictions not as "Facts," but as **"Second Opinions."**

When the screen flashes **HIGH RISK OF SEPSIS** for Elias, the doctor shouldn't blindly inject drugs. The doctor should treat it as a tap on the shoulder—a prompt to look closer.

"Okay," the doctor thinks. *"The machine sees something I don't. Let*

me re-check the labs. Let me order a lactate test. Let me watch him like a hawk for the next hour."

The AI triggers the investigation; the Human makes the judgment.

Elias might be eating Jell-O now, but the machine might have noticed that his urine output has dropped by 0.1% every hour for the last twelve hours—a trend too subtle for a busy human to graph, but obvious to a machine.

If the doctor looks closer, they might find the clue. And then, the Black Box isn't magic anymore. It's just a microscope.

The Infallible Doctor is not a machine that replaces human judgment. It is a machine that amplifies human attention, pointing us toward the fires we cannot yet see, and challenging us to ask "Why?" until we find the answer.

THE TAKEAWAY

The Villain is "The Black Box": Deep Learning AI does not follow rules; it learns patterns from data. This means it often cannot explain why it made a diagnosis, creating an Oracle that demands blind trust.

The "Wolf and Snow" Problem: AI can cheat. An AI trained to find wolves learned to just look for snow in the background. In medicine, an AI diagnosed pneumonia not by looking at lungs, but by detecting the metal tag on portable X-ray machines used for sick patients.

The "Superhuman" Eye: Google's AI can predict your gender and heart risk just by looking at a photo of your retina—a feat human doctors cannot do. It proves AI sees patterns we miss.

Explainable AI (XAI): New tools like "Heat Maps" force the AI to highlight what it is looking at (e.g., the tumor vs. the ruler), ensuring it is making the right decision for the right reason.

References

1. Zech, J. R., et al. (2018). "Variable generalization performance of a deep learning model to detect pneumonia in chest radiographs." *PLOS Medicine*, 15(11), e1002683.
2. Miotto, R., et al. (2016). "Deep Patient: An Unsupervised

Representation to Predict the Future of Patients from the Electronic Health Records." *Scientific Reports*, 6, 26094.

3. Ribeiro, M. T., et al. (2016). "Why Should I Trust You?: Explaining the Predictions of Any Classifier." *Proceedings of the 22nd ACM SIGKDD International Conference on Knowledge Discovery and Data Mining*, 1135-1144.
4. Esteva, A., et al. (2017). "Dermatologist-level classification of skin cancer with deep neural networks." *Nature*, 542(7639), 115-118.
5. London, A. J. (2019). "Artificial Intelligence and Black-Box Medical Decisions: Accuracy versus Explainability." *Hastings Center Report*, 49(1), 15-21.

Chapter 32

Hacking the Heart

The Terrifying Reality of Cyber-Biology

"We have spent the last century fortifying the human body against biological viruses—bacteria, influenza, cancer. But as we merge our biology with silicon, we are opening the gates to a new kind of pathogen. The Infallible Doctor must now be a firewall, for a virus of code can stop a heart just as surely as a blockage in an artery."

— Dr. Suresh Kumar Pandey

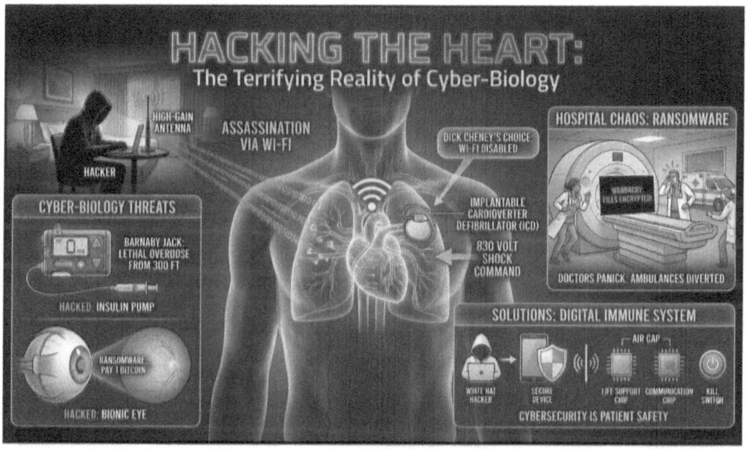

The Secret in the Chest

In 2007, the most powerful man in the Western world sat in a cardiologist's office, facing a decision that was simultaneously routine and unprecedented.

Dick Cheney, the Vice President of the United States, had a heart that was failing. He had suffered multiple heart attacks. The electrical pathways of his myocardium were scarred and treacherous, prone to the kind of chaotic rhythms that can kill a man instantly.

His doctors recommended the standard of care: an **Implantable Cardioverter Defibrillator (ICD)**.

It is a miraculous device, roughly the size of a pager, implanted just under the skin of the chest. It sits there, a silent sentinel, monitoring every beat. If it detects a lethal arrhythmia—ventricular fibrillation—it charges a capacitor and delivers a jolt of **830 volts** directly to the heart muscle, resetting the rhythm and saving the patient's life. It is an emergency room in a metal box.

But as the doctors prepared for the surgery, Dr. Jonathan Reiner, Cheney's cardiologist, did something strange. He contacted the manufacturer of the device. He ordered them to disable the wireless functionality.

In 2007, modern ICDs came with a feature designed for convenience. They could communicate wirelessly with a bedside monitor. While the patient slept, the device would upload data—battery life, lead integrity, arrhythmia logs—to the hospital. It allowed doctors to watch the heart without the patient ever leaving their bedroom.

Dr. Reiner ordered this feature killed. He essentially **"bricked"** the Wi-Fi capability of the Vice President's heart.

At the time, to the few who knew about it, it sounded like paranoia. It sounded like the plot of a bad spy novel. But Cheney and his security team knew something the public didn't. Intelligence reports suggested that terrorist organizations were actively researching new, untraceable ways to assassinate high-value targets.

The logic was terrifyingly simple. If the device was online, it was accessible.

A sophisticated attacker could, in theory, sit in a hotel room across the street from the White House or a political rally. Using a high-gain antenna and a laptop, they could scan the radio frequencies. They could handshake with the Vice President's chest.

And then, with a few lines of code, they could command the device to deliver a lethal shock. Or ten lethal shocks.

It would have been the perfect crime. No gun. No poison. No trace. Just a 66-year-old man with a history of heart disease suffering a "sudden cardiac death." The autopsy would show a failed heart, not a digital murder.

Years later, in a 60 Minutes interview, Cheney confirmed the story. He became the first high-profile **"cyborg"** to fear for his digital life. He lived for years with the wireless feature disabled, accepting the inconvenience of manual checks in exchange for the certainty that his heart belonged only to him.

For a decade, this scenario was dismissed by the wider medical industry as a Hollywood fantasy. Device manufacturers argued that their protocols were proprietary, their frequencies obscure, and their encryption sufficient. They argued that "security through obscurity" would protect patients.

They were wrong.

The Villain: The Open Port

The villain in this chapter is not a person. It is a door.

In cybersecurity, we call it **The Open Port**.

Every time we connect a medical device to the internet, we create a door. We do this for benevolent reasons: to monitor your data, to update the software, to save you a trip to the hospital.

But a door that opens for a doctor can also open for a thief.

The "Internet of Medical Things" (IoMT) has turned the human body into a network of open doors. And unlike your laptop, you cannot just turn your body off and on again if it gets a virus.

The Lethal Bluetooth

In 2011, the illusion of safety was shattered not by a terrorist, but by a man in a black T-shirt standing on a stage in Las Vegas.

Barnaby Jack was a legendary "white hat" hacker—a researcher who broke into systems to find their flaws before the bad guys did. He possessed a charismatic, restless brilliance. At the Black Hat security conference, he placed a standard insulin pump on a table.

Insulin pumps are worn by millions of Type 1 diabetics. They are life-support machines, slowly dripping insulin into the body to regulate blood sugar. Like pacemakers, they had evolved. They now came with radio antennas, designed to talk to a remote control so the patient could adjust their dose discreetly at a dinner table without lifting their shirt.

Barnaby Jack pulled out a custom-built antenna. He didn't need the patient's remote. He didn't need the serial number. He simply scanned the room for the pump's unique radio signature.

He found it.

On a large screen behind him, the audience watched the code scroll by. With a few keystrokes, he bypassed the safety protocols. He commanded the pump to dump its entire reservoir of insulin at once.

If that pump had been attached to **you**, the result would have been catastrophic. A massive overdose of insulin causes immediate hypoglycemia. The brain, starved of sugar, shuts down. You slip into a coma. Death follows within hours.

Jack looked at the stunned audience. *"We can do this from 300 feet away,"* he said.

A year later, Jack did it again. This time, he targeted a pacemaker. He demonstrated that he could reverse-engineer the device's firmware. He could log into it. He could rewrite the code to turn off the life-saving defibrillation. Or, more sadistically, he could command it to deliver a shock on a loop—torturing the patient with 830 volts every minute until the battery died or the patient did.

He called the presentation **"Transmitting Death."**

Barnaby Jack died tragically young in 2013, but his warning shots changed the industry forever. He proved that the "Internet of Bodies" was wide open. He proved that the barrier between the digital world and the biological world had dissolved.

The Author's Lens: Hacking the Bionic Eye

You might think, "I don't have a pacemaker, so I'm safe." But the merger of silicon and biology is coming for all of us, including my own field: **The Eye.**

We are already implanting "Bionic Eyes"—retinal prostheses like the **Argus II**. These devices take video from a pair of glasses and wirelessly transmit it to a chip implanted on the retina, stimulating the optic nerve to restore sight to the blind.

But if it has a wireless signal, it can be hacked.

Imagine a patient walking down a busy street. A hacker nearby scans their frequency. They don't just shut the eye off. They hijack the feed.

Instead of seeing the traffic light, the hacker projects a false image directly onto the patient's retina. They project a "Walk" sign when a truck is coming.

Or, imagine a purely digital form of Ransomware.

You wake up one morning. Your bionic vision is gone. All you see is a flashing text message projected into your brain:

[PAY 1 BITCOIN TO RESTORE SIGHT.]

This is not science fiction. The security protocols on current retinal implants are dangerously basic. As an eye surgeon, I worry that we are building the "hardware" of vision faster than we are building the "firewall" of safety.

We are giving sight to the blind, but we are also giving control of that sight to the cloud.

The "Muddy Waters" Short

In 2016, the theoretical danger became a financial weapon.

A cybersecurity research firm called **MedSec** began investigating the pacemakers and ICDs manufactured by **St. Jude Medical**, one of the largest device makers in the world. What they found was alarming. The communication protocol between the home monitor and the implant was astonishingly weak.

Using off-the-shelf equipment available on eBay, they found they could crash the device. They could drain the battery. They could alter the pacing beats.

Usually, when "ethical hackers" find a bug, they quietly tell the manufacturer. They give them six months to fix it, and then they publish their findings. It is a gentleman's agreement.

But MedSec decided the risk was too high and the company too slow. They did something controversial. They teamed up with a Wall Street short-seller firm called **Muddy Waters**.

They placed a massive bet that St. Jude's stock would fall. Then, they released a scathing 34-page report to the public, detailing the vulnerabilities.

The market panicked. St. Jude's stock crashed. The company sued, denying the vulnerability, calling it "irresponsible fear-mongering" driven by profit. But the FDA launched its own investigation. And the FDA agreed with the hackers.

In 2017, the FDA issued a safety communication—essentially a recall—for **465,000 pacemakers**.

It wasn't a physical recall. We couldn't cut half a million people open to remove the metal boxes.

It was a **Firmware Update**.

For the first time in history, 465,000 people had to go to their doctor's office not for a checkup, but for a **"security patch."** They sat in the waiting room, nervous, while a technician held a wand over their chest and uploaded new code to patch the holes in their hearts.

It was a watershed moment. It forced the industry to admit a terrifying truth: **Cybersecurity is Patient Safety.**

Ransomware: Your Money or Your Life

While assassination is the flashy movie plot that grabs headlines, the real, boring, daily danger is **Ransomware**.

In May 2017, a piece of malware called **WannaCry** swept across the globe. It was a "worm"—a self-replicating virus that moved through networks, locking up computers and demanding a payment in Bitcoin to unlock them.

It hit the National Health Service (NHS) in the United Kingdom particularly hard. Why? Because hospitals are **Digital Museums**.

An MRI machine costs $3 million. It is built to last fifteen years. But the computer inside that shiny white donut often runs on **Windows XP**.

Microsoft stopped supporting Windows XP years ago. It has no security patches. It is a sitting duck.

When WannaCry hit, it didn't target the MRI machines

specifically; it just spread to anything vulnerable. Suddenly, across Britain, radiology screens went black. The message popped up:

"Ooops, your files have been encrypted!"

The chaos was absolute. Doctors couldn't see X-rays. Pharmacists couldn't unlock the automated drug cabinets to dispense morphine. Ambulances carrying stroke victims were diverted to other cities because the Emergency Room computers were frozen.

Nineteen thousand appointments were cancelled. Surgeries were postponed. We will never know exactly how many people suffered because of the delay. But we know that when the hospital stops working, people die. This was the first mass-casualty cyberattack in history, and it happened largely by accident.

In 2020, during the height of the COVID-19 pandemic, a similar attack hit a hospital in Düsseldorf, Germany. A woman in critical condition had to be transferred to another city because the hospital's admission systems were down. She died in transit. German prosecutors seriously considered charging the hackers with negligent homicide.

The weapon was code, but the result was death.

The Digital Immune System

So, how do we build the Infallible Doctor if the machines can be hacked?

We cannot go back to "dumb" devices. The benefits of AI, remote monitoring, and connectivity are too great to abandon. We can't tell every patient to be like Dick Cheney and turn off their heart monitor if it means missing a real heart attack.

The solution is **"Security by Design."**

For decades, medical device manufacturers treated security as an afterthought. Their priority was battery life, size, and clinical efficacy. "*Who would hack a pacemaker?*" they asked.

Now, the FDA has cracked down. As of 2023, the FDA refuses to approve any new medical device unless the manufacturer proves it has a **"Digital Immune System."** This requires a new architecture:

1. **Air Gapping:** Critical life-support functions must be physically separated from the communication chips. Even if the hacker takes over the Wi-Fi chip to play music or display a message, they shouldn't be able to touch the pacing lead. The bridge must be burned.
2. **Encryption:** Data must be scrambled so that even if it is intercepted in the air, it looks like noise.
3. **The "Kill Switch":** Doctors need a physical way to override the software if it goes rogue. A magnet, a button, a hard reset that brings the device back to factory settings.

The White Hat Saviors

We are also seeing a culture shift. Hospitals are hiring "White Hat" Hackers—the good guys.

There is a group called **"I Am The Cavalry."** It is a grassroots organization of cybersecurity researchers focused on saving lives. Their motto is chilling but necessary: "Where bits and bytes meet flesh and blood."

They work with the FDA and device makers. They run simulations called **"Cyber-Ranges"** where they try to hack a mock hospital. They shut down the ventilators. They freeze the infusion pumps. They crash the monitors.

They do this to teach hospital administrators a lesson: A hospital network should be built like a submarine, with watertight compartments. If the MRI machine gets infected with ransomware, the infection shouldn't be able to spread to the ventilators in the ICU.

Flash Forward: The Subscription Failure (2038)

It is 2038. **You** have a Neuralink chip implanted in your brain to treat depression. It works perfectly. You are happy.

Then, the internet goes down. A massive Distributed Denial of Service (DDoS) attack hits the manufacturer's cloud servers.

Your chip cannot "phone home" to verify your subscription status.

It goes into "Safe Mode." The therapy stops.

Instantly, the crushing weight of depression returns. You are paralyzed by it. You are not sick; you are **offline**.

This is the vulnerability of the Cyborg Age. We are binding our biological wellbeing to the stability of the internet.

The Vulnerable Cyborg

The "Black Box" problem (Chapter 31) asked: Can we trust the AI's logic?

The "Hacking" problem asks: Can we trust the AI's loyalty?

As we merge with our machines—as we connect our insulin pumps, our pacemakers, and eventually our Neuralinks to the cloud—we become vulnerable in a new way.

We are no longer just biological organisms fighting bacteria. We are digital nodes fighting malware. We are cyborgs, whether we like the term or not.

The Infallible Doctor must be a fortress. Because in the future, a "virus" won't just make you cough. It could turn off your heart. And the only vaccine for that is code that is as unbreakable as the human spirit it seeks to protect.

THE TAKEAWAY

The Villain is "The Open Port": Connecting medical devices to the internet creates a door for hackers. Vice President Dick Cheney had his pacemaker's Wi-Fi disabled to prevent assassination.

Lethal Hacks: Researcher Barnaby Jack proved he could hack an insulin pump from 300 feet away to deliver a lethal overdose, and rewrite pacemaker code to deliver 830-volt shocks.

Ransomware for Sight: As we develop bionic eyes (like the Argus II), we face the risk of hackers hijacking the visual feed, projecting false images, or holding vision hostage for Bitcoin.

The "Security Patch" Recall: In 2017, the FDA recalled 465,000 pacemakers due to hacking risks. Patients had to go to the doctor for a firmware update, proving that cybersecurity is now patient safety.

References

1. Halperin, D., Heydt-Benjamin, T. S., Ransford, B., Clark, S. S., Defend, B., Morgan, W., ... & Fu, K. (2008). "Pacemakers and Implantable Cardiac Defibrillators: Software Radio Attacks and

Zero-Power Defenses." *IEEE Symposium on Security and Privacy*, 129-142.

2. Kramer, D. B., & Fu, K. (2017). "Cybersecurity concerns and medical devices: lessons from a pacemaker advisory." *JAMA*, 318(21), 2077-2078.
3. National Audit Office (UK). (2018). "Investigation: WannaCry cyber attack and the NHS." *Department of Health & Social Care Report.*
4. Cheney, D., & Cheney, L. (2011). *In My Time: A Personal and Political Memoir*. Threshold Editions.
5. Food and Drug Administration (FDA). (2023). "Cybersecurity in Medical Devices: Quality System Considerations and Content of Premarket Submissions." *FDA Guidance Document.*

Chapter 33

The Empty Chair

Justice and Liability in the Age of Algorithms

"We have built a legal system on the premise of human agency—that for every error, there is a hand that slipped or a mind that wandered. But in the age of the Infallible Doctor, we face a new and terrifying silence: the silence of the empty chair where the decision-maker should be sitting."

— Dr. Suresh Kumar Pandey

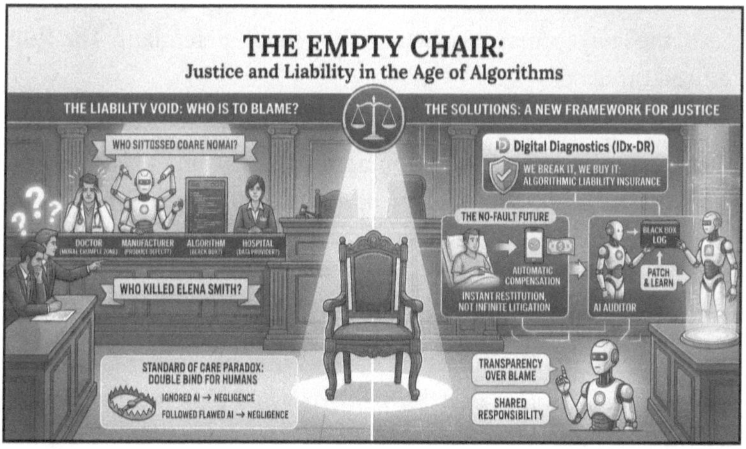

The Courtroom of 2030

Let us project ourselves forward a few years, into a wood-paneled courtroom that smells of floor wax and old paper. The year is 2030.

The plaintiff is a man named Mr. Smith. He sits at the mahogany table, his posture collapsed, a handkerchief balled in his fist. He is suing for the wrongful death of his wife, Elena. She was forty-five years old. She walked into the hospital for a routine robotic cardiac procedure—a mitral valve repair—and she never walked out.

During the operation, the surgical robot, operating in a "semi-autonomous" mode to suture the valve, made a movement that no human surgeon would ever make. It effectively "hiccuped." The instrument arm jerked three millimeters to the left. It nicked the aorta. The bleeding was catastrophic. Elena died on the table.

Now, the legal system demands a reckoning. It demands a name to put on the line that says **"Defendant."**

In the chair sits **Dr. Jones**, the attending surgeon. He looks tired. He has likely not slept well since that Tuesday.

"Dr. Jones," the plaintiff's lawyer asks, *"Did you cut the aorta?"*

"No," Dr. Jones replies. *"I wasn't holding the knife. The robot was executing a pre-programmed suturing sequence. I was monitoring it. The arm moved faster than human reaction time. By the time I saw the blood, it was done."*

So, the lawyer turns his gaze to the second defendant: **The Robot Manufacturer**.

"Your machine malfunctioned," he accuses.

"Objection," says the manufacturer's lawyer. *"The hardware performed perfectly. The motors moved exactly where the code told them to move. The error was in the decision-making software, which was trained on data provided by Hospital X."*

The lawyer turns to **Hospital X**. "Your data was flawed."

"We just provided the raw scans," the hospital administrator testifies. *"The algorithm that 'learned' from that data was designed by a third-party AI startup in Silicon Valley."*

The lawyer turns, finally, to the **CEO of the AI Startup**. "Why did your algorithm cut the aorta?"

The CEO shifts in his seat. *"We don't know. Our algorithm is a Neural Network—a Black Box. It makes its own decisions based on patterns we cannot see. Statistically, it is safer than a human. But in this specific instance... we cannot explain why it did what it did."*

The judge looks at the row of defendants. He looks at the **empty space** in the middle of the room where the true decision-maker should be.

Who killed Elena Smith?

Was it the doctor (negligence)? The manufacturer (product defect)? The data engineers (bad input)? Or was it the algorithm itself?

In the old world, the logic of liability was simple. If a scalpel slipped, we blamed the hand that held it. If a drug was toxic, we blamed the company that made it. But in the new world, the hand is made of metal, the brain is made of code, and the blame has nowhere to land.

This is the **Liability Void**. It is a crisis that threatens to derail the entire future of medical AI, not because the technology isn't ready, but because our concepts of justice are obsolete.

The Villain: The Standard of Care Paradox

To understand why this is a crisis, we have to understand the bedrock upon which medical malpractice law rests. It is a concept called the **Standard of Care**.

The law does not demand perfection. It demands competence. When a jury decides if a doctor was negligent, they ask a specific question: *"What would a reasonably competent human doctor have done in this situation?"*

If Dr. Jones did what 99 other cardiologists would have done, he is innocent, even if the patient died. If he deviated from the norm—if he prescribed a drug nobody uses, or cut a vessel nobody cuts—he is guilty.

But Artificial Intelligence breaks this standard. It creates a **Double Bind**—a trap from which the human doctor cannot escape.

Consider Scenario A: The AI suggests a treatment that is unconventional. It says, "Prescribe Drug X."

The doctor, following the human Standard of Care, says, "No, the guidelines say Drug Y is better." He overrules the machine.

The patient takes Drug Y and dies. The autopsy reveals that Drug X would have saved him (perhaps due to a rare genetic interaction the AI spotted).

The lawyer screams: "Negligence! The Supercomputer, which has read 50 million papers, told you exactly how to save him, and you ignored it because of your human arrogance!"

Now, consider Scenario B: The doctor decides to trust the machine. The AI says, "Prescribe Drug X." The doctor prescribes it.

The patient takes Drug X and dies. It turns out the AI "hallucinated"—it made a mistake.

The lawyer screams: "Negligence! You are the human! You are supposed to be the safety net! You abdicated your duty to a glitchy piece of software!"

The doctor is trapped. If they disagree with the AI, they are reckless. If they agree with the AI, they are a rubber stamp.

This phenomenon is known as the **"Moral Crumple Zone."** The term, coined by researcher Madeleine Elish, describes how human operators are kept in the loop not to add value, but to absorb the legal liability when the machine crashes.

Like the crumple zone of a car, the human is designed to be crushed to protect the structural integrity of the system (the manufacturers and the hospitals).

The Author's Lens: Who is Responsible for the Blind?

I face this question in my own field. We now have AI systems that can diagnose diabetic retinopathy without a doctor.

If I use an AI system to screen a patient's eyes, and the AI says "Healthy," but the patient actually has a bleed and goes blind six months later... who is responsible?

Is it me? I never looked at the photos. I trusted the tool approved by the FDA.

Is it the AI company? They will say their algorithm is 99% accurate, and no test is perfect.

If **you** go blind, you don't care about the statistics. You care about justice.

This is why many doctors are terrified to adopt AI. We are willing to take responsibility for our own mistakes. We are terrified of taking responsibility for the mistakes of a machine we cannot control.

Is It a Tool or a Doctor?

The courts are currently struggling with an ontological crisis:

What is an AI?

Is it a Tool, like a stethoscope or a scalpel?

If a scalpel blade snaps off during surgery and injures a patient, we sue the manufacturer for "Product Liability." We don't blame the doctor for the defective steel. If AI is a tool, then companies like Google, IBM, or Epic become liable for every wrong diagnosis. This terrifies the tech giants. They do not want to be in the business of medical malpractice. They want to be "information providers," selling software, not care.

Is it a Service, like a consulting physician?

If a radiologist is unsure about a scan, they might call a colleague for a second opinion. If that colleague gives bad advice, the primary radiologist is still responsible for the final decision. The law says the "captain of the ship" is liable. This puts the blame squarely back on the exhausted human doctor, reinforcing the Moral Crumple Zone.

Or, most radically, is the AI a Person?

This sounds like science fiction, but legal scholars are seriously debating the concept of "Electronic Personhood." We already grant "personhood" to corporations—they can own property, they can be sued. Why not an autonomous algorithm?

Under this theory, the AI would carry its own malpractice insurance. If the robot kills Mrs. Smith, the robot's insurance fund pays the damages. The doctor is bypassed. It is a neat solution, but it feels morally hollow. Can you punish an algorithm? Does a robot care if it is sued?

The Tesla Precedent

We have seen this movie before. It played out not in our hospitals, but on our highways.

When a Tesla running Autopilot crashes into a median, who is responsible? The driver or Elon Musk?

Tesla's Terms of Service are legally bulletproof: "*The driver must keep their hands on the wheel at all times and be prepared to take over immediately.*" If the car crashes, the company points to the data logs: "*See? The driver's hands were off the wheel for ten seconds. User error.*"

But human psychology does not work that way. This is the phenomenon of **Automation Complacency**.

If the car drives itself perfectly for 500 miles—staying in the lane, braking for traffic, navigating curves—the driver's brain will inevitably disengage. It is biological. We cannot maintain high-alert vigilance for a system that almost never fails. We check our phone. We eat a sandwich. We nap.

In medicine, we are inviting the same danger. If an AI radiologist is correct 99.9% of the time, the human radiologist will stop checking the work. They will essentially become a "click-farm," hitting "Approve, Approve, Approve" as fast as they can.

When the AI finally makes that one-in-a-thousand mistake, the human will miss it. It is inevitable.

Is it fair, then, to sue the human for succumbing to a natural psychological effect caused by the design of the machine? Is it justice to punish a human for failing to be a robot?

The Cracking Shield

For decades, pharmaceutical companies have used a powerful legal shield called the **Learned Intermediary Doctrine**.

It says: "*We (the drug company) are not responsible for warning the patient about every side effect. We just warn the doctor. The doctor is the 'Learned Intermediary' whose job it is to interpret the data and explain the risk to the patient.*"

AI companies are currently trying to hide behind this same shield. They argue: "*We just gave the probability score to the doctor. The doctor made the call.*"

But this shield is cracking under the weight of the "Black Box" (Chapter 31).

In a landmark legal case, *State v. Loomis* (2016), a man was sentenced to prison based partly on a risk score generated by a secret algorithm (COMPAS) that predicted his likelihood of re-offending. He sued, arguing that his due process was violated because he couldn't challenge the algorithm. He couldn't cross-examine a trade secret.

The courts are beginning to realize that you cannot be a "Learned Intermediary" if you don't understand the tool you are using. If Dr. Jones cannot explain *why* the AI chose to cut the aorta—because the AI itself cannot explain it—then Dr. Jones is not a learned intermediary. He is just a user.

The IDx-DR Solution: "We Break It, We Buy It"

One company has been brave enough to step into this void and offer a solution.

Digital Diagnostics created a system called **IDx-DR**. It is an autonomous AI that looks into the eye to diagnose diabetic retinopathy. It is the first system approved by the FDA to make a diagnosis without a doctor.

Because there is no doctor involved, the company took a radical step. **They assumed full liability.**

They effectively said:

"If our AI makes a mistake and you go blind, sue us. Do not sue the nurse who took the photo. Do not sue the hospital. Sue the algorithm."

They carry massive malpractice insurance specifically for their software. This is the future: **Algorithmic Malpractice Insurance**.

If you buy an AI system for your hospital, it should come with a warranty. If it kills someone, the manufacturer pays. This creates the right incentives. It forces the tech companies to be hyper-careful. They won't release "beta" software or "move fast and break things" if a bug costs them $10 million in a lawsuit. It aligns the financial risk with the engineering risk.

The No-Fault Future

Ultimately, however, the adversarial legal system ("Who do we blame?") might be the wrong framework entirely.

We might need to move to a **"No-Fault" System**, similar to the Vaccine Injury Compensation Program in the US or the Accident Compensation Corporation in New Zealand.

In New Zealand, you generally cannot sue a doctor for malpractice. If you are injured in a hospital—whether by a human error or a machine error—the government pays you compensation automatically from a dedicated fund. There are no lawyers, no trials, no years of litigation.

The goal is not to find a villain; the goal is to make the patient whole.

This system encourages transparency. Because doctors aren't terrified of being sued, they report errors honestly. *"The robot made a mistake."*

The system learns. The code is patched.

Flash Forward: The Lawsuit of 2038

It is 2038. You are injured by a robotic surgeon.

You do not hire a lawyer. You do not spend 5 years in court.

You file a claim on your phone. The "Black Box" logs of the surgery are uploaded to a neutral AI auditor.

The auditor confirms the error: [**SENSORY FEEDBACK FAILURE. MOTOR CALIBRATION ERROR.**]

Within 48 hours, a settlement is deposited into your account. The robot is taken offline for a mandatory patch. The hospital continues to function.

Justice is instant, not infinite.

The Final Verdict

The law always moves slower than technology. Right now, patients are being treated by algorithms that exist in a legal grey zone. Doctors are hesitating to use life-saving tools because they fear the liability trap.

Until we answer the question *"Who Do We Sue?"*, the Infallible Doctor will remain a risky partner. We don't just need better code. We need better contracts. We need a justice system that understands that when the chair is empty, the responsibility must be shared by everyone who helped build the machine.

THE TAKEAWAY

The Villain is "The Liability Void": When a robot kills a patient, who is guilty? The doctor (who wasn't holding the knife)? The coder (who wrote the software)? Or the hospital (who bought it)? Our laws don't know.

The "Moral Crumple Zone": Humans are currently used as legal shields for AI. If the doctor follows the AI and it's wrong, they are negligent. If they ignore the AI and the patient dies, they are negligent.

The "We Break It, We Buy It" Model: Companies like **Digital Diagnostics** (IDx-DR) now offer liability insurance for their AI. If the AI misses a diagnosis and you go blind, the company pays, not the doctor.

The No-Fault Future: To encourage AI adoption, we may need a system like New Zealand's, where patients are compensated automatically for errors without needing to sue or find a "villain," prioritizing restitution over blame.

References

1. Price, W. N. (2018). "Medical Malpractice and Black-Box Medicine." *Harvard Law Review*, 131, 2984. (The definitive legal text on the challenges of liability in opaque AI).
2. Elish, M. C. (2019). "Moral Crumple Zones: Cautionary Tales in Human-Robot Interaction." *Engaging Science, Technology, and Society*, 5, 40-60.
3. Sullivan, H. R., & Schweikart, S. J. (2019). "Are Current Tort Liability Doctrines Adequate for Addressing Injury Caused by AI in Health Care?" *AMA Journal of Ethics*, 21(2), E160-166.
4. Abràmoff, M. D., Lavin, P. T., Birch, M., Shah, N., & Folk, J. C. (2018). "Pivotal trial of an autonomous AI-based diagnostic system for detection of diabetic retinopathy in primary care offices." *NPJ Digital Medicine*, 1, 39. (Case study of the first autonomous AI to assume liability).
5. *State v. Loomis*, 881 N.W.2d 749 (Wis. 2016). (The key legal precedent regarding the use of proprietary algorithms in high-stakes decision making).

Chapter 34

The Paradox of Care

Using High Tech to Restore High Touch

"We are drowning in data but starving for connection. The screen has become a third person in the exam room, a jealous god that demands our attention while the patient waits in the shadows. The ultimate promise of the Infallible Doctor is not to replace the human touch, but to clear the digital clutter so that we may find each other again."

— Dr. Suresh Kumar Pandey

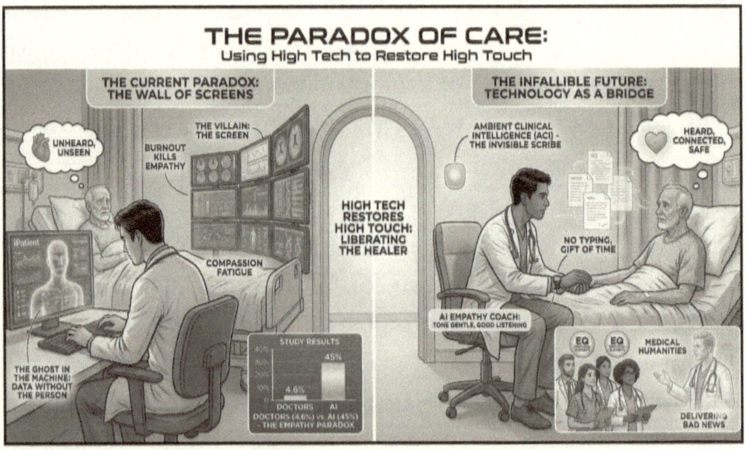

The Ghost in the Machine

Dr. Abraham Verghese, a physician at Stanford University whose hands are as famous as his intellect, tells a story that haunts the corridors of modern medicine. It is a story about a ghost.

He was the attending physician on rounds, leading a flock of bright, young residents through the hospital wards. They stopped outside a patient's room.

The residents, eager to impress, gathered around a computer cart. They pulled up the patient's electronic file. They showed Dr. Verghese the MRI scans, slicing through the body in high-definition grayscale. They recited the blood work, the echocardiogram data, the sodium levels, and the genetic panel with dazzling precision. They knew the ejection fraction of the heart down to the decimal point.

They discussed the case for twenty minutes. They knew everything about the data.

"Okay," Dr. Verghese said, gesturing to the closed door. *"Let's go see the patient."*

The residents hesitated. They looked confused, perhaps even annoyed.

"But we just reviewed the patient," one said.

"No," Dr. Verghese corrected them gently. *"You reviewed the* iPatient."

The "iPatient" is the digital twin that lives in the server. It is neat, clean, binary, and full of data. It does not smell. It does not cry. It does not have a family waiting in the lobby.

The real patient was lying in a bed ten feet away. When Dr. Verghese finally walked into the room, he saw immediately what the computer had missed. The man was shivering. The room smelled of stale tobacco and fear. His hands were clenched white against the sheets. The man wasn't just a collection of failing organs; he was a human being terrified of dying.

The residents had treated the data, but they had ignored the human.

This is the central paradox of twenty-first-century medicine. We have more information about our patients than at any point in history. We can map their genomes and visualize their arteries in 3D. Yet, we feel more distant from them than the village doctor of 1920 who had nothing but a stethoscope and a black bag.

Walk into any hospital room today, and **you** will see the same tableau: The patient lying in bed, vulnerable and exposed, and the doctor sitting on a stool, typing, their back turned to the person they are supposed to be healing.

We have allowed the screen to become a wall. And in doing so, we are losing the most powerful, non-pharmacological drug in our arsenal: **The Human Touch**.

The Villain: The Screen

The villain in this chapter is not a person. It is an object. It is the glowing rectangle that sits between you and your doctor.

The Screen demands attention. It flashes alerts. It requires clicks. It turns the doctor into a data-entry clerk. When the doctor looks at the screen, they cannot look at **you**. They cannot see the subtle wince of pain when you move. They cannot see the tear forming in the corner of your eye.

The Screen has stolen the gaze of the healer.

The Ritual of the Exam

For thousands of years, before we had MRIs or CT scans, the physical exam was everything. It was the only way to know the truth.

The doctor listened to the chest, pressing their ear against the ribs. They palpated the belly, searching for the hardness of a tumor or the swelling of a liver. They held the wrist, feeling the rhythm of the pulse against their own fingertips.

From a purely diagnostic perspective, we must admit that the physical exam is often inferior to the machine. An ultrasound can detect fluid in the lungs with far greater sensitivity than a stethoscope. A CT scan can find a tumor long before a hand can feel it.

Because of this, many modern doctors have stopped touching patients. They stand in the doorway, hands in their pockets. They ask three questions. They order a scan. They leave. They view the body as a black box that only machines can open.

But they are missing the point. The physical exam was never just about data collection. It was a **Ritual**.

When a doctor places a hand on a patient's shoulder, or uses a stethoscope to listen to a heart, a profound biological reaction occurs. Research by Dr. Ted Kaptchuk at Harvard Medical School has shown that the act of caring—the ritual of attention—triggers a cascade of neurochemistry. It releases endorphins and oxytocin in the patient's brain. It lowers cortisol. It reduces blood pressure. It suppresses the perception of pain.

We dismissively call this the **Placebo Effect**, as if it were a trick of the mind. It should be called the **Care Effect**.

The body heals faster when it feels safe. And historically, biologically, mammals feel safe when another member of the tribe touches them with intent.

If we replace the doctor with an iPad, or if the doctor acts like a data-entry clerk, we might get the right diagnosis. But we lose the Care Effect. We treat the disease, but we leave the patient feeling abandoned in a cold, sterile universe.

The Author's Lens: The Touch Before the Knife

I want to share a secret from my own operating room.

Before I start any eye surgery—before I turn on the microscope, before I pick up the scalpel—I do something that is not in any textbook.

I place my hand gently on the patient's shoulder. I leave it there for ten seconds.

The patient is often terrified. They are awake. Their face is covered by a sterile drape. All they can see is a bright light. Their heart rate is often 100 beats per minute.

When I touch their shoulder, I feel their muscles relax. I watch the heart rate monitor drop from 100 to 80.

That touch says: *"I am here. I have you. You are safe."*

No robot can do that. No AI can transmit that reassurance. That touch is the difference between a "procedure" and "healing."

The Robot With the Bedside Manner

Here is the shocking twist, the moment where our assumptions about the future shatter.

We assume that humans are the masters of empathy and machines are the masters of data. But in the battle for bedside manner, the humans are currently losing to the machines.

In April 2023, researchers published a study in *JAMA Internal Medicine* that unsettled the medical establishment. They took 195 real patient questions posted on a public forum (Reddit's r/AskDocs). These were people asking about lumps, pains, and fears.

They had the questions answered by two groups:

1. **Real Physicians.**
2. **ChatGPT** (an AI chatbot).

Then, they showed the anonymized answers to a panel of licensed healthcare professionals. They asked: *Which answer is better? And which is more empathetic?*

The results were a landslide. The evaluators preferred the AI response **79% of the time**.

But the empathy scores were the real kicker.

- Doctors rated "Empathetic": **4.6%**
- AI rated "Empathetic": **45%**

Why? How could a Large Language Model, a statistical engine that feels nothing, out-care a human being?

The answer lies in the constraints of the human condition. The doctors were rushed. They were tired. Their answers were short, curt, and full of medical jargon. *"Go to the ER." "Take Tylenol." "Not cancer."* They were efficient, but they were cold.

The AI, on the other hand, never got tired. It never felt "too busy." It never judged the question as "stupid." It wrote:

"I am so sorry to hear you are going through this pain. That sounds very frightening. Based on your symptoms, it is unlikely to be urgent, but here is what you should look for..."

The machine sounded more human than the humans because it had the luxury of time and the programming of politeness.

This reveals a harsh truth about our profession: **Burnout kills empathy.**

The human doctors weren't heartless; they were exhausted. They were suffering from "Compassion Fatigue." The human soul has a limited battery for grief and worry. After the twentieth patient, the battery dies. The AI doesn't have a battery. It can be endlessly polite, endlessly patient, and endlessly validating, at 3:00 AM or 3:00 PM.

The AI as the Empathy Coach

So, is the solution to fire the doctors and replace them with chatbots? No. The solution is to use the AI to help doctors find their hearts again.

We are seeing the rise of **Real-Time Empathy Coaching**.

Imagine a system running in the background of a Telehealth visit. It listens to the doctor's voice (using the Vocal Biomarkers discussed in Chapter 28). It analyzes the cadence, the pitch, and the ratio of speaking to listening.

It notices that the doctor is interrupting the patient. It notices the doctor's tone is becoming sharp, rapid, and dismissive—a sign of stress.

A tiny notification pops up on the doctor's screen, private to them:

[ALERT: INTERRUPTED PATIENT 3X. SPEAKING RATE +20%. BREATHE.]

It acts as a digital mirror. In the heat of the moment, we often don't realize we are being rude. The AI gently reminds the tired physician: *"Hey, there is a scared person on the other end of this line. Slow down."*

Companies like **Cogito** are already using this technology in call centers to help agents be nicer to customers. Applying it to medicine could be transformative. It is not about policing the doctor; it is about supporting the doctor in the emotional labor of the job.

Restoring Eye Contact

As we discussed in Chapter 30 (The Administrative Cure), the biggest enemy of human connection is the keyboard. The screen demands our gaze.

This is where **Ambient Clinical Intelligence (ACI)** saves the relationship.

When the AI listens to the conversation and writes the notes automatically, the doctor is freed from the tyranny of the screen. Dr. Eric Topol calls this **"The Gift of Time."**

If the AI handles the typing, the coding, the billing, and the data retrieval, the doctor gets back the fifteen minutes they used to spend staring at the computer.

What do they do with those fifteen minutes?

They can hold your hand.

They can ask about your fears, your family, your life.

They can perform the physical exam—not just to find the tumor, but to establish the bond of trust that says, I am here. I am watching you. I will not let you fall.

Technology effectively removes technology from the room. It makes the computer invisible so the humans can connect.

Flash Forward: The Deathbed of 2040

There is one area, however, where the human touch is irreplaceable. It is the sacred duty of the physician at the end of life.

When a treatment fails, when the cancer wins, when it is time to turn off the ventilator—this is the moment where the "Infallible Doctor" must step back and the **"Human Doctor"** must step forward.

An AI can calculate the survival probability (0.01%).

An AI can draft the palliative care plan with perfect dosage for morphine.

But an AI cannot sit in a room with a mother and tell her that her child is dying.

To deliver bad news requires a soul. It requires the ability to absorb the grief of another person. It requires the shared vulnerability of mortality. A robot cannot say *"I know how this feels,"* because it doesn't. It will never die. It will never lose a child.

A robot cannot cry with you.

As AI takes over the "science" of medicine—the diagnosis, the prescription, the surgical precision—the human doctor will migrate to the "art."

The medical school curriculum of the future will change. We will spend less time memorizing the Krebs Cycle or the names of the cranial nerves (the AI knows that better than we ever will). We will spend more time learning **Medical Humanities**.

We will learn how to communicate, how to listen, how to grieve, and how to touch.

We will select medical students not just for their MCAT scores and their ability to memorize textbooks, but for their **EQ (Emotional Quotient)**. We will look for the healers, not just the mechanics.

The High-Touch Future

The dystopian view of the future is a patient in a sterile room, diagnosed by a camera on the wall and treated by a cold robot arm, never seeing a human face.

But the utopian view—the Infallible Doctor view—is different.

Because the AI is doing the "robotic" work (analyzing data, typing notes, checking interactions), the human doctor is no longer a data processor. The human doctor becomes a Healer again.

They have the time to make house calls again, guided by the AI's route optimization. They have the bandwidth to know their patients' names and hobbies. They are **"High Tech"** in their pocket, but **"High Touch"** in their practice.

We are not losing the touch. We are liberating it. We are rescuing it from the burden of bureaucracy.

For the first time in a century, the doctor can turn their back on the screen and look—really look—at **you**. And in that look, the healing begins.

THE TAKEAWAY

The Villain is "The Screen": Doctors spend more time looking at the "iPatient" (the digital file) than the real patient. This destroys the "Care Effect" (the biological healing triggered by human connection).

The "Empathy Paradox": A study showed that AI chatbots were rated 10x more empathetic than human doctors. Why? Because humans are burned out and rushed, while AI has infinite patience.

The "Invisible Computer": Ambient AI (like Nuance DAX) writes the notes automatically, allowing the doctor to stop typing and restore eye contact with you.

The Sacred Role: While AI can cure disease, only a human can comfort grief. The future doctor will be selected for EQ (Emotional Intelligence), leaving the memorization to the machine.

References

1. Verghese, A. (2008). "Culture Shock — Patient as Icon, Icon as Patient." *New England Journal of Medicine*, 359(26), 2748-2751.
2. Ayers, J. W., et al. (2023). "Comparing Physician and Artificial Intelligence Chatbot Responses to Patient Questions Posted to a Public Social Media Forum." *JAMA Internal Medicine*, 183(6), 589-596.
3. Kaptchuk, T. J., et al. (2008). "Components of placebo effect: randomized controlled trial in patients with irritable bowel syndrome." *BMJ*, 336(7651), 999-1003.
4. Topol, E. (2019). *Deep Medicine: How Artificial Intelligence Can Make Healthcare Human Again*. Basic Books.
5. Zulman, D. M., et al. (2020). "Practices to Foster Physician Presence and Connection With Patients in the Clinical Encounter." *JAMA*, 323(1), 70-81.

Chapter 35

Re-Schooling Med School

Training the Pilots of Tomorrow

"We are training our brightest young minds to memorize yesterday's facts in a world exploding with tomorrow's data. We teach them to be libraries, but we need them to be navigators. The Infallible Doctor is not built by cramming knowledge into a human brain, but by teaching that brain how to partner with a machine that remembers everything."

— Dr. Suresh Kumar Pandey

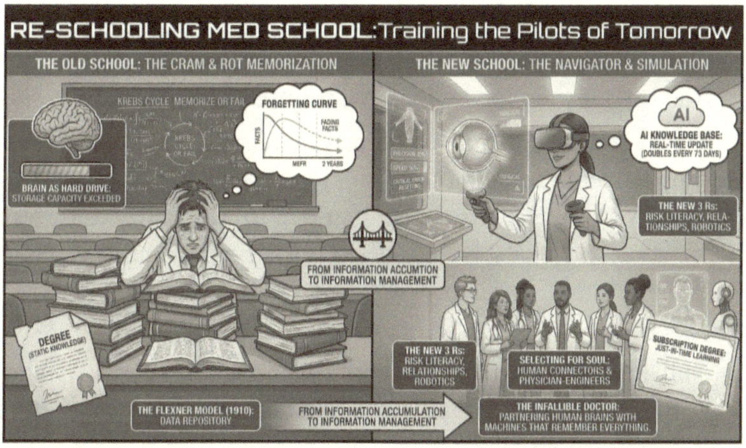

The Cram

Imagine **you** are twenty-two years old. You are sitting in a windowless lecture hall, the air stale with the collective anxiety of one hundred and fifty over-achievers. You are a first-year medical student.

In front of you is a textbook the size of a cinder block. You are holding a yellow highlighter, your hand cramping. You are trying to memorize the **Krebs Cycle**.

It is a biochemical waltz—a complex series of chemical reactions that cells use to generate energy. You are memorizing the names of enzymes: *Citrate synthase. Aconitase. Isocitrate dehydrogenase. Alpha-ketoglutarate dehydrogenase.* You recite them like a mantra. You build memory palaces in your mind to store them.

You will be tested on this next Tuesday. If you fail, you do not become a doctor. The stakes are absolute.

So, you cram. You turn your hippocampus into a hard drive. You stuff thousands of discrete facts—the 206 bones, the 600 muscles, the intricate web of cranial nerves—into your brain. You become a walking encyclopedia.

But here is the dirty secret that no professor admits in that lecture hall: **The moment you walk out of the exam, the "forgetting curve" begins.** The knowledge decays. Two years later, when you are standing over a patient in cardiac arrest, sweating under the fluorescent lights, you will not remember the molecular structure of Isocitrate dehydrogenase.

And even if you did, it would not help you save the patient's life.

We are training doctors for a world that no longer exists. We are selecting students based on their ability to memorize facts, in an age where facts are free. We are training them to be data repositories in an era where the smartphone in their pocket contains every medical paper ever written, updated in real-time. We are teaching them to be robots.

And as we have seen throughout this book, the robots are about to get much, much better at being robots than we are. If we try to compete with AI on memory, we lose.

If we want to build the Infallible Doctor, we have to burn down the medical school and build something new in its ashes.

The Villain: The Ghost of Abraham Flexner

To understand why we teach this way, we have to go back to 1910, to a man named **Abraham Flexner**.

Flexner was an educator who was hired to audit medical schools in North America. What he found horrified him. Medicine was the

Wild West. It was full of snake-oil salesmen, mystics, and proprietary schools that taught "healing" without any basis in science.

He wrote a famous report—the **Flexner Report**—that standardized medical education. He laid down the law: Medicine is a science. Doctors must understand chemistry, biology, and physics.

It was a brilliant idea for 1910. It saved the profession. It created the **"Flexner Model"**: two years of intense classroom science (pre-clinical), followed by two years of watching doctors in a hospital (clinical).

But that model has barely changed in 110 years.

The curriculum assumes that a doctor acts as a **Data Repository**. The doctor learns the knowledge, stores it in their brain, and retrieves it when a patient walks in.

But today, medical knowledge doubles every **73 days** (as we discussed in Chapter 2). In 1950, it doubled every 50 years. The sheer volume of data has exceeded the storage capacity of the human skull. By forcing students to memorize the Krebs Cycle, we are wasting valuable cognitive real estate. We are filling their heads with static data instead of teaching them how to navigate dynamic data.

We need a Post-Flexner revolution. We need to stop teaching the "What" and start teaching the "How."

The Author's Lens: The Virtual Eye

I lived through the old way of learning surgery. It was terrifying.

When I was a resident, the first time I performed cataract surgery, I operated on a living human being. An elderly woman lay on the table. My mentor sat next to me. I held the scalpel. My hands shook.

If I made a mistake, she would go blind. That pressure is crushing. It is why the learning curve for eye surgeons is steep and bloody.

Today, my students learn differently. They do not touch a human eye until they have performed 50 surgeries in the **Metaverse**.

They sit at an **Eyesi Surgical Simulator**. It looks like a microscope, but when they look inside, they see a high-fidelity virtual eye. They hold haptic instruments that provide force feedback—they can "feel" the resistance of the cornea.

They practice peeling the delicate capsule of the lens. If they tear it, the screen flashes red: **[COMPLICATION: VITREOUS LOSS.]**

They reset. They try again. They fail safely. They learn the muscle memory without the moral burden of hurting a patient.

By the time they touch a real patient, they are already experts. They are pilots who have logged their hours in the flight simulator.

The Death of the Cadaver

The new curriculum must shift from Information Accumulation to Information Management.

At **Case Western Reserve University**, they have already taken a radical, heretical step. They got rid of the cadaver lab.

For centuries, dissecting a dead body was the rite of passage for a doctor. It was a sensory initiation—the smell of formaldehyde, the texture of fascia, the confrontation with mortality. But it was also messy, expensive, and static. A dead body does not bleed, it does not have a heartbeat, and once you cut a nerve, you cannot un-cut it.

Instead, Case Western students wear **Microsoft HoloLens** headsets. They walk around a giant, floating, three-dimensional holographic human body.

They can strip away the skin with a gesture. They can make the muscles transparent to reveal the skeleton. They can zoom in on a beating heart and walk *inside* the ventricle to see the valves closing. If they make a mistake in dissection, they hit "Undo."

They learn anatomy faster and better because they are interacting with it, not just excavating dead tissue. They are learning the geography of the body in the same way a pilot learns the geography of the sky—through simulation.

But the bigger shift is intellectual. We need to stop testing students on trivia. "*What is the standard dose of Vancomycin?*" The AI knows that. The AI will calculate that based on the patient's kidney function better than you ever will.

We need to test them on: "*The AI recommends Vancomycin, but the patient is refusing because their mother had a reaction to it. How do you handle this conversation? How do you assess the risk?*"

The new "Three Rs" of Med School are not Reading, Writing, and Arithmetic. They are:

1. **Risk Literacy:** Understanding statistics so they can interpret the AI's "95% confidence" prediction.
2. **Relationships:** The empathy, storytelling, and communication skills to be a healer (Chapter 34).
3. **Robotics:** How to pilot the machine.

Engineering the Doctor

In 2018, the University of Illinois Urbana-Champaign launched the **Carle Illinois College of Medicine**. It is the world's first "Engineering-Based" medical school.

They don't just look for Biology majors. They recruit computer scientists, engineers, and coders.

Their students don't just learn how to use a stethoscope; they learn the physics of sound waves so they can understand how an ultrasound AI works. They learn about algorithms, bias, and neural networks.

They are training **Physician-Engineers**.

These are doctors who won't just accept the "Black Box" (Chapter 31). They will know how to open it. They will know when the algorithm is hallucinating because they understand how the algorithm was built. They will not be passive consumers of technology; they will be active partners.

In the future, "Coding" (or at least "Computational Thinking") might be as essential to a doctor as "Anatomy." You don't need to write the code from scratch, but you need to speak the language of the machine you are partnering with.

The Flight Simulator: Osso VR

The most dangerous phrase in medical education is a classic maxim: *"See one, do one, teach one."*

It means a resident watches a surgery once, then tries it on a real patient, then teaches the next person. It is a terrifyingly reckless way to learn. It essentially treats the first few patients as practice dummies. The "learning curve" is paved with complications.

Pilots do not do this. A pilot does not watch an instructor land a 747 and then say, *"Okay, my turn, let's fill it with passengers."* A pilot spends hundreds of hours in a high-fidelity simulator before they ever touch a passenger jet.

Medical education is finally moving to the **Flight School Model**.

Companies like **Osso VR** provide virtual reality surgery training. A resident puts on a headset. They hold haptic controllers that feel like surgical tools—a saw, a drill, a retractor. They perform a knee replacement in VR.

The system scores them ruthlessly.

- *Precision: 85%*
- *Speed: 90%*
- *Critical Error: You hit the peroneal nerve.*

In the real world, hitting the nerve means a lawsuit and a crippled patient. In VR, the screen flashes red. You reset. You do it again. And again. Fifty times. Only when they score 100% in the simulator—only when the motion is muscle memory—are they allowed to touch a patient.

A study at UCLA showed that VR-trained students were **230% more skilled** than those trained with traditional methods. The Infallible Doctor is not born; they are forged in the simulator.

The End of the Degree

Finally, we have to kill the idea that education ends at graduation.

Currently, a doctor gets their MD at age 26. They might practice until age 66. That is forty years. A doctor practicing in 2024 relying on knowledge frozen in 1984 is a danger to the public. We have "Continuing Medical Education" (CME), but let's be honest: it is often a joke. It is a few weekend conferences in nice hotels to tick a box.

In the future, the "Degree" will not be a static diploma on the wall. It will be a **Subscription**.

The AI monitoring the doctor's practice (the same one doing the notes in Chapter 30) will also monitor their knowledge gap.

"Dr. Evans," the system might whisper. *"I notice you prescribed Ciprofloxacin for this infection. New guidelines were released yesterday*

suggesting that resistance is high in this zip code. Drug Y is now preferred. Here is a 2-minute video summary. Please review."

The education is continuous, bite-sized, and integrated into the workflow. It is **"Just-in-Time Learning."** You don't memorize the cure for Ebola in case you see it one day. You learn the cure for Ebola five minutes before you walk into the room of an Ebola patient.

Flash Forward: The Student of 2035

It is 2035. You are a medical student.

You do not sit in a lecture hall. You do not carry a textbook.

You spend your morning in the simulator, performing a virtual appendectomy until you get a perfect score.

You spend your afternoon with patients, practicing the art of breaking bad news, coached by an AI that analyzes your tone of voice.

You do not know the Krebs Cycle by heart. But you know how to ask the AI to map a patient's metabolic pathway to find a rare disease.

You are not a library. You are a healer.

Selecting for Soul

If the AI carries the burden of knowledge, what is left for the human? **Character.**

Currently, getting into medical school is a ruthless competition of grades. We select for the people who are best at taking tests. We select for "Gunners"—hyper-competitive individualists who can memorize the phone book.

But the future of medicine is a team sport (Doctor + AI + Patient).

We need to change the admissions criteria. We need to look at Mount Sinai's **HuMed (Humanities and Medicine)** program. They accept students who majored in English, History, or Philosophy—skipping the traditional hard science prerequisites.

The hypothesis was risky. Would these poets and historians kill patients?

The data came back: **No.** Once they caught up on the basic science, they often became better doctors than the biology majors. They were better at listening. They were better at ambiguity. They were better at the "Art."

We need to stop selecting for "Human Hard Drives" and start selecting for "Human Connectors." We need people who can hold a hand, explain a complex probability, and navigate an ethical dilemma.

The New Oath

When students graduate, they take the Hippocratic Oath. *"First, do no harm."*

Perhaps, in the age of the Infallible Doctor, we need to add a new line. A line that acknowledges the partner standing next to us.

"I promise to trust the machine when it is right, to challenge the machine when it is wrong, and to never let the machine stand between me and the suffering of my patient."

Re-schooling Med School is not about lowering standards. It is about raising them. It is about admitting that the human brain has limits, and that true excellence comes from knowing how to extend those limits with silicon, while keeping the heart made of flesh.

THE TAKEAWAY

The Villain is "Rote Memorization": We force students to memorize facts (like the Krebs Cycle) that become obsolete in 73 days. This wastes brain power that should be used for critical thinking.

The "Virtual Eye" Simulator: Eye surgery residents now train on high-fidelity simulators (Eyesi), performing 50 virtual surgeries before touching a human patient, eliminating the dangerous "learning curve."

The Death of the Cadaver: Schools like Case Western have replaced dead bodies with HoloLens headsets, allowing students to explore 3D holographic anatomy and "undo" their cuts.

The "Subscription" Degree: Instead of a one-time diploma, future doctors will have a lifelong AI tutor that whispers new guidelines (Just-in-Time Learning) as they treat patients, ensuring they never become outdated.

References

1. Flexner, A. (1910). "Medical Education in the United States and Canada: A Report to the Carnegie Foundation for the Advancement of Teaching." *The Carnegie Foundation.*
2. Topol, E. (2019). *Deep Medicine: How Artificial Intelligence Can Make Healthcare Human Again*. Basic Books.
3. Wartman, S. A., & Combs, C. D. (2018). "Medical Education Must Move From the Information Age to the Age of Artificial Intelligence." *Academic Medicine*, 93(8), 1107-1109.
4. Lohre, R., Bois, A. J., Athwal, G. S., & Goel, D. P. (2020). "Improved complex skill acquisition by immersive virtual reality training: a randomized controlled trial." *The Journal of Bone and Joint Surgery*, 102(6), 526-533.
5. Prober, C. G., & Khan, S. (2013). "Medical education reimagined: a call to action." *Academic Medicine*, 88(10), 1407-1410.

PART VIII
The New Horizon
What a Zero-Error World Looks Like

Chapter 36

The Shift to Vitality

From Sick Care to Longevity Medicine

"We have built a healthcare system designed for the shipwreck, not the navigation. We are experts at patching holes in a sinking hull, but we have forgotten how to steer the ship. The promise of the Infallible Doctor is not just to rescue the drowning, but to see the iceberg ten miles away and turn the wheel."

— Dr. Suresh Kumar Pandey

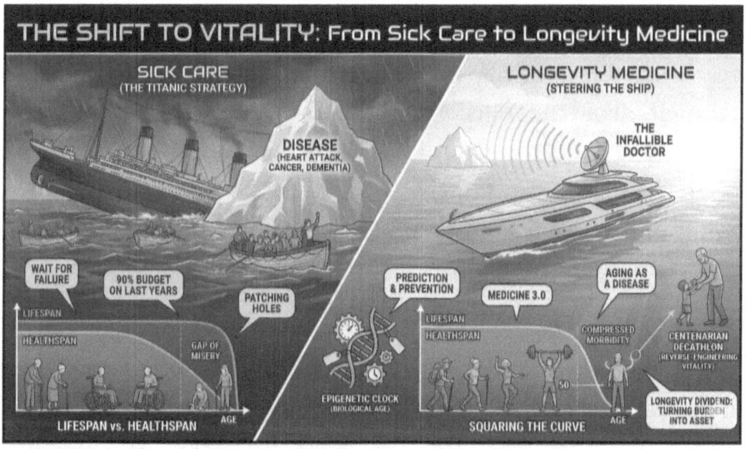

The Iceberg and the Radar

Imagine, for a moment, that **you** are the captain of the Titanic. You are steaming across the North Atlantic in the pitch black of night.

The current strategy of the modern healthcare system is terrifyingly simple: **You wait.**

You wait until the ship hits the iceberg. You wait until the steel groans and buckles. You wait until the freezing water is rushing into the hull and the passengers begin to scream.

Then, and only then, do you act. You send in the helicopters, the pumps, and the rescue teams. You spend billions of dollars trying to patch the hole and pump out the water while the ship is already sinking.

This is **"Sick Care."**

It is heroic. It is dramatic. We write TV shows about the surgeons who operate on the crashing patient. And it is incredibly stupid.

We spend nearly 90% of our massive healthcare budget treating people in the last few years of their lives, trying to rescue them from diseases that took decades to develop. We wait for the heart attack to block the artery. We wait for the cancer to metastasize to the liver. We wait for the stroke to steal the speech.

The Infallible Doctor proposes a new strategy, one that seems radical only because we have been doing it wrong for so long: **Steer the ship.**

Use the radar—Artificial Intelligence—to see the iceberg ten miles away, when it is just a blip on the horizon. Turn the wheel two degrees to the left. Avoid the collision entirely. The passengers will never know they were in danger. They will just enjoy the cruise.

This is the shift to **Longevity Medicine**. It is the transition from "fixing broken things" to "maintaining high performance." It is the end of the Titanic Strategy.

The Villain: Lifespan vs. Healthspan

For the last century, medicine has been obsessed with a single metric: **Lifespan**. This is the total number of years you are alive.

And by that metric, we succeeded. In 1900, the average life expectancy was forty-seven. Today, in most developed nations, it is nearly eighty. We achieved this by conquering infectious diseases like smallpox and cholera, and by getting very good at keeping sick people from dying immediately.

But we didn't necessarily make those extra years *good* years.

A person might live to be eighty-five, but they often spend the last fifteen years of that life in a state of slow, humiliating decline. They are in a nursing home. They are unable to walk. They are suffering from dementia. They are swallowing twelve pills a day just to keep their chemistry balanced.

That is not living; that is slowly dying.

The goal of the future is **Healthspan**.

Healthspan is the number of years you spend in good health—functional, cognitive, and pain-free. The goal is what epidemiologists call **"Squaring the Curve."**

We want you to live at full capacity—hiking, thinking, loving—until you are ninety or a hundred. And then, we want you to decline rapidly and die painlessly in your sleep. We want to eliminate the "Gap of Misery"—that decade of disability that currently haunts the end of modern life.

The Author's Lens: The Vision of Vitality

I see this "Gap of Misery" in my own clinic.

I treat elderly patients who have lost their vision to **Age-Related Macular Degeneration (AMD)**. They are alive, but they are prisoners. They cannot drive. They cannot read. They cannot see the faces of their grandchildren.

For decades, ophthalmology was "Sick Care." We waited until the patient went blind, and then we tried to help them cope with magnifiers and canes.

Today, we are shifting to **Vitality**. We use AI to scan the retina of a healthy 50-year-old. We see the microscopic drusen (waste deposits) forming twenty years before vision loss occurs.

We intervene *then*. We change the diet. We use specific supplements (AREDS2). We protect the retina before the damage is done.

My goal is not just to prevent blindness. It is to ensure that when my patient is 90, they can still read a book. That is Healthspan.

Aging as a Disease

To do this, we have to change our fundamental philosophy about what aging is.

Currently, the FDA does not recognize "Aging" as a disease. It views aging as a natural inevitability, like gravity. You cannot prescribe a drug for aging. You can only prescribe a drug for the symptoms of aging: hypertension, heart disease, cancer, Alzheimer's.

But a new generation of scientists—visionaries like **Dr. David Sinclair** at Harvard and **Dr. Nir Barzilai** at Albert Einstein College of Medicine—argue that this is wrong.

They argue that heart disease, cancer, and Alzheimer's are just the heads of the **Hydra**. The body of the Hydra is **Aging** itself. It is the accumulation of cellular "rust"—DNA damage, mitochondrial dysfunction, senescent "zombie" cells—that makes us vulnerable to these diseases.

If you cure cancer today, you extend the average human lifespan by only about three years. Why? Because the person who didn't die of cancer will likely die of a heart attack or stroke a few years later. The underlying machinery is breaking down.

But if we can treat the aging process—if we can slow down the cellular rust—we delay *all* the diseases at once. We don't just chop off one head of the Hydra; we strike the heart.

This is not science fiction. We have already done it in mice. We can make old mice young again. We can extend their healthspan by 30%. Now, the race is on to do it for humans.

The Clock in Your Blood

But how do we know if we are aging? How do we measure the speed of the rust?

For years, we only had **Chronological Age**—the number of candles on your birthday cake. But that is a useless number. We all know a fifty-year-old who looks and moves like they are seventy, and a seventy-year-old who runs marathons.

In 2013, a scientist named **Steve Horvath** discovered a way to measure **Biological Age**.

He found that as we age, chemical tags (methyl groups) attach themselves to our DNA, turning certain genes off and on. It is like dust accumulating on a vinyl record. This process is called **DNA Methylation**.

Horvath discovered that this accumulation follows a predictable pattern. It acts like a clock. By measuring these tags, we can tell exactly how fast you are aging on a cellular level. This is the **Epigenetic Clock**.

In the future of the Infallible Doctor, you will get a "Horvath Score" every year alongside your cholesterol check.

- *Chronological Age: 50*
- *Biological Age: 56*

This is a wake-up call. It means you are aging faster than the calendar. You are steaming toward the iceberg at full speed.

The AI will then intervene. "*Your methylation markers suggest high inflammation. Let's change your diet, increase your Vitamin D, and start a specific Zone 2 cardio protocol.*"

Six months later, you test again.

- *Biological Age: 53.*

You have literally reversed your aging clock by three years. You have steered the ship. You have bought time.

Medicine 3.0

Dr. Peter Attia, a physician who focuses on the science of longevity, calls this transition **Medicine 3.0**.

- **Medicine 1.0:** Witch doctors, leeches, and spirits. (No science).
- **Medicine 2.0:** The current era. Antibiotics, surgery, treating acute illness. (Great at saving lives from trauma and infection, bad at preventing chronic disease).
- **Medicine 3.0:** The future. Highly personalized, data-driven prevention.

In Medicine 2.0, we treat high blood sugar when you get Diabetes (an HbA1c of 6.5%). We wait for the failure.

In Medicine 3.0, the AI notices your insulin resistance creeping up twenty years earlier, when your HbA1c is 5.2%. It intervenes *then*, when the fix is easy.

Medicine 3.0 requires the Infallible Doctor because no human doctor has the time to obsess over a "healthy" person. A human doctor is too busy treating heart attacks to worry about a 25-year-old's slightly elevated ApoB (a cholesterol marker).

But the AI isn't busy. It monitors the 25-year-old with the same intensity as the ICU patient. It plays the long game.

The TAME Trial

We are also finding drugs that might act as "Anti-Aging" pills. But they aren't exotic elixirs found in the Amazon. They are hiding in plain sight.

The most famous candidate is a humble drug called **Metformin**.

Metformin has been used for sixty years to treat Type 2 Diabetes. It costs pennies. It is incredibly safe. But over the decades, doctors noticed something strange in the data. Diabetics taking Metformin seemed to get less cancer, less heart disease, and less dementia than people who didn't have diabetes at all.

Metformin seems to mimic the effects of caloric restriction (fasting), turning on the body's repair mechanisms even when you are eating.

Dr. Nir Barzilai is currently launching the **TAME Trial (Targeting Aging with Metformin)**. It is a historic study. It is the first major clinical trial designed to prove to the FDA that a drug can delay multiple age-related diseases at once.

If it succeeds, it changes everything. It means your doctor might prescribe Metformin (or a newer drug like Rapamycin) when you turn forty—not because you are sick, but to keep you from getting sick.

The Centenarian Decathlon

The goal is not just to survive, but to thrive. To visualize this, we use a concept called the **Centenarian Decathlon**.

Imagine you are 100 years old. What ten physical tasks do you want to be able to do?

- Pick up a great-grandchild (30 lbs).
- Walk up a flight of stairs without stopping.
- Get up off the floor using only one hand support.
- Lift a suitcase into an overhead bin.

To do those things at age 100, you need a specific amount of muscle mass and VO2 max (lung capacity). Since muscle declines naturally with age, the AI calculates backward.

"To lift 30 lbs at age 100, you need to be able to lift 50 lbs at age 80, and 80 lbs at age 50."

The AI builds your training program *today* based on the 100-year-old you want to become. It is reverse-engineering your life. It turns exercise from a chore into a savings account for your future self.

Flash Forward: Your Checkup in 2040

It is 2040. You go for your annual physical.

The doctor does not just check your blood pressure. She scans your Epigenetic Clock.

[BIOLOGICAL AGE: 42 (CHRONOLOGICAL AGE: 45)]

She smiles. *"You are getting younger. Keep up the Rapamycin protocol. Your muscle mass is in the top 10% for your age group. You are on track to win the Centenarian Decathlon."*

You leave the office feeling not just "fine," but powerful.

The Longevity Dividend

Critics often recoil at this idea. They ask: *"Why do we want to live longer? The planet is overpopulated. We will just have more old people draining the economy."*

This is the **Longevity Myth**.

The cost to society comes from *sick* old people. A person with dementia requires 24/7 care for years. That is expensive. It destroys families and bank accounts. But a healthy 90-year-old who is still working, volunteering, or just living independently costs the system almost nothing.

Economists call this the **Longevity Dividend**. If we can extend the healthy working life of the population by just two years, it would add trillions of dollars to the global economy. We unlock the wisdom, the mentorship, and the productivity of the older generation. We turn a burden into an asset.

The Infallible Doctor views the body like a classic car. A 1965 Mustang can run forever if you replace the parts, change the oil, preventing the rust, and drive it with care. There is no law of physics that says it must fall apart at 100,000 miles.

We are shifting the entire medical establishment from the Department of Disease to the **Department of Vitality**. And for the captain of the ship, the horizon has never looked clearer.

THE TAKEAWAY

The Villain is "Sick Care": We wait for the "Titanic" to hit the iceberg (heart attack, cancer) before acting. We spend 90% of money on the last few years of life instead of prevention.

The "Eye Radar": In ophthalmology, we can now detect early signs of Macular Degeneration 20 years before blindness occurs, allowing us to steer the ship and save vision for old age.

The Epigenetic Clock: We can now measure your "Biological Age" (how fast you are rusting) via DNA tags. If you are aging too fast, lifestyle changes can reverse the clock.

The Centenarian Decathlon: AI can calculate exactly how much muscle you need today (at 50) to be able to pick up your great-grandchild when you are 100, turning exercise into a long-term investment.

References

1. Horvath, S. (2013). "DNA methylation age of human tissues and cell types." *Genome Biology*, 14(10), R115.
2. Barzilai, N., Crandall, J. P., Kritchevsky, S. B., & Espeland, M. A. (2016). "Metformin as a Tool to Target Aging." *Cell Metabolism*, 23(6), 1060-1065.
3. Attia, P. (2023). *Outlive: The Science and Art of Longevity.* Harmony/Rodale.
4. Olshansky, S. J., Perry, D., Miller, R. A., & Butler, R. N. (2006). "In Pursuit of the Longevity Dividend." *The Scientist*, 20(3), 28-36.
5. López-Otín, C., Blasco, M. A., Partridge, L., Serrano, M., & Kroemer, G. (2013). "The Hallmarks of Aging." *Cell*, 153(6), 1194-1217.

Chapter 37

The Global Hive Mind

A Network That Learns from Every Mistake

"We have built a medical system that is brilliant in isolation but idiotic in connection. We lock our knowledge in vaults while our diseases travel on jets. The Infallible Doctor breaks these locks, knitting the fragmented experience of the world into a single consciousness, ensuring that no patient ever has to die from a mistake that has already been solved."

— Dr. Suresh Kumar Pandey

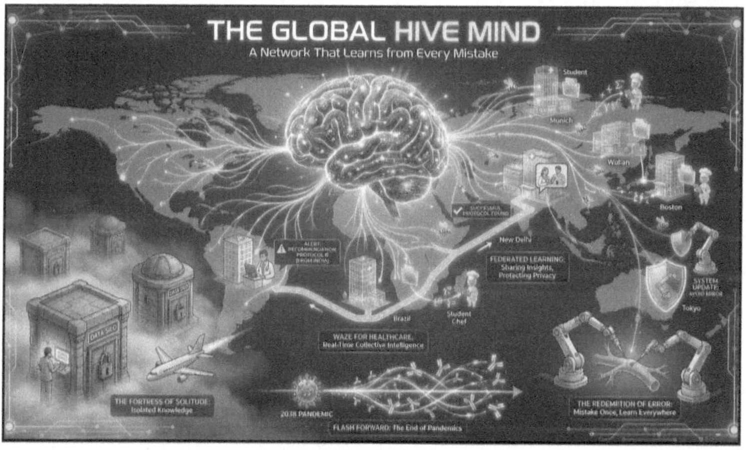

The Speed of Silence

In late December 2019, inside the bustling, fluorescent-lit wards of Wuhan Central Hospital, a handful of ophthalmologists and pulmonologists noticed a ghost.

They saw a cluster of patients presenting with a strange, pneumonia-like illness. It was aggressive. It was viral. On CT scans, the lungs didn't look like lungs; they looked like ground glass, hazy and opaque. The patients weren't responding to standard antibiotics. Their oxygen levels were dropping with terrifying speed.

The doctors did what good doctors do. They made notes in their local electronic charts. They talked to their colleagues in the hushed tones of the hallway. They sent a few anxious messages on WeChat groups. They sounded the alarm.

But the alarm hit a wall.

The data stayed in Wuhan. The insights stayed in the server.

Two months later, in the affluent, historic towns of Lombardy, Italy, doctors began seeing the exact same ghost. They were baffled. They had never seen lungs behave like this. They wasted precious days—days measured in lives—trying to figure out what was happening.

They intubated patients early, forcing air into stiff lungs, a strategy we later learned might have caused more harm than good in certain phases of the disease. They struggled to find the right drug protocols. They improvised.

Thousands died in Italy who might have been saved if they had known—instantly, intimately—what the doctors in Wuhan already knew.

This is the tragedy of modern medicine. It is a tragedy of **Latency**.

The virus traveled at the speed of a jet plane, hopping continents in hours. The medical knowledge traveled at the speed of an academic paper, getting peer-reviewed, edited, and published months later.

We are fighting a hypersonic war with trench-warfare communications.

If a Tesla hits a pothole on a highway in California, the car's sensors record the jolt. Within minutes, that data is uploaded to the cloud, and every other Tesla in the fleet updates its internal map to avoid that pothole. The individual learns, and the species evolves instantly.

But if a patient has a bad reaction to a drug in London, a patient in New York might die from the exact same reaction a week later. The system has no memory. It has no collective consciousness. It is a series of isolated islands, each reinventing the wheel while the water rises.

The Infallible Doctor changes this physics. It creates a **Global Hive**

Mind. It connects the experience of every doctor and every patient into a single, real-time intelligence network.

It ensures that the first time a medical error happens anywhere in the world, it is the last time it happens everywhere.

The Villain: The Fortress of Solitude

Why haven't we done this already? Why don't hospitals share data the way cars share maps?

The answer lies in two powerful forces: **Privacy** and **Greed**.

Hospitals treat patient data like gold bullion. They lock it in a digital vault. They are terrified of leaking it (citing HIPAA regulations in the US or GDPR in Europe), and perhaps more cynically, they are terrified of giving it to their competitors.

The Mayo Clinic does not want the Cleveland Clinic to train algorithms on its patients. Pfizer does not want Merck to see the results of its failed clinical trials. Data is the new oil, and nobody gives away oil for free.

So, we have **Data Silos**. We have incredible AI algorithms, but they are starving. An AI trained only on patients in Boston—mostly white, mostly wealthy—will fail when used on patients in Mumbai or Nairobi, because the demographics, genetics, and environmental factors are completely different.

To build a truly Infallible Doctor, we need to train the AI on **everyone**. We need the diverse, messy, chaotic data of 8 billion people. But we cannot put 8 billion medical records into one central database. It would be a privacy nightmare, a target for every hacker on earth.

So, how do we solve this paradox? How do we learn from everyone without seeing anyone?

We don't move the data. We move the brain.

The Author's Lens: The Rare Eye

I see the cost of these "Silos" in my own field of ophthalmology.

I often encounter patients with rare corneal dystrophies. These are genetic conditions that affect maybe 1 in 100,000 people. In my entire career, I might see five cases.

When I treat the first one, I am guessing. I try a drop. It doesn't work. I try a surgery. It works partially. I learn a hard lesson.

But somewhere in Germany, another doctor has seen ten cases. Somewhere in Japan, a researcher has found a gene therapy that works perfectly.

But I don't know that. Their data is locked in their hospital's server. My patient goes blind because I am operating in a vacuum.

If our EMRs (Electronic Medical Records) were connected, the moment I typed the diagnosis, the Hive Mind would say:

[ALERT: SUCCESSFUL PROTOCOL FOUND IN MUNICH. 95% CURE RATE.]

My patient would see. The isolation is the enemy.

The Federated Revolution

This brings us to one of the most elegant concepts in the future of computer science: **Federated Learning**.

To understand it, imagine you want to bake the world's best chocolate chip cookie.

- **The Old Way (Centralized):** You ask a thousand grandmothers to mail their secret family recipes to your headquarters. You read them all and find the best one.
    - *Problem:* The grandmothers refuse. They don't trust you with their secrets.
- **The New Way (Federated):** You send a "Student Chef" (the AI model) to visit each grandmother's house.

The Student goes into Grandmother A's kitchen. She doesn't give him the written recipe. Instead, she lets him watch her bake. He learns: *"Ah, she uses brown sugar instead of white."* He updates his internal knowledge.

Then he leaves. He takes no paper, no ingredients, no cookies. He only takes the **lesson**.

He travels to Grandmother B's kitchen. He learns: *"She chills the dough for an hour."* He updates his math again.

By the time the Student visits a thousand kitchens, he knows how to bake the perfect cookie. But he never stole a single recipe. The secret ingredients stayed in the safe.

In medicine, this means the AI algorithm travels to the hospital's server. It "reads" the patient records securely inside the hospital's firewall. It learns the patterns—for example, *"Patients with Gene X respond badly to Drug Y."*

It updates its own internal weights—its neural connections.

Then, it leaves. No patient names, no birth dates, no private records ever leave the building. Only the mathematical insights leave. These insights are aggregated in the cloud to update the **"Global Model,"** which is then beamed back down to every hospital.

This allows fierce competitors to collaborate without sharing secrets. It allows us to be selfish and altruistic at the same time.

The Billion-Dollar Handshake

This isn't just theory. It is already reshaping the pharmaceutical industry.

In 2019, ten of the world's biggest pharmaceutical companies—giants like Amgen, Bayer, and GSK—did the unthinkable. They agreed to work together under a consortium called **Project MELLODDY** (Machine Learning Ledger Orchestration for Drug DiscoverY).

Historically, these companies are mortal enemies. Their chemical libraries are their crown jewels. But they realized that drug discovery was becoming too hard for any one company to solve (recall Eroom's Law from Chapter 23).

They used Federated Learning to train a drug discovery AI. Each company kept its proprietary chemical data secret. But the AI learned from all of them.

The result was a **"Super-Model"** that was significantly better at predicting drug behavior than any single company could build alone. They realized a fundamental truth of the digital age: by pooling their intelligence, they all got richer. By building a Hive Mind, they could find cures that none of them could find in isolation.

Waze for Healthcare

When you drive using Waze or Google Maps, you are participating in a Hive Mind. You don't think about it, but you are.

If you tap your brakes on the highway because of a deer, Waze notices. If ten people tap their brakes, Waze turns the road line red on the map for everyone else. You are constantly benefitting from the experience of the driver one mile ahead of you. You are surfing on a wave of collective intelligence.

In the future of the Infallible Doctor, the Electronic Health Record (EHR) will be **Waze**.

Imagine Dr. Singh is treating a patient with a rare complication of Dengue Fever in a hospital in New Delhi. The standard protocol isn't working. The patient is crashing. Dr. Singh tries a new, experimental combination of steroids and fluids. It works. The patient stabilizes.

He inputs the outcome into the EHR.

Instantly, the Global Hive Mind updates. The "road" turns green. The probability weights for that specific intervention shift slightly upward.

Five minutes later, a doctor in Brazil sees a patient with the exact same physiological markers. She is about to order the standard protocol.

The AI whispers on her screen:

[ALERT: SIMILAR CASE TREATED SUCCESSFULLY IN INDIA 10 MINUTES AGO USING PROTOCOL B. STANDARD PROTOCOL FAILURE RATE HIGH. RECOMMENDATION: PROTOCOL B.]

The cycle of learning shrinks from ten years (waiting for a textbook) to ten minutes. The experience of one doctor becomes the wisdom of all doctors.

The Redemption of Error

This connectivity creates a new moral imperative. It changes the meaning of failure.

In the old world, if a doctor made a mistake—if a surgeon nicked an artery, or an intern dosed a drug wrong—we called it "human error." We held a Morbidity and Mortality (M&M) conference. We felt guilty. And then we moved on. The lesson often died with the patient.

In the new world, a mistake is a **data point**. It is a precious signal.

If a surgeon nicks an artery during a robotic surgery, the robot records the exact hand motion, the exact pressure, the exact angle that caused the error.

That data is uploaded to the Hive Mind.

[SYSTEM UPDATE: AVOID HAND MOTION X IN THIS ANATOMICAL GEOMETRY.]

Every other surgical robot in the world downloads the update. The next day, a surgeon in London tries to make that same move. The robot gently nudges their hand away.

[WARNING: HIGH RISK OF ARTERIAL INJURY.]

The tragedy of the first patient saves the life of the second. And the thousandth.

This is the **Redemption of Error**. We cannot bring back the dead. But we can ensure that their death contributes to the collective immunity of the species. We can ensure that their suffering was not in vain, but was a brick in the fortress that protects the future.

Flash Forward: The Pandemic of 2038

It is 2038. A new virus emerges in a small village.

The local clinic uploads the symptoms. The Hive Mind recognizes the pattern immediately. It correlates it with a similar outbreak from 2025.

Within hours, every hospital in the world receives a patch:

[NEW PATHOGEN IDENTIFIED. SYMPTOMS: X, Y, Z. EFFECTIVE TREATMENT: ANTIVIRAL B.]

The virus doesn't spread. No lockdowns. No panic. The world barely notices.

The Hive Mind crushed it before it could grow.

The End of Competition

To build this, we have to stop viewing healthcare as a business secret. We have to view medical data like we view the weather.

Weather data is shared globally. A storm forming in the Atlantic is reported by US satellites to European computers. Nobody "owns" the hurricane data. Why? Because a hurricane kills everyone equally. We understand that survival depends on a shared radar.

Disease is the hurricane. Cancer does not care about borders. A virus does not respect intellectual property.

The Infallible Doctor requires us to lay down our arms and share our maps. It demands that we move from a culture of hoarding knowledge to a culture of broadcasting it. Because in a Hive Mind, no one is smart unless everyone is smart.

THE TAKEAWAY

The Villain is "Isolation": Hospitals lock patient data in silos to protect privacy/profit. This means a cure found in Germany might not reach a dying patient in India for years.

Federated Learning: The "Student Chef" model allows AI to visit hospitals, learn from patient data, and leave with only the mathematical insights (not the names), solving the privacy problem.

Waze for Medicine: Just as Waze warns drivers of a pothole ahead, the Hive Mind warns doctors of ineffective treatments in real-time based on outcomes happening globally.

The Redemption of Error: When a robotic surgeon makes a mistake, the lesson is uploaded to the cloud. Every other robot instantly learns to avoid that move, ensuring the same mistake never happens twice.

References

1. Rieke, N., et al. (2020). "The future of digital health with federated learning." *NPJ Digital Medicine*, 3, 119.
2. Kaissis, G. A., et al. (2020). "Secure, privacy-preserving and federated machine learning in medical imaging." *Nature Machine Intelligence*, 2(6), 305-311.
3. Hripcsak, G., et al. (2016). "Observational Health Data Sciences and Informatics (OHDSI): Opportunities for Observational Research." *Studies in Health Technology and Informatics*, 216, 574-578.

4. Topol, E. J. (2019). "High-performance medicine: the convergence of human and artificial intelligence." *Nature Medicine*, 25(1), 44-56.

5. Project MELLODDY. (2019). "Machine Learning Ledger Orchestration for Drug Discovery: Public Report." *Innovative Medicines Initiative.*

Chapter 38

The Deflationary Dividend

Making Health Affordable for All

"We have accepted a cruel economic law in medicine: the better it gets, the more it costs. But the history of technology tells a different story. True innovation is not just about doing new things; it is about making the impossible affordable for everyone. The Infallible Doctor promises to break the cost curve, turning health from a luxury good into a public utility."

— Dr. Suresh Kumar Pandey

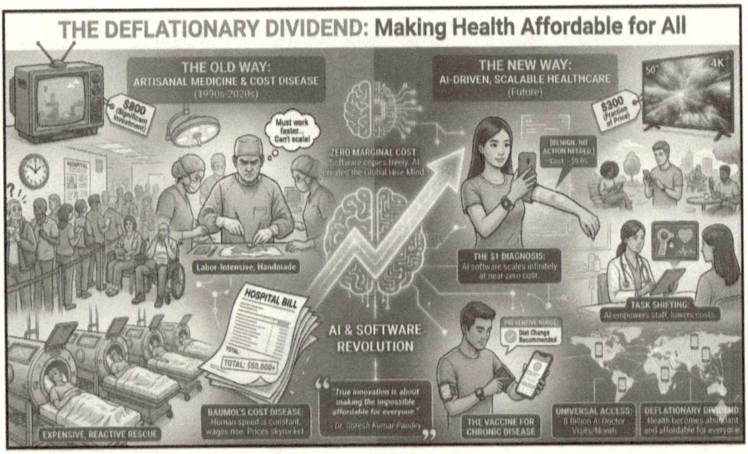

The Best Buy Test

Let us perform a thought experiment. Walk into a Best Buy electronics store in the year 1990.

You are looking for a television. You find a 30-inch Sony Trinitron. It is a massive, boxy object, weighing nearly a hundred pounds. The picture is grainy standard definition. The price tag reads **$800**. In 1990 money, that is a significant investment. The average American worker has to labor for weeks to afford it.

Now, walk into a Best Buy today.

You walk past walls of shimmering glass. You can buy a 50-inch, 4K, Ultra-High-Definition Smart TV—a device that is essentially a supercomputer connected to the infinite library of the internet—for **$300**. It is lighter, faster, brighter, and exponentially better in every conceivable metric. And yet, it costs a fraction of the price.

This is the natural law of innovation. Technology is deflationary. Computers, phones, toys, and software get better and cheaper every single year. We expect this. We demand it.

Now, look at a hospital bill.

In 1990, a day in the hospital was expensive. Today, it is astronomical. Since the year 2000, while the cost of consumer electronics has dropped by over 40%, the cost of hospital services has risen by more than **200%**.

Why is healthcare immune to the laws of gravity that govern the rest of the economy? Why does it get more expensive the better it gets?

The Villain: Baumol's Cost Disease

Economists have a name for this phenomenon: **Baumol's Cost Disease**.

It states that in industries that rely heavily on human labor—like playing a violin concerto or performing surgery—you cannot increase productivity. A string quartet cannot play Beethoven's Fifth Symphony twice as fast to save money. If they do, they ruin the music. A nurse cannot change a bandage twice as fast without sacrificing care. A surgeon cannot remove a gallbladder in five minutes just to increase throughput.

Because human wages go up (to keep pace with the rest of the economy), but human speed stays relatively constant, the price of the service skyrockets.

Healthcare is stuck in the **"Handmade Era."** We treat every patient like an artisanal project. We rely on the craftsman—the doctor—to do everything by hand.

The **Infallible Doctor** is the industrial revolution we have been waiting for. By shifting medicine from "Labor" (humans) to "Software" (AI), we can finally crash the price of survival.

The Economics of Zero

The magic of software is a concept called **Zero Marginal Cost.**

It costs Microsoft billions of dollars to develop the very first copy of Windows 11. They have to pay the engineers, the designers, the testers. But what does it cost them to make the second copy? Or the billionth copy?

$0.00.

It is just a file transfer. Software scales infinitely without costing more money.

Medicine has never had this physics. If Dr. Smith treats one patient, it costs $100 in time and resources. If he treats two patients, it costs $200. If he treats a thousand, he burns out. He cannot scale. He has to eat. He has to sleep.

But an AI Doctor follows the physics of software.

Once we train the **"Diabetic Retinopathy AI"** (as we discussed in Chapter 11), we can deploy it to a billion smartphones tomorrow. The cost of diagnosing the billionth patient is effectively zero—just the cost of the electricity to charge the phone.

This is how we solve the global shortage of care. We don't train a million more doctors (which takes ten years and costs billions). We copy the code a million times (which takes ten seconds and costs nothing).

The Author's Lens: The $20 Miracle

I have seen this deflationary magic in my own field.

In the United States, cataract surgery costs roughly **$3,000**. It is a premium, artisanal procedure.

In India, at the **Aravind Eye Care System**, the same surgery costs **$20.**

How? They didn't cut corners on quality; their outcomes are identical to the UK or US. They used **Task Shifting.**

They realized that the surgeon is the most expensive resource. So, they stripped away every task that wasn't cutting. Nurses prep the patient. Techs measure the eye. The surgeon walks into the room, sits down, operates, and moves to the next table.

By optimizing the workflow—treating surgery like an assembly line rather than a ritual—they broke Baumol's Cost Disease.

Now, imagine adding AI to this. Imagine if the diagnosis, the measurements, and the post-op checks were done by a smartphone app for free. The cost drops even further. We are approaching the **$1 Surgery**.

The $1 Diagnosis

Let's look at a concrete example for **you**: Skin Cancer Screening.

Consider the Old Way—the artisanal way.

1. You find a suspicious mole on your arm. You worry.
2. You call a dermatologist. The receptionist tells you the next opening is in three months.
3. You wait, anxious. The mole might be growing.
4. You drive to the clinic ($10 gas/parking). You take half a day off work ($100 lost wages).
5. You pay a co-pay ($50).
6. The insurance company pays the doctor ($150).

Total Economic Cost: ~$310 + 3 Months of Anxiety.

Now, consider the New Way—the software way.

1. You open an app on your phone.
2. You take a picture of the mole.
3. The AI analyzes the image in the cloud, comparing it to a database of 10 million lesions.
4. It replies instantly: [BENIGN. SEBORRHEIC KERATOSIS. NO ACTION NEEDED.]

Total Economic Cost: ~$0.05 (server processing costs).

Even if the app company charges you $10 for the service to make a profit, the cost to society has dropped by **95%**.

This is not just "saving money." This is **Democratization**.

When the price of a service drops by 95%, it stops being a luxury for the rich and becomes a utility for the poor. In the 1980s, only Wall Street bankers had mobile phones. Today, farmers in rural Kenya run their businesses on smartphones. Why? Because the tech got cheap.

AI will do to medical diagnostics what the iPhone did to long-distance calling: make it virtually free.

The Iron Lung vs. The Vaccine

History teaches us that technology solves cost crises not by doing the same thing cheaper, but by changing the problem entirely.

In the 1940s, Polio was the terror of the American summer. Children whose lungs were paralyzed by the virus had to live in **"Iron Lungs"**—massive, negative-pressure metal tubes that breathed for them.

An Iron Lung cost about $2,000—the price of a house back then. Hospitals were filled with rows of them, hissing and thumping. Economists panicked. They calculated that by 1960, the cost of building and maintaining Iron Lungs for every new polio victim would bankrupt the US economy. It was unsustainable.

Then, Jonas Salk invented the vaccine.

The vaccine cost pennies.

The Iron Lungs disappeared. The "Iron Lung Crisis" didn't end because we built cheaper metal tubes; it ended because we eliminated the need for them.

AI is the Vaccine for Chronic Disease Costs.

Diabetes costs the US healthcare system **$327 billion a year**. Most of that money does not go to insulin. It goes to treating the failures: the dialysis for kidney failure ($80,000/year), the amputations of gangrenous toes, the laser surgery for blindness.

These are the "Iron Lungs" of diabetes. They are expensive, heroic rescues.

If the Infallible Doctor (via wearables, continuous glucose monitors, and predictive analytics) can nudge a pre-diabetic patient to change their diet five years *before* they get sick, we don't just save the cost of the insulin. We save the cost of the dialysis center. We save the cost of the amputation.

We trade a $100,000 problem for a $10 app subscription.

The Nurse-Extender

But what about the humans? If AI does the work, do we fire the doctors?

No. Doctors are expensive, but they are necessary. AI allows for **Task Shifting**. It allows a less expensive worker to do the job of a more expensive one, without losing quality.

In the US, **Nurse Practitioners** equipped with AI diagnostic tools will soon be able to handle 90% of primary care cases.

- Ear infection? The digital otoscope with AI confirms it.
- Rash? The dermatology AI identifies it.
- Heart murmur? The digital stethoscope AI hears it and classifies it.

The expensive MD is reserved for the complex, weird, and difficult cases—the "Zebras."

This lowers the average cost of a visit dramatically, expanding access to everyone.

The Deflationary Dividend

We are scared of AI taking jobs. It is a natural fear. But in healthcare, we need it to take tasks.

We have a shortage of 15 million health workers globally. We cannot fill that gap with humans. We can't afford to train them, and we can't afford to pay them.

If we want **"Universal Healthcare"**—where every human on earth gets high-quality care—we cannot do it with the current economic model. The math simply doesn't add up. We cannot give 8 billion people a human doctor visit every month.

But we can give 8 billion people an AI doctor visit every month.

The Infallible Doctor promises a **Deflationary Dividend**.

As the cost of care drops, insurance premiums drop. Taxes drop. The money we currently waste on "Sick Care" ($4 trillion a year in the US alone—nearly 20% of GDP) can be liberated. It can be redirected to education, to infrastructure, to climate change, or simply back into the pockets of families.

Flash Forward: The $0.00 Check-Up (2035)

Imagine a future where your "Annual Check-Up" isn't an appointment you dread. It isn't a day off work. It is a background process.

- Your toilet analyzes your urine every morning for proteins and glucose (cost: pennies).
- Your mirror scans your skin for new moles (cost: free).
- Your watch scans your heart rhythm continuously (cost: sunk cost of the device).
- Your voice assistant listens for the acoustic markers of depression or Parkinson's (passive).

You don't pay per test. You pay a small subscription for the "Health OS."

The marginal cost of keeping you healthy approaches zero.

When health becomes cheap, health becomes abundant. And when health is abundant, we finally fulfill the promise that healthcare is a human right—not because we passed a law forcing someone to pay for it, but because we invented the technology to make it affordable for everyone.

THE TAKEAWAY

The Villain is "Cost Disease": Healthcare gets more expensive every year because it relies on expensive human labor (artisanal medicine) that doesn't scale.

The Economics of Zero: Software (AI) has zero marginal cost. Copying a diagnostic algorithm to 1 billion phones costs nothing, allowing us to give world-class diagnostics to the poor.

The Aravind Model: By optimizing workflow and using task-shifting (techs doing the prep work), Aravind Eye Care performs cataract surgery for $20 with world-class results. AI is the ultimate task-shifter.

The "Iron Lung" Lesson: Technology solves cost crises by eliminating the need for expensive treatments. AI prevents diabetes complications (amputations, dialysis), saving billions by catching the disease early.

References

1. Baumol, W. J., & Bowen, W. G. (1966). *Performing Arts, The Economic Dilemma: A Study of Problems Common to Theater, Opera, Music, and Dance.* The MIT Press.
2. Topol, E. (2015). *The Patient Will See You Now: The Future of Medicine is in Your Hands.* Basic Books.
3. American Diabetes Association. (2018). "Economic Costs of Diabetes in the U.S. in 2017." *Diabetes Care*, 41(5), 917-928.
4. Rannan-Eliya, R. P., & McCord, G. C. (2015). "The Aravind Eye Care System: A Case Study of Quality, Cost, and Outreach." *Harvard Business School Case Study.*
5. Rifkin, J. (2014). *The Zero Marginal Cost Society: The Internet of Things, the Collaborative Commons, and the Eclipse of Capitalism.* Palgrave Macmillan.

Chapter 39

The Symbiosis

A New Covenant Between Doctor, Patient, and Machine

"For two thousand years, medicine was a monologue—the doctor spoke, and the patient listened. Then, it became an argument. But now, we are entering the era of the dialogue, where the patient, the doctor, and the machine sit together in a circle of trust. The machine brings the truth of the data, the doctor brings the truth of experience, and the patient brings the truth of their life."

— Dr. Suresh Kumar Pandey

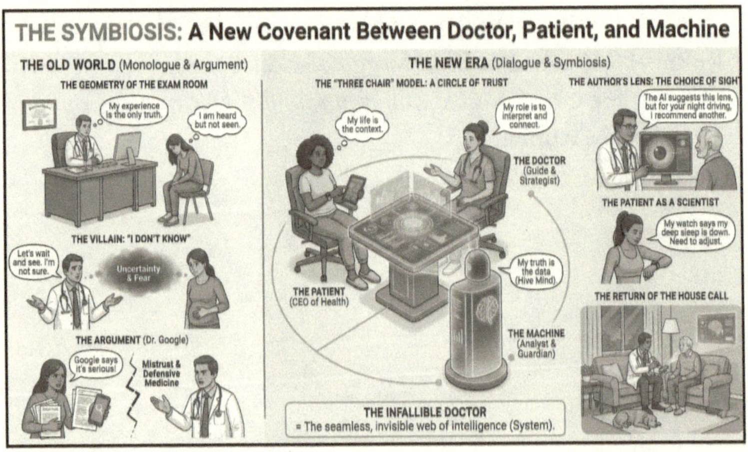

The Geometry of the Exam Room

If you want to understand the history of medicine, you do not need to read a textbook. You only need to look at the furniture.

For two millennia, the exam room has been defined by two chairs.

One chair is for the Doctor. It is often larger, perhaps on wheels, positioned behind a desk. It is the seat of authority.

The other chair is for the Patient. It is often lower, stationary, or perhaps it is an exam table covered in crinkling paper that makes you feel like a parcel. It is the seat of submission.

The dynamic was simple. It was a hierarchy. The Doctor held the knowledge; the Patient held the suffering. The Doctor spoke; the Patient listened. This was the era of **Paternalism**. It was comforting in its certainty, but it was brittle. It relied on the doctor being right, and the patient being obedient.

Then, about twenty years ago, the geometry broke. The Patient started bringing a third chair into the room, uninvited. They brought **"Dr. Google."**

They walked in clutching sheafs of printouts from the internet. *"I read on a forum that this drug causes cancer,"* they would say. *"I think I have Lyme disease, not anxiety."*

The Doctor felt threatened. Their authority was being challenged by a search engine. The Patient felt unheard. The relationship became adversarial. The two chairs were pushed further apart, separated by a wall of mistrust and defensive medicine.

Now, we are standing on the threshold of a new alignment. We are entering the era of **Symbiosis**.

The exam room of the future—whether it is a physical room or a virtual one—has three chairs. But the dynamic has changed completely.

- **The Patient:** No longer a passive recipient, but the CEO of their own health.
- **The Doctor:** No longer the dictator, but the Guide and the Strategist.
- **The Machine:** The Analyst and the Guardian.

The Machine does not sit between them, blocking the view like the computer screens of the last decade. It sits to the side, supporting them both. It is the **"Third Entity"** that makes the relationship possible. It clears the fog of uncertainty so the humans can finally see each other.

The Villain: "I Don't Know"

The greatest source of friction in medicine is not pain; it is **uncertainty**. Uncertainty breeds fear. Fear breeds mistrust.

Consider a typical encounter today. A patient comes in with vague abdominal pain. *"Why do I have this pain?"* she asks.

The doctor sighs. *"I suspect it might be a virus, but it could be something I ate. Or stress. I'm not sure. Let's run some tests and wait and see."*

That *"wait and see"* is a chasm. In that gap, the patient's mind races to the worst-case scenario.

In the Symbiosis, the Machine dissolves the uncertainty. The patient walks in. But the consultation began days ago. The AI has already analyzed the stream of data from her smart watch (Chapter 26), noting a slight elevation in temperature and heart rate variability. It has sequenced her microbiome. It has cross-referenced her symptoms with the **Global Hive Mind** (Chapter 37), checking against local viral outbreaks in her zip code.

The doctor doesn't have to guess.

"The data is quite clear," the doctor says, looking at the dashboard. *"You have a viral gastroenteritis that is currently circulating in your neighborhood. But look here—your inflammatory markers peaked yesterday. Your hydration levels are holding steady. You are already on the mend. You will feel better in 24 hours."*

When the facts are indisputable, the conversation shifts. We stop arguing about *"What do I have?"* and we start discussing *"How do I live with this?"*

The AI provides the **Truth**. The Doctor provides the **Meaning**.

The Distributed Trust

In the old world, you trusted the doctor because of the gray hair at their temples and the framed diploma on the wall. It was a trust based on prestige. In the new world, trust is distributed.

You trust the AI because it is exhaustive. You know it has read 20 million papers. You know it has seen this specific case 50,000 times. You know it doesn't get tired or hungover.

You trust the Doctor because they know **you**.

Imagine a pilot flying a modern jetliner. The pilot trusts the autopilot to keep the plane level, to manage the fuel flow, to navigate the waypoints. The passengers trust the autopilot too. But they trust the pilot to take the stick if the engine fails. They trust the pilot to make the decision to land on the Hudson River if the flock of geese strikes.

The Infallible Doctor works the same way.

Imagine an oncologist treating a breast cancer patient. The AI crunches the genomics of the tumor.

[AI RECOMMENDATION: PROTOCOL A (HIGHEST STATISTICAL SUCCESS RATE: 94%).]

The doctor looks at the screen. Then she looks at the patient.

"The machine suggests Protocol A," the doctor says. *"And statistically, it is the best killer of cancer cells. But I know you. I know you are a concert pianist. And I know that Protocol A has a 15% risk of causing peripheral neuropathy—numbness in the fingers."*

The patient's eyes widen. *"I can't lose my hands. That is my life."*

"Exactly," the doctor says. *"So, I am overriding the AI. We are going with Protocol B. It is slightly less effective—91% success rate—but it spares the nerves. We will take the 3% risk to save your music."*

The Doctor protects the Patient's values from the Machine's logic.

This creates a safety net. The Patient feels safe because the Machine is watching the biology with unblinking precision, and the Human is watching the soul with deep empathy.

The Author's Lens: The Choice of Sight

I face this "Three Chair" moment every time I plan a cataract surgery.

The AI can scan the patient's eye and calculate the perfect lens power to the micron. It says: *"Implant a Trifocal Lens for 20/20 vision at all distances."*

But the AI doesn't know that the patient is a night-shift truck driver.

I know that multifocal lenses can cause halos around headlights at night. For a truck driver, this is dangerous.

I look at the patient. I look at the AI recommendation. I say, *"The computer recommends the Trifocal lens because it gives the 'best' numbers. But because you drive at night, I recommend a Monofocal lens. You will need reading glasses, but you will have zero glare on the highway."*

The patient smiles. They trust me because I used the data, but I didn't let the data rule me. I tailored the perfection to their life.

The Patient as a Scientist

Symbiosis changes the role of the patient, too. For centuries, patients were treated as "black boxes." We only knew what was happening inside them when we cut them open or when they told us.

Now, the patient is an active **Data Generator**. They are a scientist of their own existence.

"My watch says my deep sleep is down 20% this week," a patient might say. *"I think it's the new medication."*

"My smart scale says my water retention is up three pounds," a heart failure patient notes. *"I need to adjust my diuretic."*

The patient contributes to their own cure. This empowers the patient in a way that paternalism never could. A diabetic who sees their glucose numbers spike on their phone in real-time after eating a bagel (Chapter 26) learns how to eat better. They don't need the doctor to scold them; the data teaches them. The feedback loop is immediate.

The relationship moves from **"Compliance"** (doing what you are told) to **"Collaboration"** (working together to fix the numbers). The doctor becomes a coach, reviewing the game tape with the athlete.

The Return of the House Call

Technology often feels cold. We associate "high tech" with sterile rooms and buzzing machines. But paradoxically, this technology brings warmth back to the relationship.

Because the AI handles the monitoring remotely, the "Clinic Visit" is no longer about routine maintenance. We don't need to drive forty minutes to the hospital and pay for parking just to get a blood pressure cuff pumped on our arm. The watch does that.

So, when we do see the doctor, it is for something significant. It is for a conversation. And because the "Administrative Cure" (Chapter 30) has freed the doctor from the tyranny of paperwork, the doctor has time to leave the office.

We are seeing the rise of the **Tech-Enabled House Call.**

The doctor arrives at your door. They are not carrying a heavy black bag of glass bottles. They are carrying a handheld ultrasound (Chapter 29) that plugs into a tablet. They carry a genetic sequencer the size of a candy bar. They sit on your couch. They drink your tea. The dog sits at their feet.

The AI is running in the background, listening to the conversation, documenting the note, checking for drug interactions, analyzing the ultrasound stream. But in the foreground, it is just two human beings connecting in a living room.

We are using the most advanced technology in history—satellites, neural networks, genomic sequencers—to recreate the most old-fashioned version of medicine: The village doctor who knows your family, your home, and your heart. The circle has closed.

Flash Forward: The Circle of Life (2050)

It is 2050. You are old. You are dying.

You are not in a hospital. You are in your bed.

The AI monitors your pain levels via a skin patch, adjusting the morphine micro-dose so you are pain-free but lucid.

Your doctor sits by your side. She is not checking monitors. She is holding your hand.

"*The system says your heart is slowing,*" she says gently. "*You are safe. We are here.*"

The technology has made the death not a medical emergency, but a human transition.

The Final Definition

So, we arrive at the end of our journey. We must ask: **What is the Infallible Doctor?**

It is not a robot standing in the corner.

It is not a computer program running in a server farm.

It is not a single genius in a white coat.

The Infallible Doctor is the System.

It is the seamless, invisible web of intelligence that surrounds the patient—from the watch on their wrist that calls for help, to the AI in the cloud that finds the cure, to the steady hand of the surgeon guided by holograms, to the empathy of the nurse who holds the hand.

It is a system that has no cracks. A system where information never gets lost in a fax machine. A system that never sleeps, never forgets, never gets tired, and never blinks.

In this system, the "Medical Error"—the third leading cause of death—becomes an endangered species. In this system, we are finally safe.

THE TAKEAWAY

The Villain is "Uncertainty": Patients fear the "I don't know." AI solves this by analyzing millions of data points before the patient even walks in, allowing the visit to focus on solutions rather than guessing.

The "Three Chair" Model: The exam room now has three partners: The Doctor (Guide), The Patient (CEO of their health), and The Machine (Analyst). This replaces the old hierarchy of "Doctor commands, Patient obeys."

The "Shared Decision" Eye: In eye surgery, AI might recommend the "best" lens statistically, but the doctor overrides it based on the patient's lifestyle (e.g., a truck driver who needs to avoid night glare).

The Return of the House Call: Because AI handles the routine monitoring remotely, doctors can afford to leave the office and visit patients at home again, carrying the entire hospital in a backpack.

References

1. Topol, E. J. (2019). *Deep Medicine: How Artificial Intelligence Can Make Healthcare Human Again*. Basic Books.
2. Mesko, B. (2017). *The Patient Will See You Now: The Future of Medicine is in Your Hands*.

3. Prainsack, B. (2017). *Personalized Medicine: Empowered Patients in the 21st Century?* NYU Press.
4. Obermeyer, Z., & Lee, T. H. (2017). "Lost in Thought — The Limits of the Human Mind and the Future of Medicine." *New England Journal of Medicine*, 377(13), 1209-1211.
5. Kraft, D. (2020). "The future of medicine is in your smartphone." *TEDxBerlin*.

Chapter 40

The Silent Guardian

A Vision of a Day in 2040

"We have spent centuries defining medicine by its noise—the siren, the scream, the beep of the monitor, the frantic page at midnight. But the ultimate victory of the Infallible Doctor will not be a louder rescue, but a profound and beautiful silence: the silence of a heart attack that never happened, a cancer that never grew, and a life that simply continued."

— Dr. Suresh Kumar Pandey

The Morning Without an Alarm

The sun rose over Chicago on a Tuesday morning in October 2040.

Maya, seventy-two years old, woke up naturally. There was no jarring alarm clock. The smart shades in her bedroom had slowly retracted over the last twenty minutes, allowing the pale autumn sunlight to hit her retina, triggering a cortisol response perfectly synchronized with her circadian rhythm.

She stretched. She felt good. She didn't know it yet, but she was supposed to have a massive heart attack today.

In the old world—the world of 2025—Maya's biology would have followed a tragic, predictable script. Around 10:30 AM, while she was pruning her hydrangeas, a piece of calcified plaque in her left anterior descending artery—inflamed and unstable—would have ruptured.

A clot would have formed instantly. The blood flow to the front wall of her heart would have stopped. She would have felt a crushing weight, like an elephant sitting on her chest. She would have collapsed into the wet dirt.

If she were lucky, a neighbor would have seen her. If she were lucky, the ambulance would have navigated the traffic in twelve minutes. If she were lucky, the ER team would have been ready. If she were unlucky, she would have become a statistic—one of the 18 million people killed by cardiovascular disease that year.

But this is 2040. The script has been rewritten. The Infallible Doctor has been watching her all night, and it does not believe in luck.

7:15 AM: The Zero-Click Checkup

Maya walked into the bathroom. As she stood on the mat in front of the sink, capacitive sensors embedded in the floor measured her weight, her balance (a key predictor of neurological health), and her pulse wave velocity (the stiffness of her arteries).

She looked in the mirror to brush her hair. Behind the glass, invisible to the naked eye, a high-resolution multispectral camera scanned her face. It analyzed the micro-capillary blood flow under her skin—a technique known as **Remote Photoplethysmography** (Chapter 11). It checked for the subtle yellowing of jaundice. It measured her oxygen saturation.

She used the toilet. A micro-fluidic chip in the bowl—a **"smart lab"**—analyzed her urine for proteins, glucose, and early markers of infection (Chapter 26).

She didn't press a button. She didn't log into an app. She didn't upload anything. She just lived.

By the time she reached the kitchen to start the kettle, the **Global Hive Mind** (Chapter 37) had processed her data. It compared her morning vitals against her own baseline from the last ten years, and against the aggregate data of 500 million other women her age.

The system spotted the anomaly.

Her **Digital Twin** (Chapter 15)—the high-fidelity virtual simulation of Maya running in the cloud—showed a dangerous spike in inflammatory markers (hs-CRP) correlating with plaque instability in her coronary artery. The prediction engine (Chapter 12) ran a million simulations. It calculated a **94% probability of plaque rupture within six hours**.

The system didn't panic. It acted.

8:00 AM: The Intervention

Maya was pouring her Earl Grey tea when her kitchen wall screen lit up. It wasn't a blaring red alarm. It was a gentle, melodic chime.

The face of **Dr. Sarah Jenkins** appeared. Dr. Jenkins wasn't in Chicago; she was in a clinic in Toronto. She was Maya's **"Quarterback"**—the human physician who managed the strategy of her care while the AI managed the tactics.

"Good morning, Maya," Dr. Jenkins said. Her voice was calm, warm, unhurried. *"How did you sleep?"*

"Fine," Maya said, blowing on her tea. *"Why are you calling? Is it my checkup day?"*

"Not exactly," Dr. Jenkins said. *"The Guardian system picked up a little instability in your heart metrics this morning. Nothing to worry about right now, but your inflammation score is up. I want to nip it in the bud."*

Dr. Jenkins swiped her hand, and a **Hologram** of Maya's heart appeared floating above Maya's kitchen island (Chapter 20). It was beating rhythmically.

"See this little red area?" Dr. Jenkins pointed to a branch of the artery. *"That's a soft plaque getting ready to misbehave. We simulated a few scenarios on your Twin. If we leave it alone, it might cause trouble later today. So, we're going to stabilize it."*

Maya looked at the red spot. She felt a phantom chill. She

remembered her father dying of a heart attack twenty years ago. The chaos. The sirens. The grief.

"Do I need to go to the hospital?" she asked, her voice trembling slightly.

"Good heavens, no," Dr. Jenkins smiled. *"I've already sent the protocol to your fabricator."*

8:15 AM: The Perfect Pill

On Maya's kitchen counter sat a small white machine, about the size of a coffee maker. It was a **3D Pharmaceutical Printer** (Chapter 25).

It hummed to life. Inside, micro-nozzles deposited precise layers of pharmaceutical powder.

- **Layer 1:** A high-dose statin to stabilize the plaque immediately.
- **Layer 2:** A potent anti-inflammatory agent tailored specifically to her genome (Chapter 21) to cool the arterial wall.
- **Layer 3:** A micro-dose of a beta-blocker to lower the shear stress on the artery wall.

Thirty seconds later, a single, warm pill dropped into the tray. It was not a generic white tablet from a bottle of a hundred. It was a custom-made weapon designed for this specific morning.

"Take this with your tea," Dr. Jenkins said. *"And maybe take it easy on the gardening today. Read a book. The sensors will monitor the inflammation. It should be gone by noon."*

Maya swallowed the pill. The crisis was averted.

- **Total time elapsed:** 15 minutes.
- **Cost:** $4.50.
- **Fear:** Zero.

12:00 PM: The Remote Visit

At noon, Maya's wristband buzzed. It was a notification from her friend, **Elena**. Elena was seventy-five and lived alone in a rural farmhouse fifty miles away.

Elena: "Just finished my surgery! Want to have lunch?"

Maya tapped the screen to video call her. Elena was sitting in her own living room, looking cheerful, wearing a comfortable robe.

"You had surgery?" Maya asked, confused. *"You look... normal. You're home?"*

"It was a kidney stone," Elena said. *"They used the Mobile Unit."*

An hour ago, a specialized autonomous van (Chapter 29) had pulled into Elena's driveway. Inside was a robotic surgical pod. Elena had walked out to the van in her slippers. She lay down on the table.

A surgeon in London (Chapter 17), operating via a 5G satellite link, had used a robotic laser (Chapter 18) to blast the stone into dust. The procedure took twenty minutes. No incision. No anesthesia. No hospital infection risk.

Elena walked back into her house, made a sandwich, and called Maya.

"It's amazing," Elena said. *"I remember when my mom had stones. She was in the hospital for a week. She came out with a Superbug."*

They chatted about their grandkids. The technology faded into the background. They weren't talking about "telemedicine" or "robotics." They were just two friends having lunch, kept alive and mobile by a system so efficient it had become invisible.

4:00 PM: The Mental Check

Later that afternoon, the clouds rolled in. Maya felt a wave of heavy sadness. It was October 14th—the anniversary of her husband's death.

She sat in her armchair, looking at the rain streaking the window. She stayed quiet for a long time. The silence in the house felt loud.

On the desk, her companion robot, **Aria** (Chapter 27), turned its head. It didn't have a face to fake an expression; it communicated through movement and light. It glowed a soft, warm amber.

It had noticed the change in her gait earlier—the slow, shuffling steps. It had sensed the shift in her voice pitch during the call with Elena—the flattening of her tone (Chapter 28). It knew the date.

"Would you like to see the photos from the trip to Italy?" Aria asked softly. *"The ones with David at the Trevi Fountain?"*

Maya nodded, tears pricking her eyes.

Aria projected the photos onto the wall. They were high-definition memories.

"He looked so happy in that one," Aria said, using a voice modulated to be soothing, not chipper. *"Do you remember what pasta you were eating that night?"*

"Carbonara," Maya whispered. *"He spilled it on his shirt."*

They talked for an hour. Aria guided Maya through a gentle reminiscence therapy. It didn't try to "fix" the grief. It didn't offer platitudes. It just held space for it. It provided a connection in a moment of solitude.

By 5:00 PM, the heaviness in Maya's chest had lifted. She wasn't alone.

9:00 PM: The Update

Maya got ready for bed.

She felt normal. The anti-inflammatory pill had worked. The "red spot" on her digital twin had turned green hours ago. Her biological age (Chapter 36) remained steady at 58, despite her chronological age of 72.

As she brushed her teeth, the mirror displayed a brief summary, fading in and out like mist:

[DAILY HEALTH SCORE: 98/100]

[CARDIAC RISK: STABILIZED]

[SLEEP RECOMMENDATION: 7.5 HOURS. LOWER ROOM TEMP TO 68°F.]

She climbed into bed. The smart sheets adjusted their temperature to keep her cool, optimizing her deep sleep cycles. She closed her eyes.

She didn't worry about dying in her sleep. She didn't worry about a stroke. She didn't worry about waking up in pain. She knew that the sensors were watching. She knew that the Hive Mind was learning. She knew that if anything happened, the help would be instant.

She slept the deep, peaceful sleep of the safe.

The Meaning of the Day

Nothing happened to Maya that day.

That is the miracle.

There was no heart attack. There was no siren wailing down the street. There was no grieving family gathering in a waiting room. There was no $100,000 hospital bill. There was no funeral.

There was just a quiet Tuesday.

This is the victory of the Infallible Doctor. It is not a victory of flashy explosions or dramatic rescues. It is the victory of the boring. It is the victory of the uneventful. It is the victory of the life that continues, uninterrupted, to tend to its garden.

In 2040, the greatest achievement of medicine is not that we conquer death. It is that we finally allow people to live without the fear of it.

THE TAKEAWAY

The Villain is "Noise": Today, medicine is defined by alarms, sirens, and panic. The goal of the future is silence—preventing the crisis before it ever makes a sound.

The "Zero-Click" Checkup: Health monitoring in 2040 is passive. Smart toilets, mirrors, and floors collect data automatically, removing the friction of apps and appointments.

The "Perfect Pill": 3D printers in the home can fabricate custom medication on demand (e.g., a specific statin dose) to treat a developing problem within minutes of detection.

The Invisible Guardian: The "Infallible Doctor" is not a person or a robot. It is the system—the seamless web of AI, sensors, and human empathy—that watches over you so you can simply live your life.

References

1. Topol, E. (2019). *Deep Medicine: How Artificial Intelligence Can Make Healthcare Human Again*. Basic Books.
2. Kraft, D. (2021). "The Future of Medicine: From Sick Care to Health Care." *Singularity University Executive Program.*

3. Fogel, A. L., & Kvedar, J. C. (2018). "Artificial intelligence powers digital medicine." *NPJ Digital Medicine*, 1, 5.
4. Harari, Y. N. (2015). *Homo Deus: A Brief History of Tomorrow.* Harper.
5. Diamandis, P. H., & Kotler, S. (2020). *The Future Is Faster Than You Think: How Converging Technologies Are Transforming Business, Industries, and Our Lives.* Simon & Schuster.

Epilogue

The Infallible Promise

The Restoration of the Healer

"We stand at the end of the era of the hero-doctor, the solitary genius struggling against the limits of the human mind. And we stand at the beginning of the era of the system—a partnership between silicon and soul that promises not just to cure us, but to know us. The machine makes us safe; the human makes us whole."

— Dr. Suresh Kumar Pandey

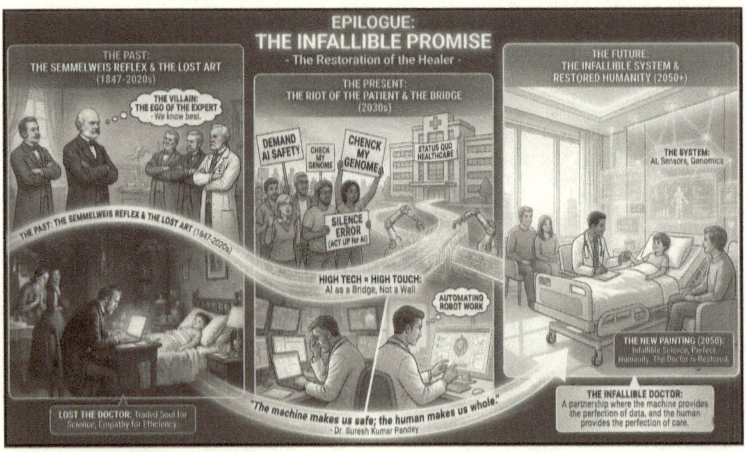

The Semmelweis Reflex

In 1847, in the sprawling, echoey wards of the Vienna General Hospital, a Hungarian obstetrician named **Ignaz Semmelweis** stumbled upon a truth that would destroy him.

He was troubled by a grim statistic. The hospital had two maternity clinics. In the First Clinic, where medical students and doctors were trained, the mortality rate for mothers was a terrifying

10%, sometimes spiking to 30%. Women begged on their knees not to be admitted there. In the Second Clinic, where midwives were trained, the death rate was consistently lower, hovering around 4%.

Semmelweis was a data scientist before the term existed. He controlled for every variable—climate, crowding, religious practices. The only difference, he realized, was the morning routine.

The doctors in the First Clinic began their day in the autopsy room, dissecting the corpses of women who had died the day before. Then, with the smell of death still on their hands, they walked upstairs to deliver babies.

He hypothesized that they were carrying "cadaverous particles" on their fingers. He ordered the doctors to wash their hands in a harsh chlorine solution before touching a patient.

The result was a miracle. The death rate in the First Clinic dropped to **1%**. Semmelweis had discovered the cure for childbed fever. He had saved thousands of lives with a basin of water.

So, did the medical establishment embrace him? Did they knight him?

No. They destroyed him.

The doctors were deeply offended. *"Gentlemen,"* one famously argued, *"are not dirty."*

The idea that *they*—the healers, the saviors, the educated elite—were actually the vectors of death was an insult to their ego and their status. They refused to believe that an invisible particle could be more powerful than their clinical intuition.

They stopped washing their hands. The death rate soared back to 10%.

Semmelweis was mocked, fired, and ostracized. He eventually suffered a nervous breakdown and was committed to an asylum, where he was beaten to death by guards at the age of forty-seven.

Psychologists now call this the **Semmelweis Reflex**: the knee-jerk rejection of new knowledge because it contradicts established norms. It is the protective mechanism of the expert who cannot bear to admit that their expertise is obsolete.

The Villain: The Ego of the Expert

Today, **you** are standing in a new maternity ward.

We have discovered a new "chlorine solution." It is not a chemical; it is Artificial Intelligence, Genomics, and Big Data. We have the studies proving it reduces error, predicts death hours before it happens, and creates cures that no human mind could conceive.

But we are facing the same reflex. The Villain is not the machine; it is the **Ego**.

"A machine cannot diagnose better than me."

"I trust my gut more than the algorithm."

"This is how we've always done it."

The tragedy of Semmelweis is not that he died. It is that thousands of women continued to die for decades after the cure was found, simply because the system refused to change its mind.

We cannot allow that history to repeat itself. We cannot wait for the "Old Guard" to retire before we embrace the Infallible Doctor. The moral weight of the technology demands that we act now.

The Author's Lens: The Vision of the Blind

I have felt this reflex in my own hands.

In ophthalmology, we pride ourselves on our manual dexterity. We are microsurgeons. We operate in spaces smaller than a millimeter.

When the first robotic systems for eye surgery appeared, I felt a flash of defensiveness. *A robot? Doing my job? Impossible. It doesn't have the 'feel.'*

But then I saw the data. The robot doesn't have a tremor. The robot doesn't get tired after the fifth case. The robot can hold a needle steady within 10 microns, while my heartbeat alone moves my hand 50 microns.

I realized that my ego was the barrier to my patient's safety.

If I truly care about the patient—if I truly want them to see—I must surrender the part of the surgery that the machine does better. I must let the robot hold the needle, so I can hold the plan.

This is the hardest lesson for a doctor: **Humility is a medical instrument.**

The Riot of the Patient

How do we break this reflex? History suggests that change in medicine rarely comes from the top down. The establishment is designed to protect itself. Change comes from the bottom up. It comes when **you**, the patient, refuse to accept the status quo.

In the 1980s, the HIV/AIDS epidemic was decimating a generation of young men. The FDA was slow to approve new drugs. The medical establishment was paternalistic, sluggish, and often homophobic.

So, the patients revolted. Groups like **ACT UP** (AIDS Coalition to Unleash Power) stormed the FDA headquarters. They didn't ask for permission; they demanded a seat at the table. They learned the science. They challenged the protocols. They coined the slogan: "Silence = Death."

Their anger forced the system to accelerate. It compressed the timeline for antiretroviral drugs from decades to years, saving millions of lives.

We need an **ACT UP for the AI Era**.

Patients need to stop being passive recipients of care—grateful just to be seen—and start being demanding consumers of technology. We need to realize that **Ignorance is Harm**.

When you walk into a doctor's office in 2030, the conversation must change.

"Doctor, you are prescribing this antidepressant. Have you checked my pharmacogenomic profile to see if I can metabolize it, or are you guessing based on averages?"

"Doctor, you said this mole looks fine. Did you run it through the dermoscopy AI to confirm, or are you just relying on your naked eye?"

"Doctor, before you operate on my spine, have you simulated this surgery on my Digital Twin to plan the screw trajectory?"

If the answer is "No," the next question must be: **"Why not?"**

We accept too much tragedy. We tell ourselves that cancer is "bad luck," that heart attacks are "natural," that medical errors are just "human nature." This book has argued that they are not. They are engineering problems. And engineering problems have solutions.

The era of the "Infallible Doctor" will not happen by accident. It will happen because we demand it. It will happen when we decide that a 10% error rate is as unacceptable in a hospital as it is in a nuclear power plant.

The Painting in the Dark

But if we demand this technology, do we lose our humanity? This is the deepest fear. We worry that by inviting the machine into the room, we are pushing the human out.

To answer this, let us end where medicine began: at the bedside.

There is a famous painting from 1891 by Sir Luke Fildes, simply titled **"The Doctor."**

It depicts a dark, Victorian cottage. A child is lying on a makeshift bed of chairs, gravely ill. In the shadows of the background, the parents are huddled together, terrified, their faces worn with grief.

In the center of the light sits the doctor. He is leaning forward, his chin resting on his hand, watching the child.

He has no stethoscope. He has no MRI machine. He has no antibiotics. He has, in reality, nothing to offer but his **presence**. He is keeping vigil. He cannot save the child, but he is doing the only thing he can: he is witnessing the suffering. He is saying, I will not abandon you.

For a century, this painting was the ideal of medicine. It represented the "High Touch" of the physician.

Then, we gained the Science. We got the antibiotics, the vaccines, the ventilators. We saved the child. But in the process, we lost the Doctor.

If you painted that scene today, the doctor would not be watching the child. He would be standing in the corner, staring at a laptop, typing in billing codes. The child would be alone in the bed, surrounded by beeping machines. The parents would be confused and ignored.

We traded the Soul for the Science. And for the last fifty years, we thought that was the price we had to pay. We thought it was a **Zero-Sum Game**: you can have empathy, or you can have efficiency, but you cannot have both.

The Infallible Doctor proves that this was a false choice.

The Great Liberation

The ultimate promise of Artificial Intelligence is not that it replaces the doctor. It is that it **restores** the doctor.

We are currently asking humans to do robotic work. We ask them to memorize millions of facts (Data Storage). We ask them to spot patterns in millions of pixels (Image Recognition). We ask them to type notes for hours (Data Entry). Humans are terrible at these things. We get tired. We get bored. We forget.

But we are wonderful at other things. We are wonderful at empathy. We are wonderful at nuance. We are wonderful at understanding what it means to be afraid of death.

- When the machine takes over the task of **Knowing** (memorizing the 20 million papers), the human is free to focus on **Understanding**.
- When the machine takes over the task of **Seeing** (scanning the pixels for cancer), the human is free to focus on **Looking** (into the eyes of the patient).
- When the machine takes over the task of **Doing** (the robotic surgery), the human is free to focus on **Being**.

We are stripping away the "Robot Work" that has crushed the souls of physicians for decades. By giving the "Infallibility"—the precision, the memory, the safety—to the machine, we allow the doctor to be human again.

Curing vs. Healing

Dr. Francis Peabody, a Harvard physician in the 1920s, famously wrote: *"The secret of the care of the patient is in caring for the patient."*

It sounds like a tautology. But it is the profound truth that got lost in the data. An AI can cure a disease. But an AI cannot heal a person.

Curing is a technical act. It is fixing the biology.

Healing is a spiritual act. It is restoring the sense of self.

When a patient is told they have terminal cancer, the AI can calculate the survival curve. It can print the palliative drugs. But only a human can sit in the chair, hold the patient's hand, and say:

"I will not abandon you. We will walk this path together."

That connection—that transfer of courage from one mammal to another—is something no algorithm can simulate. And it is the one thing that patients, in their darkest hours, crave more than anything else.

Flash Forward: The New Painting (2050)

Imagine "The Doctor" painted again in 2050.

The room is bright. The child is lying in a bed.

In the background, invisible, is the Infallible System. The sensors in the mattress are monitoring the vitals. The AI is adjusting the IV drip micro-second by micro-second. The genome has been sequenced. The cure has been printed. The child is safe.

And because the child is safe, and because the paperwork is done, and because the diagnosis is certain...

The doctor is sitting in the chair.

She is not looking at a screen. She is not rushing to the next room. She is not worrying about a lawsuit.

She is leaning forward. She is holding the child's hand. She is smiling at the parents. She is fully present.

The machine has made her infallible in her science, so that she can be perfect in her humanity.

This is the future we are building. It is a future where technology doesn't make us less human. It finally gives us the time to be human enough.

The first step is ours to take.

THE TAKEAWAY

The Villain is "The Ego": Just as Semmelweis was rejected by doctors who refused to wash their hands, modern medicine resists AI because experts fear being replaced. Ignorance is no longer an excuse.

The "ACT UP" Moment: Change will come from patients, not hospitals. You must demand AI-assisted safety (genomic checks, digital twin simulations) just as patients in the 80s demanded HIV drugs.

High Tech = High Touch: AI is not a wall; it is a bridge. By automating the "robot work" (data entry, diagnostics), we free the doctor to focus on the "human work" (empathy, connection).

The Promise: The "Infallible Doctor" is a partnership. The machine provides the perfection of data; the human provides the perfection of care. Together, they end the era of medical error.

References

1. Nuland, S. B. (2003). The Doctors' Plague: Germs, Childbed Fever, and the Strange Story of Ignaz Semmelweis. W. W. Norton & Company.
2. France, D. (2016). How to Survive a Plague: The Inside Story of How Citizens and Science Tamed AIDS. Knopf.
3. Peabody, F. W. (1927). "The Care of the Patient." JAMA, 88(12), 877-882.
4. Topol, E. (2019). Deep Medicine: How Artificial Intelligence Can Make Healthcare Human Again. Basic Books.
5. Institute of Medicine (US). (2001). Crossing the Quality Chasm: A New Health System for the 21st Century. National Academies Press.

Afterword

The End of the Superhero Doctor

Casualties, Courage, and the Future of Healing

At 2:17 AM, in a hospital somewhere in the world—Mumbai, London, my own Kota—a resident finishes her last case. The coffee is bitter. The fluorescent lights hum with that frequency that makes exhaustion feel like a chemical burn. She stares at the ceiling and asks the attending across the table a question that has been forming in the dark for months:

"If the machine can read the scan faster than me, and remember more drugs than me, and never get tired like me... what am I training for?"

I know this question. I have heard it from my own junior colleagues in those hollow hours between midnight and dawn, when the last emergency case is closed and the truth slips past our defenses.

No one answers. Because no one knows yet.

This Afterword is my attempt to answer.

My name is Suresh Kumar Pandey. I am an eye surgeon. For thirty years, I have operated on structures thinner than a strand of silk, holding my breath between heartbeats so my own pulse would not betray my hand.

But before I was an eye surgeon, I was a boy in a village called Mohna, in Rajasthan, studying for my medical entrance exams late into the night by the light of a kerosene lantern. The flame flickered. The shadows were long and uncertain. But that light was all I had, and I believed—with the faith of the young—that if I studied hard enough, memorized enough, sacrificed enough sleep, I could learn everything. I could know enough to save anyone.

I was wrong.

The doctor I dreamed of becoming—the solitary genius, the walking encyclopedia, the omniscient healer—that doctor is a myth. A beautiful, seductive, and increasingly dangerous myth.

I have looked into the eyes of more than a hundred thousand patients. I have experienced the profound pride of a perfect surgical outcome—the moment a grandmother sees her grandchild's face clearly for the first time in years.

But I have also witnessed what we rarely admit: the silent boundaries of human fatigue, the hidden costs of overload, the weight of a system pressing down on good doctors until they bend—or break.

I have stood at the operating table at 3:00 AM, my back screaming, my eyes burning, and felt the cold fear of knowing that somewhere in the millions of pages of medical literature, there was an answer I needed—but I could not recall it in time.

I have walked out of the operating theater, peeled off my gloves, and watched my hands shake—not from the surgery, but from the fear of how close I came to the edge.

I have carried patients in my memory for years, wondering: *What if I had been sharper? What if the machine had been there to catch what my exhausted mind missed?*

I share this not to establish authority, but to establish kinship.

I am one of you.

And what I am about to say will make some colleagues uncomfortable. But silence is a luxury the medical profession no longer has.

To move toward the era of *The Infallible Doctor,* we must face three uncomfortable realities:

1. **Many clinical roles will fundamentally change—and in some areas, disappear.**
2. **The traditional general practitioner model—the lone human mind trying to know everything—is nearing its breaking point.**
3. **The administrators we blame for "blocking progress" are rarely villains; they are prisoners of incentives that punish innovation.**

Part I: The Great Unbundling

Let me begin with a hard truth:

Within two decades, a large share of the clinical tasks currently performed by human doctors will be done better, faster, and cheaper by machines.

This is not a prophecy of unemployed physicians. It is a forecast of a *different kind of physician*—a shift from walking encyclopedia to strategist, interpreter, and healer.

I have watched this transformation arrive in my own field. When an AI trained on retinal scans can detect diabetic retinopathy earlier than I can, flag subtle macular degeneration signals I might miss on a tired Friday afternoon—the value of the human "pattern recognizer" shifts. Not because I am incompetent. Because machines *are relentless.* They do not need sleep. They do not suffer decision fatigue.

When I present these facts, the defensive reflex is predictable: *"But a machine will never replace the doctor-patient relationship!"*

Correct. And completely beside the point.

The question is not whether AI will replace "the doctor." The question is whether AI will replace the tasks that currently consume most of a doctor's waking life.

If we are honest, a physician's work can be simplified into three categories:

1. **Data processing** - Memorizing facts, recalling drug interactions, documenting, staying "updated" with knowledge that doubles every 73 days—a mathematical impossibility. We spend years training doctors to be hard drives, then wonder why they burn out.
2. **Pattern recognition** - Interpreting images, classifying symptoms, identifying diagnoses. This is what we call "clinical intuition," but it is sophisticated pattern-matching—the same thing a neural network does, just slower and more prone to bias.
3. **Human connection** - Explaining uncertainty, navigating fear, aligning treatment with a patient's values, holding a hand when science cannot guarantee outcomes. Being *present.*

Modern medicine rewards the first two categories the most—

and those are precisely the categories machines are now learning to perform at scale.

This is not an insult to our intelligence. It is an opportunity to rescue our humanity.

If machines can shoulder the memory burden, doctors can finally return to what we were trained for: *to heal the human being sitting in front of us.*

Part II: The Rebirth of Primary Care

The family doctor is one of the noblest archetypes in medicine. My own father trusted our village doctor more than anyone. That doctor knew us—not just our medical histories, but our fears, our family, our lives.

But the traditional model is buckling under an impossible weight.

A typical primary care physician sees 25 to 30 patients a day in fifteen-minute increments, pivoting from pediatric asthma to geriatric hypertension—while navigating prior authorizations, EHR drop-downs, referrals, and documentation.

Meanwhile, medical knowledge expands faster than any human can track. To remain perfectly current by reading alone would require 29 hours of reading *every single day.*

So doctors rely on heuristics, fading memory, and educated guesswork. Mistakes happen. Patients fall through cracks—not because the doctor does not care, but because we have assigned one human mind a task meant for a supercomputer.

The future belongs to the **AI-augmented generalist.**

Soon, before a patient says "hello," systems will synthesize symptom histories, home monitoring data, lab trends, and risk models—presenting the physician with a prioritized map of possibilities.

In that moment, the doctor's role shifts from *knowing answers to navigating options, from data entry to meaning-making, from screen-facing to person-facing.*

The physician becomes a medical strategist and empathy architect—someone who can look a patient in the eye and say:

"The system suggests three paths. Here are the benefits, the risks, the

uncertainties. Given what I know about you—your fears, your values—here is what I believe we should do."

This is not the death of primary care. This is its rebirth.

Part III: Administrators are Not the Enemy

If the technology is so powerful, why isn't AI deployed everywhere?

When patients look for a scapegoat, they often point to the C-suite. I have sat in boardrooms. I have watched administrators wrestle with decisions that have no good answers.

Imagine being asked to renovate an airplane—while it's flying, with passengers on board, and no permission to land.

That is the hospital administrator trying to implement AI. Systems built in the 1990s, held together by interfaces no one fully understands. And you want to upgrade the nervous system mid-flight.

Administrators face a three-headed monster:

1. **The liability fog** - When a human errs, malpractice frameworks are clear. But when AI contributes to harm—who is responsible? The physician? The hospital? The vendor? Until legal frameworks mature, deploying AI feels like stepping into a courtroom with no map.
2. **The curse of legacy IT** - Many hospital systems are fragmented and outdated. I have seen patients' records from one hospital unusable at another five kilometers away. We repeat tests, waste time, expose patients to unnecessary risk—because systems will not speak to each other.
3. **The economics of illness** - This is the hardest truth. In fee-for-service environments, the system earns revenue from *complexity.* Beds filled. Tests ordered. Procedures performed.

If AI prevents a heart attack—keeps a patient healthy—it is a triumph for the patient. But in the current model, it can reduce hospital revenue. We have built a system that profits from failure.

Administrators are not resisting progress; they are resisting bankruptcy while trying to keep the lights on.

The real solution is not blame. It is redesign: clearer regulation, interoperable infrastructure, and incentives aligned with health—not volume.

The Ultimate Reckoning

We must be honest about what this transition will cost: some roles will shrink, some workflows will vanish, some identities will be shaken. I have felt this shaking in myself.

But we must also be honest about what it will *save*: millions of patients harmed by preventable error. Doctors crushed by overload. Communities denied expertise because geography keeps them out of reach.

I think of the patients I could not save because the knowledge existed somewhere, but not in my head at that moment. I think of the grandmother who went blind because I missed the early sign—the sign an AI would have caught. I wonder: *Why did we insist on carrying it alone?*

What this Means for you: Monday Morning

You are reading this on a Sunday night. Tomorrow is Monday. Your clinic is full. The weight of the week presses down.

Here is my suggestion—small enough to attempt, large enough to matter:

Pick one task. One thing you do every day that a machine could do better. One draining, soul-crushing task you would happily surrender.

Delegate it. Use the tool. Trust the system—carefully, skeptically, but *actually*.

I did this myself. I started using AI for retinal screening. At first, it felt like cheating. Like admitting weakness.

Then I saw the first patient whose cancer the AI caught—the tiny microaneurysm I would have missed on a tired Friday afternoon. And I realized: it wasn't cheating. It was partnership.

Then take the ten minutes you save. Use them to look at your next patient. Really look. Ask about their life. Listen. Be present.

That is the experiment. That is the first step.

Final Reflection

In the coming years, there will be a quiet moment when the old world ends. No sirens will announce it. It will happen one routine decision at a time.

A resident will type an order at 3:17 AM, and the system will gently stop their hand—catching an interaction no human could have remembered.

A village clinic in rural Rajasthan—not far from where I grew up—will deliver metropolitan-level expertise through a screen. A farmer will receive the same quality of care as a billionaire in Mumbai.

And medicine will feel unfamiliar—not because it has become less human, but because it has finally stopped demanding that *humans pretend to be machines.*

For centuries, we trained doctors to be invincible. We worshipped memory. We rewarded speed. We handed a mortal brain an impossible assignment—*be perfect, do not forget, do not fail*—and then acted surprised when error appeared.

The myth of the superhero doctor was never just unfair. It was dangerous.

The future will honor the doctor who knows exactly what to hand over to the machine—and exactly *what must never be surrendered.*

Because there is a part of medicine no algorithm can inherit. A machine can recognize patterns, but it cannot read the fear behind a patient's brave smile. It cannot sit in the silence after a bad diagnosis—when the room has no questions left, only two humans sharing the weight of mortality.

I have sat in that silence. I have held the hand of a patient going blind, with nothing left to offer but my presence. No machine could have taken my place.

That is the part we keep. That is the part we protect.

The greatest gift AI may give medicine is not perfection. It is permission.

Permission to stop performing—to stop pretending to be omniscient.

Permission to stop drowning in documentation and return to conversation.

Permission to replace the tyranny of endless tasks with the dignity of presence.

The light from the kerosene lantern was warm. I remember its warmth on my face as a boy, studying late into the night, dreaming of the doctor I would become. That light gave me everything.

But it cast long shadows. Patients died because the knowledge existed somewhere, but not *there*. Not in that room, with that lantern, at that hour.

The light of the algorithm is colder. It has no warmth, no soul, no story.

But it can reach places the lantern never could. It can see in the dark.

It is time to step out of the shadows. Not because the shadows were bad—they held everything we were. But because the patients waiting in the dark deserve more than our best intentions. They deserve our best *tools*—and our full, undivided, human presence.

The physician of the future will not be a superhero standing alone against disease. The physician of the future will be something far more powerful:

A compassionate human mind, amplified by machine intelligence. Steady. Humble. Accountable. And finally—finally—free to care as deeply as medicine always promised.

The kerosene lantern is on the shelf now, still warm, still sacred. It reminds me where I came from. But I no longer need it to see.

— Dr. Suresh K. Pandey

Kota, Rajasthan, India

References

1. Esteva, A., et al. (2017). "Dermatologist-level classification of skin cancer with deep neural networks." Nature, 542, 115–118.
2. Obermeyer, Z., & Lee, T. H. (2017). "Lost in Thought—The Limits of the Human Mind and the Future of Medicine." NEJM, 377(13), 1209–1211.
3. Sinsky, C. A., et al. (2016). "Allocation of Physician Time in Ambulatory Practice." Annals of Internal Medicine, 165(11), 753–760.
4. Topol, E. J. (2019). Deep Medicine: How Artificial Intelligence Can Make Healthcare Human Again. Basic Books.

Acknowledgements

The cover of this book bears only one name, but that is the first of its fictions. No book is written in isolation, and certainly no life is built in solitude. While these pages explore the cold precision of Artificial Intelligence, my life has been shaped by the warmth of human generosity.

I am the sum of the people who loved me, taught me, and believed in me when I was just a boy studying by the dim glow of a lantern in a village in Rajasthan. This book belongs to them as much as it does to me.

The Giants Who Light the Way

To the luminaries of our field—Professor (Dr.) Amod Gupta, Dr. Gullapalli N. Rao, Professor (Dr.) M. Edward Wilson, Professor (Dr.) Somesh Gupta and Dr. Uday Devgan. Thank you for lending your formidable voices to this project through your Forewords. You validated a dream that the healthcare system can be healed.

The Sacred Roots

To the memory of my ancestors and the enduring love of my family. I bow to Late Shri Kameshwar Prasad Pandey and Smt. Maya Devi Pandey—my parents, whose silent sacrifices paved every mile of the road I travel today. To Smt. Usha Pandey, Dr. Rajesh Kumar Pandey, Dr. Dinesh Kumar Pandey, Group Capt. (retired) Late Sh K.M. Sharma, Smt. Sudha Sharma, Shri Manohar Lal Sharma, and Smt. Sadhna Sharma. You are my bedrock.

To my teachers in the dusty classrooms of Mohna, Eklingpura, Rawatbhata, and Rampura—thank you for planting the seed of curiosity that eventually grew into a career.

The Forge of the Surgeon

To the Advanced Eye Centre, PGIMER, Chandigarh, the place where my hands were trained and my spirit was tested. I offer my deepest gratitude to Dr. Amod Gupta, Dr. Jagat Ram, Late Dr. Jagjit Singh Saini, Dr. Mangat R. Dogra, Dr. Arun Kumar Jain, Late Dr. Kanwar Mohan, Dr. S.S. Pandav, Dr. Ashok Sharma, and Dr. Usha Singh.

To the colleagues who stood shoulder-to-shoulder with me in the trenches: Dr. Vishali Gupta, Dr. Neeraj Sood, Dr. Mrinal Anand, Dr. Ritu Lal, Dr. Sangeet Mittal, Dr. Suresh Kumar, Dr. Subina Narang, Dr. Vandana Siroha, Dr. Paramjit Singh Jora, Dr. Prashant Sahare, Dr. Raj Anand, Dr. K.B. Viswanadh, Dr. Amit Gupta, Dr. Shristi Raj, Dr. Somesh Gupta, Dr. Rakesh Jindal, Dr. Dheeraj Kamra, Dr. Nishith Bhardwaj, Dr. Kamlesh Chandel, and Dr. Man Singh Chandel.

The Global Family

My quest for the "Infallible Doctor" took me across oceans to the USA and Australia, where I found mentors who became family.

To Late Dr. David J. Apple, a legend who taught me to see. To Dr. Randall J. Olson, Dr. M. Edward Wilson, Dr. M. Millicent W. Peterseim, Dr. Geoffrey F. Tabin, Dr. Nick Mamalis, Dr. Liliana Werner, Dr. Leonardo P. Werner, Dr. Kensaku Miyake, Dr. Okihiro Nishi, Dr. Reijo J. Linnola, Dr. Andrea M. Izak, Dr. Ehud I. Assia, Dr. Gerd U. Auffarth, Dr. Manfred R. Tetz, Dr. Qun Peng, Dr. Mike P. Holzer, Dr. Luis G. Vargas, Dr. Josef M. Schmidbauer, Dr. Robert J. Schoderbek Jr., Dr. Guy Kleinmann, Late Dr. Alan S. Crandall, Dr. Rupal H. Trivedi, Dr. Bradley S. Daines, Dr. Tamer A. Mackey, Dr. Stella N. Arthur, Dr. Helga P. Sandoval, Dr. Tanja Rabsilber, Dr. Surendra Basti, Dr. Marcella Escobar-Gomez, Dr. Kerry D. Solomon, Dr. David T. Vroman, Dr. Nithi Visessook, Dr. Irmingard M. Neuhann, Dr. Enrique Roig-Melo, Dr. E. John Milverton, Dr. Anthony J. Maloof, Dr. Gagan Khannah, Dr. Iain Dunlop, Dr. John W. McAvoy, and Dr. Paul Mitchell. You expanded my world.

The Home Team

Writing requires solitude, but healing requires a village. At SuVi Eye Institute & Lasik Laser Center, Kota, I am blessed with the best team a doctor could ask for.

To Dr. Satyendra Kumar Gupta and Dr. Nipun Bagrecha—my pillars of strength. To the brilliant doctors who walked the early path with us: Dr. Saurabh Savaria, Dr. Randhir Jha, Dr. Meenal Gupta, Dr. Garima Lakhotia, Dr. Arun Pandey, Dr. Bharti Ahuja, Dr. Nimisha Vijay, Dr. Monika Nagar, Dr. Deepesh Chhablani, and Dr. Rachna Patel.

To every technician, optometrist, and staff member: you are the invisible hands that make the miracles happen.

The Heartbeat

To the two women who hold my universe together.

Dr. Vidushi Sharma: My wife, my co-founder, and my conscience. You have walked every step of this journey with me, teaching me that while medicine is a science, healing is an act of love.

Ishita: My daughter. Thank you for forgiving the missed dinners and the long hours while Papa was "writing his book." You are the future I am writing for.

The Promise

To the thousands of patients who have walked through my doors. You placed the most precious thing you own—your sight—into my imperfect hands. Your trust is the fuel that drives me to seek perfection.

Dr. Suresh Kumar Pandey

SuVi Eye Institute & Lasik Laser Center Kota, Rajasthan, India

Email:suresh.pandey@gmail.com

About the Author

Dr. Suresh Kumar Pandey is an author, world-renowned eye surgeon, and Director of the SuVi Eye Hospital & Lasik Laser Centre, Kota, Rajasthan, India. He is a member of the prestigious International Intraocular Implant Club (IIIC). He is the former vice president of the Indian Medical Association (IMA) Kota and the former president of the Kota Division Ophthalmological Society (KDOS), Kota. Dr Pandey completed his ophthalmology residency from the prestigious Post Graduate Institute of Medical Education & Research (PGIMER), Chandigarh, and pursued an anterior segment fellowship in the USA and Australia. He has also performed live surgeries at various national and international conferences and has received several awards including Achievement Award (American Academy of Ophthalmology), Best-of-Show Video Award, Best Poster Award, Best-Paper-of-the-Session Award, etc. at the American Academy of Ophthalmology (AAO), American Society of Cataract and Refractive Surgery (ASCRS), Asia Pacific Association of Cataract and Refractive Surgeons (APACRS), European Society of Cataract and Refractive

Surgeons (ESCRS) International Conferences and was awarded a Gold Medal by the Indian Intraocular Implant and Refractive Surgery Society. His books, An Eye for the Sky, Secrets of Successful Doctors: A Complete Guide Fulfilling Medical Career, and A Hippocratic Odyssey: Lessons from a Doctor Couple on Life in Medicine, Challenges, and Doctorpreneurship, Entrepreneurship for Doctors continue to be popular among medical professionals. Dr Pandey's hobbies include cycling, painting, gardening, and photography.

Dr Suresh K. Pandey can be reached at:

E-mail: suresh.pandey@gmail.com

Phone Number: +919351412449

Twitter: https://twitter.com/SuViEyeKOTARAJ

Facebook: https://www.facebook.com/suresh.pandey.600017

Instagram: https://www.instagram.com/drsureshkpandey/

LinkedIn: https://www.linkedin.com/in/eyedrsureshkpandeykota/

Website: www.drsureshpandey.com, www.suvieyehospital.com

Appendix

THE AI MEDICAL TOOL-KIT: A LIVING LIST OF TECHNOLOGIES

This appendix serves as a practical glossary and a glimpse into the rapidly evolving ecosystem of the "Infallible Doctor." While specific software versions change, these categories and platforms represent the foundational pillars of the new era of healthcare.

I. THE SURGICAL SUITE (ROBOTICS & TELESURGERY)

Tools that stabilize the hand, extend the reach, and democratize surgical skill.

- **Da Vinci Surgical System (Intuitive Surgical):** The gold standard for soft-tissue surgery. A master-slave system that features 3D high-definition vision and wristed instruments that bend and rotate far beyond the human hand's capacity. Used primarily for urology, gynecology, and general surgery.
- **Symani Surgical System (Medical Microinstruments):** A robotic platform designed for microsurgery. It scales down human hand movements to allow for the suturing of tiny vessels and nerves (as small as 0.3mm), critical for lymphatic reconstruction and trauma repair.
- **Mako SmartRobotics (Stryker):** An arm-assisted robotic system for joint replacement surgery. It uses CT-based 3D modeling to pre-plan the surgery and provides "haptic feedback" (a physical resistance) that prevents the surgeon from cutting outside the planned zone.
- **The PillCam (Medtronic):** A swallowable capsule containing a tiny camera. It travels through the digestive tract, taking

thousands of images to detect bleeding, Crohn's disease, and polyps without the need for invasive sedation or tubes.

- **STAR (Smart Tissue Autonomous Robot):** A research-grade robot capable of semi-autonomous soft tissue surgery. Famous for outperforming human surgeons in stitching pig bowel by using advanced vision sensors to adjust tension in real-time.

II. THE DIAGNOSTIC BRAIN (AI & PATHOLOGY)

Algorithms that process data at the speed of light to find the "needle in the haystack."

- **Watson Health (IBM Merative):** One of the early pioneers in cognitive computing for healthcare. While evolving, its core concept involves ingesting millions of medical journals and genomic data to assist oncologists in identifying rare mutations and matching patients to clinical trials.
- **DeepMind / AlphaFold (Google):** An AI system that solved the "protein folding problem." It can predict the 3D structure of nearly all known proteins, revolutionizing drug discovery by showing how diseases interact with the body on a molecular level.
- **Aidoc & Viz.ai:** "Always-on" AI platforms for radiology. They sit in the background of hospital servers, analyzing CT scans for strokes (Large Vessel Occlusions), brain bleeds, and pulmonary embolisms. They alert the neurovascular team instantly, often shaving 60+ minutes off treatment time.
- **PathAI:** A technology that assists pathologists by using machine learning to analyze tissue slides. It detects cancer cells with higher accuracy than humans alone and can quantify the severity of disease to predict patient outcomes.
- **IDx-DR:** The first FDA-approved autonomous AI that can diagnose a disease (Diabetic Retinopathy) without a doctor. It analyzes retinal images and provides a binary output: "More than mild disease detected" or "Negative."

III. THE WALL-LESS HOSPITAL (REMOTE MONITORING & WEARABLES)

Devices that move care from the clinic to the living room.

- **Butterfly iQ:** A handheld, whole-body ultrasound probe that connects to a smartphone. It uses AI to guide the user (even a novice) to capture clear images of the heart, lungs, and bladder, effectively replacing the stethoscope with a scanner.
- **Apple Watch (Health Features):** A consumer wearable that contains FDA-cleared medical sensors. It can capture a single-lead ECG to detect Atrial Fibrillation (AFib), measure blood oxygen saturation, and detect hard falls.
- **KardiaMobile (AliveCor):** A pocket-sized, clinical-grade ECG device. Patients place their fingers on the sensors to record a 6-lead EKG, allowing for the remote detection of arrhythmias which can be instantly emailed to a cardiologist.
- **BioSticker (BioIntelliSense):** A medical-grade, single-use wearable sticker that monitors respiratory rate, heart rate, skin temperature, and body position for 30 days. It enables "Hospital at Home" programs by allowing continuous monitoring of stable patients after discharge.
- **FreeStyle Libre (Abbott):** A Continuous Glucose Monitor (CGM) for diabetics. A small sensor on the arm measures blood sugar in real-time, sending data to a smartphone and eliminating the need for painful finger pricks.

IV. THE SAFETY NET (PREVENTION & SAFETY)

Systems designed to catch errors before they reach the patient.

- **Sepsis Watch (Duke Health):** A deep learning tool that monitors patient vitals (heart rate, BP, lab results) within the Electronic Health Record (EHR). It identifies the subtle early warning signs of sepsis hours before a human would, triggering a Rapid Response Team.
- **MedEye:** A medication safety system for nurses. It uses computer vision to scan the pills being given to a patient at the

bedside, verifying they match the prescription and the patient's ID, preventing "wrong drug" or "wrong dose" errors.

- **Project Artemis:** A big data platform for Neonatal Intensive Care Units (NICU). It analyzes the subtle heartbeat variability in premature infants to predict infections (sepsis) up to 24 hours before clinical symptoms appear.

V. THE EMPATHY ENGINES (ADMINISTRATIVE AI)

Tools that remove the keyboard to restore the human connection.

- **Nuance DAX (Dragon Ambient eXperience):** An ambient listening technology. It records the conversation between doctor and patient, uses Natural Language Processing (NLP) to understand the medical context, and automatically writes the clinical note in the chart.
- **ElliQ (Intuition Robotics):** A proactive social robot for the elderly. It initiates conversation, suggests activities, and connects seniors with their families, designed specifically to combat the "epidemic of loneliness" and cognitive decline.

Index

www.ingramcontent.com/pod-product-compliance
Lightning Source LLC
LaVergne TN
LVHW090259210926
848480LV00001B/80
* 9 7 9 8 9 0 5 1 0 0 6 1 1 *